Baltic Capitals

Tallinn • Riga • Vilnius • Kaliningrad

the Bradt Travel Guide

contributing author
Neil Taylor

additional authors
Stephen Baister
Howard Jarvis
Chris Patrick

edition
3

www.bradtguides.com

Bradt Travel Guides Ltd, UK
The Globe Pequot Press Inc, USA

Baltic Capitals
Don't miss...

Vibrant cafés and bars
Pilies gatve, Vilnius (GT)

Fascinating architecture
Eisenstein's building,
10b Elizabetes iela, Riga
(CN) page 93

Beautiful parks and gardens
Kadriorg Park,
Tallinn (JV) page 59

Festivals
Song Festival,
Riga (CN)

Museums and galleries
The Amber Museum,
Kaliningrad
(JS) page 201

above **Pregel River and the old German red-brick Gothic cathedral, Kaliningrad** (JS) page 194

centre **Skārņu iela, Riga** (CN) page 90

left **St Anne's Church, Vilnius** (GT) page 165

top left **Europa Tower, Vilnius** (GT) page 167
top right **Overview of Tallinn Old Town** (TH) page 39
above left **Decorated door, Tallinn** (TH)
above right **Art nouveau or Jungendstil door, Riga** (SC) page 93

top Sailors crossing the bridge over the Pregel River, Kaliningrad (JS)
above left Amber, commonly found in all the Baltic states (ACZ) page 86
above right Lithuanian folk costume at a song festival, Vilnius (JS)
below Blackheads' House, Riga (CN) page 100

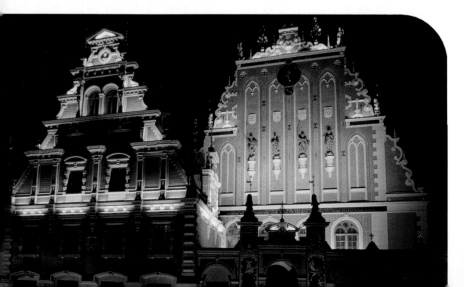

above **Vilnius Cathedral**
(CN) page 163

centre **Christmas market,
Tallinn** (CN)

right **Hearts adorn the walls
of the Church of St Teresa,
Vilnius** (RW) page 154

above **St Brigitta Convent, Pirita**
(JV) page 57

centre **Rācenes Spa near the beach at Majori, Jūrmala**
(CN) page 117

left **Trakai Castle, near Vilnius**
(GT) page 173

Authors and Contributors

Neil Taylor was from 1975–2005 director of Regent Holidays, a British tour company that has specialised in travel to the Baltic states and Kaliningrad since 1991. He visits the area about four times a year and in 1999 his Bradt guide to Estonia was first published. It is now in its fourth edition. He is on the Board of the Association of Independent Tour Operators (AITO) and writes and broadcasts on general travel trade topics. In 2000, Neil was awarded the Lifetime Achievement Award by the British Guild of Travel Writers.

Stephen Baister studied modern languages at Oxford and London universities and worked as a publisher before becoming a solicitor. While in practice, he represented a number of clients with interests in eastern and central Europe. He is the co-author of the Bradt guide to Latvia of which the fourth edition was published in 2005. He has a doctorate in east European law from University College London. He is now a Registrar in Bankruptcy in the High Court.

Howard Jarvis has been the chief editor of a number of publications in the Baltic countries, including the region's only weekly newspaper the *Baltic Times* and the travel trade magazine *Baltic Stand By*. He has been a contributor at Jane's Information Group since 2000 and has written numerous articles on developments in the Baltic region and Belarus. Now based in Vilnius he is the editor of a monthly magazine for business travellers called *VilniusNOW!* while still finding a little time for freelance work.

Chris Patrick has a degree in French and German from Oxford University. After graduation she lived and worked in Japan and travelled extensively in the Far East. She works now in international research and consultancy and has assisted a number of organisations from eastern Europe in doing business in the Far East. She first visited Latvia in 1989 and has returned many times since. She is co-author of the Bradt guide to Latvia, of which the fourth edition was published in 2005.

PUBLISHER'S FOREWORD

Hilary Bradt

The first Bradt travel guide was written in 1974 by George and Hilary Bradt on a river barge floating down a tributary of the Amazon. In the 1980s and '90s the focus shifted away from hiking to broader-based guides covering new destinations – usually the first to be published about these places. In the 21st century Bradt continues to publish such ground-breaking guides, as well as others to established holiday destinations, incorporating in-depth information on culture and natural history with the nuts and bolts of where to stay and what to see.

Bradt authors support responsible travel, and provide advice not only on minimum impact but also on how to give something back through local charities. In this way a true synergy is achieved between the traveller and local communities.

When we published our first guides to the Baltic states in 1995 we never imagined that the region would become so popular. The last Soviet troops had only left the three republics during the previous year, and their psychological presence was still felt. My own visit to Tallinn a few years later showed me a vibrant city rejoicing in its independence. Now, of course, the Baltic capitals are drawing thousands of discerning travellers looking for something a little different for a short break. It's been quite a Cinderella story!

Third edition May 2006 First published 2001

Bradt Travel Guides Ltd, 23 High Street, Chalfont St Peter, Bucks SL9 9QE, England.
www.bradtguides.com
Published in the USA by The Globe Pequot Press Inc, 246 Goose Lane,
PO Box 480, Guilford, Connecticut 06475-0480

Introduction, Kaliningrad and Tallinn copyright © 2006 Neil Taylor
Riga copyright © 2006 Stephen Baister
Vilnius copyright © 2006 Neil Taylor and Howard Jarvis
Photographs copyright © 2006 Individual photographers
Maps copyright © 2006 Bradt Travel Guides

British Library Cataloguing in Publication Data
A catalogue record for this book is available from the British Library
ISBN-10: 1 84162 139 0   ISBN-13: 978 1 84162 139 5

Photographs Stephen Baister and Chris Patrick (SC), Anne Croquet-Zouridakis (ACZ), Tricia Hayne (TH), Christian Nowak (CN), Matt Rudd (MR), Jonathan Smith (JS), Gediminas Treciokas (GT), Joanna Vaughan (JV), Rob Watkins (RW)
Front cover Viru Gate (TH), Blackheads' House (TH), Angel Statue, Bernardine Cemetery (ACZ), Cosmonaut Memorial (MR)
Back cover Eisenstein's building, 10b Elizabetes iela, Riga (CN), Alexander Nevsky Cathedral, Tallinn (JS)
Title page Amber (ACZ), Kadriorg Park pavilion (JV), Art nouveau building, Alberta iela 13 (CN)

Maps David Priestley

Typeset from the author's disc by Wakewing
Printed and bound in Italy by Legoprint SpA, Trento

Acknowledgements

In preparing the text on Königsberg, I must give particular thanks to Lorenz Grimoni, Director of the Königsberg Museum in Duisburg. He gave me access to the museum archives which cover all aspects of pre-war life in the city and which house research done by Germans in Kaliningrad since 1990 when they were able to return there. Future generations in particular will be grateful for all the work done in the museum to preserve the memory of what had been an important German city. In Kaliningrad itself, my guide, Olga Danilova, has shared her enthusiasm, realism and knowledge on each of my visits. I owe Olga a great debt, as do most English-speaking visitors. The staff at Baltma Tours always seemed to meet my increasingly complicated requests and must be congratulated on reducing the Soviet visa bureaucracy that still plagues the rest of Russia.

FEEDBACK REQUEST

We are always pleased to hear from readers, whether they send bouquets, brickbats or suggested changes. All that matters is that they leave the Baltic capitals with a positive impression. Please write to Bradt Travel Guides, 23 High Street, Chalfont St Peter, Bucks SL9 9QE; e info@bradtguides.com.

Contents

Introduction

The late 1990s saw the term 'short break' take on a totally new dimension in the travel business. Tourists who previously limited their horizons to Paris and Amsterdam were suddenly offered shopping weekends in Minneapolis or a glimpse of the Taj Mahal. The three Baltic capitals soon realised that they could fill a gap between these two extremes.

EU and NATO entry in 2004, plus earlier Eurovision Song Contest victories for Estonia and Latvia, gave the area tremendous, and very positive publicity.

With a flying time of three hours from London, Manchester or Dublin, with the abolition of visas and with the 'Westernisation' of hotels, each capital offers a fulfilling three or four days either on its own or as part of a longer visit to two or three of them. Except perhaps in December and January, the weather is good enough for walking between the major attractions, all of which now cater for the English-speaking visitor.

The time difference is always two hours from Britain, the airports are close to the city centres and immigration procedures are very quick so a visitor might well reach a hotel in one of the Baltic capitals more quickly than one in Berlin or Rome.

Kaliningrad is taking longer to realise the potential of catering for short-stay visitors. From 1999 visas were issued on arrival at the Polish border and at the airport, but visitors arriving from Lithuania still have to face the obstacle course set by Russian embassies abroad. Travel was often complicated with little non-Russian material available and in the early 1990s tourists had been treated with suspicion and fear. Neither the shops nor the few open museums could really offer any temptations. Seeing, however, the success of Vilnius to the north and Krakow to the south has been a major stimulus to compete. The year 2005 gave Kaliningrad a welcome opportunity to promote itself as it celebrated the 750th anniversary of the founding of Königsberg and welcomed Gerhard Schröder and Jacques Chirac to a summit with Vladimir Putin. There is much still to do and older visitors will quickly find some similarities with the Soviet Union but regular visitors who came in 2005 were able to see the month by month changes. There is now a genuine need for a guidebook; seven years ago this claim could not have been made.

Parallels with many other parts of Europe will immediately strike the visitor. The towering Gothic steeples in Tallinn, Riga and Kaliningrad emphasise the importance of the Baltic German community. The domes and colour of the Russian orthodox churches are constant reminders of the 200 years the Baltic republics spent in the Russian Empire. The use of mobile phones by all generations is one of many habits picked up by the renewed links to Sweden and Finland. France, Italy and Spain have made their mark in the local restaurants, whilst Britain has concentrated on the pubs. Local footballers, of course, play not only in Europe but for teams all over the world!

Allow time in all four capitals for evening concerts; in the winter the architecture of the buildings will be as much an attraction as the music. Most date from the late 19th century and avoided damage both from bombing and from over-zealous modernisers during the Soviet period. In the summer, music moves to the lakes, to the parks, to the riverside and to the coast. The concert repertoire mixes local music with Western classics and high standards can be guaranteed. Allow time too for shopping since local materials and craftsmanship stand out in all the local markets. Wool, linen, copper and amber are all transformed into original gifts. Local photographers, historians and translators have now finally got together to publish excellent souvenirs of each city. With efficient postal services, they can easily be sent home. Above all, take in the changes that have taken place in the last 15 years. There is no longer the need to look on a visit to the Baltics as an adventure. The best compliment that can be paid to them is to regard them as ordinary European capitals.

KEY TO STANDARD SYMBOLS

Bradt

---·---· International boundary	ℹ Tourist information
▬▬▬▬ Railway	✉ Post office
--🚗-- Car ferry	Historic building
🚌 Bus station etc	Stadium
⌂ Hotel, inn etc	• Other attraction
✕ Restaurant	Statue/monument
☕ Café	Bird nesting site
☆ Night club/Casino	Zoo
$ Bank	✝ Church or cathedral
Theatre	✡ Synagogue
Museum/gallery	☾ Mosque
e Internet café	← Direction arrow
	Pedestrianised road

I

Overview

WHEN TO GO

Most tourists to the Baltic states visit in the summer months between late April and early October. July and early August are very busy in the cheaper hotels since this is the German and Scandinavian school holiday period. Temperatures in the summer can reach 25°C/80°F quite regularly, though they often hover around 20°C/70°F. Good weather can never be guaranteed in this area. Clouds can quickly congregate, turning a sunny morning into a dismal afternoon, but the reverse is equally true. Day trips should never be undertaken without a coat and strong shoes. Tallinn barely sees night-time around midsummer and the days are long in all four countries from May until September. The de-luxe and business-class hotels often reduce their prices in July and August to attract tourists at a time when their normal clientele is absent.

More tourists are now seeing the attractions of winter visits to these four cities. Culture flourishes then, temperatures do not fall much below freezing, and queues are non-existent at the major sites. From western Europe, winter air fares have now dropped to a level which makes weekend breaks in these cities very popular. January and early February should be avoided because of the short hours of daylight then and the occasional bitter day, but other months should offer a pleasant stay. Christmas is now taken seriously in the Baltics and a well-planned short shopping trip around the Christmas markets should more than make up for the air fare.

PUBLIC HOLIDAYS

New Year	1 January
Orthodox Christmas (Kaliningrad)	7 January
Independence Day (Lithuania)	16 February
International Women's Day	8 March
Restoration of Independence Day (Lithuania)	11 March
Easter	March/April
May Day (Estonia, Kaliningrad and Latvia)	1 May
Victory in Europe Day (Kaliningrad)	9 May
Independence Day (Kaliningrad)	12 June
Midsummer (Estonia and Latvia)	23–4 June
Mindaugas Day (Lithuania)	6 July
Assumption (Lithuania)	15 August
Restoration of Independence Day (Estonia)	20 August
All Saints Day (Lithuania)	1 November
Day of Reconciliation (Kaliningrad)	7 November
Independence Day (Latvia)	18 November
Christmas	24–5 December

Flags are displayed in the Baltic countries on 14 June, to commemorate those deported to Siberia on 14 June 1941 and in later deportations. They are also displayed on 23 August, to commemorate the signing between Germany and the USSR of the Molotov–Ribbentrop Pact on 23 August 1939, which enabled the USSR to incorporate the three Baltic states in June 1940.

① TIME ZONES

Before World War II, Estonia and Latvia were two hours ahead of GMT and Lithuania one hour ahead, as was East Prussia. During the Soviet occupation the three Baltic republics and the Kaliningrad region were forced to use Moscow time which is three hours ahead of GMT. Courageous local nationalists during this period would often keep their watches an hour behind Moscow time as an act of defiance to the USSR and of loyalty to the former regime. On regaining independence changing back the time was one of the first acts of the new governments and in the early '90s they all kept in step, to be joined later by Kaliningrad. In the mid-90s they tended to go their separate ways, causing havoc with bus and plane timetables, but fortunately since 2000 they have all agreed to work within the EU framework, so they are always two hours ahead of the time in Britain and one hour ahead of most of Europe.

RED TAPE

Estonia, Latvia and Lithuania abolished the Soviet visa system immediately after their independence in 1991. Since joining the EU they have implemented the same visa exemptions so citizens from all other EU countries, as well as from Australia, Canada, New Zealand and the USA do not need visas. Citizens of many other countries also do not need visas, but South Africans do, although a visa issued to them by one Baltic state is valid in the other two. Visa procedures for people who do need them are cumbersome, expensive and time-consuming.

Kaliningrad initially followed Russia by adopting the former Soviet visa system but a fall in the number of tourists forced them to break away from this in 1999. All tourists still need a visa, which is only granted on the basis of pre-booked accommodation, but it is now issued on arrival at the airport and at the land borders with Poland. They are NOT issued on the Lithuanian border so visitors entering Kaliningrad this way will need to apply several weeks in advance through a Russian embassy. Although the local authorities in Kaliningrad are eager to abolish visas for EU citizens, Moscow was still in 2005 refusing to let them do so.

CONSULAR HELP IN THE BALTICS Australia, Britain and the United States have consulates in each of the Baltic capitals except Kaliningrad. The British consulates can provide assistance to nationals of most Commonwealth countries in emergencies and also to nationals of EU countries that do not have their own consulates. Kaliningrad has six consulates representing Belarus, Denmark, Germany, Lithuania, Poland and Sweden. The Danish one, situated in the Scandinavian Airlines office (*Sovietsky 1;* ⤷ *0112 55 0105*) handles emergencies for all Western tourists. The German government had expressed interest all through the 1990s in opening a consulate but this wish was only granted by the Russian government in 2004, so reluctant were they to make even a hotel room German territory again. It was to take until autumn 2005, after a visit to the area by Chancellor Schröder, for a whole house to be given diplomatic status and therefore to again become German territory. Many buildings suggested for this were turned down, but in the end, presumably to cause the Germans maximum embarrassment, the Russians agreed to the use of a house situated in Thälmann Ulitsa. Ernst Thälmann was the pre-war leader of the German Communist

Party who was killed in a concentration camp. In early 2005, there had been seven consulates in Kaliningrad, but the Latvians left in the autumn, still not having been granted a building for their use. See also pages 20, 68, 132 and 189.

$ MONEY AND BUDGETING

CURRENCY AND CHANGING MONEY Each country has its own currency and payment in any other one is impossible. All four currencies are convertible and can be exchanged throughout the Baltic countries. As banks and exchange bureaux do not usually charge commission, small amounts left over can be re-exchanged without difficulty. In Tallinn, Riga and Vilnius, banks and exchange bureaux change all major Western currencies. Those at airports are always open for incoming flights but at land borders and at railway and bus stations they tend to close between 20.00 and 08.00, even though many international buses and trains travel through the night. Exchange bureaux in the towns are usually open seven days a week from around 09.00 to 19.00. Most hotels change money, some at any time of day, but rates are always better in exchange bureaux. On day trips out of town, remember to change sufficient money before departure since exchange and credit card facilities may not be available *en route*. In the Kaliningrad oblast, apart from at the land border with Lithuania, it is often only possible to exchange euro or US dollars into roubles. It is forbidden to make any payments in foreign currency. Thomas Cook and HSBC sell all four currencies in the UK, but it is otherwise difficult to obtain them in advance in western Europe. Estonia, Latvia and Lithuania had originally planned to convert to the euro in 2007 but in late 2005 it was thought that this would be postponed until 2008, although all three currencies were already tied to the euro by then. Tourists from Britain can obtain all three Baltic currencies at one of several exchange bureaux at Heathrow, Gatwick and Stansted airports before they leave and from all major banks. They are also available in Helsinki. It is always important to insist on receiving low-value notes when changing money as notes worth more than about £5/US$8 are often difficult to exchange in museums, cafés and kiosks where tourists are likely to spend most of their cash. For the latest exchange rates, check your daily newspaper or www.xe.com. The following gives an indication of the exchange rates at the time of publication.

Exchange rates
Estonia The Estonian kroon has a fixed rate with the euro of 15.65EEK. In April 2006 exchange rates against the pound and US dollar were £1 = 22.60EEK, and US$1 = 13.00EEK. Notes are issued for 1, 2, 5, 10, 25, 50, 100 and 500EEK although those for 1 and 2 kroon are now being replaced with coins. There are also coins for 10, 20 and 50 sents.

Latvia The lat is the official currency of Latvia (in Latvian the singular is *lats*, the plural *lati*). There are 100 santimi to the lat (the singular is *santims*, the plural *santimi*). The lat (Ls) is fixed to the euro with one euro being worth 0.70 lat and a dollar being worth around 0.58 lats in 2006. In contrast to Estonia, coins are issued up to Ls2 and notes from Ls5 upwards. As the lat is worth almost exactly £1, the money there is very convenient for British tourists to calculate as coins and notes exactly match their British counterparts. Coins are issued for 1, 2, 5, 10, 20 and 50 santimi and for Ls1 and Ls2; notes for Ls5, Ls10, Ls20 and Ls50. (Gamblers and money-launderers may also find the Ls100 and Ls500 notes of use.) Outside Latvia, it is sometimes difficult to exchange coins so these should be re-exchanged before departure, and on the Latvian side of land borders.

Lithuania Having for nine years been tied to the US dollar, since February 2002 the lit has been tied instead to the euro. The fixed rate is 3.45Lt = €1, so in early 2006 the

Overview MONEY AND BUDGETING

3

pound was worth about 5.05Lt and the dollar about 2.85Lt. There are coins for 1, 2, 5, 10, 20 and 50 cents and also for 1Lt, 2Lt and 5Lt. There are notes for 10, 20, 50 and 100 lits. Those formerly in circulation for 1, 2 and 5 lits have been largely replaced by coins.

Kaliningrad Through much of the 1990s the Russian rouble fluctuated wildly against other currencies, but since 1998 it has been very stable against the US dollar at a rate of US$1 = RUB28. In April 2006, £1 = RUB50, and €1 = RUB34.26. Coins are issued for 10, 20 and 50 kopeks and for 1, 2 and 5 roubles. Given the very low prices for most items of interest to tourists, the only notes likely to be of use are those for 10, 20 and 50 roubles, although higher denominations are issued.

Cash machines These are easily found all over Tallinn, Riga and Vilnius. Their use is spreading all the time in these three cities. In Kaliningrad, reliable ATMs are becoming more readily available. Cash machines generally take major credit cards such as MasterCard and Visa. Do, however, check before leaving home what charges your bank will make for such use.

Credit cards In Tallinn, Riga and Vilnius the use of cards is as widespread as elsewhere with all major shops, restaurants and hotels taking them. They can be used in hotels in Kaliningrad, but not in shops and only in a few restaurants. The Eurolines offices at Tallinn and at Riga bus stations accept credit cards, but otherwise they cannot be used at railway or bus stations. As even long-distance fares are very low, this is not a major problem. In Tallinn, few museums and galleries are able to accept them, although those that have opened recently usually do.

Travellers' cheques These are useless throughout the Baltics. Only a few banks can exchange them; shops hotels, restaurants and exchange bureaux will invariably refuse them. The easy availability of cash machines in Estonia, Latvia and Lithuania, and the very low cost of incidentals in Kaliningrad, makes their use superfluous. (Many local people do not write cheques any more as they only use electronic banking.)

BUDGETING Whilst hotel costs are similar to those in western Europe, other expenses will be much lower, except at restaurants and clubs clearly geared to affluent foreigners. A bus or train ride of 200km may well cost only £4/US$7, a light lunch £3/US$5 and a taxi across town £4/US$7.50. With low sales taxes, petrol is about half the UK price and a carton of 200 cigarettes costs scarcely more than the price of a packet in Britain. In Kaliningrad, prices are even lower than in the other three cities. Museums do charge admission fees, usually with reductions for children and for the elderly. The full charge is rarely more than £1/US$1.80 and often much less. Locally produced books and maps in English often offer good value. On day trips out, incidental costs will be much lower than in the capitals and on these occasions it is worth looking out for souvenirs since their prices will be geared to local consumers.

Shoppers visiting more than one of the cities will save money by finishing their tour in Kaliningrad, where all the obvious souvenirs are much cheaper than further north. Amber is of course the obvious buy there, together with linen and vodka. Lithuania and Estonia produce tasteful items carved from juniper wood, whereas the best china and glass is sold in Riga.

Tipping Up to 10% is very welcome in restaurants, cafés and hairdressers if the service deserves it, but not otherwise. In Tallinn, many expats make a point of not tipping if the service does not deserve it, in the hope that it will improve on future occasions. In Riga and in some more expensive restaurants in Vilnius, menus will indicate whether service is included so in such circumstances be sure not to tip twice!

WHAT TO TAKE

The shops are now so well stocked in all four countries, with prices usually much lower than those in western Europe, that there is no need to stock up with supplies before departure. Long gone are the days when travellers took iron rations and a medicine chest to safeguard their survival. An umbrella is essential year-round as clouds can suddenly appear on even the nicest of days. Be prepared similarly for changes in temperature: a sweater may be needed in summer and a spring day can become a winter one. Tough footwear is always essential because of the uneven pavements and the number of sites away from main roads. Relatively formal wear is still the custom for concerts and plays. Westerners attending performances often stand out with their untidy, casual dress.

The foreign-language bookshops in three of the Baltic capitals are well supplied with English-language, light and serious reading matter but few English (or even German) books are sold in Kaliningrad. Local guides in Kaliningrad are always pleased to receive books in English and many find their way into school and college libraries.

GETTING THERE

✈ BY AIR During 2004 and 2005 there was an enormous increase in direct flights from the UK to the Baltics and they also began from Ireland during this time. Air Baltic started daily services to Riga from Heathrow and Dublin, and to Vilnius from Gatwick and Dublin. They also operate a Manchester to Riga flight. Lithuanian Airlines increased their daily Gatwick–Vilnius service to twice a day and began a Dublin service. British Airways returned to the Gatwick–Vilnius route in 2005. In the autumn of 2005 Ryanair started a daily flight to Kaunas from Stansted and one from Liverpool to Riga. Lithuanian Airlines was privatised in the summer of 2005 but there were no immediate changes in its operational procedures. The Estonian Air monopoly on London–Tallinn was broken by easyJet. In the autumn of 2004 and during 2005 they both enjoyed good load factors on their daily flights. In the summer of 2005 Estonian Air started services from Manchester and Dublin to Tallinn.

The growth in services from western Europe to each of the Baltic states also grew dramatically from 2004 with Belgium, France, Holland and Germany all being well served with direct flights. The first direct link with the USA came thanks to Uzbekistan Airways whose flights transit Riga en route from Tashkent to New York.

SAS Scandinavian Airlines have several services a day from Tallinn, Riga and Vilnius to both Copenhagen and Stockholm and then these connect with flights to Britain, Ireland and to the USA. SAS offer 'open-jaw' fares, which allow travel into one city and back from another. This facility is also available to towns in Poland and Russia, so that it is possible to fly into Gdańsk, for example, and out of Tallinn. SAS is particularly convenient for travellers from Great Britain and Ireland as it serves seven airports – London Heathrow, London Gatwick, Birmingham, Manchester, Edinburgh, Glasgow and Dublin – so a journey from any of them to the Baltics should not take more than five hours.

In 2004 CSA Czech Airlines started to serve the Baltic capitals and their connections to the UK were by 2005 almost as extensive as those offered by SAS as they fly to London Heathrow, London Stansted, Birmingham, Manchester and Edinburgh.

LOT Polish Airlines is the only airline to serve Kaliningrad from the west and they also fly to the three Baltic capitals. From Warsaw they have an extensive network of services to the UK, Ireland and North America. Finnair have several flights a day to Tallinn from Helsinki and also daily services to Riga and Vilnius. These connect with the services they jointly operate with BA between Helsinki, London, Edinburgh and Manchester and also with their flights to Dublin and to the USA.

Riga Airport was traditionally notorious for its high airport taxes but the arrival of no-frills airlines and the competition offered by Tallinn forced them down in 2004 and in fact in the same year those at Tallinn dropped too as a result. Travellers leaving any Baltic airport should now not have to pay much more than about £12/US$20 in taxes.

Flights between Vilnius, Riga and Tallinn are operated by Lithuanian Airlines and Air Baltic. Air Baltic is a subsidiary of SAS. These used to be very expensive, but from 2004 became much cheaper if booked by a tour operator in conjunction with other flights or if booked several months in advance.

Minimal air services now operate from the Baltics to Russia and Ukraine although the abolition of visas for EU passport holders travelling to Ukraine might increase flights to Kiev.

BY TRAIN With the continuing reduction in air fares and the worsening services on international trains, this is unlikely to be a means of transport used by many visitors to reach this area. Customs and immigration procedures can take many hours, usually in the middle of the night. Trains still operate from Kaliningrad to Warsaw and from Tallinn to Moscow. There are also trains from Kaliningrad and the Baltic cities to Moscow and Kiev. Belarussian transit visas are now needed for these, as well as the appropriate Russian visas. The Tallinn–St Petersburg service was abandoned in 2005, probably for good.

BY BUS Eurolines has an extensive network of services to western Europe from the Baltics and some services to Russia. Eurolines and other local companies also run express buses between the Baltic states. These operate several times a day and are the most practical way of land travel between the major cities. They jump the queue at the frontiers so timings are virtually guaranteed. The journey takes around five hours from Riga to either Vilnius or Tallinn. There is a through service from Vilnius to Tallinn and also routes from Riga to Kaunas and to Tartu. Reservations can be made abroad through travel agents (see page 7) but tickets are collected from the Eurolines office in the relevant bus station. The fare from Riga to either Tallinn or Vilnius is around £8/US$14 one-way. English is spoken in all Eurolines offices. Online booking is likely to be possible in 2006.

Local companies operate services from Kaliningrad to Nida, Vilnius and Riga which should be pre-booked in view of the visa stipulations. These, too, jump border queues so passengers who may have spent around £5/US$8 for their fare can have the pleasure of overtaking rich businessmen fuming in their Mercedes. There are some similar services to Poland but these are less regular nowadays as local travellers now require visas.

BY CAR The entry of the three Baltic states into the EU has made car driving from western Europe much easier. Basic UK insurance cover is now valid there (although still not in Kaliningrad). However with the massive reduction in air fares that took place in 2004–05, flying and then hiring a car locally makes much more sense. UK tour operators can easily arrange a fly-drive package, but for visitors staying largely in the capital cities cars are unlikely to be of use. Many of the sites are within walking distance of hotels and others are within easy reach by bus or taxi. For day trips off the beaten track hiring may be worthwhile but as prices for local guides and drivers are very reasonable it is often sensible to consider hiring a car on this basis. Minor roads are not well signposted and local people in the countryside do not usually speak foreign languages.

BY FERRY In the summer, hovercraft and catamarans take between an hour and 90 minutes to link Tallinn and Helsinki. Larger boats, taking about three hours, operate year-round. Services start around 08.00 in the morning and finish around 21.00 at night. Competition between the many companies operating these routes keeps prices down to about £12 one-way and £20 return. Some carriers offer a business class for about double this price and this offers a private lounge and free refreshments. A day and overnight ferry operates between Tallinn and Stockholm and a day one between Riga and Stockholm. Visitors from Britain and Ireland wanting to visit Sweden and the Baltic states can obtain a three-sector ticket from SAS agents and then use one of these ferries. Several cruise liners visit Kaliningrad, Riga and Tallinn as part of a tour around the Baltic Sea.

TOUR OPERATORS
UK

Baltic Adventures 1 Hyde Cl, Harpenden, Herts AL5 4NB; ℡ 01582 462283; f 01582 764339; e info@balticadventures.co.uk; www.balticadventures.co.uk. Specialists for activity groups, stag and hen weekends.

Baltic Holidays 40 Princess St, Manchester M1 6DE; ℡ 0870 757 9233; f 0870 120 2973; e info@balticholidays.com; www.balticholidays.com. Offers a very wide range of individual and group tours to all 3 Baltic states.

Exodus Travels Grange Mills, 9 Weir Rd, London SW12 OLT; ℡ 020 8673 0859; f 020 8673 0779; e info@exodus.co.uk; www.exodus.co.uk. Cycling groups to Latvia and Estonia, plus general tours covering the 3 Baltic states.

Explore Worldwide Nelson Hse, 55 Victoria Rd, Farnborough, Hants GU4 7PA; ℡ 0870 333 4001; f 01252 391110; e info@explore.co.uk; www.exploreworldwide.com. Operates a 2-week group tour through the 3 Baltic states, with departures throughout the summer.

Kirker Holidays 4 Waterloo Ct, 10 Theed St, London SE1 8ST; ℡ 0870 112 3333; f 0870 066 0628; e travel@kirkerholidays.com; www.kirkerholidays.com. De-luxe individual short breaks to the 3 Baltic capitals.

Martin Randall Travel Voysey Hse, Barley Mow Passage, London W4 4GF; ℡ 020 8742 3355; f 020 8742 7766; e info@martinrandall.co.uk; www.martinrandall.com. Group tours to the Baltic states for those interested in art, architecture and music, including a tour each year to the Riga Opera Festival.

Opera Tours The Tower, Mill La, Rainhill, Prescot, Merseyside L35 6NE; ℡/f 0151 493 0382; e info@operasabroad.com; www.operasabroad.com. Individual packages including opera or concert tickets.

Regent Holidays 15 John St, Bristol BS1 2HR; ℡ 0117 921 1711; f 0117 925 4866; e regent@regent-holidays.co.uk; www.regent-holidays.co.uk. The only UK operator to promote Kaliningrad as well as the Baltic states. Group tours cover the four capitals; city breaks are available to each of them and tailor-made individual itineraries can cover any combination of the cities with the surrounding areas. Itineraries can also include Belarus, Finland, Poland and Russia.

Scantours 73 Mornington St, London NW1 7QE; ℡ 020 7554 3530; f 020 7387 4496; e info@scantoursUK.com; www.scantoursuk.com. Offer city breaks, group tours and individual arrangements to 3 of the Baltic capitals and also combinations with Denmark, Sweden and Finland.

Specialised Tours 4 Copthorne Bank, Copthorne, Crawley, West Sussex RH10 3QX; ℡ 01342 712785; f 01342 717042; e info@specialisedtours.com; www.specialisedtours.com. Arrange short breaks to 3 of the Baltic capitals, a Classical Baltics tour linking the 3, and individual arrangements throughout the Baltics.

Travel Editions 69–85 Tabernacle St, London EC2A 4BD; ℡ 020 7251 0045; f 020 7251 7399; e tours@traveleditions.co.uk; www.traveleditions.co.uk. Group tours, many arranged as newspaper readers' offers.

Vamos Travel 2 Styles Cl, Leamington Spa Warks CV31 1LS; ℡ 0870 762 4017; f 0870 762 1016; e info@vamostravel.com; www.vamostravel.com. Specialises in stag weekends and sporting breaks.

Ireland As direct flights started from Dublin to the Baltic capitals in 2004, tour operators soon followed with appropriate programmes for city breaks and longer stays. The two with the widest range of possibilities in 2005 were:

Citiescapes 6 Castle St, Bray, Co Wicklow; ℡ 01 276 1222; f 01 276 0101; e book@citiescapes.ie; www.citiescapes.ie

Home & Abroad 1 Wexford St, Dublin 2; ℡ 01 475 1177; f 01 475 4683; e sales@homeandabroad.ie; www.homeandabroad.ie

GETTING AROUND

BY AIR Domestic flights in Estonia operate between Tallinn and the islands of Hiiumaa and Saaremaa. In Lithuania they operate in the summer between Vilnius and Palanga on the coast. In Latvia Air Baltic started flights from Riga to Liepaja in the summer of 2005. From Monday to Friday there are flights three times a day between Tallinn and Riga and Riga and Vilnius. A morning and evening flight operates between Tallinn and Vilnius. There are no flights to Kaliningrad from the other Baltic capitals, only from Warsaw and St Petersburg.

BY TRAIN Most tourists never use the rail services in the Baltic states as so few meet their needs. None operates between the three capitals. Normally buses are quicker and more regular, both between the countries and on domestic routes. The only train routes likely to be of use to tourists are from Tallinn to Paldiski, from Riga to Jurmala, and from Kaliningrad to Svetlogorsk, in each case from the capital to a nearby town on the coast. Day trains do, however, operate between Vilnius and Kaliningrad and can be considered as an alternative to the bus.

English is not often spoken in railway stations but timetables are clearly displayed, although in Kaliningrad this is of course in the Cyrillic alphabet. Russian is in fact the first language of most railway employees throughout the Baltics. Tickets for the suburban services mentioned above are sold on the train.

BY BUS The most convenient way to travel between all four cities is by bus. Most services are run by Eurolines and Baltic specialists abroad can pre-book these. In the winter, it is often possible to buy a seat on the spot before departure. The journey time between Tallinn and Riga and also between Riga and Vilnius is around five hours. Buses operate about six times a day on both sectors and the one-way fare is around £8/US$15. There is a daily bus from Kaliningrad to Riga which takes around nine hours and one night bus between Kaliningrad and Vilnius which takes eight hours. The one-way fare on these routes is also around £7/US$10. For those in no rush between Kaliningrad and Vilnius, there are six buses a day between Kaliningrad and Klaipeda which run along the Curonian Spit. These then connect with hourly services between Klaipeda and Vilnius. Allow about ten hours for the whole journey.

Extensive services operate in all four cities and local maps will give details of current routings. In Tallinn, where several competing companies operate, service numbers change quite frequently so it is important to get an up-to-date map. In the other cities, a regular pattern has now been set so few changes are likely in the near future. In Riga and Vilnius, the airports are served by a good local bus service. This is less regular in Tallinn, but as several hotels have a minibus service and a taxi into town should not cost more than £4/US$7, this does not matter so much. In Kaliningrad the local bus that serves the airport does not pass close to any of the hotels so most tourists are collected by their local travel agent.

Tickets bought at kiosks in Tallinn and Vilnius are cheaper than those bought on the bus and in Tallinn 2005 saw the introduction of bus passes for various durations from 2 to 72 hours. Visitors staying for several days at hotels in the outskirts should investigate season tickets. Riga and Tallinn have tourist passes which include free local transport as part of the total package but, as the price of these is rather high, visitors will normally save money by paying fares and admission charges as they go.

Buses link the capitals with all other major cities in their respective countries on a very regular basis. For instance between Tallinn and Tartu, or Vilnius and Kaunas, services operate every half-hour. Timetables are displayed in the bus stations and in most cases the fare is paid directly to the driver.

BY TAXI Taxis used to be a nightmare throughout the Baltics but are now properly regulated in all four cities. Within city limits, meter fares apply and this is also the case to and from the airports. Taxis can be easily hailed in the streets and with the lively nightlife for which all four cities are now renowned, they operate almost round the clock. Taxis ordered by phone are usually cheaper than those hailed on the street so visitors planning to make many such journeys should enquire on arrival about reliable companies. These all use meters. Some of the de-luxe hotels operate their own fleets. These are metered; prices tend to be higher but then so is the comfort of the vehicles! Lengthy journeys which would be unthinkable by taxi in western Europe can be undertaken in the Baltics with costs being so much lower.

ACCOMMODATION

A massive programme of hotel renovation took place throughout the area following the demise of the Soviet Union. The cities approached this task in different ways. Tallinn and Riga started by renovating the large tower blocks bequeathed by the Soviet Union and several have now gone through two separate renovations since 1991. From the mid 1990s, smaller hotels opened in the old town centres and also in the more affluent suburbs. In Vilnius, the reverse process operated with new small hotels opening first and only in 2002 did renovation begin at the Lietuva Hotel. In all three cities, visitors have now, for many years, taken for granted proper plumbing, satellite television, English-speaking reception staff and varied menus in the restaurants. In Kaliningrad, the lack of investment incentives and the lower number of visitors has let modernisation proceed at a much slower pace so most hotels remain large and impersonal. The year 2006 will see a large number of new hotels opening in Tallinn and Riga; some will be enormous new buildings, others renovations of older ones. Given the occupancy rates hotels in both cities enjoyed in 2005, there will be no problem in filling these new rooms, at least during the summer. Vilnius is likely to have its second hotel boom in 2007.

The bigger hotels rarely expect visitors to pay the prices given on their websites as most book through agents who have negotiated lower rates. Many smaller hotels now also prefer to use agents since the volume of regular business they provide compensates for the lower prices they pay. Four- and five-star hotels reduce their prices at weekends, over public holidays and in July–August when business traffic drops. Three-star hotels tend to raise their prices then since they cater largely for tourists.

It is always wise to pre-book hotels not only for the lower prices but also simply to secure a room. A relatively small conference or sporting event may lead to the whole town being full. Pre-booking in Kaliningrad is in any case essential to secure a Russian visa.

In their renovations many hotels are only putting in showers and not baths in the rooms. Tourists who prefer baths should ask their tour operator to stipulate this when making the booking.

EATING AND DRINKING

It is perhaps in restaurants and bars that the transformation from the old days is most apparent in Tallinn, Riga and Vilnius. *In Your Pocket* and the *City Paper* now list hundreds of choices in each city and what is gratifying is the number that still exist five or six years after opening. Every major cuisine is represented and, with the numbers of restaurants now available, advance booking is often not necessary. It is worth venturing outside the old city areas: the best food is often to be found in their immediate vicinity and there is little risk of seeing other tourists there, and certainly not large groups. One has to be brutally honest about local food. Whilst there are many perfectly acceptable dishes, few are memorable. However, they should at least be made from fresh ingredients, now that these are available year-round. Thick soups can be recommended in winter as meals in themselves, and pancakes are served with a variety of savoury or sweet fillings. The ranges of coffee, cakes and ice cream available are one positive legacy of Soviet and German times.

Kaliningrad has made progress recently and there is sufficient choice to cover a stay of a week or so. Prices are so low that it would be invidious to complain about the quality; a wide menu can now be taken for granted but do not yet expect many non-Russian restaurants.

Wine is quite expensive throughout the region and the quality unexciting. It is often better (and much cheaper) to drink local beer. Spirits are good everywhere with a wide local and international choice. Tourists who knew the old USSR will still find it hard to adjust to a small café in the Baltics offering a choice of malt whiskies, at prices half those charged in Scotland.

MEDIA AND COMMUNICATIONS

TELEPHONES AND POST Public telephones in all four countries are operated by cards which can be bought at local kiosks. Cards are not interchangeable so new ones have to be bought for each country. It is not possible to use credit cards, nor do any phones accept coins. Instructions are usually given in English in the phone booths. The procedure is the same in all four countries: the receiver is lifted, the card inserted and then the number dialled. As the call continues, the reducing value of the card is shown on the screen. Calls to western Europe cost around £0.60/US$1 a minute with reductions in the evenings and at weekends. With competition from mobile phone companies, prices are tending to fall. Prices from hotel rooms are of course higher than this but they are rarely exorbitant. Calls to local mobile phones can cost almost as much as international calls, particularly in Estonia. Calls can be made from all major post offices.

Dialling codes and information specific to the various countries are given in the individual city chapters later in the book. However, to make an international call from all four countries, dial 00 followed by the country code:

Australia	61	Ireland	353
Canada	1	Italy	39
Estonia	372	Lithuania	370
Finland	358	UK	44
France	33	USA	1
Germany	49		

Post from the three Baltic states is transmitted quickly, reaching western Europe or America within four or five days. From Kaliningrad, post has to travel via Moscow so tends to take at least two weeks. Postage rates are fairly similar in all four countries, with higher charges applying for cards and letters sent out of Europe. As they sell thick envelopes and parcel paper, it is easy to send home books and other bulky items bought during a tour. Post offices sell cards at very reasonable rates. The one at the top of Tallinn Old Town charges less than half the price demanded by sellers in the street outside! Stamps can naturally only be used in their country of origin so do not forget to use them before moving on!

All major courier companies such as DHL, Fedex and UPS have offices in each of the capitals.

NEWSPAPERS AND MAGAZINES The *In Your Pocket* series of mini-guides to each of the capitals provides invaluable information for each city, including listings of restaurants, museum opening hours, postage rates and details of public transport. Their irreverent style is a pleasant contrast to the minimal official tourist material that is produced locally. Where appropriate they can be highly critical. For Tallinn, Riga and Vilnius the guides are produced locally every couple of months, so are always up to date. The Kaliningrad one is produced on an irregular basis, if at all, from Vilnius so is less reliable. Guides cost the equivalent of £1.50/US$2.50 and are available at many hotels and kiosks. They are published in full on the website (*www.inyourpocket.com*) so this is worth consulting before departure.

The *Baltic Times* is published weekly in Riga (in English) and covers contemporary politics in the three main Baltic countries. The *Königsberg Express*, published monthly in German in Kaliningrad, fulfils a similar role there. European editions of the main American and British newspapers are available on the morning of publication in Tallinn, Riga and Vilnius. German papers occasionally reach Kaliningrad. In the winter they are sold in the Kaliningrad Hotel and in the summer also in Svetlogorsk.

The *City Paper*, published monthly in Tallinn, in a sense combines the *Baltic Times* and the *In Your Pocket* guides. Each issue costs about £1.30/US$2. It has useful background articles on contemporary politics, thoughtful restaurant reviews and excellent practical information on the three main Baltic capitals. It is an excellent introduction to the area and earlier issues are covered on its website (*www.balticsworldwide.com*).

TELEVISION All hotels used regularly by foreign tourists now have satellite television, offering at least one English-language channel. Many offer both American and British channels, realising that most visitors have a clear preference for one or the other.

MUSEUMS

In all four countries, museums tend to have short opening hours and close at least one day a week. Monday is the most likely day for closure. Although opening times tend to change frequently, the *In Your Pocket* guides carry this information, as do the local tourist offices. Where museums have useful websites with details of their current opening hours, these are listed. It is rare for museums to open before 10.30 in the morning. Smaller ones are happy to open specially for groups and tour operators usually arrange this so that their party can have the building to themselves. This arrangement is particularly attractive at the Mentzendorf House and at the Rozentals Museum in Riga, both of which can take around 25 people in comfort, but not more. Most have an admission charge, though this is rarely higher than the equivalent of £1/US$1.50. Pensioners are often admitted free of charge.

HEALTH

No inoculations are required for visits to this area and hygiene standards in hotels and restaurants are high. Nevertheless, it would be wise here, as at home, to be up to date with immunisations against diphtheria and polio. Tap water should not be drunk in Kaliningrad but is safe elsewhere in the Baltic states. It is wise to carry around a good insect repellent and to use it day and night if mosquitoes are around. Local hospitals can be trusted to deal with any emergency; long gone are the days when foreigners flew to Helsinki or Stockholm for any minor ailment. EU passport holders are entitled to use health facilities in the Baltic states on the same basis as residents.

TRAVEL CLINICS AND HEALTH INFORMATION A full list of current travel clinic websites worldwide is available on www.istm.org. For other journey preparation information, consult www.tripprep.com. Information about various medications may be found on www.emedicine.com/wild/topiclist.htm.

CRIME

This is much less of a problem than in most European capitals, although pickpockets are a threat in Tallinn and Riga old towns where the maze of small streets makes for an easy getaway. There have recently been attacks on rich foreigners in Tallinn leaving clubs late at night. Car theft is common throughout the area and cars should always be left overnight in a guarded hotel parking lot.

Passports and air tickets can fairly safely be left in hotel rooms, locked in cases. Otherwise usual sensible precautions apply. Do not take out large sums of cash when walking around the main tourist areas. What might be a modest sum to a Western tourist can be a month's pay for a local youngster so it is not surprising that some will succumb to temptation when offered the chance.

MAJOR DATES IN BALTIC HISTORY

1201	Riga founded.
1221	First recorded demonstration in Riga against occupation.
1323	Vilnius documented for the first time in a letter by Grand Duke Gediminas, who made it Lithuania's capital.
1386	Royal union of Poland and Lithuania.
1410	Polish-Lithuanian army defeats the Teutonic Knights, ending German hegemony over the Baltic region.
1544	Founding of Königsberg University.
1569	Polish-Lithuanian Commonwealth formed.
1579	Founding of Vilnius University.
1581	Riga falls to the Polish-Lithuanian Commonwealth.
1600	Tallinn seized by the Swedes.
1621	Riga seized by the Swedes.
1710	Riga and Tallinn seized by the Russians.
1758–62	Russians occupy Königsberg for four years.
1794	Vilnius seized by the Russians.
1795	Polish-Lithuanian Commonwealth is wiped off the map; Vilnius becomes a provincial capital of the Tsarist Empire.
1812	Napoleon seizes Vilnius but his forces are driven back a few months later. Riga's wooden suburbs were burnt to prepare to defend the Old Town against Napoleon, who instead advanced towards Moscow.
1836	Richard Wagner moves to Königsberg from Magdeburg to marry and to escape his creditors. The following year he would move to Riga to take up an appointment as Director of Music (and also to be further from his creditors).
1873	First Song Festival held in Riga.
1918	Lithuanian independence is declared in Vilnius on 16 February, Estonian independence declared on 24 February in Tallinn, and Latvian independence in Riga on 18 November.
1920	In the Treaty of Tartu of 2 February 1920, the Treaty of Moscow of 12 July, and the Treaty of Riga of 1 August, the Soviet Union recognises the independence of each of the Baltic states. Polish troops seize Vilnius on 9 October and it will remain under Polish occupation until autumn 1939. Kaunas is established as a temporary capital of Lithuania.
1924	On 1 December an attempted coup d'état by the Communist Party of Estonia fails.
1933	In elections held on 5 March, the Nazis win 53% of the vote in Königsberg, one of the highest percentages anywhere in Germany.

1939	Molotov-Ribbentrop pact signed on 23 August. On 9 October, Hitler summons the Baltic-German communities of Tallinn and Riga 'back home' even though most had been settled in the Baltics for centuries.
1940	Between 14 and 16 June, Tallinn, Riga and Vilnius are occupied by Soviet troops. The three Baltic states would be formally incorporated into the USSR on 21 July.
1941	The Baltic capitals each fall to the German army as it advances into Russia; Vilnius on 23 June, Riga on 1 July and Tallinn on 28 August.
1944	Reoccupation by Soviet troops of Vilnius on 7 July, of Tallinn on 22 September and of Riga on 13 October.
1945	On 10 April, General Lasch surrenders Königsberg to the Red Army.
1946	In July Königsberg is renamed Kaliningrad.
1947	In October the deportation begins of all remaining Germans in Kaliningrad.
1960	Tallinn, Riga and Vilnius are opened to foreign tourists for stays of no more than three nights. Kaliningrad will stay closed until 1988.
1965	A twice-weekly ferry service opens between Tallinn and Helsinki, which will remain the only link with the West until 1989.
1980	Olympic Games sailing and yachting events held in Tallinn.
1986	On 14 June, the first demonstration since the return of Soviet power in 1944 is held beside the Freedom Monument in Riga.
1988	On 11 September Trivimi Velliste, a future Foreign Minister, publicly demands Estonian independence in front of an audience of 300,000 at the Song Festival Amphitheatre in Tallinn.
1989	A human chain of two million people links Vilnius, Riga and Tallinn on 23 August, the 50th anniversary of the signing of the Molotov-Ribbentrop Pact.
1990	11 March. The restoration of Lithuanian independence is declared in Vilnius by Vytautas Landsbergis from the same balcony used on 16 February 1918.
1991	Fourteen protestors defending the Vilnius Television Tower are killed by Soviet troops on 13 January. On 20 January five protestors would be similarly killed in Riga. 20–21 August. Following the unsuccessful coup in Moscow against President Gorbachev, Estonia and Latvia declare independence. Worldwide diplomatic recognition for all three Baltic states follows within the next few days.
1993	On 31 August the last Soviet troops leave Lithuania; they would finally leave Latvia and Estonia in 1994.
2002	Eurovision Song Contest held in Tallinn. The 2003 one took place in Riga.
2004	The three Baltic states join NATO in April and the EU in May.
2005	3 July. Gerhard Schröder and Jacques Chirac visit Kaliningrad, the first foreign heads of state to do so.
2006	On 14 March the former Estonian President, Lennart Meri, dies.
2008	Likely introduction of the euro in the three Baltic states.

2

Tallinn

Whether approached by air, land or sea, Tallinn is immediately identifiable as a capital that looks West rather than East. The departure board at the airport lists London, Copenhagen and Stockholm but rarely St Petersburg. The boats that fill the harbour, be they massive ferries or small yachts, head for Finland and Sweden, not Russia. The traffic jams that are beginning to block the main streets are caused by Volkswagens, Land Rovers and Saabs, not by Ladas. Links with the West are celebrated, those with Russia are commemorated. In May 1998, Tallinn celebrated its 750th anniversary since on 15 May 1248 it adopted Lübeck Town Law, which united most members of the Hanseatic League. A month later, as on every 14 June, flags were lowered in memory of those deported to the Soviet Union on 14 June 1941.

Immediately after independence Western goods started pouring into the shops, and Russian ones are now very hard to find. There is a similar reluctance to buy from any of the other former Soviet Republics. Travel agents offer the same tempting prices for holidays in Turkey, Greece and Italy that are available in western Europe, but nobody is interested in St Petersburg or the Crimea. Architecturally, with the exception of the Alexander Nevsky Cathedral, it is the Germans, Swedes and Danes who have left their imposing mark on the churches and fortifications of the Old Town. Tallinn was always ready to defend itself but in the end never did so. The nearest it came to a major battle was at the conclusion of the Northern War in 1710, but plague had reduced the population from 10,000 to 2,000 so the Swedes offered little resistance to the army of Peter the Great. It has suffered many occupations but, apart from a Soviet bombing raid in 1944, the city has not been physically harmed as no battles were ever fought there.

The division in Tallinn between what is now the Old Town on the hill (Toompea) and the newer town around the port has survived political administrations of every hue. It has divided God from Mammon, Tsarist and Soviet governors from their reluctant Estonian subjects, and now the Estonian parliament from successful bankers, merchants and manufacturers who thrive on whatever coalition happens to be in power. Tallinn has no Capitol Hill or Whitehall. The parliament building is one of the most modest in the Old Town, dwarfed by the town walls and surrounding churches. When fully restored, the Old Town will be an outstanding permanent monument to Gothic and baroque architecture, and a suitable backcloth to formal political and religious activity. Outside its formidable wall, contemporary Tallinn will change rapidly according to the demands of the new business ethos.

HISTORY

Written records on Tallinn date only from the 12th century although it is clear that a small port existed well before then. In 1219 the Danes occupied Tallinn and much of what is now northern Estonia, on the pretext of spreading Christianity. The name Tallinn dates from this time and in Estonian actually means 'Danish city'. Although this name was chosen to suggest only temporary occupation, it has been maintained. The first German merchants settled in 1228 and they were to maintain their economic domination until 1939, even during the long periods of Swedish and Tsarist rule. Their elaborate coats of arms, displayed in the Dome and Niguliste churches, were a formal expression of this power. When, for instance, the Swedes surrendered to the Russians in 1710, the capitulation documents confirmed that German would remain the official language of commerce. Reval, the German name for Tallinn, is sometimes seen in English publications; it probably comes from *Revala*, the old Estonian name for the surrounding area. A more colourful explanation is that it comes from the two German words *Reh* and *Fall*, meaning the falling of the deer as they attempt to escape the Danish occupation.

Peter the Great visited Tallinn on 11 different occasions, so crucial was the city as an ice-free port to his empire. In 1711 he joined Christmas celebrations in Town Hall Square. He instigated the permanent expansion of Tallinn beyond the city walls by building Kadriorg Palace near the coast about two miles from the Old Town. The previous history of constant warfare at least in the vicinity of the town had led to all buildings being makeshift wooden houses which could easily be burnt as a preliminary defence to the city. Tallinn was then to enjoy 200 years of peace and increasing prosperity. Architecturally, though, the Old Town has always remained the centre of Tallinn and its main attraction. Gert Walter, a Baltic German who settled in East Germany and could therefore return to Tallinn during the Soviet period, describes the Old Town as having 0.5% of the surface area of Tallinn but giving it its entire magic.

The completion of the railway link with St Petersburg in 1870 turned Tallinn into a major city. The port was enlarged to handle the increasing volume of goods that could now be brought there and factories were established to take advantage of the larger markets. In the 20th century, most events that would determine Estonia's future took place in Tallinn. Independence was declared there in 1918 and in 1991, German occupations were imposed there also in 1918 and again in 1941. The Soviets came in 1940 and then chased the Germans out in 1944. In the 20th century, the Russians and Germans between them occupied Tallinn seven times, and the country has been independent three times, although it has to be admitted that independence on the first occasion in 1918 lasted only for one day. Britain can claim considerable credit for ensuring that the next period of independence would last much longer – 20 years. Intervention by the Royal Navy during 1918–19 in the Gulf of Finland near Tallinn ensured that neither the Bolsheviks nor the Germans were able to conquer Estonia at that time.

The port always adapted to the political circumstances in which it found itself. During the first independence period from 1920 to 1940 it exported large quantities of timber and dairy products to Britain as the market to the new Soviet Union was lost. Passenger services linked it with all its Baltic neighbours. It would suffer a moribund 45 years from 1945 until 1990 with little international trade being allowed. The twice-weekly ferry service that operated for Finnish visitors from the 1960s rapidly increased to a boat an hour during the 1990s as the notorious 'vodka tourists' poured in, together with some other visitors who had broader interests. Whilst 2.5 million passengers a year come to Tallinn on this route, the port has to battle hard with Russian, Latvian and Lithuanian ports for the transit traffic in goods from Russia and central Asia.

Between 1945 and 1990 the city's population doubled in size to 500,000, about 30% of the total population of Estonia. Since then, Tallinn's population, like that of the whole country, has dropped considerably as couples delay starting families and living on one's own becomes more popular. It is now approximately 380,000. The year 2002 was the first year since 1990 when more births than deaths were registered.

Michael Bourdeaux

For 15 years after World War II, Tallinn was a closed city, nestling amongst the forest of defensive (offensive) weaponry trained on the NATO countries. Suddenly in 1960 it was opened to Western visitors. I was lucky enough to have been a student at Moscow University at the time, so in May 1960 I was perhaps the first British visitor. I not only went there by train from Leningrad but also stayed illegally in a private house for the first and only time during the 25 years that I knew the Soviet Union. Far from being worried that I would bring trouble on their heads, the occupants barred the exit and refused to let me out until I had agreed to stay for three nights, having found my own photograph displayed on their wall!

All of us, as if by common agreement, steered clear of the topic of the Soviet occupation but the family thoroughly organised my time for the next three days. After eight months in drab winter Moscow, the élan of ancient Tallinn in its bright spring colours took me into a new world. A visit on Sunday to Kaide's Lutheran church, St Charles' Church, left mixed impressions. Strangely, the family did not want to accompany me. This huge church was about half full, with 40% of the congregation younger people, a far higher proportion than one saw in Russia. I tried to see the pastor after the service, but the corridor was blocked by dozens of young people waiting outside his door. None of these, to my surprise, would speak to me, although most must have known Russian. I surmised they were waiting for religious instruction, illegal under the Soviet system at the time, and were unwilling for a foreigner (or a Russian if they took me for one) to intrude.

On my final day, having purchased an air ticket to Riga, I was waiting on the tarmac beside a small aeroplane. An official came up to me, demanded my documents, took me inside and told me my intended flight was illegal for a foreigner. 'Our rules are less strict than yours in Britain for Soviet citizens,' he said. 'When I was there, I was prevented from visiting many places. You can go where you like, but not always by your chosen route. Visit Riga by all means, but you must do so by train via Leningrad.'

SUGGESTED ITINERARIES

ONE DAY Spend the whole day in the Old Town starting at the top of the Toompea Hill around 09.00 when the churches open but before the cruise passengers are brought there. Start at the Alexander Nevsky Cathedral (page 52), continue to the Dome Church (page 52), walk down Lühike jalg ('Short Leg') and drop into the Adamson-Eric Museum (page 45) at the bottom of the hill to be amazed at how one man can produce art in so many shapes and forms. A visit to Niguliste Church (St Nicholas') (page 53) should finish the morning.

Spend midday around Town Hall Square and, if the weather permits, climb the Town Hall Tower for a view of contemporary Tallinn before going down to the basement (page 51) to see the exhibition on how the square has looked over the last 800 years. Do not forget to use the toilets here as they offer the best views of the foundations.

Continue the afternoon at the City Museum (page 45) and allow an hour to watch all the films which relive the bombing in 1944 and the independence demonstrations in 1988–91. Have a cup of tea in the café at the top and then finish up at the Maritime Museum (page 49) to see how and why so many nations fought for control of the harbour. Only the British (and the Estonians!) are presented in a favourable light. The latest exhibit covers the tragedy of the *Estonia* which sank in September 1994, claiming 850 lives. The two streets that link the museum to the Viru Gate, Uus and Müürivahe, are ideal for a final stroll, as they have a range of buildings to admire, but also small cafés and shops. Do take a walk around the Old Town after sunset to see the major buildings bathed in floodlight.

TWO DAYS After a totally urban day, some greenery is called for, so start by taking the tram to Kadriorg Palace (page 59) and linger in the gardens before going in. Do not miss the porcelain at the Mikkeli Museum (page 60) before walking on to KUMU (page 59), the new art museum that opened in February 2006. A rest will be needed before setting off further out of town to the Song Festival Grounds (page 58). Try to imagine 5,000 people singing here, or come in July 2009 and see the real thing. Take the bus back to Vabaduse Väljak (Freedom Square), an area where there are many cafés for lunch. Look in at the Tallinn Art Hall to see which contemporary artists are in favour, and then face the Occupation Museum (page 50) which shows the horrors and banalities of life under the Soviet and German occupations between 1940 and 1991. Finish the afternoon at the National Library (page 49). Hopefully there will be a concert in the early evening either at Niguliste (page 53) or at the Dome Church (page 52).

PRACTICALITIES

MONEY AND BANKING
Currency The Estonian kroon is tied to the euro at the rate of 15.65EEK. In April 2006 exchange rates against the pound and US dollar were £1 = 22.60EEK and US$1 = 13.00EEK.

Banks and credit cards The **Hansapank** at Vanu Turg 2 and the **Äripank** at Vana Viru 7, close to the Viru Gate, usually give the best exchange rate for pounds and dollars. The nearby **Tavid** exchange at Aia 5 is very useful for getting rid of unwanted notes from all over the world. During the day, their rates are as good as those at Äripank and they do not charge commission so even small amounts can sensibly be exchanged. Tavid is open around the clock but from 19.00 until 09.00 the following day during the week, and from 17.00 at the weekends, their rates worsen considerably, often by as much as 10%. In December 2005, Tavid opened a new office at Kullassepa 2, beside Town Hall Square, but their good rates only apply for transactions equivalent to €200 or more. Elsewhere in the town, both at banks and exchange bureaux, the rate for pounds can vary enormously whereas that for dollars is less erratic. There are many exchange bureaux and banks along Viru which leads from Viru Square to Town Hall Square. Check the rates before deciding which to use. The exchange bureaux are open daily from 10.00 until 19.00. Banks close at 17.00 or 18.00 and do not usually open at weekends, except for those branches based in large shopping centres which open on both Saturday and Sunday. ATMs (cashpoints) are available throughout the town.

Appalling rates for all currencies can always be guaranteed at the 'airside' bureau in Tallinn Airport and at the bus station so these two outlets should be avoided. The banks 'landside' at the airport and those at the railway station offer reasonable rates. Tourists are advised not to accept notes of 500EEK when changing money since they are often difficult to use as most transactions will involve much smaller sums or can be paid by credit card. At the time of publication, it was still uncertain whether Estonia would join the euro in 2007 or 2008.

LOCAL MEDIA The *Baltic Times*, published weekly on a Thursday, is the best English-language source of news for the three Baltic republics. It also lists exhibitions and concerts. *Tallinn In Your Pocket*, published every two months, is invaluable for its independent – and therefore irreverent – reviews on restaurants, museums and other sites. *The City Paper*, published monthly, covers Tallinn, Riga and Vilnius together in a similar way to *Tallinn In Your Pocket* but with the addition of political articles. The printed publication now concentrates more on background articles, but their website has a full and critical list of hotels and restaurants. Both *The City Paper* and *Tallinn In Your Pocket* are a welcome contrast to many worthy but dull local guidebooks. Travel agents abroad who specialise in the Baltics will be able to provide copies of both publications or they are available online (*www.inyourpocket.com* and *www.balticsworldwide.com*). Several free-of-charge listings magazines are circulated by hotels and local travel agents but as these are supported totally by advertising, they cannot really be trusted.

European editions of British and American newspapers are on sale in Tallinn at the larger hotels on the day of publication.

There are no local radio or television stations that transmit in English.

COMMUNICATIONS

Telephones Public phone boxes take phone cards, which can be bought at kiosks; they do not take cash or credit cards. Calls can also be made from post offices. Mark-ups on phone calls from hotel rooms vary enormously. Some hotels have wisely reduced prices to persuade visitors not to use their mobile phones; others have kept charges that were acceptable in the 1990s but are not any longer. As in Britain, there is now no distinction in Estonia between costs for local or national calls, although some hotels still maintain one. From a phone box, reckon to spend about 40p/70c a minute to phone a landline in Britain or North America.

Dialling To reach Tallinn by phone from abroad, first dial the international code 00, second the Estonia country code 372, and then the Tallinn seven-digit number. This will always begin with a '6'. A similar system operates in other areas of Estonia. For instance, all Tartu numbers begin with a '7'. To reach phones abroad from Tallinn dial 00 and then the relevant country code.

Mobile phones Many Estonians now have mobile phones, which are operated by a number of different companies. They each have a separate access code which is dialled after the 372 and which replaces the city code of 6. Despite the popularity of mobile phones, calls to and from them are still much more expensive than those to and from landlines.

The SMS craze has hit Tallinn more vigorously than most other cities. Such was the variety of services already then available that in autumn 2003 *Tallinn In Your Pocket* devoted a special section to this topic. Paying for car parks and checking bank balances this way is now old hat for Tallinners, as is checking the weather and finding a recipe for dinner. Recent additions include donating food for a baby elephant at Tallinn Zoo and buying condoms from machines that used to accept cash.

Useful telephone numbers

Ambulance and Fire Brigade 112	Police 110
Central Hospital 620 7015	Telephone Information 626 1111
City Tourist Office 645 7777	

Post The **Central Post Office** is at Narva mnt 1, opposite the Viru Hotel. It has relatively short opening hours (*Mon–Fri 08.00–20.00, Sat 08.00–18.00*). It is closed on Sunday. It sells postcards, changes money and provides telephone services. Tourists often use the post office at the top of the Old Town at Lossi plats 4 beside the Alexander Nevsky Cathedral but this is only open 09.00–17.00 Monday–Friday. For collectors, it has a wide selection of stamps, and postcards are sold at much lower prices than those charged elsewhere in the Old Town. The postal service is extremely efficient, with cards reaching anywhere in Europe within a few days.

Internet All major hotels have a business centre offering a full range of services including internet access but the charges are high – usually around 100EEK per half hour. Terminals are free of charge, but therefore often in use, at the National Library. Kaubamaja, the department store at the back of the Viru Hotel, charges 40EEK an hour; the store is open seven days a week (*Mon–Fri 09.00–21.00, Sat 09.00–20.00 and Sun 10.00–18.00*). By far the cheapest centre in Tallinn is **Matrix** at Tartu 31, on the road to the bus station and airport. It charges only 15EEK an hour and is open day and night. The clientele is largely teenagers playing computer games and looking at sites which their parents would probably try to ban at home. The café beside the bus station under the Viru Centre can be recommended for those who prefer to make frequent short use of internet cafés. They have a 'season ticket' for ten hours costing only EEK100 which allows unlimited access for that time-frame.

The computers which used to be available for free public use at the airport have been withdrawn. Only those passengers with access to the business lounges now have this facility.

EMBASSIES

Canada Toom-Kooli 13; ✆ 627 3311; f 627 3312; e tallinn@canada.ee

Ireland Vene 2; ✆ 681 1888; f 681 1899; e embassytallinn@eircom.net

Latvia Tõnismägi 10; ✆ 646 1313; f 631 1366

Lithuania Uus 15; ✆ 631 4030; f 641 2013; e amber@anet.ee; www.hot.ee/lietambasada

Russia Pikk 19; ✆ 646 4175; f 646 4178; e vensaat@online.ee; www.estonia.mid.ru

UK Wismari 6; ✆ 667 4700; f 667 4723; e information@britishembassy.ee; www.britishembassy.ee

USA Kentmanni 20; ✆ 668 8100; f 668 8134; e tallinn@usemb.ee; www.usemb.ee

HOSPITALS AND PHARMACIES
The Central Hospital (✆ *620 7015*) on Ravi provides 24-hour emergency care and the 24-hour pharmacy (✆ *644 2282*) is at Tõnismägi 5. Long gone are the days when foreigners who fell ill demanded to be taken immediately to Helsinki.

RELIGIOUS SERVICES
Tallinn now has an active religious life, with services held regularly at all the re-functioning churches in the Old Town. An English-language service is held every Sunday at 15.00 at the Holy Ghost Church. Full details are available on www.eelk.ee/tallinna.puhavaimu. The synagogue is on Karu near the harbour. There is currently no mosque in Tallinn.

TOURIST INFORMATION
The **Tallinn Tourist Board** has a shopfront office on the corner of Kullassepa and Niguliste (St Nicholas') which sells a small range of books, maps and cards. They have up-to-date editions of *Tallinn In Your Pocket* and *The City Paper*. There is also a large reference folder with timetables for ferries to Finland, buses out of Tallinn and local railways. There is a similar office in the ticket hall by the harbour. This office, like all other tourist offices around Estonia, has a website (*www.visitestonia.com*). Visiting these sites before departure will save a lot of time on arrival.

For tourists who arrive without having pre-booked any excursions, or who need to book further accommodation in the Baltic area, this tourist office (on the corner of Kullassepa 4/Niguliste 2) can advise on local operators with regular programmes. Recommended ones include:

Baltic Tours Pikk 31; ✆ 630 0460; f 630 0411;
e incoming@baltictours.ee; www.bt.ee
Estonian Holidays Rüütli 28/30; ✆ 627 0500; f 627

0501; e holidays@holidays.ee; www.holidays.ee
Estravel Suur-Karja 15; ✆ 626 6266; f 626 6262;
e sales@estravel.ee; www.estravel.ee

The Tallinn Card Vigorously promoted by the Tourist Board and in many hotels, the Tallinn Card will suit visitors keen to visit many museums and to travel to the outlying attractions. The cost includes a free sightseeing tour, free use of public transport and free admission to all museums. For those still active in the evenings it also includes free admission to the Hollywood nightclub. However, it has to be said that for those taking a more leisurely approach to their stay and who are based in the town centre, it may well be cheaper to pay as you go. No reductions in the cost are made on Mondays or Tuesdays when many museums are closed. Full details of what is included can be seen on www.tallinn.ee/tallinncard. From April 2006 the cost is 130EEK for 6 hours, 350EEK for 24 hours, 400EEK for 48 hours and 450EEK for 72 hours.

TRANSPORT

TALLINN AIRPORT The airport is only 3–4km from the town centre. The current building dates originally from 1980 as Tallinn suddenly needed to show an international face for the Olympics (sailing events were held in the Baltic) and has been modernised on several occasions to meet the demands of Western travellers since independence. Major renovation is again underway in 2006, with plans to name it after Lennart Meri, Estonia's first president who died in March 2006. He will always be remembered there for holding a press conference outside the gents' toilets to show his dissatisfaction with their lack of cleanliness.

A local bus service operates to the town centre every quarter of an hour with the final stop behind the Viru Hotel. Several other hotels such as the Radisson and the Central are within walking distance of this stop. Tickets bought from the driver cost 15EEK and only local currency can be used. (Tickets bought from kiosks cost 10EEK individually or 85EEK if bought in a block of ten; these are available at the landside kiosk where arriving passengers leave the baggage hall.) During the day taxis are easily available. They are all metered and cost about 100EEK into town. Passengers arriving on late-evening flights should pre-book a transfer through their travel agent as few taxis operate then and the bus service usually finishes around 23.30. The local bus from the airport passes the main bus station (*Autobussijaam*), which is useful for those wanting to continue journeys beyond Tallinn. Local buses, transfer coaches and taxis must be paid for in local currency.

There is an exchange bureau airside and also one landside in the arrivals area. The airside one offered outrageous rates throughout 2005, about EEK17.50 to the pound, when EEK23 was easily available in the town centre. There are two banks landside and the one nearer to the departures area usually offers better rates. For travellers arriving from Britain on an Estonian Air flight from Gatwick, the Thomas Cook exchange bureau at Gatwick handles Estonian kroon. There is a cashpoint in the arrivals area. There is no tourist information office or hotel-booking agency at the airport. American and British tourists plagued by high airport taxes at home will be relieved to hear that at Tallinn airport they are minimal. Flight schedules are available on the website (*www.tallinn-airport.ee*).

TAXIS Taxis are all metered and have a minimum fare of 35EEK. Journeys within the town centre should not cost more than 50EEK. As taxis are reasonably priced and always metered, they can be considered for long journeys. For instance, one to Lahemaa National Park, about 100km from Tallinn, is unlikely to cost more than 900EEK.

Taxi companies called by phone are always cheaper than those that ply for hire on the street or park at ranks. Their cars are a little older but perfectly safe and all have meters. Taxi Raadio (☏ 601 5111) are reliable and a journey to the airport with them rarely costs more than 60EEK.

LOCAL BUSES/TRAMS AND TROLLEYBUSES Many tourists to Tallinn never take either a bus or a taxi during their stay as the Old Town is very close to most of the hotels and the steep narrow roads conveniently restrict traffic to pedestrians anyway. Such visitors, however, miss everything that is cheaply and easily accessible by bus outside the Old Town. There are competing bus companies so exact routes and numbers change from time to time but services are frequent and the public transport map *Tallinn Ühistranspordi kaart*, published by Regio, is reprinted sufficiently often to be up to date. Some stops have maps but not all do and the names of the stops listed in the timetables are unlikely to mean much to visitors. The tram and trolleybus routes are of course fixed. In spring 2006 the flat fare was 10EEK for individual tickets bought from kiosks or 15EEK for tickets bought on the bus. A book of ten tickets bought at kiosks cost 85EEK, so buying one of these halves the cost of travel. Passes are available for stays of four days or longer. (See also *Tallinn Card*, page 21.) Good bus services operate to Pirita and Rocca al Mare and also to the cheaper suburban hotels such as the Dzingel and Susi. Tram enthusiasts will be pleased at the number of places relevant to tourists which their routes pass.

CAR HIRE This is not advisable within Tallinn. Distances are so short and parking so difficult that public transport, taxis and bicycles are the sensible way to get around. Visitors planning to travel to other towns can easily rely on buses but cars are very useful for seeing the coast and national parks. In the summer it is important to pre-book cars as demand invariably exceeds supply. Tour operators abroad can easily do this, as can the local agents listed above, or bookings can be made directly with the many international and local companies now involved in this business.

CYCLING This is a very sensible way of visiting the city, particularly as many places in the Old Town are difficult to reach by car and buses of course cannot travel on the narrow roads there. Much of the town is very flat and the rides out to Pirita or Rocca al Mare offer scenic and architectural perspectives not available in the centre. **City Bike** (☏ 511 1819 or 683 6383; e *mail@citybike.ee; www.citybike.ee*) have daily group tours around Tallinn and also arrange transport for cyclists to Lahemaa National Park or Paldiski. In April 2006 they opened an offive and a hostel at Uus 33 in the Old Town, where all their tours start and where their bicycles are kept.

🏠 **ACCOMMODATION**   *Hotel Bern*

Tallinn now has about 60 hotels but they are often fully booked at weekends, during trade fairs and in the peak summer season. Pre-booking is therefore always advisable. Specialist travel agents abroad often have access to lower prices than those quoted by the hotels directly, and they may also have allocations at several hotels specifically reserved for them. February 2001 saw the opening of the Radisson and during 2002 and 2003 several smaller hotels opened in the Old Town and just outside it. In 2004 the 200-room Tallink Hotel opened opposite the Viru Hotel, L'Ermitage next to the National Library and the Ülemiste beside the airport. There was little new in 2005 with only one major development, the Merchant's House, which may well have many successors in future years as hotels convert Old Town properties into quiet oases from the bustle outside. The years 2006 and 2007 will see several hotels taking advantage of the laxer planning environment recently introduced in Tallinn. The council is happy to see more skyscrapers and less control over renovation in the Old Town.

The recommendations that follow are obviously rather arbitrary and the omission of a hotel should in general be taken as resulting from lack of space rather than necessarily as a criticism. An ethical tour operator will be able to warn visitors away from the fortunately few hotels that have degenerated into brothels, which sadly cannot be listed as such here, much as one is tempted to take the risk. It can be assumed in all cases that the rooms in the hotels mentioned below have private facilities, that the hotel accepts credit cards, and that it has a restaurant and bar. Many hotels have saunas which guests can use free of charge. Baths are rare in Estonian hotels, even in four-star establishments, so should be specifically requested. By the time this book is published, probably all the hotels will be giving free WiFi access to their guests.

Luxury

🏨 **Parkconsul Schlössle** (27 rooms) Pühavaimu 13/15; ☎ 699 7700; f 699 7777; e schossle@consul-hotels.com; www.consul-hotels.com. For several years, this hotel was in a class on its own but competition finally came in 2003 with the opening of the Three Sisters (see opposite) and more will come with the opening of the Telegraaf in September 2006. A townhouse owned by many successful Baltic Germans over the years, the Parkconsul Schlössle was converted into Tallinn's first truly luxurious hotel and any senior government minister from abroad has always stayed here. It is small enough to maintain the air of a gracious private residence. There is a small conference centre, but it seems incongruous. The hotel is a setting for constant but unostentatious indulgence, for cigars rather than cigarettes, for champagne rather than wine. The restaurant, like all the best ones in Tallinn, is in a cellar and has an extensive menu. For those able briefly to abandon all this, the hotel is within walking distance of all the attractions in the Old Town. *Dbl 3,350EEK.*

🏨 **Telegraaf** (80 rooms) Vene 9; ☎ 600 0600; f 600 0601; e info@telegraafhotel.ee; www.telegraafhotel.ee. When this opens in September 2006, it will be Tallinn's largest 5-star hotel. Hopefully strict planning controls

will ensure that the 19th-century façade, from what was the main post office, will be maintained. *Rates unavailable at time of publication.*

🏨 **Three Sisters** (23 rooms) Pikk 71; ☎ 630 6300; f 630 6301; e info@threesistershotel.com; www.threesistershotel.com. Perhaps because it is so luxurious, the hotel does not bother with an Estonian name as no Estonian could afford it. It is clearly aiming to rival the Parkconsul and is to some extent modelled on it. Both buildings have a history of over 500 years and both can claim famous rather than notorious owners. Here a library is the dominating public room and a member of staff escorts guests into the lift for the one-floor journey down to the restaurant. With only a small number of rooms, one even with a piano, the atmosphere of a 19th-century townhouse can still be maintained. Computers and plenty of other 21st-century paraphernalia are available if needed, but it seems a pity to let modernity intrude. Estonians who wish to impress their friends on the cheap come for lunch here and linger over a £5/US$8 club sandwich. Foreigners come in the evening for pumpkin soup, pork with chanterelle mushrooms and a particular rarity in Estonia, homemade ice cream. *Dbl 5,550EEK.*

First class

🏨 **Barons** (34 rooms) Suur-Karja 7; ☎ 699 9700; f 699 9710; e barons@baronshotel.ee; www.baronshotel.ee. For every bank that closes in Tallinn, a new hotel opens, but in this case it is on the same site. Thirteen different banks in fact occupied the building during the 20th century. Some doors as a result do seem excessively secure. Visitors will find it hard to believe that Barons opened in 2003 rather than 1903, since the panelling, the minute lift, the sombre colour schemes and the illustrations of Tallinn are all from the earlier date. So is the name of the road: 'karja' means 'to herd', as cattle used to be led to pasture along it. Whenever renovation is carried out, more and more papers from the early 20th century come to light. The view from many rooms and from the restaurant over

the Old Town will again keep the 21st century away. For once it is sensible to go upstairs to eat in Tallinn, rather than downstairs. Do however avoid Friday and Saturday nights here, when the hotel is an oasis of quiet against a backdrop of raucous behaviour in the surrounding bars. No rooms have baths but the suites have jacuzzis. *Dbl 2,500EEK.*

🏨 **Domina City** (68 rooms) Vana-Posti 11–13; ☎ 681 3900; f 681 3901; e city@domina.ee; www.dominahotels.com. As one of the few hotels to open in 2002, the Domina, with its Old Town location, its size and its standards, was bound to succeed and few of those that have opened since can claim to compete with it. Many rooms have a bath as well as shower, and for those that do not, the computers built into the TV

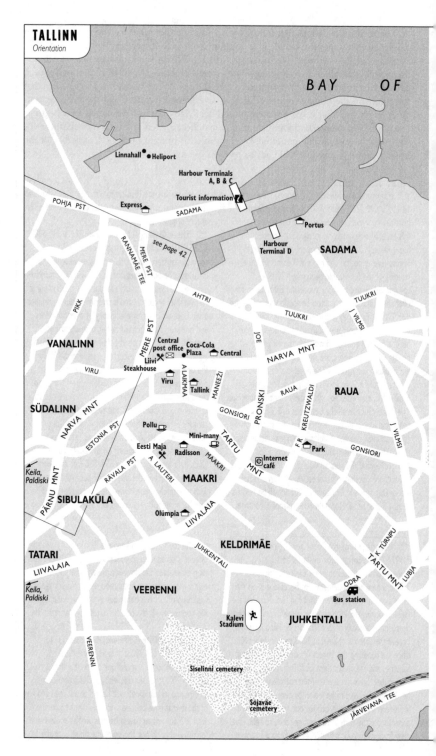

TALLINN
Orientation

BAY OF

Linnahall • Heliport

Harbour Terminals
A, B & C

Tourist information

POHJA PST

Express

SADAMA

Portus

see page 42

Harbour
Terminal D

SADAMA

RANNAMÄE TEE

MERE PST

AHTRI

TUUKRI

TUUKRI

J VILMSI

PIKK

MERE PST

VANALINN

Central
post office

Coca-Cola
Plaza

Central

JOE

NARVA MNT

VIRU

Liivi
Steakhouse

Viru

A LAIKMAA

Tallink

MANEEŽI

GONSIORI

PRONSKI

RAUA

F R KREUTZWALDI

RAUA

J VILMSI

SÜDALINN

NARVA MNT

ESTONIA PST

Pollu

Mini-many

TARTU

Park

GONSIORI

Keila,
Paldiski

RÄVALA PST

Eesti Maja

Radisson

MAAKRI

A LAUTERI

MAAKRI

MNT

Internet
café

PÄRNU MNT

SIBULAKÜLA

Olümpia

LIIVALAIA

KELDRIMÄE

K TÜRNPU

TARTU MNT

LUBJA

TATARI

LIIVALAIA

JUHKENTALI

Keila,
Paldiski

VEERENNI

ODRA

Bus station

VEERENNI

Kalevi
Stadium

JUHKENTALI

Siselinni cemetery

Sõjaväe
cemetery

JÄRVEVANA TEE

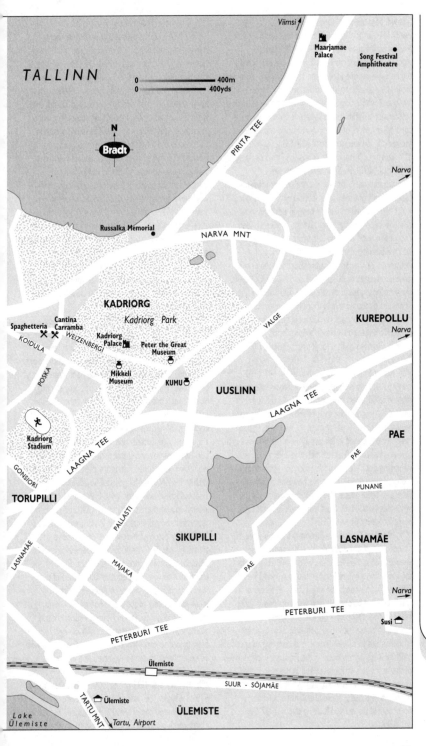

TALLINN

Viimsi ↑

Maarjamae Palace

Song Festival Amphitheatre

0 ————— 400m
0 ————— 400yds

N

Bradt

PIRITA TEE

Narva →

Russalka Memorial

NARVA MNT

KADRIORG

Kadriorg Park

VALGE

KUREPOLLU

Narva →

Spaghetteria   Cantina Carramba
KOIDULA   WEIZENBERGI

Kadriorg Palace

Peter the Great Museum

Mikkeli Museum

KUMU

UUSLINN

LAAGNA TEE

PAE

PAE

POSKA

Kadriorg Stadium

LAAGNA TEE

PUNANE

GONSIORI

TORUPILLI

PALLASTI

SIKUPILLI

LASNAMÄE

MAJAKA

PAE

Narva →

LASNAMÄE

PETERBURI TEE

Susi

PETERBURI TEE

Ülemiste

SUUR - SÕJAMÄE

Lake Ülemiste

TARTU MNT

Ülemiste

Tartu, Airport

ÜLEMISTE

sets will be more than adequate compensation. The British will like the choice of Sky as well as BBC TV. Full AC will be installed during 2007–08. The Italian management is reflected in the ample use of marble in the reception area and with the range of wildly abstract art in the restaurant. What is distinctly not Italian is the fact that 2 whole floors are non-smoking. Like all good restaurants in Tallinn, the one here is built into a brick-lined cellar. Lovers of Soviet memorabilia should note the red star on the roof. *Dbl 2,400EEK.*

⌂ **Domina Ilmarine** (150 rooms) Pohja 23; ☎ 614 0900; f 614 0901; e ilmarine@domina.ee; dominahotels.ee. What was Estonia's major machine-tool factory from the Tsarist period until World War II, which then turned to making hearing aids in Soviet times, is an unlikely background for a modern, hygienic and well-lit hotel but that is the fact. So well regarded was the business during Estonia's first period of independence that both the president and the prime minister invested in it. Being just outside the Old Town, the hotel has space and uses it well. The rooms are big, as are the public areas, and there is ample parking for coaches and for private cars. Double glazing prevents any traffic noise from causing a disturbance. Part of the hotel is allocated to flats for long-stay guests. *Dbl 2,000EEK.*

⌂ **Kalev Spa** (100 rooms) Aia 18; ☎ 649 3300; f 649 3301; e kalevspa@kalevspa.ee; www.kalevspa.ee. Around 2000, Estonians suddenly discovered they needed to keep healthy, so spas and gyms sprung up around the country, particularly on the coast. This spa hotel, which opened in January 2006, is the first one in a town centre so its facilities, including a very welcome swimming pool, are geared as much to residents as to visitors from outside. Their use, however, is free of charge to hotel guests. The restaurant overlooks the swimming pool, which must make over-indulgent guests there feel guilty. *Dbl 1,900EEK.*

⌂ **Meriton Grand** (165 rooms) Toompuiestee 27; ☎ 667 7000; f 667 7001; e hotel@grandhotel.ee; www.grandhotel.ee. Travellers who came to Tallinn in the early 1990s will remember the grim Hotel Tallinn that used to besmirch this site. Luckily all traces of it were removed before this new hotel opened in 1999. Being immediately below the Old Town and having more than ample rooms, it appeals both to business travellers and to tourist groups. It is tempting to spend much of a stay in this hotel in the lift, since it offers one of the best views of Toompea Hill at the top of the Old Town. British tourists are drawn by the high proportion of rooms with baths. There are plans to build a spa hotel behind the current building during 2007. *Dbl 3,000EEK.*

⌂ **Olümpia** (400 rooms) Liivalaia 33; ☎ 631 5333; f 631 5325; e olympia@revalhotels.com; www.revalhotels.com. Built originally for the Olympic Games in 1980, this hotel is now the firm favourite of foreign business visitors to Tallinn. With the range of restaurants and conference facilities it offers, some never leave the hotel during their stay in Tallinn. They are often joined by the local expat community which has a particular affinity for the '60s music played in the Bonnie and Clyde nightclub. At weekends and during the summer, rates drop to attract tourists paying their own way. All of the rooms are now at least of four-star standard and the reception staff work very quickly during the arrival and departure 'rush hours'. The restaurant on the top floor offers excellent views of the Old Town and many rooms do so as well. The newspaper shop always stocks up-to-date British newspapers, a rarity in Tallinn. Tourists who want to arrive or leave in greater style than a local taxi is able to provide can hire the hotel's 9m-long Lincoln which costs about £50/US$80 an hour. *Dbl 2,300EEK.*

⌂ **Radisson** (280 rooms) Rävala pst 3; ☎ 682 3000; f 682 3001; e info.tallinn@radissonsas.com; Tallinn.radissonsas.com. All the main central Tallinn hotels that opened during the 1990s were conversions of existing buildings. In 2000, the Radisson dramatically broke away from that tradition by not only starting from scratch but also by constructing what is still in early 2006 the tallest building in Tallinn. This gave it the advantage of not having to make any compromises and a purpose-built formula was worked out to appeal to both the business and the leisure traveller. It has often pioneered what other hotels are then forced to copy, such as free WiFi for all guests. The 2005 novelty was a special low check-in for small children, with toys around should there be any delay. Cultured guests will appreciate the paintings in the lobby area by Kaido Ole, one of Estonia's best-known contemporary artists. In that year the hotel also opened its Lounge 24, a rooftop café which gives excellent photo opportunities towards both the Old Town and the new financial area growing up (literally) in the immediate vicinity of the hotel. For tourists wanting a more unusual photo, Tallinn Central Prison is easily visible from here. The restaurants and Lounge 24 have been priced to cater for local patrons, too, so are not as expensive as might be expected in a 4-star hotel. *Dbl 2,500EEK.*

⌂ **Reval Park** (121 rooms) Kreutzwaldi 23; ☎ 630 5305; f 630 5315; e sales@revalhotels.com; www.revalhotels.com. Formerly the dreaded Kungla Hotel which could barely claim 2-star status, the site transformed itself within a few weeks during the summer of 1997 and has never looked back. It has pioneered rooms for non-smokers, for the disabled and for those with allergies as well as round-the-clock gambling, fortunately in a casino with a separate entrance. Rooms are larger here than in most other hotels and the restaurant has very low prices for excellent food. Walking to the Old Town is just about possible and indeed essential as the surroundings are very bleak. The guarded car park is free of charge to hotel guests. *Dbl 2,000EEK.*

⌂ **St Petersbourg** (27 rooms) Rataskaevu 7; 🕿 628 6500; f 628 6565; e stpetersbourg@schlosse-hotels.com; www.schlosse-hotels.com. The St Petersbourg is under the same management as the de-luxe Schlössle Hotel and suits those who want a comfortable Old Town address and who do not miss luxury. The small number of rooms is certainly a draw. It may well be the oldest hotel in Tallinn, as it has had this leading position under every single regime of the 20th century. Its location near to many famous clubs and restaurants appeals to visitors who can dispense with sleep for much of the night. It is one of the very few hotels in Tallinn to offer a babysitting service. *Dbl 5,000EEK.*

⌂ **Santa Barbara** (53 rooms) Roosikrantsi 2a; 🕿 640 7600; f 631 3992; e st_barbara.res@scandic-hotels.ee; www.scandic-hotels.com. The austere limestone façade from the turn of the century hides a very professional operation which is run by the Scandic group who also operate the nearby Scandic Palace Hotel. The cellar restaurant is completely German, with no intrusion from Estonia or anywhere else. The staff get to know all the guests, many of whom are now regulars, which makes the hotel difficult to book for first-time visitors. *Dbl 1,600EEK.*

⌂ **Scandic Palace** (87 rooms) Vabaduse Väljak; 🕿 640 7300; f 640 7299; e palace@scandic-hotels.com; www.scandic-hotels.com. The hotel brochure claims it has offered 'excellent service since 1937' and this is probably true. Although many other hotels now match its facilities, Estonians are very loyal to it as the hotel was one of the few links from the first independence period that remained throughout the Soviet era. Embassies were briefly set up in the hotel in 1991 before foreign legations could reclaim their pre-war buildings. It is now equally conveniently situated for tourists interested in the Old Town and business visitors needing the government ministries. In 1997 President Meri opened the new presidential suite which will doubtless for decades remain one of the most expensive in Tallinn at £250/US$400 per night, but the remaining 86 rooms are more modestly priced. The

hotel is run by the Scandic group that also operates the Santa Barbara in Tallinn, the Ranna in Pärnu. *Dbl 2,600EEK.*

⌂ **Tallink** (300 rooms) Laikmaa 5; 🕿 630 0800; f 630 0810; e hotel@tallink.ee; www.bwhoteltallink.com. If this hotel had been located anywhere else in Tallinn, it would have been considered enormous, with its 300 rooms. However, as it overlooks the Viru with 500 rooms, it seems merely large. Being closely linked to the ferry company that operates to Helsinki, it is very much an outpost of Finland in Tallinn. Everything works and the light colours are appealing, particularly in winter, but perhaps more could have been done to broaden its appeal. The bus from the airport stops outside its door and some higher rooms have good views over the Old Town. *Dbl 2,300EEK.*

⌂ **Viru** (500 rooms) Viru Väljak 4; 🕿 630 1390; f 630 1303; e viru.reservation@sok.fi; www.viru.ee. Being the centre of the tourism trade for much of the Soviet era, the enormous Viru initially found it hard to redefine its role in the face of competition and ever-rising standards. By 2000 it had finally undergone a complete renovation and can now serve both business clients and fastidious tourists. It has become very biased towards Finnish clients, particularly since its takeover by the Finnish chain Sokos. Some of these guests can provide unwanted liveliness late on Friday and Saturday evenings. Its location is excellent for the Old Town and for local shops. Tourists determined to have a bath rather than a shower are more likely to succeed here. Although the hotel already had over 400 rooms, it opened an extension with a further 100 rooms in spring 2004. In late 2005 it was fighting the town council for permission to build a complete new extension to the hotel in the neighbouring Tammsaare Park. *Dbl 2,500EEK.*

⌂ **Viruinn** (15 rooms) Viru 8; 🕿/f 644 9167; e viruinn@viruinn.ee; www.viruinn.ee It is perhaps surprising that this is the first hotel in Tallinn to convert an old townhouse as carefully as possible into a boutique hotel. It is opening in May 2006, with beams obstructing everywhere and access difficult for both the old and the very young, given the number of stairs and corridors. Needless to say, there is no lift. However the fit middle-aged will enjoy an escape from all-too-modern Viru Street back into the 19th century. Good sound-proofing ensures their isolation. The Al Sole café downstairs provides a halfway house between the old and the new with light meals and cakes worthy of its more famous competitors. *Dbl 2,500EEK*

🏠 **Central** (247 rooms) Narva mnt 7; ☎ 633 9800; f 633 9900; e sales@revalhotels.com; www.revalhotels.com. This hotel became an immediate favourite of tour operators from abroad when it opened in 1995 as it had no Soviet past to eliminate. Regular improvements have followed ever since. Staff were immediately aware of the demands and eccentricities of Western tourists, who have been catered for in the café/restaurant ever since. The hotel offers disabled access and one room in the new wing is adapted for use by disabled guests. A computer is available free of charge to guests. It is within easy walking distance of the Old Town and the main post office. Having opened in what was then a rundown part of town, the surrounding area is becoming increasingly attractive, with more shops and restaurants opening every year. *Dbl 1,500EEK.*

🏠 **Dzingel** (200 rooms) Männiku 89; ☎ 610 5201; f 610 5245; e hotell@dzingel.ee; www.dzingel.ee. Situated in Nõmme, Tallinn's most exclusive suburb, the Dzingel is in fact one of the town's simplest and largest hotels. Regular long-stay visitors find its facilities perfectly adequate in view of the low prices charged and many tourists are happy both in winter and in summer with its quiet location beside a pine forest. Modernisation in 2002 made a great difference. The bus journey north into the town centre takes about 20 minutes. It is one of the few hotels where the staff happily and openly speak Russian although they can manage basic English. The restaurant is dull and surprisingly expensive but there is a late-night supermarket in the same block which can provide the ingredients for a varied picnic. *Dbl 800 EEK.*

🏠 **L'Ermitage** (91 rooms) Toompuiestee 19; ☎ 699 6400; f 699 6401; e reservations@lermitagehotel.ee; www.lermitagehotel.ee. Although on a main road, this hotel is in many respects quieter than others as it is so well soundproofed; late-night revellers do not get this far from the Old Town as they would actually have to walk for 10 mins. It appeals to groups as coaches can stop directly in front and isn't too big to seem impersonal. Those lucky enough to get a high room at the front will be rewarded with excellent views of the town walls. *Dbl 2,000EEK.*

🏠 **Imperial** (32 rooms) Nunne 14; ☎ 627 4800; f 627 4801; e imperial@baltichotelgroup.com; www.baltichotelgroup.com. Like the Konventa Seta in Riga and the Rūdninkų in Vilnius, this hotel is built into the town wall, which is therefore being preserved as part of it. Although on one of the few real roads in the Old Town, the location is quiet. During 2005 the hotel was considerably upgraded which led to the demise of

the stag parties who previously had been tolerated here. Rooms vary greatly in size and protruding beams sometimes add more of the medieval ambience than some guests would wish. Massive discounts are often available in winter here, together with late check-outs, useful for those booked on the afternoon flight to London. *Dbl 2,200EEK.*

🏠 **Merchant's House** (37 rooms) Dunkri 4–6; ☎ 697 7500; f 697 7501; e info@merchantshousehotel.com; www.merchantshouse.com. In summer 2005 a formula that has worked so well in Riga at the Gutenbergs finally reached Tallinn – 14th–16th-century woodwork and frescoes have been integrated into a hotel that will satisfy even the most fastidious customer. Rooms of course vary in size and shape, as do the corridors, but small detours to reach them are a small price to pay for such a special environment. Given the round-the-clock activity on Dunkri it is good that only 3 of the rooms face it, and that the library, which also does so, is well soundproofed. The 'winter' restaurant is amongst the cellars of the basement, the 'summer' one in the courtyard onto which most rooms look. Tallinn's first ice bar is on the ground floor and on a similar theme it is worth mentioning that all rooms are air-conditioned, an important asset for several weeks during the summer. The temptations at the ice bar can be viewed on the obvious website address (*www.icebar.ee*). *Dbl 2,400EEK.*

🏠 **Meriton Old Town** (40 rooms) Lai 49; ☎ 614 1300; f 614 1311; e hotel@grandhotel.ee. This hotel opened in March 2004 and is under the same management as the Meriton Grand, but has deliberately been pitched at a very different clientele. Those who normally shun 2- or 3-star hotels may well accept such a standard here, given the view that most rooms have over the Old Town, of St Olav's Church, or towards the harbour. There is also the added appeal of the hotel being built into the city wall. Being on the edge of the Old Town, the place is quiet yet with a reasonably central location, within walking distance of many museums and shops. It is worth paying the slightly higher costs for the rooms on the fourth floor, with their larger size, their baths rather than showers and above all for the views. The basement rooms make up for the total lack of a view with the skilfully implanted use of the old city wall. For anyone willing to risk turning up after midnight without a reservation, rooms are then sold at half-price. *Dbl 1,200EEK.*

🏠 **Mihkli** (77 rooms) Endla 23; ☎ 666 4800; f 666 4888; e mihkli@anet.ee; www.mihkli.ee. The location on one of the main roads leading from the town centre is certainly drab and the hotel itself used to be as well. From around 1998, however, serious attempts were made to improve the décor and the staff and these have been largely successful. It is within walking distance of the Old Town and on the doorstep of the National Library. Long-stay visitors are now here and locals use the restaurant, both of which are always good signs. It is probably the closest hotel to the Old Town with a parking lot and the number of dedicated sgl rooms is helpful. The repeat business that the hotel enjoys is also evidence of a complete turn-around. The live music at the weekends in the restaurant is of a consistently high standard and is well soundproofed from the rest of the hotel. The Uniquestay group took over the hotel in February 2006 so changes are to be expected. *Dbl 1,100EEK.*

🏠 **Old Town Maestro** (23 rooms) Suur-Karja 10; ☎ 626 2000; f 631 3333; e maestro@maestrohotel.ee; www.maestrohotel.ee. Having opened in 2001, this small hotel now has its regulars who want straightforward furnishings, peace and quiet and yet an Old Town location. Rooms are much bigger than might be expected from a converted townhouse but the lift is much smaller – it can take only one person with a case at a time. The road is traffic-free but that does mean wheeling cases along the cobbles on arrival and departure. The reception area doubles up as a bar, which adds to the family atmosphere. The sauna and the business centre are, surprisingly, side by side on the top floor. Photographers should bring their cameras for the unusual views over the town from the staircase and from the sauna. *Dbl 1,900EEK.*

🏠 **Pirita Convent Guesthouse** (21 rooms) Merivälja 18; ☎ 605 5000; f 605 5010; e pirita@osss.ee; www.osss.ee. For anyone determined to have quiet at night, this is undoubtedly the place to go for. The nuns stay up for latecomers so ideal guests are those who have dinner here and then go to their rooms. The yachting harbour of Pirita is 3km northeast of the town and the ruined convent with this new guesthouse is set well back from the main road. Prices, too, are provincial rather than Tallinn. Tourists with a car will be happy with the space here and others will be pleased that after 500 years a religious order is finally active on the site again. An extensive programme of concerts takes places in the chapel. *Dbl 1,200EEK.*

🏠 **Portus** (107 rooms) Uus Sadama 23; ☎ 680 6600; f 680 6601; e tallinnhotels@tallinnhotels.ee; www.tallinnhotels.ee. Regular visitors to Tallinn will remember this hotel as the Saku, named after the brewery and which provided a glass of beer at check-in. If the ambience is slightly more sober now, this is undoubtedly a hotel for the young and lively. Rooms

have their numbers painted on them, so that guests with uncertain late-night vision can still hopefully find the right one. The beer store has been converted into a children's playroom but the corridors are still painted red, orange and yellow. It is in the port so convenient for those also visiting Helsinki. Bus number 20 stops outside the door for those who would rather avoid the 15-min walk to the Old Town. The Italian restaurant offers a surprisingly good meal for starting or finishing a visit to Tallinn. *Dbl 1,000EEK.*

🏠 **Savoy** (40 rooms) Suur-Karja 17–19; ☎ 680 6604; f 680 6601; e tallinnhotels@tallinnhotels.ee; www.tallinnhotels.ee. This hotel, due to open in May 2006, is under the same management as the City Portus in the harbour, but the style is completely different so it is probably just as well that the 2 hotels are a good mile apart. Their respective clients would mix as well as beer on wine. The Old Town location and baths in nearly all of the rooms will appeal to older tourists wanting a leisurely stay. Particular selling points are a free supply of drinks in the minibar and free landline phone calls throughout Estonia. *Dbl 2,500EEK.*

🏠 **Shnelli** (124 rooms) Toompuiestee 37; ☎ 631 0100; f 631 0101; e reservations@gohotels.ee; www.gohotels.ee. As part of the much-needed renovation of the railway station, this hotel opened beside it in 2005. It is a straightforward 3-star hotel with the 'Green' rooms facing the park below the Old Town and the 'Blue' hopefully facing a sea and sky which display this colour, but which also overlook the platforms of the railway station. The former obviously cost rather more. The railway theme predominates in the photos on the walls and even in the design of the corridor carpets. A covered walkway links the hotel to the station and its restaurant; as with stations everywhere now, the trains are less important than the shops to which most of the space has been let. The restaurant is much cheaper than any in the Old Town and particularly at weekends offers a pleasantly quiet environment for a meal. The few trains now running from here will certainly not provide any disturbance. *Single visitors hoping to change their status whilst in Tallinn may want to take advantage of the rooms let only to 2 people after midnight for 500EEK. Otherwise: Green Dbl 1,250EEK, Blue Dbl 950EEK.*

🏠 **Skane** (38 rooms) Kopli 2c; ☎ 667 8300; f 667 8301; e skane@nordichotels.ee; www.nordichotels.ee. Being just over the railway and the tramlines from the Old Town, this hotel is literally on the wrong side of the tracks. Hopefully gentrification of the surrounding area does not take too long and it can then look the Old Town in the face. In the meantime, guests can enjoy prices that are half of those charged by hotels just

500m away and the walk into the Old Town is very short. A tram and bus stop are on the doorstep. No rooms have baths, but all have BBC TV. *Dbl 900EEK.*

🏠 **Susi** (100 rooms) Peterburi 48; ✆ 630 3300; f 630 3400; e susi@susi.ee; www.susi.ee. An estate agent would probably describe the location as 'unprepossessing' since it is surrounded by factories and a petrol station and is on the wide St Petersburg motorway. It is literally the high point of Tallinn at 55m above sea level. On 14 May 1343, the St George's Night rebellion took place here. It had started further north on 23 April and this was the nearest point to Tallinn that Estonian forces would reach. Over 10,000 were killed in a desperate attempt to overthrow the Teutonic Knights. A plaque in the hotel lobby commemorates the battle, as does the park on the other side of the road where there are several further monuments. The hotel is more comfortable and more modern than any of the other tourist-class hotels outside the centre and is easily accessible by tram. The pictures displayed on its staircase put many of Tallinn's museums to shame. There are oils, lithographs and watercolours showing contemporary and historical Tallinn; other pictures are of country scenes. They are well lit and sensibly framed and of course can be seen 24 hours a day. Should the lift break down, this gallery is more than adequate compensation. The hotel suits many groups as parking is easy, as are access to the airport and the Tartu road. *Dbl 1,000EEK.*

🏠 **Taanilinna** (20 rooms) Uus 6; ✆ 640 6700; f 646 4306; e info@taanilinna.ee; www.taanilinna.ee. Perhaps they were daring, perhaps they were foolish, but in June 2002 Tallinn saw its first hotel with Russian-speaking reception staff and with brochures in English and Russian. The spelling 'Hotell' was the only concession made to Estonia at the time, although the website now has an Estonian section. Visitors who do not care about this will like the prices, the small number of rooms, the location in one of the few quiet streets in the Old Town and the use of wood rather than of stone. The terrace sadly looks out on to the back of a supermarket and a dreary block of flats but in future years this view may well change. The wine cellar is an unexpected bonus in a hotel of this size and category and is most welcome given the lack of other watering holes in the immediate vicinity. *Dbl 2,200EEK.*

🏠 **Ülemiste** (120 rooms) Lennijamaa tee 2; ✆ 603 2600; f 603 2601; e sales@ylemistehotel.ee; www.ylemistehotel.ee. This hotel opened beside the airport in 2004 in what was then a very bleak location but the development since then of the Ülemiste shopping centre beside it has greatly enhanced the potential pleasure of a stay here. Prices in these shops are of course much lower than those charged in the

town centre. Great advantage has been taken of all the space available so expect a larger lobby, rooms and even corridors than elsewhere in Tallinn. Those able to indulge in the more expensive rooms at the top of the hotel will be rewarded with views across Ülemiste Lake. The location is very convenient given the number of flights arriving late and leaving early. It is a 400m walk to the terminal or one stop on the local bus. In the winter the hotel offers a late check-out at 15.00 to passengers taking the London flight at 16.15. For those prepared to take quite a risk, rooms are offered at half-price to walk-in passengers who arrive after midnight. *Dbl 1,400EEK.*

🏠 **Unique** (67 rooms) Paldiski mnt 3; ✆ 660 0700; f 661 6176; e info@uniquestay.com; www.uniquestay.com. Tallinn hotels have tended to copy each other once a successful formula has been found. The larger ones inevitably copy models from abroad and the smaller ones try to recreate a 1930s ambience even though modern technology is around if guests need it. When the Unique opened in spring 2003, it clearly wanted to break away from anything that had ever been tried before. Each room has its own flat-screen computer which can be used free of charge around the clock. It also has tea and coffee. The lighting in the corridors comes from the floor rather than the ceiling. Orange rather than green or brown is the predominant colour. Originally restricted to 17 rooms at Paldiski 3, the hotel added another 50 in April 2004 in its new building on the corner of Paldiski and Toompuiestee and plans a further extension in 2006. Several of these rooms, the Zen rooms, are as original as their predecessors, with whirlpool baths, adjustable lighting and gravity-free chairs. This is also the first hotel in Tallinn with an Estonian restaurant! The chain plans to expand both within Tallinn and to the neighbouring Baltic states. *Dbl EEK1,600.*

🏠 **Vana Wiru** (80 rooms) Viru 11; ✆ 669 1500; f 669 1501; e hotel@vanawiru.ee; www.vanawiru.ee. Viru St is always full of tourists but most will not know of the existence of this hotel as its entrance is at the back. Potential guests should not be deterred by the fact that the building dates from the 1950s, normally the worst period of Soviet architecture. Its vast marble lobby suggests luxury but in fact most of the rooms are of a standard size and with showers rather than baths. Few have good views but with a location beside the city wall, one can forgive anything. It is certainly worth paying more for the junior suites on the 5th floor which do have extensive views over the Old Town. Shopaholics should enquire about the 10% discount the hotel arranges for its guests at the nearby Kaubamaja department store. Groups will like the convenient coach park right beside the entrance. *Dbl 1,700EEK.*

There is now such a choice of restaurants in Tallinn that it is invidious to attempt a shortlist. Every major nation is represented and more unusual ones include Argentina, Georgia, Lithuania and Scotland. Hawaiian and Thai food appeared for the first time in 2000, Czech and Arabic food followed in 2002 and by 2003 Russian food had also staged a comeback, having been completely rejected in the years immediately following independence. By 2005, they were joined by an African, an Armenian and a Korean one. All restaurants and bars have to provide a non-smoking section. In April 2004 there was serous discussion about following the Irish and banning smoking altogether but this had not come about by early 2006.

Detailed descriptions of restaurants appear in the *City Paper*, shorter ones in *Tallinn In Your Pocket*. A dark entrance, down poorly maintained stairs in a side street, is usually a clear indication that good food and value lies ahead. Bright lights at street level should be avoided. Exploration need no longer be limited to the Old Town; competition there is driving many new entrants to open up in the suburbs. At the time of writing, nobody has opened a revivalist Soviet restaurant, though the success of such ventures in Riga and in former East Berlin must in due course tempt some embittered members of the Russian-speaking community in Tallinn.

Most of the following restaurants have been open for several years and are popular with tourists, expats and local residents. I have, however, deliberately tried to include some that are not well known abroad and which cannot afford to advertise. I have also gambled on some recent openings in the expectation that they will outlive this edition of the book. Apologies in advance to the many other excellent restaurants that, with more space, would also have been included. Websites are listed so that menu planning can begin abroad and not just at the table. Restaurants are on the whole very good at keeping these up to date, and for those in a rush it is possible to pre-book not only a table but also the meal. Eating in hotels is popular in Tallinn and some of their restaurants are covered in the hotel descriptions in the previous chapter.

RESTAURANTS

✖ **African Kitchen** Uus 34; ☎ 644 2555; www.africankitchen.ee. This restaurant became so popular during 2005 that it was hard to believe that it only opened around Christmas 2004. It is cheap and cheerful, but so much more as well. The menu is diverse, the website to the point and equality across the continent is assured by offering one cocktail, and only one, from each of 25 different African countries and all at the same price. Come here with a group, or be willing to become part of one. This is not the place for dining à deux. Live music is played, with no extra costs, every Fri and Sat evening. *200EEK.*

✖ **Balthasar** Raekoja Plats 11; ☎ 627 6400; www.restaurant.ee. Garlic dominates every course here, even the ice cream, but above all in the salads. Whilst other dishes do appear on the menu, they tend to be as appetising as a vegetarian option in a steakhouse. Opening in early 2000, the restaurant took over the top floor of the former pharmacy (see page 50) and has kept as much of the original wooden furnishings as was practical. With the restaurant's views over Town Hall Square, it is tempting to linger here but it also offers a quiet respite over lunch between morning and afternoon sightseeing tours. The range of short drinks at the bar can be equally tempting at other times of day. *350EEK.*

✖ **Bocca** Olevimägi 9; ☎ 641 2610; www.bocca.ee. A passer-by on the pavement here who happened to notice the plain glass windows with the 2 canvas panels behind them would not believe that during 2003 Bocca got more publicity abroad than all other Tallinn restaurants put together. Only the cars parked outside suggest considerable opulence inside. Critics liked the modern minimalist layout against the medieval backdrop of very solid limestone. They liked the changing lighting schemes – and the fact that plenty of modest pasta dishes were available if octopus and veal seemed unnecessarily extravagant. The glitterati have moved on now, but standards here have stayed the same. *500EEK.*

✖ **Le Bonaparte** Pikk 45; ☎ 646 4444; www.bonaparte.ee. The formal restaurant at the back and the easy-going café at the front are both French through and through. The décor is very domestic and totally unpretentious. The care and flair all go into the food, which is still too rare in Tallinn, whether it is a simple cake in the café or an elaborate pâté at the start

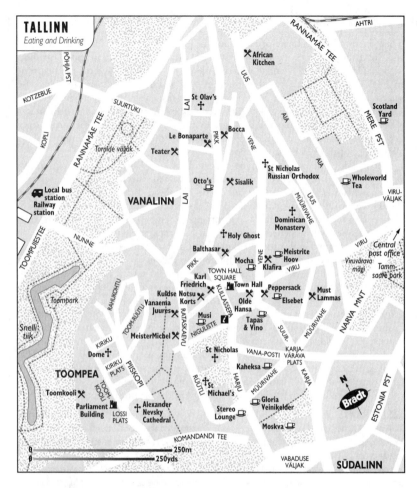

AHTRI

RANNAMÄE TEE

POHJA PST

KOTZEBUE

SUURTÜKI

St Olav's ✝

✗ African
Kitchen

UUS

LAI

AIA

Scotland
Yard

MERE PST

RANNAMÄE TEE

Torolde väljak

Le Bonaparte

Teater ✗

PIKK

✗ Bocca

VENE

AIA

St Nicholas
Russian Orthodox ✝

✗ Wholeworld
Tea

VIRU-
VÄLJAK

Local bus
station
Railway
station

Otto's

✗ Sisalik

VANALINN

LAI

MÜÜRIVAHE

UUS

Dominican
Monastery ✝

TOOMPUIESTEE

NUNNE

✝ Holy Ghost

VIRU

Central
post office

Toompark

RAHUKOHTU

PIKK

Balthasar ✗

Mocha
Klafira

Meistrite
Hoov

VENE

VIRU

Viruvärava
mägi

Tamm-
saare park

TOWN HALL
SQUARE

Snelli
tiik

Karl
Friedrich

Town Hall

Peppersack

Must
✗ Lammas

NARVA MNT

MÜÜRIVAHE

Kuldse Notsu
Korts
Vanaenia
Juures ✗

RATASKAEVU

KULLASSEPA

Olde
Hansa

Elsebet

Musi

NIGULISTE

Tapas
& Vino

SUUR

MeisterMichel ✗

St Nicholas ✝

VANA-POSTI

KARJA-
VÄRAVA
PLATS

Dome ✝

KIRIKU

Kaheksa

HARJU

MÜÜRIVAHE

KARJA

TOOMPEA

KIRIKU
PLATS

PIISKOPI

RÜÜTLI

✝ St
Michael's

N

ESTONIA PST

Toomkooli ✗

TOOM-
KOOLI

Gloria
Veinikelder

Bradt

Parliament
Building

LOSSI
PLATS

✝ Alexander
Nevsky
Cathedral

Stereo
Lounge

Moskva

KOMANDANDI TEE

0 ————— 250m
0 ————— 250yds

VABADUSE
VÄLJAK

SÜDALINN

of a serious meal. Other unusual touches are the individual towels in the toilets and coat-warmers for visitors in winter. Prices in both the restaurant and the café are fortunately very Estonian. Those who want to take France home with them can buy a range of cheeses and bread at the counter. *450EEK*.

✗ **Cantina Carramba** Weizenbergi 20a; ☎ 601 3431; www.carramba.ee. Opening in Kadriorg outside the town centre in 2004 was certainly a gamble, but it has definitely paid off. The variety of Mexican food, not to mention its low cost, is certainly worth the 10-min tram ride it may take to get here. Onion rings in beer dough is one of many original dishes served. Helpful to newcomers are the little pepper symbols beside many dishes on the menu. One indicates a medium dose where three is really strong. Being open through the day, an afternoon at the Palace or KUMU could pleasantly end with an early supper here. Do bear in

mind that although the cuisine is Mexican, the portions are certainly American. *250EEK*.

✗ **Controvento** Katariina käik; ☎ 644 0470; www.controvento.ee. Uniquely in Tallinn, this restaurant could maintain a review written when it first opened in 1992. It has retained the same menu, the same décor and probably many of the same clients, who want no-nonsense home cooking in an Italian bistro and no attempts to emulate temporary culinary fads. Prices have had to increase somewhat but they remain modest in comparison with the competition in the Old Town. *300EEK*.

✗ **Eesti Maja** Lauteri 1; ☎ 645 5252; www.eestimaja.ee. Do not expect quick service here or even staff with much English, but instead be ready for enormous portions and rich food at each course. It will be hard to spend more than £6/US$10 a head and many eat their fill for much less. Side rooms seating around 8–10 people are useful for private functions. One houses a collection of photographs from the 1920s. The vegetable soup makes a good meal in itself at lunchtime. The building also houses *Global Estonian*, an English-language bi-annual magazine well worth buying for the tough interviews they give to local politicians willing to meet them. *150EEK*.

✗ **Golden Dragon** Pikk 37; ✆ 631 3506; www.goldendragon.ee. This is a straightforward Chinese restaurant in the best sense of the term. The cooking is fine, the menu enormous and the service adequate. Do not expect delicate cooking, but with the prices so reasonable, it would be unfair to ask for this. The lanterns dangle against a background of Estonian limestone. Modern China and modern Estonia of course share an obsession for piped music so be ready for any meal to be spoilt on this score. The entrance is in a courtyard, through a heavy door and down a tortuous staircase. This complication fortunately keeps out the more raucous tourists. *180EEK*.

✗ **Karl Friedrich** Raekoja Plats 5; ✆ 627 2413; www.restaurant.ee. The grand location on Town Hall Square might suggest ostentation and prices to match but fortunately this has not happened. Each floor caters for a different age group but it is the top floor that is recommended; the long walk up and down is well worthwhile. Oldies should book well in advance for a table overlooking the square and enjoy a lingering lunch or dinner. It became a pepper restaurant in 2005 so expect this ingredient even in a crème brulée or a chocolate mousse. At the same time, the kitchen moved upstairs so diners on that floor see all their food being prepared. Perhaps they went for pepper to compete with the garlic restaurant over the square? *400EEK*.

✗ **Klafira** Vene 4; ✆ 667 5144; www.klafira.ee. If Soviet Russia has been banished for good from Estonia, the Tsarist aristocracy is making an effective comeback here instead. Perhaps they were wise to wait until 2000, nine years after the re-establishment of Estonian independence, before doing so. Their food is strictly Russian, their wine is sensibly French. That rich Estonians are firstly willing to come and then secondly even to speak Russian to the staff shows the high standards the restaurant has set. Allow a full evening here and do not consider the cost beforehand. It will be expensive by Estonian standards, but not by London or New York ones. *400EEK*.

✗ **Kuldse Notsu Korts** (The Golden Pig) Dunkri 8; ✆ 628 6567; www.notsu.ee. Although this restaurant belongs to the luxury St Petersbourg Hotel next door, the two establishments have nothing in common. This country restaurant, with low ceilings and long wooden tables, seems pleasantly incongruous in the middle of the Old Town. However, this is precisely its appeal. It offers varied Estonian fare – thick mushroom soups, pork in innumerable guises and apples in almost as many. Drink apple juice or beer rather than wine. Few tourists venture in, but many Estonians do and this must be its best recommendation. *250EEK*.

✗ **Liivi Steakhouse** Narva mnt 1; ✆ 625 7377; www.steakhouse.ee. Everything is wonderfully predictable here, so this is the place to be unadventurous. All styles of steak are on the menu and they can be accompanied by a wide range of red wines. The starters are pâtés and soups and the sweets apple pie or ice cream. Being situated opposite the Viru Hotel in a complex that also houses the main post office, the clientele is very varied but always conventional. *350EEK*.

✗ **MeisterMichel** Rataskaevu 22; ✆ 641 3414; www.meistermichel.ee. This house belonged to Michel Sittow (1469–1525), an artist who lived for most of his life in Tallinn. He is best remembered for his portraits but sadly none of his work has remained in Tallinn itself. His portrait of Catherine of Aragon is in the Art History Museum in Vienna. Given his travels, he would have known quite of few of the varied dishes now served in this restaurant. Apples are the theme of most of them, so the results are inevitably more straightforward than in the Tallinn restaurants that take garlic or pepper as their leitmotiv instead. Children are encouraged with their special menu. *400EEK*.

✗ **Must Lammas** (The Black Sheep) Sauna 2; ✆ 644 2031; www.mustlammas.ee. For years this Georgian restaurant was called Exit but it changed its name in early 2001. Luckily little else has changed in the intervening years. All guests are greeted with portions of firewater and strips of salted beef as the menus are handed out. Eat meat, meat and more meat all evening, topped, if you did not have lunch, with some ice cream drenched in brandy. Start with stuffed vine leaves and move on to beef and pork stews. Vegetarians keep out. *250EEK*.

✗ **Olde Hansa** Vanaturg 1; ✆ 627 9020; www.oldehansa.com. Ignore the silly name and the silly costumes worn by the staff but enjoy the candles (there is no electric light) and the genuinely Estonian live music. Some tables are for two but don't venture in for a quiet, intimate evening. This is really a party venue so come as a group and with a very empty stomach. Portions are enormous, even for soup and ice cream. *300EEK*.

✗ **Peppersack** Viru tänav 2; ✆ 646 6900; www.peppersack.ee. Johan Peppersack was one of Tallinn's best mayors when Estonia was ruled by the Swedes in the 16th and 17th centuries. He fought the occupiers for money and for autonomy with a tenacity that no other mayor could equal in the subsequent 400 years. He would not have tolerated the mess Polish restorers, local Estonians and the Soviet occupiers got into when they tried and failed to restore the building in time for the 1980 Olympics. The compromise between Polish baroque and the former Gothic is still there. Perhaps it is better to look at the live entertainment, which can feature fencers, troubadours or martial artists (check the website if it matters which). The menu is extensive but many find it easiest just to order one of the feasts at a fixed price which includes 3 courses and drink. Several of these are fish-based and one is vegetarian. *350EEK.*

✗ **Sisalik (Lizard)** Pikk 30; ☎ 646 6542; www.sisaliku.ee. This is probably the only restaurant in Tallinn that has the linguistic and gastronomic daring to have a website in French. It is quite right that they should, since this is provincial France transposed to medieval Tallinn. The frogs' legs on the menu prove the point. The tortuous stone steps leading down to the basement location are distinctly Estonian (or Scots) but then France takes over. Those who know 'Les Amis' in Vilnius (page 142) will appreciate the need for a similar restaurant here. The menu is large enough to meet all tastes but small enough to ensure that mistakes are not made and that nothing synthetic is ever offered. The really greedy do not immediately walk out onto Pikk after eating here. They 'go to Belgium' upstairs at the café **Anneli Viik** for coffee and chocolate. *300 EEK.*

✗ **Spaghetteria** Weizenbergi 18; ☎ 601 3636; www.restorankadriorg.ee. People-watching from restaurants in the town centre tends to involve horror at the misbehaving foreigners or concern for the rushing Estonians. The location of this restaurant, on a first floor above the tram stop for Kadriorg Park, gives views of a totally different kind. People who come here have time, and are relaxed. Raucous stag parties would never find their way here. Looking inwards is the

kitchen, which forms the centre of this floor. The food is of course Italian, but it is perhaps significant that the wine list is much longer than the menu. Priorities here are clearly Italian, too. *250EEK.*

✗ **Teater** Lai 31; ☎ 646 6261. Coming into this basement from the stairs will often seem like an intrusion, so glued to their cigarettes and to TV are the staff and their close friends. However, walk through to a back alcove and the gathering will be interrupted to bring a menu of mixed Creole and Estonian influence. Start with the grilled dishes from the former and finish with the pancakes from the latter. Do not expect any tender loving care here but the cheapness and the variety of the menu will be ample compensation. *200EEK.*

✗ **Toomkooli** Toomkooli 13; ☎ 644 6613; www.toomkooli.ee. Those who are not deterred by the awkward location at the back of the Old Town are rewarded on arrival with an extensive international menu and wine list but prices that have stayed Estonian. Minimal music and very heavy wooden chairs give a more formal air to the surroundings than is now common in many Tallinn restaurants, but in a town now so geared to the young, this should be taken as a compliment. *350EEK.*

✗ **Vanaema Juures** (Grandma's Place) Rataskaevu 10/12; ☎ 626 9080. This is probably Tallinn's most famous restaurant but not even a visit from Hillary Clinton has gone to its head. The valid and repeated descriptions of it – good home cooking, a traditional décor and a cosy atmosphere – degenerate into cliché but few would dispute them. The furnishings and photographs from the previous independence period (1918–40), together with discreet music from that time, deter the young and raucous, but others will immediately appreciate the originality of total Estonian surroundings. Unfortunately, Grandma has not got around yet to having a website. *300EEK.*

CAFES AND BARS There is little distinction between cafés and bars in Tallinn as no licences are needed to serve alcohol. Self-service at a counter remains common although practice varies as to whether clients then wait for the drinks or whether they are brought to the table. Those that open only in the evening are listed in the entertainment section. Those below are open all day and usually in the evening as well. Piped music is largely unavoidable but perhaps readers can help find a café where all music is banned so peace and quiet is assured. The success of those listed below should ensure that they are all around during the currency of this book, although be prepared for name changes if a new owner takes over.

🏠 **Café Anglais** This section sadly has to start with an obituary rather than with a recommendation. Most of the expat community in Tallinn would come here regularly to eat cheaply but to still benefit from a view

over Town Hall Square. At the threat of closure, protests were as vigorous from the Quai d'Orsay as they were from Whitehall and Foggy Bottom, but all to no avail. The landlords could not agree a rent with the restaurant owners and so, at the time of writing, they were still looking for premises while some of the staff have set up the Basso Lounge at Pikk 13.

✕ **Elsebet** Viru 2. Lunch on the run is not yet a Tallinn phenomenon, despite the serious business environment. However, those who want to bring London practice with them can race into the ground floor here and will be out in 5 mins at most with a range of sandwiches, quiches and cakes. The more sensible visitor will forget breakfast in the hotel for once to arrive here with a camera at 08.00 so that a window table on the first floor will be theirs. Stay for a couple of hours to see the last of yesterday's drunks being picked up, the Tallinn elite coming out of their expensive flats and the first of the cruise parties meandering towards Town Hall Square. Don't forget a zoom lens to catch unsuspecting faces and Tallinn's windows and roofs.

♀ **Gloria Veinikelder** Müürivahe 2; www.gloria.ee. It seems a shame to ignore Estonia while in Tallinn but that is what anyone who comes here has to do. Forget vodka or the local Vana Tallinn and concentrate on the 2,000 different bottles not only of wine but also of cognac and whisky. Many foreigners justify their presence in this wine bar by pointing out that they can enjoy their 'own' drinks here at prices much lower than those charged at home. That the bar is called 'Napoleon' shows where most of these 2,000 bottles come from.

🍺 **Jõujaam** (Power Station) Vaike Karja 8. Perhaps where Stereo Lounge (see page 36) started many others will follow, but for the moment it is only here that a white background has again emerged in the heart of the Old Town. The pictures and the décor all centre on the theme of generation and high and low voltage reveal the size of the dishes. The smaller ones are in fact the most original; a hot salad of beans, pears and ham or a cheese-based vegetarian wrap will be remembered for longer than the Adenauer pork chop or the Kekkonen steak. Hopefully these references to politicians famous in the 1950s will keep the clientele quieter and older than those usually seen in Old Town bars.

🍺 **Kaheksa** Vana-Posti 8. Kaheksa means 'eight' but nobody seems to know the reason for this name. The austere granite Sõprus Cinema to which this is an adjunct is a surprising backcloth but indoors a totally tropical environment is created. The décor is light, as are the drinks, most of which are rum and coconut based. Teetotallers can hide their abstinence behind fruit-smoothies which really are light desserts. From about 2002, a Caribbean theme hit Tallinn and here it is at its best. Perhaps a visit here in midwinter is inadvisable as leaving will be a blow; wait until the summer when the outside will from time to time rival

the interior. Given its proximity to Hollywood, one of Tallinn's largest nightclubs, the clientele here is inevitably young, particularly in the early evening.

☕ **Kohvicum** Uus 16. This is in the basement of the Music Academy (Muusikamajas) but is open to the public although few tourists track it down. Its warmth is welcome in winter and so is the opposite in summer. It is run by the Kehrwieder group who own a number of dependable cafés around Tallinn. The location is most useful, given the few other cafes in this part of the Old Town. The website (www.kohvik.ee) gives a full list of them and a map showing their locations.

☕ **Maiasmokk** (Sweet Tooth) Pikk 16. It is nice to find a café that is unashamedly old-fashioned. The panelling is dark, the staff middle-aged and the food prepared on the spot. It is provincial in the best sense of the word, being one of the very few cafés in Tallinn that are spared piped music. Prices also stay 2 or 3 years behind those charged elsewhere, particularly surprising given its location on the tourist beat in the centre of the Old Town. There is a separate entrance to the restaurant, which consists of small dining rooms on the first floor that can be booked for private groups of 8 to 10. Choose the view carefully: one overlooks the balcony of the Russian Embassy from which the occupation of Estonia was proclaimed in 1940. In summer 2004 the Kalev Chocolate Museum moved to the top floor of the restaurant but still had not opened in spring 2006, although a small exhibition on the history of marzipan has done so.

☕ **Meistrite Hoov** (Masters' Courtyard) Vene 6. Lavish chocolates are usually expected in boutiques or at least in department stores. Here, too, they are available, and in fact are the main attraction. Suits in a café called Chocolaterie are unknown, self-service is the norm and soft cushions cover the chairs. Expect to be surrounded by modern art, both in painting and in ceramics. The size of the exhibition depends on the weather; it rapidly expands outdoors whenever it can. A few simple rooms above the café are now let out for between 800 and 1,500EEK to non-smokers only. They have kitchen facilities so are useful for visitors wanting to stay longer than a few days in the town centre.

☕ **Mini-many** Maakri 22. This wooden house could not be a greater contrast to the Radisson Hotel on the other side of the road. It has only 5 tables and serves plain home cooking on traditional black-and-white tablecloths. The clientele is largely local but the occasional foreigner is now seen here.

☕ **Mocha** Vene 1. Return visitors to Tallinn will remember this as the Mary and there seems little need for a name change. The selection of teas remains as extensive as that of the coffees and for those who would be happier in Austria or Germany, the Mocha provides perfect solace. After a cake or two here there is no need for lunch or supper. Papers to read abound, there is no rush and the music is much quieter than elsewhere. The neighbouring shops change frequently; let us hope that Mocha sees no need to follow suit. The Irish and Italian embassies share a building over the road so their flags plus the EU one make the café easy to find.

Moskva Vabaduse Väljak 10; ☏ 640 4694; www.moskva.ee. Some cafés survive in Tallinn on sheer cheek and this must be one of them. The name is as risky as ever given the poisonous level of relations with Russia and the location of this café on Freedom Square. The décor remains gloomy and the website is in dark brown, with no foreign language translations. Yet local expats and Estonians return again and again. Perhaps it is for a sense of security as much as for the 1990s prices. The food will always be dependable, as is the company; the music, if noticeable at all, will not intrude.

Musi (Kiss) Niguliste 6; ☏ 644 3100; www.musi.ee. This wine bar opened almost without anybody noticing in spring 2005. It has to be said that the chipped stairs and the formidable wooden door (always closed) are hardly an encouragement. As it is situated on one of the main tourist routes, this scenario is perhaps just as well, so tourists who do track it down will be rewarded with suburban prices and an almost homely feel, so small are the rooms. The abstemious will be able to have a meal here from the salads and pies on offer and nobody need worry about being over 25. It is probably a good sign, if a surprising one, that 9 months after opening, the menu and the website are still only in Estonian. Do not ask for a wine list as what is offered changes frequently, but positively. Just ask the staff for current offerings and prices. However high or low the bill, it will come in a jewellery box. Foreigners are welcome, but they must fit in.

Otto's Pikk 35. For the moment cafés are few and far between on Pikk, although it is a central street in the Old Town. Although the décor here is modern, this one generally attracts an older clientele which is rewarded with lower prices and larger portions than those usually offered elsewhere. They may also prefer the smaller size as there are only 5 tables.

Pollu Rävala 8. The headquarters of the Estonian Civil Aviation Administration, close to the Radisson and Viru hotels, is an unusual place to look for coffee but for those on a tight budget and not the least interested in atmosphere, the public café in the basement rewards those who track it down, with coffee for 4EEK, light snacks for 12EEK and hot meals for around 22EEK. The hot dishes come straight from the freezer and the

flowers on the tables are guaranteed to be artificial, but at these prices who should care?

Scotland Yard Mere pst 6e; ☏ 653 5190; www.scotlandyard.ee. Many British antique shops must have been plundered to recreate the 1890s here, though whether gunsmiths needed to relinquish so much of their old stock is a moot point. The guns worn by the staff are fortunately fakes. Proximity to the port attracts the wilder, rougher crowd on Fri and Sat nights, but more conventional guests will feel happy here during the day and might even want to stay for a meal. Despite the old-fashioned décor, it is very much a young set who come here.

Stereo Lounge Harju 6; ☏ 631 0549; www.stereolounge.ee. Older visitors will remember George Browne's that used to be at this address. While pubs remained a novelty in Tallinn, its formula worked, but Stereo has shown that by 2004 a change was very necessary. The décor is totally white here, except for the staff who are in easyJet orange and the bottles which have stayed as their manufacturers produced them. There is no longer any need to battle to the bar for a drink; it and a healthy range of light dishes can quickly be brought to any table, but for those able to support themselves on a bar stool, the array of drinks served and the breadth of the TV screen will provide an enticing vista.

Tapas & Vino Suur Karja 4; ☏ 631 3232. Suur Karja is notorious for the number of bars on it catering only to loud-mouthed stag parties. It was courageous for a serious wine bar to open here early in 2005 but the gamble has paid off. The cracks in the ceiling beams and the Soviet dark-brown panelling under the bar cleverly deters those who would not be welcome. The pile of Estonian literary journals, laid ready for customers at the entrance, is probably a further no-no to such people. The middle-aged, those who like to talk, or the experimenters willing to try Israeli wine or Canadian whiskey will doubtless linger here. Maybe the tapas can soon be enlarged into full meals and a stay in one of the deep armchairs extended from one hour to two.

Tristan ja Isolde Raekoja Plats 1. Although part of the Town Hall, its entrance is so well concealed that, even at the height of the tourist season, space is often available. However, the most enticing time to come is in midwinter late in the evening. Stride across the deserted snow-covered square, pull open the squeaking door and enjoy glühwein in what looks like a Swiss country inn. Follow this with Irish coffee and chocolate cake and hopefully the warmth will last until you get back to your hotel.

Wholeword Tea Aia 4. A slight misnomer as the

shop really specialises in China tea and offers a full tea ceremony for those who have the time. It is part of a larger shop selling a wide range of holistic products and is the greatest contrast to any other Tallinn café a visitor is likely to find. Do not ask for the tea to be laced, do not ask for it to be served quickly and do not ask for milk. Accept these restrictions and linger over your pot for an hour or so. Therapy does not come cheaper or more congenially than it does here.

ENTERTAINMENT AND NIGHTLIFE

On regaining independence, Tallinn immediately rebelled against the limited and formal entertainment that had previously been available. Out went dance bands, string quartets and folk dancing; in came discothèques, striptease and jazz. Private enterprise immediately seized the Finnish market that came every weekend laden with money and determined to spend it – not necessarily in the most sensible of ways; vodka at a quarter of the price it is at home is bound to lead to grief. Above all, the night went on until breakfast. No club now dares to close before 02.00. Admission fees are rare so it is common to sample quite a few different places in one evening. Now that Tallinn has a large middle class, the clientele is very mixed in most clubs as Estonians no longer feel excluded from them. None are yet typecast but go for smart-casual dress. Anything torn or ill-fitting is frowned on in Estonia. Better to be out of date than out of figure.

Before the clubs open, rock and pop concerts draw large crowds to **Linnahall**, near the harbour. It has performances most evenings.

OPERA AND CONCERTS The **Estonian National Opera** (*www.opera.ee*) has performances three or four times a week. Specialist tour operators can pre-book tickets as the programme is fixed about six months in advance. Given the inevitable government cutbacks in this field, it is remarkable how up to date the building now is following its 1998–2005 reconstruction, with the stage lighting being particularly impressive. Unlike Riga, Estonia's opera rarely attracts world-famous performers – and indeed some Estonian performers, especially in this field, have been attracted abroad by the much higher fees paid there. The fact that about 30% of the opera's tickets year-round are sold to non-Estonians shows the high standard that it offers, as well as the very reasonable prices charged. Even after the Opera House reopened in December 2005 following its restoration, the highest ticket price was usually 300EEK, about £13/US$20, and many cost much less. Performances are always in the original language; 20% or so are of contemporary Estonian works, the remainder are popular classics. The opera is closed in July and August.

Classical concerts are held in the **Old Town Hall**, the **Estonia Concert Hall**, the **House of Blackheads** and in **St Nicholas' Church,** all of these venues being in the Old Town. In most cases tickets are sold only on the day or the day before the concert so there is no need (or possibility) to pre-book from abroad. Whilst some performances take place in midsummer, music-lovers are well advised to come at other times of year when the choice is wider and the standard higher.

Young people congregate at **Linnahall**, the concert hall beside the heliport near the harbour, where live music is staged most evenings. Performers are always local. Sometimes this is replaced by family shows and sometimes by raucous Russian plays not genteel enough for the main Russian Theatre. The website (*www.linnahall.ee*) is only in Estonian (*Pileti hind* are the ticket prices and *Jäähalli* is the ice-skating rink).

Films are always subtitled and never dubbed so tourists can see films missed at home without any problem. The **Sõprus Cinema** (*www.kino.ee*) in the Old Town at Vana-Posti 8 is easily accessible from many hotels. It is now part of a Baltic chain called Cinamon which is the name used for the complexes that have opened in Vilnius and Kaunas. Younger people flock to **Coca-Cola Plaza** (*www.superkinod.ee*), a

2

combination of 11 separate cinemas and a shopping mall. It is situated behind the Central Post Office on Viru Square and so is also close to many hotels.

NIGHTLIFE Tallinn prides itself on its nightlife and some tour operators promote it extensively. It does tend to attract some people who should really have kept their vomiting and urinating back home in Britain and Finland. As a major stag destination from 2003, perhaps it will finally fall from popularity in 2006 when these crowds move on.

Fortunately, nightclubs do not go in and out of favour as quickly in Tallinn as they do elsewhere and many clubs that were thriving six or seven years ago still do so now. Many do not charge an entrance fee, particularly midweek, so if you find you have stumbled into somewhere not to your taste, it won't cost much to move on.

The clubs listed below are all totally different, and this is deliberate. *Tallinn In Your Pocket* keeps very up to date on this topic as it is published six times a year and not being dependent on advertising can be objective. To whet your appetite, check their website (*www.inyourpocket.com*) before leaving home.

☆ **Bonnie & Clyde** Olümpia Hotel, Liivalaia 33. As this club is safely ensconced in a 4-star hotel, it is never a mistake to suggest a date here. Do, however, dress up properly, firstly to get in and secondly not to lower the tone. If you are under 25, you may well not want to try unless you can be sure of being taken for at least 30. If you are 45, do not worry. Nearly everybody else is too.

☆ **Eiffel** Grand Hotel, Toompuiestee 27. The hotel caters for staid, elderly tourist groups wanting a quiet base near the Old Town, but this rooftop club is far more broad minded, both in its music and in its clientele. The music is normally live, which makes the volume sensible for those wanting to be able to talk with their guests. The view up to the floodlit Tall Hermann Tower is a pleasant contrast to the cellar walls on offer in so many other clubs, as is the space to move around. Smart-casual dress is the norm, though extremes in either direction can sometimes be seen.

☆ **Harley Davidson** Dunkri 11. This club must clearly be a rebellion against the de-luxe St Petersbourg Hotel on the other side of the road. Nobody here has any dress sense at all and if they cannot arrive on a motorbike, will certainly not choose a taxi instead. Pretend to be under 25 to be comfortable here and,

yes, a leather jacket is the common currency. Probably to stop endless protests from hotel grandees, the club closes at midnight during the week and at the comparatively early time of 02.00 on Fri and Sat nights.

☆ **La Casa del Habano** Dunkri 2. For those who hate nightlife but for business reasons have to pretend otherwise, Tallinn's first cigar lounge provided the perfect answer. To impress, insist on a Cuban cigar, but the miserly can also order Danish and Dutch ones. Sit at the window during the evening and see all of single Tallinn go by, some to the de-luxe St Petersbourg Hotel and some to the Harley Davidson described above. As the lounge is also open during the day, come back then for a different view of families and cruise passengers.

☆ **Molly Malone's** Mündi 2. Yes, the old aluminium Guinness advertisements are corny, yes the music can be dated and yes, because of the location on Town Hall Square it can get very crowded in summer, but nonetheless a visit to Tallinn is not complete without a look-in at Molly's. Expats regularly congregated here, even before fish and chips came onto the menu. In the summer, spilling on to the square is normal so relative peace can alternate with Irish liveliness.

GAY TALLINN Visitors to Tallinn may be surprised at how limited the gay scene is. Whilst the legal restraints they faced in Soviet times have all of course been abolished, the hostility the gay community then faced has still not been eradicated. As a result, open affection outside the few gay clubs is very unusual and visitors are advised to avoid this. Some clubs even function behind closed doors and it is necessary to ring a bell to gain admission. Opening hours can often change, as can nights on which women are admitted. This should be checked on their websites. Three well-established clubs are:

☆ **Nightman** Vineeri 4; www.nightman.ee. This club just southwest of the Old Town off Liivalaia started as

one strictly for gays but now both straights and gays happily mix here. It makes no effort to attract foreigners – its website is still only in Estonian – and it opens only on Fri and Sat, but nonetheless consistently fills up, so arrive on the dot of 22.00 or wait until around 03.00 to be sure of admission.

☆ **Ring Club** Juhkentali 11; www.ringclub.ee. Women and striptease are strictly segregated here but do check the explicit and detailed English-language website before setting off. Juhkentali is close to the bus station and is hardly the most salubrious road in Tallinn, which perhaps suits the risqué approach of this club and the gloomy underground surroundings in which its activities take place.

☆ **X-Baar** Sauna 1; www.zone.ee/xbaar. With its central location, comparatively long history and small size, this is probably the place to go first in Tallinn. The jazz and the pink décor will provide reassuring surroundings.

SHOPPING

Monday to Friday most shops open 10.00–18.00 and on Saturday they close earlier, usually around 16.00. On Sundays they stay closed. However those in the Old Town of interest to tourists open in the summer 10.00–19.00 seven days a week. Supermarkets open every day, usually 09.00–21.00. Only the smallest shops now refuse credit cards. Some may take euros or dollars, even though this is technically illegal. However the exchange rate is likely to be very poor so local currency should always be used for small items where credit cards are not applicable.

Postcards are best bought at the **post office** at the top of the Old Town at Lossi Plats 4, beside the Alexander Nevsky Cathedral. Here they tend to cost about half the price charged by the sellers on the street. It also sells a wide selection of stamps for collectors.

Apollo at Viru 23 is the best source for **books** in English on Tallinn, Estonia and the neighbouring Baltic states. It usually stocks a wide selection of Bradt guides and also paperback fiction in English.

It is hard to support ethnic cleansing, but with the purchase of **souvenirs** it can probably be justified at **Meistrite Hoov** (Masters' Courtyard) at Vene 6 where a condition of trading is that anything sold is produced in Estonia. There is nothing wrong with Russian wooden dolls, Lithuanian amber and Chinese paper-cuts, but Tallinn Old Town is not the place where they should be promoted, as they all too often are. Come here for a range of small outlets selling locally produced beeswax candles, woollen sweaters, juniper butter knives and hand-painted ceramics. Expect considerable renovation, but no change in principles, during 2006 and 2007. For **chocolate** it is important to go to the **Kalev** shop at Lai 1, rather than to their other shops in the Old Town since prices here are much lower. The shop at Lai 5, **Puupood**, has a wide range of tasteful souvenirs with very few made outside Estonia. Being in a basement, and with a precariously low entrance from the street, its prices are much lower than those charged a few steps away on Old Town Square.

Those who shop for necessity rather than for pleasure usually call in at the hypermarket **Ulemiste**, beside the hotel of the same name a few hundred yards from the airport. It sells a wide range of souvenirs, cheap household goods, black bread and vodka which can be picked up just before checking in for a flight. Shopaholics, however, should go instead to the **Viru Centre**, a shopping complex beside the hotel of the same name and now linked to Tallinn's largest department store, **Kaubamaja**. Its multilingual website (*www.virukeskus.com*) gives full details of all the shops it includes. Being completely enclosed, and with the bus station in the basement, the outside weather is irrelevant year-round.

WALKING TOUR

Tourists tend to concentrate on the Old Town but many modern buildings are of interest, too. While the main sights in the Old Town can be covered in one day, more time is needed for others. A route for a day-long walking tour is suggested.

Lennart Meri

Old Tallinn… It looks at us in the morning when we are hurrying to work and in the evening as we return home, always with the same good-natured glance of a friendly old man. But we scarcely notice it. We scarcely notice the thousand-year history of these streets. Why should we? These ancient stones are a part of ourselves, flesh of our flesh. We were born and grew up among them. We fell in love, fought, dreamed, took part in strikes, died, built monuments to ourselves and never lost heart. Yes, we have always been rather cramped for space. But it is of course a joy to us to see how every year the cloud of romantic legend thickens over our city and it is an even greater joy to tourists. Some of these legends are not totally devoid of truth. It is quite true for instance that kings and princes, admirals and pirates once galloped along these uneven cobbles, that swords clashed in knightly tournaments and the sweet wine of Portugal flowed plentifully. Kings, rulers… Where are they now? But we remain, we with our thousand-year-old town, its legends, secrets, subterranean passages, walled-up windows, enchanted doors. So pause for a while before them, feel their surfaces that the centuries have polished smooth. Perhaps they have something to tell you? Perhaps you will be able to hear the clatter of hooves at midnight, the clash of swords, the stifled sighs, the grim song of troops on the march? Then hold your breath and listen, for these stones speak of our distant childhood.

Lennart Meri was President of Estonia 1992–2001 and died in March 2006

Start at the final Soviet architectural legacy to Estonia, the **National Library** (*Eesti Rahvusraamatukogu*), begun in 1986 and completed in 1993 (page 49). It is situated on the intersection of Endla and Tõnismägi close to the Mihkli and Santa Barbara hotels.

Cross the road to **St Charles's Church** (*Kaarlikirik*). With its almost Episcopalian simplicity it is the perfect antidote to what is to come later in the walk (page 52). On leaving the church, turn right into Kaarli and then take the first road on the left, Toompea. The **Occupation Museum** opened here in summer 2003 (page 50).

Continuing up the hill, at the first crossroads, note the simple monument to 20 August 1991, the date Estonia declared independence during the failed Moscow coup. Had it been necessary, Estonians were ready to use the walls and towers to defend the Old Town from possible Soviet attack but the quick collapse of the coup and the immediate recognition by the USSR of Estonian independence prevented this. Looking ahead is a monument that dates from the 15th century, **Pikk Hermann** (Tall Hermann Tower). It has withstood numerous invasions and remains intact. Its height of nearly 50m is supported by foundations 15m deep. The first Estonian flag was flown from here in 1884, 34 years before the country was to become independent. Subsequent conquerors always marked their success by raising a flag here. A German guidebook printed in 1942 lists 12 major dates in Tallinn's history, the last being 28 August 1941, when the German flag was raised over Pikk Hermann. During the Soviet occupation, the Estonian SSR flag was flown, but the Estonian national flag returned in 1989. It is raised at sunrise and lowered at sunset, except at midsummer when it is not lowered at all on the night of 23/24 June. The blue in the flag represents the sky, black the soil, and white the aspirations of the Estonian people.

Turn right down the hill (Komandandi) to **Kiek in de Kök** ('Peep in the Kitchen', page 48). The reason for the name becomes obvious as one climbs the 45m tower to the sixth floor and peers into more and more houses; only the steeples of St Nicholas and St Olav are higher. Kiek in de Kök does not have any catering but the nearest tower to it, **Megedi**, can be recommended in this respect. This tower, like most in the city wall, dates from the late 14th century and was continually enlarged during the 15th century. From around 1800 when its defensive potential declined, it was converted into a barracks. In 1980 the top floor became a café which uses the name Megedi, and the ground floor a restaurant, called Neitsitorn.

On leaving Kiek in de Kök turn back up the hill and turn right into Toompea, which ends in the square between **Parliament** (Riigikogu, page 50) and the **Alexander Nevsky Cathedral** (page 51). The juxtaposition of these two buildings appropriately contrasts official Estonian and Russian architecture. The one is simple, small and functional, the other elaborate and deliberately powerful, a completely Russian architectural outpost dominating the Tallinn skyline. The **Parliament Building**, the interior of which dates from 1921, is one of very few in the Old Town to have seen frequent reconstruction, the last one resulting from a fire in 1917 which may have been started by the Bolsheviks.

Continue up the hill along Toomkooli with the post office on your right. By the end of 2006, this street should be completely restored, the first one to be back to its 1920s glory. Straight ahead, on Kiriku Square, is the **Dome Church** (Toomkirik), sometimes called St Mary's Cathedral (page 52).

As you turn left out of the church, the **Estonian Knighthood Building** dominates the opposite side of Kiriku Square. From 1992 until 2006 it provided temporary shelter for the Estonia Art Museum that now has its own building in Kadriorg. Turning sharp right from the museum along Toom Rüütli leads, after 150m, to the main viewpoint across Tallinn. It is inevitably crowded during the tourist season so an alternative can be recommended along Rahukohtu, on the corner of Rüütli. Rahukohtu also starts on the right-hand side of the gallery. To reach the lower town, it is necessary in either case to return along Piiskopi towards the Russian cathedral and then to walk down the steps of Lühike Jalg ('Short Leg'), rather a misnomer as there are in fact about 100 steps. At the top, though, are several tempting cafés, souvenir shops and well-maintained toilets which can provide a respite before continuing the walk. Before starting the descent, look to the left along Pikk Jalg ('Long Leg'). The façade which commands one of the best views over Tallinn is modelled on the main building of Tartu University. Perhaps appropriately, in view of the current strength of the Estonian economy, this imposing building houses the Ministry of Finance. On the right at the end of Lühike Jalg is the **Adamson-Eric Museum** (page 45).

Continuing down the hill, the steps become a road which continues to a junction. To the left is Rataskaevu and to the right, Rüütli, both roads which house some of Tallinn's most famous restaurants. Ahead is **Niguliste** (St Nicholas' Church, page 53), which, like many other early churches in Tallinn, was a military installation as well as a church, with ample hiding places and secret exits to the city walls. Coming out of the church and turning left along Rüütli, the next building on the left is the Swedish **Church of St Michael** (page 53).

On leaving the church, turn right to the memorial to the writer **Eduard Vilde** (1865–1933). The illustrations depict scenes from his novels and plays, and the two stones represent an open book. Between 1918 and 1920 he served as Estonian ambassador in Copenhagen and Berlin, convincing both governments that an independent Estonia was here to stay. The **Tallinn Tourist Information Centre** is on the other side of the road. Proceed down the steps to Harju. Ahead, until late 2005, was the bookshop, Felix and Fabian, but a new branch of another bookshop Raamatukoi, will open here during 2006. On the corner of Harju and Kuninga note the plaque on the wall to the writer Juhan Smuul (1922–71) who lived here because the building belongs to the Writers' Union. Despite winning both Stalin and Lenin prizes and being chairman of the Writers' Union, he was a genuinely popular writer at the time which is why the plaque has not been removed. Hopefully, his works will soon be republished.

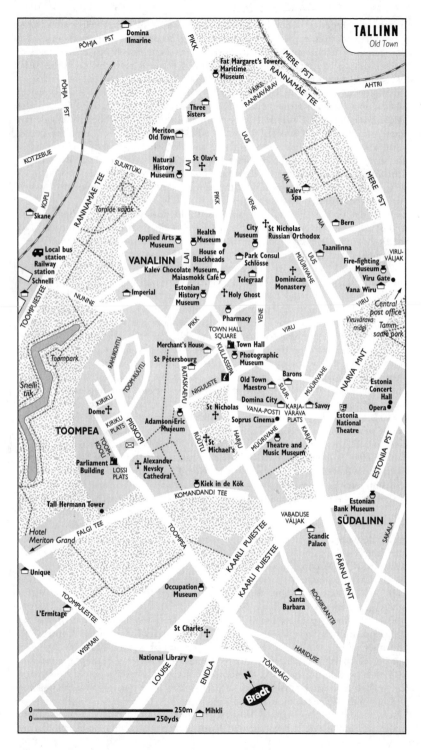

TALLINN
Old Town

PÕHJA PST
Domina Ilmarine
PIKK
Fat Margaret's Tower, Maritime Museum
MERE PST
RANNAMÄE TEE
VÄIKE-RANNAVÄRAV
AHTRI
PÕHJA PST
Three Sisters
UUS
KOTZEBUE
RANNAMÄE TEE
SUURTÜKI
Meriton Old Town
Natural History Museum
St Olav's
LAI
PIKK
VENE
Kalev Spa
AIA
MERE PST
Skane
Tornide väljak
KOPLI
Applied Arts Museum
Health Museum
City Museum
St Nicholas Russian Orthodox
AIA
Bern
Local bus station
Railway station
Schnelli
VANALINN
House of Blackheads
Park Consul Schlösse
Taanilinna
UUS
VIRU-VÄLJAK
Fire-fighting Museum
Kalev Chocolate Museum, Maiasmokk Café
Telegraaf
MÜÜRIVAHE
Viru Wiru
NUNNE
Imperial
Estonian History Museum
Holy Ghost
Dominican Monastery
Vana Wiru
Viru Gate
TOOMPUIESTEE
PIKK
Pharmacy
VENE
VIRU
Central post office
RAHUKOHTU
TOWN HALL SQUARE
Viruvärava mägi
Tamm-saare park
Toompark
Merchant's House
Town Hall
VIRU
Snelli tiik
St Petersburg
TOOM-RÜÜTLI
RATASKAEVU
NIGULISTE
Photographic Museum
Old Town Maestro
KULLASSEPA
Barons
SUUR
MÜÜRIVAHE
NARVA MNT
Estonia Concert Hall
Dome
KIRIKU
KIRIKU PLATS
Adamson-Eric Museum
St Nicholas
Domina City
VANA-POSTI
KARJA-VÄRAVA PLATS
Savoy
Opera
TOOMPEA
PIISKOPI
TOOM-KOOLI
Soprus Cinema
HARJU
St Michael's
RÜÜTLI
MÜÜRIVAHE
Theatre and Music Museum
KARJA
Estonia National Theatre
Parliament Building
LOSSI PLATS
Alexander Nevsky Cathedral
ESTONIA PST
Kiek in de Kök
KOMANDANDI TEE
Estonian Bank Museum
SAKALA
Tall Hermann Tower
FALGI TEE
TOOMPEA
VABADUSE VÄLJAK
SÜDALINN
Hotel Meriton Grand
KAARLI PUIESTEE
Scandic Palace
PÄRNU MNT
Unique
KAARLI PUIESTEE
TOOMPUIESTEE
Occupation Museum
Santa Barbara
ROOSIKRANTSI
L'Ermitage
WISMARI
St Charles
HARIDUSE
National Library
LOUISE
ENDLA
TÕNISMÄGI
N
Bradt

| 0 | | 250m | Mihkli |
| 0 | | 250yds | |

Jaan Kross (born 1920), Estonia's most famous contemporary writer, still (in early 2006) lives in this complex and is fit enough to reach his fourth-floor flat without a lift. (In Soviet times, only buildings with five floors or more had lifts installed.)

Turn into Harju. The bombed site on the right has deliberately been left as it was, following the bombing raid of 9 March 1944. The inscription commemorates the 463 people killed that night. In June 2002 a referendum was held in Tallinn about the future of this site. Only 2% of the population turned out to vote, but 87% of them wanted to keep the site as a memorial and not let it fall into the hands of developers. Returning along Harju and then Kullassepa brings one into **Raekoja Plats**, or Town Hall Square. Just before reaching the square, it is worth turning right for a few minutes into the small alley, Raekoja. The building on the right, which now houses the **Photographic Museum** (page 51), was the town's main prison until the early 19th century.

The Town Hall Square is similar to many in northern Germany as it was the commercial centre for the Baltic Germans. In the 16th century, the Germans accounted for about 1,500 of Tallinn's total population of around 5,000. They maintained all positions of authority, ruling from the Town Hall and the surrounding buildings. The square was the centre for all major events in the town, happy and tragic. Carnivals, weddings and Christmas have all been regularly celebrated here and the Tallinn Old Days Festival, held each year in early June, recreates the carnival atmosphere with its musical and artistic events. What was probably the world's first Christmas tree was displayed here in 1441. Yet the square was also the site for frequent executions and floggings, its grimmest day being in 1806 when 72 peasants were executed following a failed uprising. Nowadays it is hard to imagine such a background as work and punishment have given way to total relaxation. Cafés surround the square and spread into it during the summer. From 2001, a Christmas market has taken place here throughout December. One of the few buildings on the square that has kept its original function is the **Pharmacy** (page 50), which dates from 1422. The **Town Hall** (page 51) is the only late Gothic building still intact in Estonia, dating largely from the 15th century.

Across the square, opposite the Town Hall, are several short streets which lead to Pikk. On the corner of Mündi and Town Hall Square is a millennium clock which counted down the seconds until midnight on 31 December 1999. Saiakäik is the smallest street in Tallinn. Take either Mündi or Saiakäik and turn right to the junction of Pikk and Pühavaimu for the **Holy Ghost Church** (*Pühavaimu*, page 53). Cross Pikk for the **Estonian History Museum** (*Ajaloomuuseum*, page 47), whose building is as impressive as any of the contents, perhaps more so. As you turn left into Pikk, the new Russian Embassy is on the left and on the right is Maiasmokk, a café that has deliberately stayed old-fashioned both in décor and in prices. The name translates appropriately as 'sweet tooth'. In summer 2004 the **Kalev Chocolate Museum** moved here too (page 48). Pikk has two of the few notable *Jugendstil* or art nouveau buildings in Tallinn, both designed by Jacques Rosenbaum. Number 18, next to Maiasmokk, has a flamboyant Egyptian theme; number 25 on the corner of Hobusepea is more modest. Number 61, built across Pagari, and probably the blandest building in the Old Town, was the KGB headquarters in Soviet times and now houses the Interior Ministry. Unlike its opposite number in Vilnius, it has not been opened to the public.

Next on the left is **St Olav's Church** (*Oleviste*, page 54), named after the King of Norway and now a Baptist church. A few yards further down on the right is **Fat Margaret's Tower** which houses the **Maritime Museum** (*Meremuuseum*, page 49). Outside is a plaque unveiled by Prince Andrew in May 1998 which commemorates British naval involvement in the battles between Estonian forces and the Bolsheviks from 1918 to 1920.

Turn right out of the museum and leave the Old Town on Suur Rannavärara, the continuation of Pikk. On the right is the monument to those who died in the *Estonia* tragedy in 1994. It can be interpreted in a number of ways, perhaps symbolising the boat breaking into two or the total divide between life and death. Cross Põhja puiestee to the disused power station, now ironically the **Energy Museum** (*Energeetikamuuseum*, page 46). Built originally in the late 1920s, it then had some claim to *Jugendstil* influence but many subsequent alterations have completely removed any hint of beauty and style.

Return into the Old Town and walk behind Fat Margaret's Tower along Uus. Number 37 is the **Marine Mine Museum** which opened in 2003. The mines displayed here (and the objects made out of them) all come from Naissaar Island off the coast from Tallinn, which was the centre of production for the whole of the Soviet Union. Number 31 is the **Scottish Club**, in fact a restaurant open to all. It has the best-maintained lawn in Estonia. Next door is a whisky shop, a clear testimony to Tallinn's affluence and passion for Western consumer goods. It is hard to believe that until 1989 whisky was available only in foreign currency shops. Turn right into Olevimägi and then left into Vene. On the left is a smaller, but no less Russian version of the Alexander Nevsky Cathedral, **St Nicholas' Russian Orthodox Church**. Again no concessions are made to Estonia; everything is written, spoken and sung in Russian. It dates from the early 19th century. On the right at number 17 is the **City Museum** (*Linnamuuseum*, page 45). As with the History Museum, the building is of as much interest as the contents. Having escaped the fires that ravaged so many buildings in the Old Town, this 14th-century merchant's house still has examples of 16th-century wooden panelling, windows and furniture.

On the right are the ruins of the Dominican Monastery, founded in 1246 but destroyed during the Reformation in 1524 when the monks were forced to flee. Extensive archaeological excavations were carried out between 1954 and 1968 when the ruins were first opened to the public. Take a torch and wear sturdy shoes as the surviving ambulatories are poorly lit. Of most interest are the stone carvings by the 16th-century Dutch sculptor Arent Passer. Chamber music concerts take place here during the summer. On leaving the monastery, turn left into Vene and left again into Katariina Käik. Gravestones from the monastery are lined up along the left-hand wall. This tiny alleyway is where local expats buy their souvenirs of Tallinn, as few tourists find it. It is also used as a film set. Turn right at the end into Müürivahe, which runs below the city walls. Elderly Russians have stalls here, selling woollen sweaters, gloves and socks both in midsummer and in midwinter. The walk ends at the junction with Viru Street. To the left is the 15th-century Viru Gate, as formidable as the fortifications seen at the start of the walk. To the right is McDonald's; will it also last five centuries?

Visitors with more time can see many museums in addition to those mentioned in the walk. Close to the Viru Gate at Vana Viru 14 and opposite the Viru Hotel is the **Fire-Fighting Museum** (page 47). Back in the Old Town, in Lai, are the **Applied Arts Museum** (page 45) at number 17 and the **Health Museum** (page 45) at numbers 28–30.

Next to the Applied Arts Museum is the **Natural History Museum** (page 50) at Lai 29, and then the **Theatre and Music Museum** (page 51) at Müürivahe 12. Just outside the Old Town, behind the railway station at Kotzebue 16, is the **Dolls' Museum** (page 46).

WHAT TO SEE AND DO

MUSEUMS Most museums close at least one day a week – usually Monday or Tuesday – and some for two days; they also close on public holidays. Many do not open until 11.00 and only one, the Architecture Museum, stays open until 20.00 and this is only in the summer. Churches are open every day from around 09.00.

The most popular ones for foreign visitors, such as the City Museum, Kadriorg Palace and KUMU, charge around £2/US$3.50 for adults. Others charge around £1/US$1.75. Most museums give reductions for children and for senior citizens. There is no charge on 21 February (International Guides Day) and 18 May (International Museums Day) for many of the museums listed. There is also often one day a month when free admission is granted, although the day in question varies from museum to museum. Several state museums share the website www.ekm.ee, and several city ones www.linnamuuseum.ee. These and the individual sites listed below give current information on opening hours and on charges. The Tallinn Card gives free admission to all the museums listed.

Adamson-Eric Museum (*Lühike Jalg 3;* ℡ *644 5838; www.ekm.ee; open Wed–Sun 11.00–18.00*) Adamson-Eric (1902–68) was without doubt the most famous Estonian artist who worked during both the independence period and the Soviet era. This house has no links with him, although before being used as a museum it did have workshops for coppersmiths. The museum opened in 1983 and the collection is based on around 1,000 works bequeathed by his widow. These cover his whole life in both painting and applied art. Gifts from abroad have recently been added to the collection. Labels are in English. Adamson-Eric's parents were able to pay for long periods of study during the 1920s in both Paris and Berlin. Elements of Fauvism and Cubism can be seen in many of his pictures but he was equally drawn to the Bauhaus and worked closely with Walter Gropius, George Grosz and Otto Dix. On his return to Estonia he first specialised in portraits, then added landscapes and broadened into applied arts. In this field, his work became as diverse as his painting. Around 1930 he began with tapestries and textiles and then added ceramics and metalwork to his range. Shortly before the war he diversified even more, starting to work with leather and to design stage sets. He retreated with the Soviet army in 1941 and managed to maintain his artistic integrity despite the stringent demands of Soviet officialdom. With the inevitable lack of materials for applied art at this time, he concentrated again on painting. In 1949, the political tide finally turned against him and he was expelled from the Communist Party, forced to give up his posts and sent into factory work. Although released in 1953 on Stalin's death, his health had deteriorated and he suffered a stroke in 1955. His reaction was simply to learn to paint as well with his left hand as he had previously done with his right! His health slowly improved and he was able to add porcelain painting and tile design to his work in the field of applied art. He remained active until shortly before his death in 1968.

Applied Arts Museum (*Lai 17;* ℡ *641 1927; www.ekm.ee; open Wed–Sun 11.00–18.00*) The ticket desk still sells the Soviet guidebook which boasts that the exhibits 'are really wonderful, conspicuous in their originality and can bear comparison with the best items of the world'. Exhibits from the Soviet period are now on the upper floors, and modern ones on the ground floor, so visitors can judge the changes for themselves and whether such hyperbole applies to either era. In all fields the collections are extensive and show the Estonian dedication to pottery, weaving, glassmaking and woodwork that has surmounted all political regimes. The modern section is largely made up nowadays of temporary exhibitions so it is worth checking the website before going to see what is currently on show.

City Museum (*Vene 17;* ℡ *644 6553; www.linnamuuseum.ee; open Mon, Wed–Sun 10.30–18.00*) The ground floor is taken up with a model of the Old Town in 1825 and it is remarkable how close this is to the town today. The Alexander Nevsky Cathedral is the only major addition and there is the section of Harju Street destroyed by Russian bombing in 1944.

Many of the exhibits on the upper floors here would now be regarded as politically incorrect in the West as they concentrate on the accoutrements of the rich; life below stairs and outside the guilds and churches is ignored. Part of the museum is quite understandably called the 'Treasury', given the quantity of tapestries, silverware, pewter and porcelain displayed there. Nonetheless, the collection shows the breadth of industry and culture that developed in Tallinn from 1860 onwards. The arrival in 1870 of the railway from St Petersburg led to an increase in the population from 30,000 to 160,000 by 1917. One anniversary the Estonians were forced to celebrate in 1910 was the 200th anniversary of the Russian conquest. The museum was closed in 2000 for extensive renovations which included proper lighting and the addition of considerable visual material. It now shows videos of pre-war and Soviet Estonia, of the 1944 bombing, the 1980 Olympics and the 1989 demonstrations that would in due course lead to independence. Allow at least an hour to see these properly. A room of Soviet and Nazi posters has also been added. The café on the top floor is unusual in offering only homemade food. This museum is well labelled in English and the postcard sets they sell are excellent value.

Dolls' Museum (*Kotzebue 16;* ✆ *641 3491; www.linnamuuseum.ee; open Wed–Sun 10.30–18.00*) Opened in 1985 as a memorial to one of Lenin's closest colleagues, Mikhail Kalinin, the Dolls' Museum nonetheless even then had a small collection of toys. Kalinin is now completely forgotten (in Tallinn at least, if not in Kaliningrad!) and toys have taken over completely. The collection of dolls and dolls' houses goes back as far as the 18th century, but there are also board games, teddy bears and general toys from 1900 onwards since this is one of the few elements of Estonian life unaffected by the changing political environment. The walk from the Old Town behind the Hotel Skane offers a completely changed architectural environment; Tallinn on the wrong side of the tracks becomes a town of poorly maintained wooden houses and an abandoned factory. The market beside the station is worth a stop of a few minutes. Excellent light refreshments are available at prices well below those elsewhere in the town and the choice of clothes, CDs and gadgets is a good reflection of mass Estonian taste.

Energy Museum (*Põhja pst 29;* ✆ *612 4500; www.energiakeskus.ee; open Mon–Sat 10.00–17.00*) For tourists who never had the chance to visit Tirana's 'Albania Today' or Chinese museums during the Cultural Revolution, this is a splendidly flamboyant substitute. Ironically for an energy museum, many of the lights do not work but those that do illuminate graphs that all start at zero in 1945 and shoot up to the stratosphere throughout the 1950s, 1960s and 1970s. Engineers will be interested in the various meters and generators on display. The only hint of modern Estonia is an occasional photograph. The basement could not provide a greater contrast with all its striplights working and its displays of contemporary abstract art. Modern Estonia does indeed have energy but it is now portrayed more metaphorically than literally. Demonstrations of the machinery take place several afternoons a week. Check at the entrance for details.

Estonian Art Museum (KUMU Eesti Kunstimuuseum) (*Weizenbergi 34/ Valge 1;* ✆ *602 6001; www.kumu.ee and www.ekm.ee; open May–Sep Tue–Sun 11.00–18.00; Oct–Apr Wed–Sun 11.00–18.00*) Having searched for a home since 1919, the collection now finally has one, purpose-built and opened with appropriate fanfare in February 2006. In size and scope, it dwarfs any other museum in Estonia and perhaps any elsewhere in the Baltic states as well. Some of the pictures displayed here were in its last temporary home, the Estonian Knighthood building beside the Dome Church in the Old Town. Many are on show for the first time, including a large collection from the Soviet period (1944–91). The names of the 19th- and 20th-century artists displayed here are sadly unknown outside Estonia, but many styles will be recognised by visitors. Both in the Tsarist period and under independence, most Estonian artists of note studied in Paris so the prevalent style there is reflected in their pictures. Konrad Mägi (1878–1925) is the country's most famous landscape artist and his pictures here are of many regions in Estonia. It is hard to overstate the importance of this building to Estonian culture. Given the struggle for survival Estonians so often had to endure in the 20th century, it is not surprising that museums and galleries had a low priority under all regimes, whether Estonian or under a foreign power. Collections tended to be placed in buildings that happened to be available or which were seized from an ancient regime. The country can now afford to look after its history and its modern artists. Hopefully KUMU is seen as a model to be copied around Estonia. Vilnius is planning to follow suit with its modern art gallery in 2007 which will in turn force Riga to offer something similar.

Estonian Bank Museum (*Estonia pst 11;* ☎ *668 0760; www.eestipank.info; open only Wed–Fri 12.00–17.00; admission free*) The political history of the country is mirrored in this museum through its currency. In 1928 the kroon was tied to the British pound but it floated after 1933 when Britain left the Gold Standard. The current building dates from 1935 and manages to combine elements of neo-Gothic, neo-renaissance and functionalism. In its predecessor, Estonian independence was proclaimed on 24 February 1918 and in this one a temporary Estonian government was formed in September 1944 between the German and the Russian occupations. The collections here are always bang up to date, so include not only the bank notes issued since 1992, but also designs for recent credit cards and even those for Estonian euro coins unlikely to be introduced until 2008.

Estonian History Museum (*Pikk 17;* ☎ *641 1630; www.eam.ee; open Thu–Tue 11.00–18.00*) Dating from 1410, it was the headquarters of the Great Guild and has changed little since. Visitors who arrive when the museum is shut can at least be consoled by the sight of the 15th-century door knockers. Exhibits inside are well labelled in English and concentrate on archaeology and costumes. Take a look at the film that is always running in the alcove off the main exhibition hall. It shows all the archaeological links the country has with most of its neighbours, and then the buildings which resulted from the influence of the Hanseatic League. Of more contemporary interest is the Tsarist banknote and coin collection and a section on the founding of the local freemasons in the late 1770s. They were later banned by Alexander I in 1822. It has to be admitted however, that Estonian history is better covered in Tartu than in Tallinn.

Fire-Fighting Museum (*Vana-Viru 14;* ☎ *644 4251; www.rescue.ee; open Tue–Sat 12.00–17.00*) Like the Energy Museum, it has not changed since the Soviet era so combines the didactic with the heroic. Dolls' houses show every possible cause of an accident in each room. Macabre photos abound of charred bodies, exploding television sets and open fires out of control. A panel lists medals awarded to local firemen until 1988 but none are listed after that year. It is a cruel comment to suggest that heroism in the Estonian fire service ceased at the restoration of independence in 1991. A number of horse-drawn and early motor fire engines are displayed. Although captions to all exhibits are only in Estonian and Russian, the staff hand out translation cards in English and German.

Health Museum (*Lai 28-30;* ☎ *641 1732; www.tervishoiumuuseum.ee; open Tue–Sat 11.00–18.00*) The building here dates from 1377 and a spiral stone staircase dates from

2

that time. The Health Museum is one of the few totally contemporary museums in Tallinn and uses a range of models, toys, visual aids and colourful charts to show both adults and children the importance of healthy living. One cabinet shows the ideal weekly diet for a ten-year-old child. Some visitors may find the explicit illustrations of the effects of syphilis disturbing. Overall it is a brightly lit and well-thought-out display, a vivid contrast to many other museums. The mummified remains of an alcoholic chain-smoking 54-year-old are compared with the healthy organs of a car-crash victim and if this is not warning enough, the lungs of active and passive smokers are shown, together with a cirrhosis-ridden liver. It may well be the only museum in the country with a hands-on element – two exercise bicycles are available for visitors. One section has been translated into Russian – that on sexually transmitted diseases. More conventional museum exhibits include medical equipment from a hundred years or so ago.

Kalev Chocolate Museum (*Pikk 16;* ☎ *628 3811; www.kalev.ee; open Mon–Sat 09.30–18.00; admission free*) Now based at Pikk 16, above Maiasmokk café, the Kalev Chocolate Museum originally opened in December 2000 beside the Kalev factory on the Pärnu road to the south of Tallinn, near the tram terminus. An extensive (and cheap) Kalev shop still remains there. In 2003 the factory moved out of Tallinn and that part of the building was taken over by the police, although the amount of computer theft that accompanied this move caused them considerable embarrassment and the local population considerable amusement. Whilst the museum gives a thorough coverage of the different production techniques used in its 200-year history and visitors have the chance to smell eight different flavours, the real interest is in the political history revealed in the designs on the boxes issued during the Soviet period. In 1950, the tenth anniversary of Estonia 'joining' the USSR warranted a special box-top, even though three of those years had been spent under German occupation. Later in the 1950s, pre-war pictures of Narva were used, even though it was the Soviet army that destroyed the city in 1944. By the 1980s the authorities became aware of the knowledge Estonians now had of the West, so Mickey Mouse and Finnish television characters were allowed to join traditional Russian role models.

The history of chewing-gum in the former USSR deserves a book to itself since different politburos all devoted endless sessions to this topic. Puritans wanted it banned but the realists wanted to prove that whatever the USA could do, the USSR could do better. Production was first authorised in 1968, banned again and then reintroduced for the Olympics. Only the Kalev factory ever received the necessary authorisation to produce it.

The factory is proud that following independence in 1991 it has been able to re-establish export markets, even as far away as the United States. Perhaps a few elderly consumers there remember the Shirley Temple portrait used on boxes produced in the 1930s. Not even famous German factories are likely to be able to match the 237 varieties of marzipan produced by Kalev now. Prices in this new museum are a little higher than in most local shops, but of course the choice available is greater. At the time of writing in early 2006, some of the museum had still not reopened on the new site, but now that the restaurant above it has closed, this situation should soon be remedied.

Kiek in de Kök (*Komandandi 2;* ☎ *644 6686; www.linnamuuseum.ee/kiekindekok; open Tue–Sun 10.30–18.00*) From its initial construction in the 15th century until its completion in the late 17th century, the tower grew in height and width with walls and floors as thick as 4m, but ironically, after a Russian attack in 1577, it never saw military action again. The last time it was prepared for war was in the 1850s when the

Russians feared a British invasion during the Crimean War. On the top floor, note the model of the 'plague doctor' with a waxed tunic and cape impregnated with herbs. He carries a cane with which to touch patients to avoid any risk of infection. The main exhibition on the top three floors covers Tallinn's military history. The lower floors are now used as an art gallery.

Maritime Museum (*Pikk 70;* ✆ *641 1408; www.tallinn.ee/meremuuseum; open Wed–Sun 10.00–18.00*) Fat Margaret, the tower which holds this museum, was built between 1510 and 1529. Some walls are as much as 6m thick. In 1830 it became a prison but after being stormed in 1917 it was left as a ruin for the next 60 years. Polish restorers, famous throughout the former Soviet block, finally came to the rescue in 1978. Climb to the roof for very photogenic views of St Olav's and the town gates. The museum covers shipbuilding, cartography, port-construction and fish-breeding. There is a recent exhibit on the *Estonia* which sank off the Finnish coast on 28 September 1994 with the loss of 850 lives. A model of one of the boats has political interest. It was originally named after Viktor Kingissepp, leader of the underground Estonian Communist Party in the early 1920s, who was executed in 1922 after leading a failed attempt to overthrow the government. In 1990 it was renamed after Gustav Sule, who was Estonian javelin champion in the 1930s.

National Library (*Tõnismägi 2;* ✆ *630 7611; www.nlib.ee; open Mon–Fri 10.00–20.00, Sat 12.00–19.00, closed Sat in Jul and Aug*) Day tickets for the National Library may be bought in the entrance hall, a section of which is decorated with prints by one of Estonia's most famous contemporary artists, Eduard Wiiralt. Sadly these are not lit as well as they should be. To encourage regular use, the library has several music rooms, antiquarian and modern bookshops, a café and even piped music. On a bitter winter's day tourists may wish to await a change in the weather amongst the many English-language books and journals now available there. As one of Estonia's many preparations for entry into the EU, there are also large French, German and Scandinavian reading rooms. Normally, however, visitors should head straight for the eighth floor to view two contrasting Tallinns. To the north and east is the Tallinn of the travel posters – the spires, turrets and golden domes. In the other direction is a part of the town best seen at this distance, consisting of abandoned factories and fading tower blocks, with minimal intrusion of any colour. This area is still changing too slowly.

The predecessor to this library was opened in 1918 in the parliament building on Toompea and had 2,000 books, a number that only increased to 6,000 during the 1930s. After World War II, the history of the library mirrored that of the country as a whole. Its bleakest period was until 1953 when most of the collection was of Russian books translated into Estonian. On Stalin's death the library was renamed after one of Estonia's most famous authors, Friedrich Reinhold Kreutzwald, a clear sign of a more liberal climate. By 1967 funds were specifically allocated for books in the Estonian language and in 1988, shortly before this new building was supposed to open, it was renamed the National Library and the formerly restricted sections were opened to all. The design seems to symbolise glasnost: light streams in through many massive windows and large open shelves display a wide cross-section of the two million books stored there. It will remain a grandiose memorial to massive public sector investment. Yet it was almost not completed. The fading Soviet government was not eager to continue funding projects outside Russia and the new Estonian one was faced with bills it could not pay. On 28 June 1989, between four and five thousand volunteers joined the building works under the slogan 'Dig a grave for Stalinism'. The director, Ivi Eenmaa, later to become mayor of Tallinn, single-handedly fought Moscow and then each new Estonian government for adequate funds and was finally able to open the library on 22 February 1993, two days before National Day. Many Estonians would have liked to remove the Soviet War Memorial from the front of the museum, particularly as the sculpture is of a Red Army soldier. After much deliberation, it has been kept out of respect for the Russian-speaking population.

Natural History Museum (*Lai 29a;* ☎ *641 1738; www.loodusmuuseum.ee; open Wed–Sun 10.00–17.00*) The surprise here is that most of the exhibits are contemporary rather than historical. Whilst there is an impressive array of stuffed animals, of far greater interest is the collection of photographs of the Estonian countryside, all well lit and well labelled. The standard of English is particularly high here.

Occupation Museum (*Toompea 8;* ☎ *650 5281; www.okupatsioon.ee; open Tue–Sun 11.00–18.00*) This museum could only be opened thanks to funds provided by an Estonian-American, Olga Ritso, who fled abroad in 1944 after both her father and her uncle had been killed by the Soviets. When the museum was formally opened by her and Prime Minister Juhan Parts, they cut not a ribbon but barbed wire. The pathetically inadequate clothing of the prison camps is perhaps the most moving exhibit though the sight of small cases into which thousands of Estonians had to pack belongings for their Siberian exile must run a close second. The red star and a swastika are always shown side by side. To the Estonians, the Russians and the Germans are equally guilty. There are also display cases showing day-to-day life in Estonia under Soviet rule. It seems hard to believe that these items were all most Estonians knew until 1991. The cellars are now being used to display statues from Soviet times, which had all been pulled down when Estonian independence was restored in 1991. One earlier one is however missing. A statue of Stalin which had survived since 1956 could not be included; being 4m high there was no way it could be brought into the museum for display. The entrance to the museum is on Toompea, not on Pärnu.

Parliament (*Lossi plats 1a;* ☎ *631 6331; www.riigikogu.ee; open when parliament is in session*) The façade is a simple classicist one, and all the stone and wooden materials are local. Earlier buildings on this site had usually served as a governor's residence although, in the late 19th century, the building became a prison. The earliest fort was built on this site in 1227 and the northern and western walls date from this time.

The most famous room within the building is the White Hall, with its balcony overlooking the square. The current décor, with white cornices and a yellow ceiling, dates from 1935. From 1922 there had been a more elaborate neo-classicist design, including ceiling mirrors and elaborate panelling. The current parliamentary chamber was rebuilt in 1998 and members of the public can attend debates there, but no interpretation from Estonian is provided. There are 101 members of parliament, representing ten parties, and around 20% of its members are women. Visitors are forbidden to enter 'with cold steel, firearms and pungent-smelling substances'.

Pharmacy (*Raekoja plats 11;* ☎ *631 4860; open daily 10.00–18.00*) Tour guides often like to point out that this business opened 70 years before Columbus discovered America. The coat of arms of the Burchart family, who ran the pharmacy for 400 years, can be seen over the entrance. Amongst the medicines they dispensed which are unlikely to find contemporary favour were fishes' eyes, lambswool and ground rubies, but patients were at least offered these potions with a glass of hot wine to help digestion. In 1725 Peter the Great summoned Burchart to St Petersburg, but he died before Burchart could reach him. In 2000 the pharmacy was extensively refurbished. Part of it is a museum and part a modern chemist's shop.

Photographic Museum (*Raekoja tn 4–6; 644 8767; www.linnamuuseum.ee; open Thu–Tue 10.30–18.00*) Estonia has always had a strong photographic tradition and this museum displays not only cameras produced in the country but photographs from the 19th and early 20th century. The earliest date from 1840. We tend to think of business cards with photos as fairly new but the museum displays one printed in 1859. April fools with cameras started a little later, in the 1890s, so canals in Pisa and leaning towers in Venice date from then. The Minox camera was produced commercially in Riga from 1938, but the first ones to be made came from Tallinn in 1936, with several prototypes being displayed here. It is fortunate that many pictures from the first independence period have survived. One British custom has been taken over by Estonian photographers: everybody says 'cheese' in English and it is also the name of the local photographic journal. The basement is a gallery for the display and sale of contemporary photographs.

Theatre and Music Museum (*Müürivahe 12; 644 6407; www.tallinn.ee/teatrijamuusikamuuseum; open Wed–Sun 10.00–17.30*) Despite its name, this museum in fact covers only music. A violin-maker's workshop has been reconstructed and the display features most instruments of the orchestra, all of which have at some time been made in Estonia. The production of violins and pianos has a long and distinguished history in Tallinn. Very few labels are in English but, fortunately, this does not matter too much given the self-explanatory nature of the exhibits. Estonians are often accused of taking themselves too seriously; from the cartoons on the stairs, it is clear that Estonian musicians, at least, do not. No famous 20th-century conductor is spared portrayal in irreverent clothes. One violinist, Hugo Schuts, is even drawn in a bathing costume.

Town Hall (*Raekoja plats 1; 645 7900; www.tallinn.ee/raekoda; open 15 May–15 Sep 11.00–18.00*) The exterior and the interior are equally impressive. It was the administrative and judicial centre of the town and the extensive range of woodwork and paintings in the council chamber mainly reflect judicial themes. Six centuries of Tallinn's history have been determined in this room and, with the restoration of independence, its role will now increase. For much of this time there were clearly ample funds in the public treasury, as is shown by the opulence of the candelabra, the money-chests and the size of the wine cellars. One of the carvings on the magistrates' bench, of David and Goliath, is often taken to symbolise the relationship between Tallinn Council and its nominal masters on Toompea in the Old Town. The council chamber has always been heated, unlike the neighbouring Citizens' Hall. Dancing, eating and drinking at winter receptions tend to be particularly vigorous to compensate for this. The original weathervane on the top of the spire, known as Old Thomas, was destroyed in the 1944 raid but the rest of the building was spared. German architects, artists and craftsmen were employed for the Town Hall and all documents were written only in German, even during the long periods of Swedish and Russian rule. Only the tapestries have a non-German origin, being Flemish. The originals are not in fact displayed any more, because of their fragile condition, but two exact copies woven over a six-month period in 2003 by the British company Hines of Oxford now hang in the Citizens' Hall. Both are over 8m long and show scenes from the legend of King Solomon.

It is sometimes possible to climb up the spire; the view from the top offers excellent shots of the Old Town for photographers but the stairs are steep so this is only recommended for the fit and determined. A large exhibition opened in the basement in summer 2003 and it is worth braving the extremely narrow staircase down to it. Plans and photographs of the square are shown as it has been, as it might have been and as it may be, together with many fragments unearthed in recent excavations. Do not forget to use the toilets here as they have been skilfully placed within the foundations.

Another exhibition opened in summer 2004 in the attic behind the clock. Its main exhibit is a model of Tallinn as it was in 1825, but more important is the fact that this attic has been cleared. Restoration that started in 1952 finally came to an end 52 years later. It generated 273 tonnes of debris, much of which had been stored here. Some of the smaller, more valuable finds in wood, earthenware and textiles are now on display beside the model.

CHURCHES

Alexander Nevsky Cathedral (644 3484; open daily 08.00–19.00) The cathedral

was built in 1900 on a former garden which had housed a statue of Martin Luther. It was Alexander Nevsky who defeated the Teutonic Knights in 1242 so the building had a dual role in pretending to show Russian superiority over both the Baltic Germans and the local Estonians. It was hoped that it would help to stifle the burgeoning nationalistic movements in Estonia, too. Ironically, the Tsarist power that it represented was to last only a further 17 years. Entering the cathedral represents a symbolic departure from Estonia. No-one speaks Estonian and no Estonian-language books are sold. The icons, the mosaics and the 15-tonne bell were all imported from St Petersburg. Occasionally plans are discussed, as they were in the 1930s, for the removal of the cathedral as it is so architecturally and politically incompatible with everything else in Toompea, but it is unlikely that any government would risk the inevitable hostility that would arise amongst the Russian-speaking population of Tallinn.

Charles's Church (611 9100; www.eelk.ee/tallinna.kaarli; open daily 10.00–17.00)

This massive and austere late 19th-century limestone building seats 1,500 people and is the centre of the Estonian Lutheran Church. At a time when Russian rule was becoming more oppressive, its size discreetly symbolised Estonian nationalism. The name comes from an original wooden church built in the late 17th century during the reign of the Swedish King Charles XI. Although the church took 20 years to build, the large altar fresco was completed in ten days in 1879 by the well-known artist Johann Köler.

Dome Church (644 4140; www.eelk.ee/tallinna.toom; open daily 09.00–17.00) Work

started on the Dome Church soon after the Danish invasion in the early 13th century and the first church was consecrated by King Waldemar II in 1240. It was slowly enlarged over the next four centuries as funds became available but much of the interior was destroyed in the fire of 1684 which devastated the whole of the Old Town. The Swedish King Charles XI imposed a special tax for the rebuilding of Tallinn and within two years the church had been largely restored. The baroque spire was added in 1778 so in all the church has an architectural history of over 600 years. The altarpiece, painted in 1866, is the work of the Baltic-German artist Eduard von Gebhardt. The organ, probably the most powerful in Estonia, was made in Frankfurt an der Oder in 1913 and is the last to have been imported from Germany before World War I.

The Dome Church was the religious centre for the main families of the Tallinn Baltic-German community; their coats of arms cover the church walls and their tombstones cover the floor, although a few are of Swedish origin. At the back of the church are two tombstones commemorating the butchers' and the shoemakers' guilds. The most impressive tomb, which is beside the altar, is that of the French mercenary Pontus de la Gardie who served in the Swedish army in many battles with the Russians. In the north aisle is a monument to Samuel Greig, a Scottish admiral who served in the Tsarist navy from 1763 until his death in 1788. The inscription expresses the sorrow of Catherine II at his death. Like many Scottish predecessors and successors, he had a distinguished career in this navy. He helped to destroy the Turkish fleet at the battle of Chesme in 1770 and to build up Kronstadt into a major naval base. Next to this monument is one to Adam von Krusenstern, the Baltic German who led the first Russian expedition to sail around the world, in 1803. Note the two globes, both of which omit New Zealand.

Holy Ghost Church (644 1487; www.eelk.ee/tallinna.puhavaimu; open daily 10.00–16.00)
That this church does not face due east suggests that there was already a complex street layout by 1300 when building began. It was the first church to hold services in Estonian and the first extracts from the catechism in the Estonian language were printed for use here in 1535. The pulpit is the original one dating from this time. Some of the panels along the balcony, under restoration during 2003, depict Old and New Testament themes, others the life of St Elizabeth of Thuringen, the patron saint of beggars and orphans. The 1684 fire destroyed much of the interior and the original spire but the next spire was for many years the oldest in Tallinn, dating from 1688. It was badly damaged in a fire in 2002 but was quickly replaced. Of the same age inside the church is the large wooden clock on the north wall, carved by Christian Ackermann from Königsberg. Spared from the fire was the folding altar carved in 1483 by the Lübeck artist Bernt Notke, whose *Dance Macabre* at St Nicholas is noted below. Only the organ is modern, dating from 1929; it is one of the few in Tallinn's churches built by an Estonian and not imported from Germany. To the left of the altar, the White Ensign and the plaque below it commemorate the British sailors who gave their lives between 1918 and 1920 fighting the Bolsheviks. A replica of this plaque was unveiled at Portsmouth Cathedral by Prince Andrew in December 2005.

St Michael's Swedish Church (644 1938; www.eelk.ee/tallinna.rootsi; open daily 10.00–18.00)
St Michael's does not have a tower as it was first built in the early 16th century as an almshouse and hospital. Only in the 18th century was it consecrated. The Swedish community all fled in 1944 which gave the Soviet authorities a pretext for converting the building into a sports centre, mainly used for boxing and wrestling. Generous support from the Swedish Lutheran community enabled it to be reconsecrated in 1993.

St Nicholas' Church (Niguliste) (644 9911; www.ekm.ee; open Wed–Sun 10.00–18.00)
In common with many other Tallinn churches, St Nicholas' was first built in the 13th century and then expanded over the next 400 years. The original spire dated from 1696 and, being outside the town walls, the church was spared from the 1684 fire. It was, however, badly damaged during the Soviet air raid on Tallinn of 9 March 1944, having had its last service the day before. The spire was firmly restored only in 1984. An earlier replacement collapsed in 1982 and the Soviet authorities flooded the streets with police to stop photographs being taken of this humiliation. (They did not completely succeed.) The carvings, chandeliers and pictures, many dating from the 16th century, had fortunately been removed before the bombing. They are all now on display again and are particularly valuable given that so much similar work in Tallinn was either destroyed in the 1684 fire or suffered from neglect in more recent times. The silver collection suffered a more precarious fate, with much being looted during World War II, but with the addition of some donations, the current exhibition is a very representative collection of Estonian work in this field from the 15th century onwards.

The interior of the church was slowly restored during the Soviet period in 1953. A new exhibition was opened in 2005 which describes this work and captions are in English. St Nicholas' has kept its role as a museum and concert hall so has not been reconsecrated. The life of St Nicholas is portrayed in the altarpiece, over 6m wide and painted in Lübeck by Hermen Rode between 1478 and 1482. The *Dance Macabre* by Bernt Notke, another Lübeck artist, was painted a decade or so earlier and shows how nobody escapes death, whatever their powers when alive. Note the one very modern addition – a stained-glass window by the contemporary artist, Rait Prääts, whose glass can also be seen at the National Library and the Sakala Conference Centre.

St Olav's Church (⟍ 641 2241; www.oleviste.ee; church open daily 10.00–14.00. Tower open May–Sep 11.00–17.00) When first built in 1267, St Olav's 140m-high steeple made it one of the tallest buildings in the world. This steeple caught fire in 1820, having been struck by lightning, and its replacement reaches 'only' 120m. It is still, however, a major feature of the Tallinn skyline and since the summer of 2002 has been open to the public. Much of the interior of the church was destroyed in the 1820 fire, as it had been in an earlier one in 1625. The rebuilding, completed in 1840, provides a contrast to most other churches in Tallinn for its plain interior. Tsar Nicholas I donated a large bell in 1850 and his generosity is noted in an inscription written, with no trace of irony, in German. The organ dates from this time but the chandeliers are earlier and have been donated from other buildings.

EXCURSIONS FROM TALLINN

Where Tallinn is keen to show either how medieval or how modern it is, trips outside will reveal an Estonia either still trapped in the Soviet period or much more content to return to nature. Ideally, add an extra day to a Tallinn visit to allow time for some of these very different experiences.

The island described, Aegna, can be visited only in the summer, but Rocca al Mare, Kadriorg and Pirita are equally attractive under snow. The former Soviet naval base at Paldiski is macabre all year round.

ROCCA AL MARE OPEN AIR MUSEUM (*Vabaõhumuuseumi tee 12;* ⟍ *654 9100; www.evm.ee; open May–Oct daily 10.00–18.00, although the buildings close at 16.00; open Nov–Apr daily 10.00–17.00 but the buildings are closed then*) This museum deserves a half-day to itself, ideally in balmy summer weather or after a heavy fall of snow. Take the 21 or 21b bus from the railway station and also take a sweater as protection against the wind on the many non-balmy days. A winter excursion on a sunny day is worthwhile to get some impression of what most Estonians used to endure month in, month out, every winter. Visitors at midsummer on 23 June can enjoy the all-night celebrations held here. The name in Italian means 'cliff beside the sea' and was given by the original owner of the estate when it was bought in 1863.

The museum was founded in 1957 and first opened to the public in 1964. The descriptive panels throughout are in English. It now consists of around 70 buildings and when complete should have a hundred. The aim is to show all aspects of Estonian rural architecture, with houses of both rich and poor. Most date from the 19th century but one of the chapels was built in 1699. The whole of Estonia is represented – windmills are, of course, from the island of Saaremaa but in contrast there are fishermen's cottages from Lake Peipsi on the Russian border. Even the poorest families managed to afford a sauna since to Estonians it is as crucial to living as a cooking pot. The interiors have all been appropriately furnished with kitchen utensils, weaving looms and chests of drawers.

Amongst the more unusual buildings is a tabernacle from the Herrnhut movement, a strict offshoot of the Lutheran Church. Future plans include the restoration of a Swedish cottage – about 8,000 Swedes lived in Estonia before World War II. There is already a Swedish church here, brought from the formerly Swedish-speaking village of Sutlepa. The exterior is 17th century and the interior 19th century. Inside there is a permanent exhibition of drawings from all the other Swedish churches in Estonia. In bad weather, finish your tour at the Kolu Tavern. Kolu is a village between Tallinn and Tartu, and the tavern here still has two separate bars, one originally for the gentry and one for the peasants. It serves filling, hot food such as pea soup and mashed potatoes with bacon, but do not expect any concessions to the 21st century; it remains firmly in the 19th, although a more conventional restaurant will in due course be built for more fastidious diners.

PALDISKI Since independence, an uneasy quiet has descended on this former Soviet naval base situated 40km west of Tallinn. Unusually for Estonia, a regular train service operates from here to Tallinn, with eight services a day, the journey lasting a little over one hour. However, individual tourists would be well advised to take a car and guide for a half-day excursion as several en-route stops can be made. Estonians are more than happy to see the back of the Russian sailors but have yet to find a new role for this harbour. A daily car-ferry service to Kappelskär in Sweden started in summer 2000 which provided much-needed employment and the switching of cargo services from Tallinn soon followed, which is helping to bring a sense of hope back into the town.

Peter the Great inspected the site personally in 1715 before authorising the building of a harbour which was originally planned as the largest in the Russian Empire and for defending the country against the Swedes. It was better protected than Tallinn and ice-free for much longer. This first point was brought home to Peter very forcefully in 1717 when two boats sank in a storm whilst moored in Tallinn harbour. From then until his death in 1825 he became obsessed with this project; the workforce was around 2,500 men supported by around 300 horses. A dam over 300m long was built. The harbour would never in fact be completed although innumerable attempts were made in the 18th century. Much of the labour was supplied by prisoners; so many died of ill-treatment that Paldiski became known as the 'second Siberia'. The final straw came in 1757 when the workers' pay was reduced from two kopeks to one kopek a day and over 200 died of starvation in the months of March and April 1758 alone. The dam soon collapsed and what remained of the harbour was destroyed in a storm in 1818. Now only some of the fort remains.

In September 1939 the USSR imposed a mutual assistance pact on Estonia under which Paldiski was seized as a naval base. In May 1940, shortly before the full occupation of the country, all Estonians were expelled from the town, a practice that would be repeated all too often from 1945 in many other towns and villages along the coast. Paldiski is now the largest Soviet blot on the Estonian landscape; only the dustbins, brightly coloured and modelled on penguins with their beaks open, provide relief from piles of rubble, barbed wire and ransacked blocks of flats. Improvements are very slow to come here.

The first building to be seen on the way into the town is the former prison, but it can hardly be distinguished from much of what follows. When the Russian forces finally left in September 1995, having been granted dispensation to stay after independence, a population of around 4,000 was left with only 10% of them speaking Estonian; the remainder were Russian-speaking civilians. A curtain behind a window, an irregular light or even the sight of an occasional human being, shows that life has not totally died out here but the slogan in the town's English-language brochure, *A Town with a Future*, seemed at the time to be a joke in particularly bad taste. However, in 2000 a new hotel was opened, the **White Ship** (*Valge Laev*) (*Rae 32;* ℡ *674 2095; www.weekends.ee*). 'Welcome aboard' mats are behind each entrance, a porthole is on the door of every room and maritime memorabilia cover all the walls. It would be possible to commute into Tallinn from here, and when Tallinn hotels are full, late bookers will have no choice.

Returning to Tallinn, two very contrasting stops can be made. Shortly after independence, a monument was erected in the forest at **Klooga** to commemorate the massacre of 2,000 Jews there on 19 September 1944, just before the German withdrawal. The small Estonian-Jewish community had already been killed by then;

these victims were largely from other eastern European countries. The former village of **Tabasalu** is now the first of Tallinn's suburbs, most of whose inhabitants have much more money than sense or taste. The money stands out, but it is well protected by high walls and Rottweilers. A few poultry farmers remain on the outskirts of the village but it cannot be long before they are bought out.

AROUND TALLINN BAY Allow a full day to visit the island of Aegna, the yacht harbour at Pirita and the park at Kadriorg. Several buses serve Pirita from the town centre and the journey takes about ten minutes. The relevant bus stop is one beyond that for the hotel.

Aegna Boats to and from Aegna operate out of Pirita harbour from a small jetty beside the café, not from the larger jetty beside the hotel and yacht club. Boats leave for the island around 09.00, at 12.00 and in the early evening. Check timings at the tourist office or via a hotel reception before setting off and do not forget an umbrella in case the weather suddenly changes. Tickets cost 80EEK for the round trip.

Aegna is so quiet that even Estonians are prepared to turn off their mobile phones, and neither the Germans nor the Russians were able to leave their mark. Conifer trees abound, as do minute beaches, and the few open areas have been made available for camping. Much of the island can be seen in the three hours allowed by the morning boat schedule though a full day of peace and quiet is what most local visitors seek. Paths are clearly marked and a detailed map is displayed at the harbour.

Pirita, Viimsi and Kadriorg Palace Pirita was built as the Olympic village for the yachting and sailing events of the 1980 Olympics. For a precious three weeks Tallinn briefly returned to being an international city. An array of consumer goods, Western newspapers and direct international telephone dialling suddenly came to Tallinn and left equally suddenly when the games were over. Only the buildings have remained and they are so obviously of Soviet design that the harbour hardly seems to belong to modern Estonia. On returning to Pirita, visitors of Estonian origin may wish to take the 34 bus for 2km inland to **Metsakalmistu**, the Forest Cemetery. Most famous Estonians are buried in this pine forest, including the writer A H Tammsaare, the poetess Lydia Koidula, the chess player Paul Keres and most recently Lennart Meri, the President from 1992-2001. Since independence, the body of Konstantin Päts, president until the Soviet occupation, has been returned and he is now buried here together with his immediate family. He died in a Soviet psychiatric hospital in 1956. The body of General Laidoner, however, still lies in 2001 in a communal grave in Vladimir Prison where he died in March 1953, despite strong pressure from the Estonian government for it to be formally identified and returned. His wife was released from prison in 1954 after his death but was only allowed to return to Estonia after her 70th birthday. She had been a pianist and took some music with her to Siberia, practising on walls and tables to keep her fingers fit. Johan Laidoner was commander-in-chief for much of the pre-war period and his former house on the Viimsi Peninsula, about 5km from Pirita, is now the **Laidoner Museum** (*Mõisa tee 1; \ 621 7410; www.laidoner.ee; open Wed–Sun 11.00–18.00*). The most moving exhibit is a French–Russian dictionary given to him during his imprisonment in 1944; he used several pages of it to compose his political testament. It ends, in English, with the words 'Estonia, with all thy faults, I love thee still. Johan Laidoner'. Considering how jealous Stalin was of his reputation, it is remarkable how many items associated with him and with this house have survived. During Soviet times the KGB had taken it over in order to break completely the links with Estonian independence. Estonians are pleased to point out that Laidoner did in the end outlive Stalin, even if only by a few days in March 1953.

The museum was greatly expanded in 2001 and again in 2003. With the help of the Imperial War Museum in London there is now a British room, covering the navy's role in helping to establish Estonian independence in 1918–20. (There are two memorials to this, one in the Holy Ghost Church in Tallinn, see page 53, and one in Portsmouth Cathedral. Both were unveiled by Prince Andrew.) It is expected that many more exhibits will soon come from Britain. This would be appropriate in view of Laidoner's often quoted remark, 'Without the arrival of the British fleet in Tallinn in December 1918, Estonia and the other Baltic states would have found themselves in the hands of the Bolsheviks.' The Poles have likewise opened a room in honour of Marshal Pilsudski who played a similar role to Laidoner in ensuring his country's independence from Russia.

The walk back to the centre of Tallinn is two or three miles. Cross the main road from the harbour to the site of **St Birgitta's Convent**. Although the convent is included in most sightseeing tours, walking here can be a precarious experience as the surroundings of the ruin are so badly maintained. The convent lasted intact for only 170 years, from 1407 until the siege of 1577 when it was largely destroyed by troops of Ivan IV in the Livonian Wars. The outline of the main body of the church is clear; the western gable together with the vestry, cloister and refectories can be identified. Minor restoration and excavation work started in 1960 and was brought to a close only in 2001. The new convent on the north side was completed in 2000 and part of the building is used as a hotel (see page 29).

Staying on the land side of the main road, after half a mile is the **Soviet War Memorial**. It could hardly be anything else, given its size and the military themes of the bronze statues. The Estonians carry out minimal maintenance here but, as with all Soviet war memorials, they are not removed and Russians congregate on the days of the old Soviet holidays such as May Day and 7 November. The text is particularly offensive to Estonians as the monument is dedicated to 'Fighters for Soviet Power'. It was completed only in 1975. A Soviet guidebook excuses this long delay by claiming 'at last Estonian artists had enough skill and adequate economic means to complete such an ensemble'. The obelisk dates from 1960 and commemorates the hurried departure from Tallinn of the Bolshevik fleet in 1918 when German forces occupied the town.

An even more dominant landmark from the Soviet era is the **TV Tower** (*www.teletorn.ee*) about a mile inland from Pirita on Kloostrimetsa. Going there by bus, expect to be surrounded by elderly Russians with flowers since the Russian cemetery and crematorium are nearby. The few tourists who now visit the tower also seem to be Russian. This is a pity as it does provide an extensive view of the town and port not available elsewhere. The entrance is as flamboyant as one would expect: the windows are of stained glass, with portraits of valiant industrial workers; covered aisles surround basins of fountains which in turn are surrounded by lawns. However, nothing has been maintained properly (except for the lifts inside) so moss and weeds become ever more prominent. Nobody has bothered to put Estonian signs in the lift or change the menu in the revolving-tower restaurant from smoked fish and chicken Kiev. The telescope still takes kopek coins. However, prices are almost as dated too; it is many years since liqueurs in central Tallinn cost only 25EEK a glass.

A few hundred yards further along this road is **Maarjamäe Palace** (*Pirita tee 56; 621 7410; www.eam.ee*), which has probably had one of the most turbulent ownership histories of any site in Tallinn. Maarjamäe means 'Mary's Hill' but the German name, Streitberg ('Hill of Strife'), was for many centuries more appropriate. The only consolation is that the blood shed here spared Tallinn itself from many battles. The final one took place in the early 18th century as Russia seized the Baltics from the Swedes during the Northern Wars. To set the seal on his conquest, Peter the Great established Kadriorg Park as a summer residence, so many of the St Petersburg nobility felt obliged to followed suit. Those who could not immediately afford the luxury of a suitable building subsidised it with a factory, so lime kilns and sugar refineries adjoined the manor houses. The sugar was sold in Riga and St Petersburg and the plant was run on British coal. A fire in 1868 destroyed much of the factory and it was never rebuilt. In the 1870s, when the estate was bought by Count Anatoli Orlov-Davydov from St Petersburg, the rebuilding he ordered came to deserve the title 'palace'. Terraces, a gateway decorated with copper eagles and the Gothic tower gave it an almost regal air. The Dutch Consulate bought it in the 1920s when the Orlov-Davydovs emigrated to France and continued its use as a summer residence. It was to lose its appeal in this role when in 1926 the road to Pirita was built across the grounds, cutting off the manor house from direct and private access to the sea. However, the road brought with it commercial potential which was eventually realised in a hotel and restaurant called the Riviera Palace. In 1937 the Estonian air force took it over as a training school and they are sadly responsible for the dreary façade. From 1940 until 1975, when Maarjamäe became a museum, the Soviet military used but did not abuse it. During the 1980s, Polish restorers finally brought the building back to its turn-of-the-century glory, turning their attention to the chandeliers, fireplaces, parquet floors and ceilings. It is ironic that one of the last Soviet legacies to Tallinn should be the perfect surroundings for a museum which chronicles Estonian independence.

Although few labels are in English and the one available guidebook is now badly out of date, this is without doubt the best museum in Tallinn. New rooms are constantly being added, exhibits are generously displayed, the layout is sensibly planned and there is the complete absence of benign neglect that seems to permeate so many other Tallinn museums. It covers Estonian history from the mid 19th century until the present day. It amply contrasts the lifestyles of rich and poor and shows the diversity of industrial products and international contacts that the country enjoyed during the first period of independence between the two world wars. It even had a thriving tourist board whose brochures displayed here sold Estonia as 'The Cheapest and Most Interesting Country in Europe'. One room opened in the summer of 1998 is devoted to the life of Konstantin Päts, Estonia's president between the two world wars. On more contemporary themes, the anti-Soviet guerrilla movement and the return to independence are covered movingly but not bombastically. Amongst new themes covered in rooms opened in 2000 are the battle for Tallinn in early 1918 and the German occupation of 1941–44.

At the back of the palace are some Soviet statues too big (and too boring) to drag to the Occupation Museum in the town centre. It is perhaps a pity that they cannot at least be lifted so that visitors fortunate enough not to have known that era can at least have an idea of its constant physical domination.

Continuing towards the town centre is one of the few late-1950s constructions of which Estonians can be fiercely proud – the **Song Festival Amphitheatre**. It has the massive grandeur to be expected from that time but is not wasteful of materials and does not dominate the surrounding area. The parabola provides cover for 5,000 singers and up to 20,000 more have often taken part. The most famous recent festival took place in 1989, when the previously banned national anthem, 'My Native Land', was sung by an audience of around 300,000 people, 20% of the entire population of the country. In winter, the steep slope at the back of the parabola provides Tallinn's only ski- and toboggan-run. Note the plaques at the top of the slope which commemorate each of the Song Festivals held every five years since 1869. The 2004 Festival was commemorated by a statue at the top of the auditorium to Gustav Ernesaks (1908–93) who did more than anyone else to keep the Estonian element alive in the Song Festivals held during Soviet times. The tower was opened to the public in 2000 and gives photographers good shots of the Old Town and the port combined.

Returning to the shoreline, at the junction of the roads to Pirita and to Narva, note the **Russalka (Mermaid) Memorial**, which commemorates the sinking of a battleship with this name in 1893. It depicts an angel looking out to sea. In 2005 replica gas lamps were installed around the monument. Do not be surprised to see Russian-speaking wedding couples laying flowers here on a Saturday. The sculptor, Amandus Adamson, is one of Estonia's most famous, and perhaps because of this monument he was granted official respect in the Soviet period and a memorial bronze bust of him stands in Kadriorg Park.

Inland, the vista is now dominated by **KUMU** which well deserves all four capital letters given the size of the building. It looks down from the hill at the eastern end of **Kadriorg Park**. This is the **Eesti Kunstimuuseum** (*www.kumu.ee*), the Estonian Art Museum, which opened in February 2006. Everything will be 'big' about it; even the lifts will hold 122 people. A small selection of the art shown here will come from the Knighthood Building where it has been on temporary display since 1992 but much will be seen for the first time, including a collection dedicated to the Soviet period. The atmosphere is totally different to that in the cramped buildings of the Old Town; there should finally be some outreach to the many people who feel intimidated from entering other museums in Estonia. Cafés, a children's centre and an auditorium will all help in this endeavour, as will regular temporary exhibitions by contemporary artists.

The park is the next stage of the walk and one corner is just behind the Russalka Memorial. The park, and **Kadriorg Palace** which forms its centrepiece, was built immediately following Peter the Great's first visit to Tallinn in 1718 with his Italian architect Niccolo Michetti. The triumphal decoration of the ceiling in the Great Hall celebrates his defeat of the Swedes in the Northern War and is loosely based on Rembrandt's *Diana and Actaeon*. The hunter being torn apart by his dogs can be seen to symbolise the Swedish King Charles XII being let down by his army. Sadly the building was not completed by 1725 when Peter the Great died and no subsequent Tsar ever showed the commitment that he did. In fact Catherine I never came to Tallinn again after his death. Perhaps the description often given of the palace as a 'mini-Versailles' is fair, as what was carried out does show some French and Italian influence. A fire destroyed much of the interior in 1750 and it was subsequently never again used by the Russian royal family. In 1930 Kadriorg Palace became the official residence of the Estonian president but now houses the Foreign Art Museum, the collection being mainly Flemish and Baltic German.

None of the furniture was originally here. The Russian royal family took furniture with them as they travelled between their palaces and also 'borrowed' extensively from the local nobility. Much of this collection is what the Baltic Germans had to leave in their manor houses when Hitler 'called them home' in October 1939. Despite the cool personal and state relations with the Russians, a lot of furniture was still ordered from St Petersburg during the first independence period (1920–40). However, the room devoted to Soviet art from the 1920s is likely to be of most interest to visitors. The designs on the porcelain show the most immediate break with the past as all the themes are 100% political. It would take another ten years before painting was similarly controlled. Some of this porcelain was prepared for the first Soviet Art Exhibition held in St Petersburg in 1923, by which time the St Petersburg Imperial Porcelain Factory had become the State Porcelain Factory. It came to be known as 'agitation porcelain'. Many rooms have been restored to their original 1930s layout, when President Päts lived here. The Danzig-Baroque library is the most elaborate room and was completed only in 1939, a year before the Soviet takeover. The salon has a wooden drinks cabinet with panels portraying scenes from *Kalevipoeg,* the 19th-century Estonian national epic. The palace reopened in 2000 and then work started on re-landscaping the surrounding gardens. Much of this exterior work was completed in 2005.

Kadriorg Park is a year-round joy for local people and tourists alike. In winter the combination of sun and snow amidst the trees and sculptures offers a peaceful contrast to the hectic commercial life of Tallinn just a few hundred metres away. Spring brings out the blossom of the cherry and ash trees, summer the swans, the squirrels and the fountains and autumn the blends of gold and red as the trees shed their leaves. A cottage in the park used by Peter the Great during the construction of the palace now poses as a museum but the paucity of exhibits perhaps redefines the word 'minimalist'. A bare main room, a few photographs and some haphazard items of furniture would be best concealed from tourists entitled to expect much more.

A hundred metres back towards town, on Weizenbergi opposite the main entrance to Kadriorg Palace, the **Mikkeli Museum** will quickly restore the enthusiasm of a visitor. This building was the palace kitchen but in 1997 was opened to house the collection of Estonia's most fortunate private art collector, Johannes Mikkel. Born in 1907, he was able to start buying during the first independence period when departing Baltic Germans and Russian nobles abandoned enormous quantities of paintings, porcelain and prints. He was allowed to trade during the Soviet period and enhanced his collection with items bought in the Caucasus and central Asia. There is no predominant theme, but the quality and taste of every item stands out, be it a piece of Kangxi or Meissen porcelain, a Dürer woodcut, a Rembrandt etching or any one of his 20 Flemish paintings. Folders in English are available in every room with descriptions of all major exhibits and modern lighting ensures that each item is viewed as well as possible. Mikkeli died in January 2006 so perhaps the museum will soon be enhanced with further pieces from his private collection.

On leaving the museum and turning left, a slight detour can first be made to the far side of the lake behind the Mikkeli building. The splendidly isolated house at Roheline 3 is the **Eduard Vilde House Museum** where Estonia's most prolific writer, both at home and in exile all over Europe, spent the final six years of his life between 1927 and 1933. Typically for most established Estonians at that time, the furnishings are simple and there are many empty spaces. Return to Weizenbergi to continue back into town. At the corner of Poska on the left, house number 20a has some baroque imitation of the palace although it was built only in 1939. Weizenbergi lasts a further 300m or so before joining Narva mnt. Every house is probably now owned, or was before World War II, by a famous Estonian. Ladas or small Toyotas may be parked in the street, but considerable wealth is discreetly hidden behind the lace curtains. The turn-of-the-century, four-storey houses display hints of *Jugendstil*, whilst the wooden ones are characteristic of middle-class suburbs throughout Estonia. On a neighbouring street, Koidula, one of the largest wooden houses belonged to Estonia's most famous author, A H Tammsaare, who died in March 1940. In his honour it is now the **Tammsaare Museum** but labelling is only in Estonian and Russian. The only English translations of his work were published in Moscow in the 1970s and are now out of print. The exhibition has hardly been changed since the Soviet era so it presents him as far more of a 'man of the people' than was really the case. Tammsaare is depicted on the 25EEK note and it is perhaps significant that it is his farm that is pictured on the reverse, not this townhouse. Some downstairs rooms are now used for modern art exhibitions, which provide a much-needed splash of colour in contrast to the gloom upstairs.

At the junction of Weizenbergi and Narva mnt there is a taxi rank and bus stop. A large Methodist church has recently been built on the far side; otherwise Narva mnt from here back to the Viru Gate is totally devoted to Mammon. There is no point in describing any of the buildings since they are mainly being pulled down to give way to glass skyscrapers. This area will soon be Tallinn's Wall Street or Square Mile. A Japanese restaurant has already opened to ensure a serious and affluent gastronomic ambience.

3

Riga

Riga is the largest and most cosmopolitan of all the Baltic capitals and is by a long way the most interesting town or city in Latvia. It is located on the Daugava River about 15km from the point where the Daugava meets the Baltic Sea in the southeastern corner of the Gulf of Riga. Riga can trace its history to the beginning of the 13th century, but it was in the course of the Middle Ages that it developed into a Hanseatic city, and by the 18th and 19th centuries it had grown into one of Europe's leading ports and industrial centres. By the late 19th/early 20th century it had also become a cultural centre, famous for its opera, theatre and music. Riga celebrated its 800th anniversary in 2001 with a year-long series of special events and also with the rebuilding of the Blackheads' House (see page 65).

THE CITY

The modern city is divided into two parts by the city canal which flows through the elegant parks that separate the historic Old Town from most of the New Town, with its shops, offices and suburbs. The air of elegance and spaciousness created by the area of open space in what is otherwise the centre of a busy capital has led to Riga being compared to Paris by a number of guidebooks and travel writers. There is some justification in the comparison. Even when Latvia was part of the Soviet Union, Riga was more sophisticated than Russian Soviet cities and towns, since it had better shops and the odd decent restaurant and café. Now its medieval and art nouveau architecture and well-kept parks allow the comparison to continue. There are modern international hotels, many good cafés and restaurants, and small and pleasant shops stocking local art and international brands. In 1992–93 the local authority privatised about 90% of Riga's shops, from the old GUM (State Universal Store) in the Old Town, to the small bookshops and tobacconists.

Between 1945 and 1991 Riga grew enormously, largely as a result of Soviet expansion which generally took the form of building large, drab, low-quality blocks of flats in the suburbs. One of the first, called Kengarags, can be seen along the Daugava and plenty can also be seen on the trip from the airport to the city centre.

The present population is estimated at just under 800,000, but even now about 40% is Latvian and about 55% Russian (the balance is made up of Poles, Belarussians and Ukrainians). Over half the population (about 54%) is female.

Until Latvia's independence from the Soviet Union in 1991 Russian was the predominant language heard in Riga. Now, as can be seen from the signposts, Latvian is regaining ground, but Russian is still widely spoken (as are English and German, as second languages).

HISTORY

In 2001 Riga celebrated 800 years of recorded history. In all these years Riga has been the capital of an independent country, presided over by Latvians, for a mere 35 years:

for 20 years between 1920 and 1940 and again since 1991. The remainder of the time it has been fought over and ruled by peoples from all over northern Europe, but predominantly by the Germans and Russians. What is remarkable is that while other peoples have disappeared or been swallowed up into larger states, a people known as the Latvians have survived to establish themselves with a distinct national identity and their own government and to emerge into the 21st century as an independent nation with Riga as its capital.

Archaeological excavations indicate that the area now occupied by Riga was probably inhabited and operated as a trading centre as early as the 2nd century BC or even well before: it is thought that the name Riga may originate from a local word 'ringa', meaning a winding river, and it is clear that well before 1201 Riga was already developing as a small harbour. The first mention of the modern city can however be traced to 1201 when Bishop Albert von Buxhoevden (or Buksherden) of Bremen established the first German fortress here as part of his crusade to introduce Christianity to the local Livs. Religious life was quickly established, with several churches, including the Dome Cathedral, founded in the early years of German domination. During the 13th century Riga suffered from no fewer than five major fires, which eventually gave rise to a law prohibiting the construction of wooden houses inside the town walls, but overall the town prospered as a trading centre, joining the Hanseatic League in 1282. Despite the prosperity, there was constant tension between the citizens and their rulers, giving rise to numerous battles and reprisals.

In 1521 St Peter's Church began to operate as a centre for Reformation doctrine; in 1524 the first Latvian Evangelical Lutheran congregation was formed at St James' Church. As Lutheran teachings gained a foothold in Riga, Catholicism retreated: Catholic churches were demolished, and religious paintings and carvings were destroyed. Lutheranism has been the dominant religion ever since. Teutonic influence gradually waned and in 1561 Riga fell into the hands of the Polish/Lithuanian Empire. The end of the 16th century marked a period of instability, and Russia (under Ivan the Terrible), Poland, Denmark and Sweden all laid claim to the city.

The Polish–Swedish War of 1599–1629 ended as far as Riga was concerned when the city fell to Gustavus Adolphus II in 1621. Following the Peace of Oliva of 1660, Riga became the second capital of Sweden. Again there was a period of commercial success and prosperity. In 1663 a water supply was established using wooden pipes. In 1681 Riga's first newspaper, the *Rigische Nouvellen*, was established. In 1685 the first Bible was printed in Latvian. In the same year a number of large rocks that blocked navigation of the Daugava were removed by explosion. In 1701 a pontoon bridge was built over the Daugava – it was the longest in the world.

Swedish rule continued until 1710, when after an eight-month siege by the Russians, Riga surrendered to the Russian general, Count Sheremetyer. For the next 200 years Riga remained under Russian control, although it continued to be heavily dominated by the Baltic Germans who lived throughout most of Latvia. This period was by no means a bad one for Riga. Peter I married the fourth daughter of Ernst Glück, the Lutheran pastor who translated the Bible into Latvian. She became Catherine I of Russia. Writing in German of the time he spent in Riga between 1764 and 1789 Johann Gottfried Herder wrote 'I lived, taught and behaved in such a free and such an unrestrained way in Livonia such that I can hardly imagine living and behaving again.' In 1743 street lighting was introduced. In 1782 a theatre was established (where Wagner conducted from 1837–39). Riga was also a place of intellectual and scientific enlightenment in the 18th century. In 1798 Dr Otto Herr introduced vaccination against smallpox, and in 1802 the Latvian pharmacist Grindels founded the Society of Pharmacy, which started a trend for the formation of a whole range of medical and scientific associations. In 1801 torture was abolished as part of the legal process, as was public execution.

The 18th century also saw a growth of Latvian cultural awareness. Whilst Herder wrote his *Fragmente über die neuere deutsche Literatur* (*Fragments Concerning Recent German Literature*) in Riga, in 1774 he published a number of Latvian folk songs in German translation.

Riga avoided the effects of the Napoleonic Wars; although Napoleon had threatened to attack 'this suburb of London', he never reached it. As Napoleon's troops approached Riga in 1812, the governor-general of Riga set the wooden houses of the Riga suburbs on fire to deflect the invaders. In the wake of the French Revolution, the wave of liberation that swept across Europe made itself felt in Riga too, and in 1817 serfs were emancipated, 40 years before those in Russia. In 1830 farmers gained the right to live in the cities. In 1840 a rural education law was passed. Soon an educated rural class grew up, starting up trade in Riga and other towns. Jews were given residency rights in Riga only in the mid 19th century, before which most were itinerant traders. By the outbreak of World War I in 1914, their numbers in Riga had reached about 100,000 and they were active both in commerce and in the academic world.

In 1857–58 the town walls were dismantled to allow expansion. In 1861 the railway came and the postal service was expanded. Riga gradually developed into a major industrial centre and the first shipyard opened in 1869. Telephones arrived in 1877; horse-drawn trams appeared, and a major bicycle factory was established. In 1887 an electric power generation station was built. This industrialisation also brought a huge increase in the population of Riga: in 1767 the town had 16,300 inhabitants; 100 years later the population had grown to 102,590 (of whom about 20–25% were Latvian). By 1897 the population more than doubled to 255,879, but the Latvian population now accounted for almost 50%. A prosperous Latvian working class and middle class began to emerge.

Parallel to this industrial expansion came a growth in Latvian nationalism. Latvian newspapers, notably *Tas Latviešu Ļaužu Draugs* (The Friend of the Latvian People), had appeared since the 1820s and 1830s, but Russian remained the language of education, government and the legal system. However, Krišjānis Barons' work in collecting Latvia's *dainas*, traditional four-line folksongs, and the establishment of a folk song festival in Riga in 1873, gave impetus to the movement called the Latvian Awakening, which grew out of the Riga Latvian Association. The Latvian Association published a Latvian encyclopedia, founded a national opera and a national theatre. The folk song festival gave birth to a national anthem, *Dievs Svētī Latviju* (God Bless Latvia).

The end of the 19th century was also a time of growing working-class political awareness. In 1899 women workers at the Džuta textile mill went on strike. The police intervened, and before long demonstrations began in the course of which five workers were shot dead and 31 wounded. A full-scale riot soon ensued. In 1904 the Latvian Social Democratic Party was formed, the most significant movement of its kind in imperial Russia.

On 13 January 1905 a demonstration of the poor and working classes was put down with force in Moscow. The demonstrators had wanted to show solidarity with demonstrators who had gathered four days earlier in front of the tsar's palace in St Petersburg to hand in a petition seeking political reform. A demonstration in support also began in Riga, but again it was put down by force of arms and over 70 people were killed. The Social Democratic Party began to organise resistance, and by October Riga was in the grip of a general strike. Armed peasants attacked German landowners, and other strikers attacked the prison, aiming to free a number of political prisoners.

Before the end of the year Russian troops moved to regain control, putting the revolution down with particular brutality in which over 900 peasants and teachers were executed under martial law, and thousands were exiled to Siberia. The Russian authorities aimed their vengeance especially at teachers who were known for their social-democratic leanings. Many Latvian intellectuals escaped only by fleeing to the West. The writer, Jānis Rainis, fled to Switzerland; Kārlis Ulmanis, the chairman of the Peasants' Party, who was later to become president of Latvia, sought refuge in the United States.

The outbreak of World War I drove Latvia into the arms of the Russians with whom they allied themselves against the German foe. In 1915 German forces were approaching Riga. In a manic evacuation, the Russians moved Riga's industry and about 96,000 workers to Russia. Even the power station was dismantled and moved. In all, about one-third of the total population of Latvia was forced to leave the country. In 1917 German troops crossed the Daugava, and the capital surrendered to them.

In the same year, however, the Russian Revolution was making its consequences felt. Whilst some political elements in Riga sought the annexation of Latvia to the German Empire, others were looking to Soviet power to free their country from the Germans. In spring 1918 Latvia was split into three: Kurzeme and Riga went to Germany, Latgale to Russia, and the rest of Vidzeme was left unmolested. However, following the defeat of Germany, on 18 November 1918, in the Riga national theatre an independent republic of Latvia was proclaimed, and Kārlis Ulmanis was given the task of forming a provisional government. A period of what amounted to civil war ensued, the Russians supporting Latvia against the persistent exercise of German military force. Only on 11 August 1920 was a peace treaty signed between Latvia and the Soviet Union following the final expulsion of German troops from Latvia in December 1919.

The period between the two world wars is often referred to as the first period of Latvian independence. The 1920 treaty provided for the Soviet Union and Latvia to recognise each other as states. In 1922 Latvia adopted its own constitution and issued its own currency. Jānis Čakste was elected as the first president of the republic.

Riga was not immune to the Depression that gripped most of Europe during the 1930s and unemployment rose to high levels. On 15 May 1934 Ulmanis mounted a coup and formed an authoritarian administration. Democratic socialists were imprisoned, political parties of both left and right were banned, and freedom of the press was curtailed. In 1935, the Freedom Monument was erected in the centre of Riga (see page 113).

Under the terms of the pact between Hitler and Stalin of 23 August 1939 it was agreed that the Baltic states would fall under the sphere of influence of the Soviet Union. By the end of that year the Soviet Union had already begun to establish a military presence in Latvia. On 17 June 1940 Soviet troops marched in to take over the country and establish a pro-Soviet regime. On 21 July 'elections' were held under Soviet auspices and a new government and parliament declared Latvia to be a republic of the USSR. Ulmanis was deported, as were thousands of citizens from Riga and elsewhere in Latvia, many of them to Siberia or central Asia.

In June 1941 the USSR was forced to join in the war when attacked by Germany. Latvia was unprepared, and on 1 July 1941 Hitler's troops arrived in Riga to 'liberate' it from Stalin's USSR, causing the Soviets to retreat, leaving devastation in their wake. Stalin had murdered or deported a substantial proportion of the Jewish population in Riga as enemies of the people; Hitler imposed his anti-Semitic policies, massacring Jews at Rumbula and Biķernieki, and establishing concentration camps. Riga was 'liberated' on 13 October 1944. The German occupation of Kurzeme continued until May 1945 when the Red Army arrived again to 'liberate' Riga from the Germans. The retreating Germans destroyed houses, factories, roads and bridges, and thousands of Latvians fled to the West.

After the end of World War II the USSR provided economic assistance to Latvia, and Russian immigrants took the places left by the fleeing or slaughtered native Latvian population. However, the Soviet 'liberators' were not welcomed: many Latvians formed resistance groups and fighting ensued until Stalin intervened with his usual brutality, ordering mass deportations to Siberia in 1949 and acts of destruction including the blowing up of the Blackheads' House (see page 100) in May 1948.

However, Latvian nationalism whilst repressed was not extinguished. In 1988 5,000 demonstrators gathered in Riga on 14 June to commemorate the deportations, and on 23 August 10,000 demonstrators gathered to mark the anniversary of the Hitler–Stalin pact. In the mean time in June at a meeting of the Latvian Writers' Union a resolution was passed that led to the founding of the Popular Front of Latvia in October 1988 that was to campaign for political, cultural and economic independence.

In 1989 Latvia experienced its first free elections of deputies to the Supreme Soviet of the USSR. This event was followed by the passing of laws in the Latvian Supreme Soviet proclaiming the sovereignty of the Latvian Soviet Socialist Republic and declaring Latvian the official language of the country. Latvia was again on the road to independence. On 18 November 1989 over 500,000 people gathered on the banks of the Daugava in Riga to mark the 71st anniversary of Latvia's independence.

On 4 May 1990 the Supreme Soviet of Latvia met in the pre-war Saeima building and passed a resolution on 'the renewal of Independence of the Republic of Latvia'.

A period of instability followed as the Latvian Communist Party endeavoured to take back the helm of government, staging a failed coup in January 1991 in which five people were killed. A plebiscite held in March 1991 resulted in three-quarters of the population voting to secede from the Soviet Union. On 19 and 20 August Soviet troops blocked roads leading to Riga and seized the Interior Ministry building. The Moscow coup failed, however, and on 21 August the Latvian parliament voted to restore independence. On 25 August 1991 Iceland became the first country to recognise the new independent Baltic state, but others soon followed, and by the end of the year the Republic of Latvia had been granted admission to the UN. A new constitution proclaiming Latvia as an independent democratic republic was adopted in 1992. Riga was once more the capital of an independent democratic state.

Since then Riga has made huge efforts to establish itself not only as a vibrant capital of Latvia but also as the major city in the Baltics. Although in terms of size it is the largest of the Baltic capitals, in terms of influence it faces tough competition from the others. Even within Latvia, its trading status is frequently under threat from the port of Ventspils. Major strides have however been made in improving the city. Many buildings have been restored or rebuilt (most notably the Blackheads' House), infrastructure has been improved and the economy expanded. Since its accession to NATO and the European Union in 2004, the city has looked forward to consolidating this progress and establishing itself as a major European capital.

SUGGESTED ITINERARIES

ONE DAY

- Walk through the Old Town (see *Walking tours*, page 87)
- Have a coffee at one of Riga's new coffee houses
- Try a traditional Latvian lunch
- Spend the afternoon in the art nouveau district (page 93)
- Have a cocktail on the 26th floor of the Reval Hotel Latvija (page 75)
- Have dinner in a restaurant in the Old Town
- Visit the opera or a concert

TWO DAYS In addition to the suggestions on page 65:
- Take your time over visiting the Old Town, incorporating visits to museums
- Visit the National Museum of Art (page 99) and the Russian Orthodox Cathedral (page 108)
- Take an afternoon trip to the Open Air Ethnographic Museum (page 104)
- Visit some of the art galleries and antiques shops in the Old and New towns
- Treat yourself to handmade chocolates
- Choose from a wide variety of evening entertainments

THREE DAYS In addition to the above:
- Take a trip outside Riga, either to Jūrmala on the coast (see page 117) or to Rundāle Palace (page 119)
- Wander through the parks and gardens in central Riga
- Visit the Central Market (page 96) and stock up on local produce
- Take a final look at the city by night

PRACTICALITIES

MONEY AND BANKING

Currency In April 2006 exchange rates were £1 = Ls1.00, US$1 = Ls0.55, €1 = Ls0.68. See page 3 for further information on the currency.

Changing money You can change money easily: there is a bureau de change at Riga Airport, which is always open for flight arrivals, but slightly better exchange rates are available in the town. The bureaux de change at the railway station and the bus station are open every day, but not late in the evening. Banks are always dependable for reasonable exchange rates. The bureaux de change in the town vary enormously in the rates they offer. Some are more competitive than the banks but others may charge up to 20% commission. A nasty trick amongst many exchange bureaux that became prevalent in 2005 was to advertise the selling (*pārdošana*) rates for foreign currencies but not the buying (*pirkšana*) rate. It is therefore always important to check the buying rates before making any commitment. In 2005 the shop Latvijas Balzāms at Vaļņu 21, behind the Riga Hotel, consistently offered good rates and also good prices of course for alcohol. The exchange bureau there is open seven days a week 10.00–19.00 but the shop stays open until 22.00.

Try to carry most cash in small change since museum entrance charges are low (usually no more than Ls1), as are most things you are likely to need on a day-to-day basis (drinks, bus fares and so on); large denomination notes are rarely welcome. Therefore when changing money, always ask for Ls5 notes and coins. As prices are low, avoid changing large sums. Street crime is rare in Latvia, and the atmosphere is generally relaxed. However, you should avoid carrying large sums in cash, and it is wise to leave money and valuables in a hotel safe; carry some cash in a money belt.

LOCAL MEDIA Riga is extremely well provided with up-to-date English-language information for visitors. However, visitors should treat warily the listings magazines often distributed in hotels, of which there are now a large number. Being totally dependent on advertising, much of it from nightclubs, their coverage of the city is inevitably biased. Under pressure from the Tourist Board, one of these, *Riga This Week*, now has a totally separate publication, *Riga This Night*, to cover that market. It is better to pay the moderate costs for the *Baltic Times*, *Riga In Your Pocket* and *The City Paper* for a detached view and a much higher standard of writing. One new free magazine, *Riga Now*, does however offer several background articles in each issue which are not simply advertorials.

European editions of British and American newspapers are on sale in Riga at the larger hotels on the day of publication.

Although there are no local radio or television stations that transmit in English, if you have access to FM radio you may be interested in:

96.2	**Radio Naba** A student station playing all types of non-classical music	100.5	**BBC World Service**
		103.7	**Klassika** Classical music
99.5	**Russkoje Radio** Easy listening Russian channel	105.2	**Radio SWH** Popular Latvian music

COMMUNICATIONS

Telephones The country code for Latvia, for calls from outside the country, is 371. To call Riga from abroad therefore dial 371, and then the seven-digit number.

To use a public payphone in Riga you normally need a phonecard (Telekarte). These can be bought at kiosks, stores, post offices, etc, wherever you see the sign Telekarte, and are available for Ls2, 3 or 5. Some phones also take coins. The post office at 1 Stacijas laukums and Plus Punkts kiosks also sell Interkarte, an international prepaid calling card that can also be used with mobile phones (☏ 707 3434; *www.baltia.net*).

To call towns outside Riga from Riga, prefix the city code:

Bauska 39   Cēsis 41

Mobile phones More Latvians now have mobile phones than landline ones. To call mobile phones in Riga, just dial the seven-digit code. Contact your service provider before leaving in order to set up international roaming. If your own mobile phone does not operate in Latvia, it is possible to rent one from many shops in the centre of the town or from the better hotels. For further information on telephoning contact Lattelkom (☏ 800 80 40; *www.lattelkom.lv*).

Useful telephone numbers

Fire	01	Directory enquiries	118 or 117
Police	02	Tourist information	704 4377
Ambulance	03		

Post The most convenient post office (Latvijas Pasts) is at 19 Brīvības bulvāris (*www.pasts.lv*) and is open 07.00–22.00 Monday to Friday, 08.00–20.00 Saturday and Sunday. It sells phonecards and postcards, and can help with international calls. Other post offices are at Stacijas laukums (Station Square) and 41–43 Elizabetes iela. In 2005 a new post office opened in the Old Town at Grēcinieku 1 which also sells maps and books at very reasonable prices.

Rates for postcards are Ls0.10 within the Baltics, Ls0.20 for Europe and Ls0.30 for North America. For letters (minimum weight) the rates are Ls0.15 within the Baltics, Ls0.30 for Europe and Ls0.40 for North America (correct in early 2006).

Internet All major hotels have a business centre offering a full range of services including internet access, but the charges are high. An alternative is internet cafés, of which Riga has a generous sprinkling, including the sample listed below. Most offer internet access for Ls0.45–0.50 per hour.

In the Old Town

⊜ Dualnet Café 17 Peldu iela (next to the Ainavas Hotel); ☏ 781 44 40. *Open 24 hours.*

⊜ Planeta 14 Pils iela; ☏ 722 6673. *Open 24 hours.*

C&I Internet Club 11-308 Merķeļa iela; ☎ 721 2040; e club@icc-info.lv. *Open Mon–Fri 8.00–20.00, Sat 09.00–17.00, closed Sun.*

Elizabete 75 Elizabetes iela; ☎ 728 2876. *Open Mon–Fri 09.30–22.00, Sat & Sun 10.00–21.00.*

WiFi The number of wireless hotspots in Riga is growing all the time. If your laptop is equipped with a Wireless LAN card, you should be able to go on-line at all the larger hotels free of charge. The Radisson was one of the first to offer this service, so others quickly followed. By the end of 2005 many cafés in the Old Town were providing this service as well.

EMBASSIES

Canada Doma Laukums 4; ☎ 722 6315; f 783 0140

Germany Raiņa 13; ☎722 9096; f 782 0223

Russia Antonijas 2; ☎ 721 2579; f 783 0209

UK Alunana 5; ☎ 777 4700; f 777 4707

US Raiņa 7; ☎703 6200; f 782 0047

HOSPITALS AND PHARMACIES

✚ **Hospital** Gaiļezeva; Hipokrāta iela 2

✚ **Dentist** Elladent; Vilandes iela 18 *(open 09.00–23.00 Mon–Fri, 09.00–14.00 Sat–Sun)*

Pharmacy *(aptiek)*:

✚ **Rudens Aptieka** Ģertrūdes iela 105. 24hr.

✚ **Vecpilsētas Aptieka** Audlēju iela 20. 24hr.

✚ **Drogas** numerous branches across the city

RELIGIOUS SERVICES The majority of churches are Lutheran, with Orthodox churches coming in second place. Few offer services in languages other than Latvian or Russian. There is currently no mosque in Riga.

✝ **Church of England** St Saviour's, 2a Anglikāņu iela *(service in English 11.00 Sun)*

✝ **Lutheran** The Dome *(Sun 12.00)*; St John's *(Sun 08.00, 09.00, 11.00)*; and many others

✝ **Old Believers** Grebenščikova Church, 73 Krasta iela *(services in Church Slavonic at 08.00 and 17.00 on Sun)*

✝ **Orthodox** Orthodox Cathedral, 23 Brīvības iela *(services in Church Slavonic at 08.00 and 17.00 Mon–Fri,*

07.00, 09.30 and 17.00 on Sat, and 08.00, 10.00 and 17.00 on Sun)

✝ **Roman Catholic** St Jacob's/St James' *(page 108)*, 7 Jāņa iela *(the Roman Catholic Cathedral – service in English 10.00 Sun)*; Our Lady of Sorrows, Lielā Pils iela

✡ **Synagogue** 6–8 Peitavas iela *(Hebrew service at 09.30 Sat)*

TOILETS Men's toilets are often marked ▼, women's ▲. V (*vīrieši*) or K (*kungi*) are also used for men, and S (*sievietes*) or D (*dāmas*) for women.

TOURIST INFORMATION If you need detailed information, suggestions for particular trips or other specialist information, the staff at the tourist office will be pleased to help. The tourist office can also arrange guides. It is located in the Old Town in the Blackheads' House at 7 Rātslaukums (☎ *704 4377;* f *704 4378;* e *tourinfo@rcc.lv; www.rigatourism.com; open 10.00–18.00*).

Riga In Your Pocket and *The City Paper* have detailed coverage of forthcoming events.

The Riga Card The Riga Card provides access without further charge to trams, buses and trains in Riga and Jūrmala, as well as entitling the holder to free admission or a discount at certain museums. The card costs Ls8 for 24 hours, Ls12 for 48 hours and Ls16 for 72 hours (half price for children under 16). It can be purchased from most hotels, the airport (arrivals hall) and the tourist information office. Although it is convenient, most tourists do not spend this amount of money per day if they pay for individual journeys and tickets as they go.

TRANSPORT

RIGA AIRPORT The airport (Lidosta Riga) is about 8km from Riga. A taxi from the airport to the capital should cost a maximum of Ls10 and all taxis operating there have to be metered. There is also a bus service between the airport and the central bus station. The A22 leaves from a bus stop in front of the terminal slightly to the right and on the far side of the airport car park. In 2005 it ran every half-hour from 05.50 to 23.15, but the frequency is likely to be extended in 2006, given the enormous increase in flights now operating from the airport. Buy your ticket (Ls0.20) from the information booth in the terminal building or on board. There is a charge of Ls0.20 for cases. The journey from the airport to the centre of Riga should take no more than about 20 minutes by taxi, and about 30 minutes by bus.

TAXIS Taxis are plentiful. You can flag them down anywhere in Riga but in the Old Town there are normally several waiting at both ends of Kaļķu iela, just near the Hotel de Rome and just beyond the Riflemen's Monument. Licensed cabs (these all have yellow licence plates) are fairly reliable provided you check that the meter is on. Rates are 30 santīmi per kilometre during the day, rising to 40 santīmi per kilometre between 22.00 and 6.00. If you want to save money, avoid using taxis waiting outside hotels, as these tend to charge above average rates. To book a taxi, use one of the following free 24-hour numbers: Bona Taxi ☏ 800 5050; Riga Taxi ☏ 800 1010; Rigas Taksometru parks ☏ 800 1313.

DRIVING IN RIGA It is best to see Riga on foot. The Old Town is a relatively small area and most places you are likely to want to visit in the New Town are also most easily reached on foot. A car is therefore not much use for short stays in the city. Note too that access to the Old Town is restricted for cars. To enter the Old Town you need a special pass which costs Ls5 per hour, plus a Ls5 deposit. You can buy the pass at Statoil (1c Eksporta iela) or at Marika Exchange (14 Basteja bulvāris). Note too that on-street parking in the New Town can be hard to find. There are some multi-storey/underground car parks, including 50 K Valdemāra iela (entrance opposite Antonijas iela) and the Ģertrūdes Centrs near St Gertrude's Church.

If you do drive, be aware that the maximum speed in Riga is 50km/h, seat belts are compulsory, you must always drive with headlights on, various on-the-spot fines are imposed for traffic violations, and that road markings, traffic signs and other drivers' behaviour are not always of the same standard you would expect at home.

Car hire For visiting areas outside Riga a car is useful, although public transport and organised tours are usually available. Car hire is relatively easy to organise but is quite expensive, as it is in the other Baltic states.

🚗 **Avis** 3 Krasta iela; ☏ 722 5876; f 782 0441; e avis@avis.lv; www.avis.lv and at Riga Airport; ☏ 720 7353
🚗 **Baltic Car Lease – Sixt franchisee** 28 Kaļķu iela (Hotel de Rome); ☏ 722 4022; and at Riga Airport; ☏ 720 7121; f 720 7131; e car.rent@carlease.lv; www.e-sixt.lv
🚗 **Budget Rent A Car** Riga Airport; ☏ 720 7327; f 720 7627; e budget@delfi.lv; www.budget.lv

🚗 **Easyrent** 52 Daugavpils iela; ☏ 919 3198; e office@easyrent.lv; www.easyrent.lv
🚗 **Europcar** 10 Basteja bulvāris; ☏ 721 2652; f 782 0360; e www.europcar.lv, and at Riga Airport; ☏ 720 7825
🚗 **Hertz** 24 Aspāzijas bulvāris; ☏ 722 4223 and at Riga Airport; ☏ 720 7980; f 720 7981; www.hertz.lv
🚗 **National Car Rental** Riga Airport; ☏ 720 7710

BUSES AND TRAMS Riga has a well-developed transport system of eight tram lines, 24 trolleybus lines and 39 bus lines. The fare is charged at a flat rate of 20 santīmi (Ls0.20)

Riga TRANSPORT **3**

a journey. Different tickets are needed for each mode of transport and can only be bought on board from the *konduktors*. In addition to the bus, tram and trolleybus, there is another form of transport, the *taksobuss* or *mikroautobuss*, which covers longer distances and costs more, depending on the length of the journey.

The maps in *Riga In Your Pocket* and the yellow Jāņa Sēta Riga map contain information showing public transport routes. There are no route maps at bus/tram stops or inside the buses and trams, but the driver normally announces the name of the approaching stop and other passengers are generally helpful if you ask for directions.

The bus station (*autoosta*) is in Prāgas iela, close to the main market and on the other side of the railway station (under the bridge) away from the city centre. You can telephone for information (☎ *900 0009*), but may find it advisable to attend in person: timetables are on display; otherwise apply to window 1 for information. Some ticket sellers also speak English.

TRAINS Riga has a brand-new, sparkling railway station (*Stacijas laukums;* ☎ *583 2134 for information, or* ☎ *583 3397 for advance booking*), although the same cannot be said of the local trains. Tickets can be bought in the main ticket hall from counters 1 to 13. Most staff selling tickets speak English. The timetables show the track (*ceļš*) the train leaves from. When you go to your train, you will also see the word *perons* (platform) with a number. Ignore this and look for the right track. Timetables and other information are available in English on the Latvian Railways website (*www.ldz.lv*).

TOUR BUSES A number of firms offer city tours by coach. It is probably best to organise these through your hotel if you are staying in one that offers this facility. Otherwise you can contact one of the agencies below:

Latvia Tours 8 Kaļķu iela; ☎ 708 5057, and 13 Marijas iela; ☎ 724 3391. Does city tours from 10.00 to 13.00 on Mon and Sat from May to Sep, and also offers regular trips to the Open Air Museum (see page 104) and Motor Museum (see page 103), Rundāle (see page 119) and Sigulda. Trips to Cēsis, Jūrmala and Liepāja can also be arranged.
Patricia LTD 22 Elizabetes iela; ☎ 728 4868;

e tour@balticguide.net. Various tours for groups – minibus tours, walking tours, Jewish Riga tours, etc. Also offers trips to Sigulda.
Riga Sightseeing Amber Way; ☎ 703 7900; e amberway@inbox.lv. Daily departures from the Latvian Riflemen's Monument and individual sightseeing around Latvia and the Baltic states. Walking tours as well as tours by bus.

BOATS In summer you can take boat trips on the Daugava departing from 11. Novembra krastmala, close to Akmens bridge. Departures are at 11.00, 13.00, 15.00, 17.00 and 19.00. These last an hour. A longer trip to Mežaparks and back takes about two hours and costs Ls2. It is possible to take this trip one-way and then to return by tram (☎ *953 9184*).

CYCLING Sharing Riga's roads with their notoriously aggressive car drivers is only an activity for the brave, although a growing number of people seem to be cycling in areas away from the city centre. If you do want to hire a bike or a scooter you can do so from:

🚲 **Gandrs** 28 Kalnciema iela; ☎ 761 4775; e gandrs@gandrslv; www.gandrs.lv (in Pārdaugava; cross the Vanšu bridge on foot or take bus number 22). Bikes costs Ls1 per hour or Ls5 for the day, plus a deposit of Ls20.

🚲 **Suzuki** 51 Tallinas iela; ☎ 731 2926; e ekstrom@ekstrom.lv; www.ekstrom.lv. Scooter hire from Ls12–15 per day, plus a deposit of Ls50–100, depending on the scooter.

Riga offers a wide choice of accommodation. If money is no object, you can choose from an ever-growing number of luxury hotels, many conveniently situated in the Old Town. For budget travellers there are some very acceptable options, too: some of these are located away from the centre but most are on tram routes, which makes getting into the Old Town an easy and relatively quick matter. During 2005, many hotels were being built in all categories and in different parts of the town which should reduce prices in 2006. In newer hotels air conditioning can be taken for granted. It is rarely needed, but on Riga's few really hot days during the summer, it is a great asset. Free of charge WiFi access can also be taken for granted in most four–five-star hotels and in many three-star ones too. It is advisable to book well ahead if you want a room in a particular price range or location, especially in summer. Otherwise, although you will always find somewhere to stay, it may not be exactly what you want.

An alternative to staying in Riga, particularly in summer, is to book a hotel in nearby Jūrmala, Riga's seaside resort. Jūrmala is about 20 minutes from Riga by car and about 40 minutes by train (see page 117). Jūrmala has some attractive and recently restored small hotels, as well as larger hotels with views over the Gulf of Riga. However, if you have only a few days in Riga, you probably won't want to travel backwards and forwards every day.

There is currently (at time of publication in May 2006) no tourist information service at the airport, although there are plenty of telephones if you want to find a hotel yourself before going into town. Prices of Riga hotels are often quoted in US dollars and/or euro on websites and in brochures but you will always need to make payment in lats. The rates quoted by hotels generally include a buffet breakfast and VAT, unless otherwise specified.

All the quality hotels take credit cards. In practice, there tends to be little difference between prices for single rooms and prices for doubles, and single travellers will often be given a double room anyway.

Luxury

Hotel Bergs (38 apartments) In the Berga Bazārs, 83–85 Elizabetes iela; ↘ 777 0900; f 777 0940; e reservation@hotelbergs.lv; www.hotelbergs.lv. One of Riga's most recently opened hotels, the Hotel Bergs is in the Berga Bazārs shopping area on the edge of the New Town. The hotel and surrounding area is named after the Bergs family who lived in Riga before World War II and whose descendants now run the hotel. The monumental exterior is in contrast to the subtler interior décor. Most of the apartments have kitchenettes; all are spacious and tastefully decorated. The hotel is suitable for tourists, many of whom will also enjoy the handmade chocolates and other exclusive products on sale in the adjoining shopping area, but it also has some of Riga's most comprehensive business facilities, as well as an elegant and acclaimed restaurant. *Prices for suites range from Ls89 to Ls199. Lower rates may be available at the weekend.*

Europa Royal (60 rooms) Kr Barona iela 12 (↘ 707 9444; f 707 9449; e riga@europaroyale.com; www.europaroyale.com. This hotel will open in May 2006 in a building as interesting for its political history

as for its architecture. In 1919 the occupying German army used what will be the car park as an execution ground. It was a newspaper publishing house between the wars, with an interior designed by one of the most famous architects of the time, Eizens Laube. His quarrels with the owners were so bitter that Laube continued to write about them in exile in the US until his death there in 1967. In the 1980s the building housed the Latvian Writers' Union, a major force behind the burgeoning independence movement. Its opening has been delayed for so long to ensure that as much of the late 19th-century Renaissance exterior is preserved as possible. The Europa group also run two similar hotels in Lithuania, one near the Gates of Dawn in Vilnius and the other in Klaipeda.

Grand Palace Hotel (56 rooms) 12 Pils iela; ↘ 704 4000; f 704 4001; e grandpalace@schlossle-hotels.com; www.schlossle-hotels.com. Superbly located near the Dome Cathedral, this luxury hotel opened in 2001 and is probably the most expensive in the Old Town. Although the building is old, the hotel has all modern facilities, including a fitness centre,

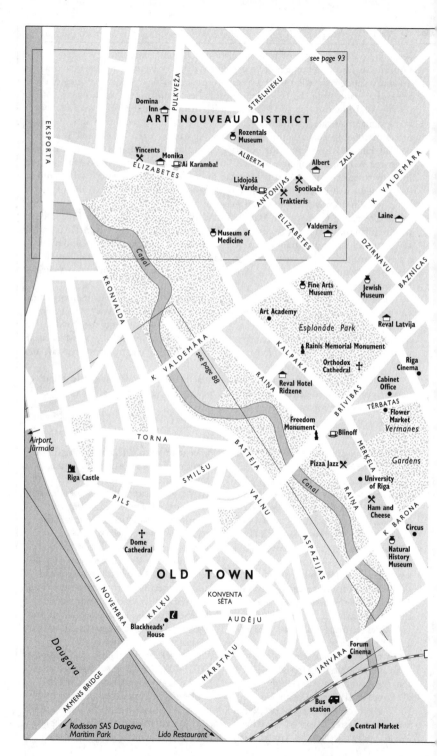

see page 93

Domina
Inn

ART NOUVEAU DISTRICT

PULKVEŽA

STRĒLNIEKU

Rozentals
Museum

EKSPORTA

Vincents   Monika
    Ai Karamba!
ELIZABETES

ALBERTA

Albert

ZALA

K VALDEMĀRA

Lidojošā
Varde   Spotikačs

ANTONIJAS

Traktieris

ELIZABETES

Valdemārs

Laine

DZIRNAVU

Museum of
Medicine

BAZNĪCAS

Canal

KRONVALDA

Fine Arts
Museum

Jewish
Museum

Art Academy

Esplanāde Park

Reval Latvija

KALPAKA

Rainis Memorial Monument

Riga
Cinema

K VALDEMĀRA

see page 88

Orthodox
Cathedral

RAINA

Reval Hotel
Ridzene

Cabinet
Office

BRĪVĪBAS

TĒRBATAS

Flower
Market

Airport,
Jūrmala

TORNA

Freedom
Monument   Blinoff

Vermanes

Gardens

Riga Castle

SMILŠU

BASTEJA

Pizza Jazz

University
of Riga

MERĶEĻA

RAINA

PILS

VAĻŅU

Canal

Ham and
Cheese

K BARONA

Circus

Dome
Cathedral

OLD TOWN

ASPĀZIJAS

Natural
History
Museum

II NOVEMBRA

KONVENTA
SĒTA

KALĶU

AUDĒJU

Blackheads'
House

Forum
Cinema

MARSTAĻU

13 JANVĀRA

Daugava

Bus
station

AKMENS BRIDGE

Radisson SAS Daugava,
Maritim Park

Lido Restaurant

Central Market

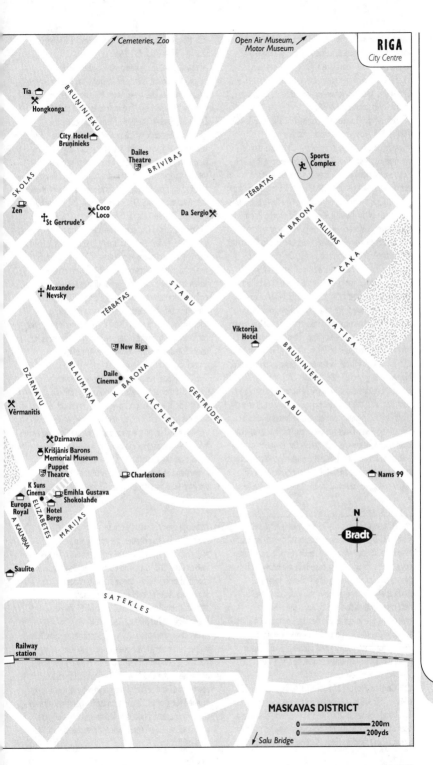

Cemeteries, Zoo

Open Air Museum,
Motor Museum

Tia
Hongkonga

BRUŅINIEKU

City Hotel
Bruņinieks

Dailes
Theatre

BRĪVĪBAS

Sports
Complex

TĒRBATAS

SKOLAS

Zen

St Gertrude's

Coco
Loco

Da Sergio

K BARONA

TALLINAS

A ČAKA

Alexander
Nevsky

TĒRBATAS

S T A B U

MATISA

Viktorija
Hotel

New Riga

Daile
Cinema

K BARONA

BRUŅINIEKU

DZIRNAVU

BLAUMAŅA

LĀČPLĒŠA

GERTRŪDES

S T A B U

Vērmanitis

Dzirnavas

Krišjānis Barons
Memorial Museum

Puppet
Theatre

Charlestons

Nams 99

K Suns
Cinema

Emihla Gustava
Shokolahde

Europa
Royal

ELIZABETES

Hotel
Bergs

N

A KALNIŅA

MARIJAS

Bradt

Saulite

SATEKLES

Railway
station

MASKAVAS DISTRICT

0		200m
0		200yds

Salu Bridge

sauna and steam room. Each room has a gold, white and blue decorative scheme and antique-style furniture but also satellite TV and internet access. There are two restaurants, the light and airy Orangerie and the velvet-curtained Seasons. *Rooms Ls130–172, suites Ls263–367.*

🏠 **Hotel de Rome** (90 rooms) 28 Kaļķu iela; 📞 708 7600; f 708 7606; e reservation@derome.lv; www.derome.lv. At the edge of the Old Town, this German-run 4-star hotel is one of the best in Riga. The location, overlooking the Freedom Monument and surrounding parks – of which there is a terrific view from the restaurant – on the edge of the Old Town but within easy reach of the New, is ideal for the tourist. But it is also within easy reach of all the government offices, ministries and many company headquarters, so is suitable for anyone visiting Riga on business. The standard of accommodation and of the common parts is high. The German Otto Schwarz restaurant offers an excellent breakfast and first-class meals at other times of day. Tourists who would like to enjoy its view towards the Freedom Monument should take advantage of the lower meal prices offered at lunchtime. *Prices start from about Ls91 for a sgl room, and Ls100 for a dbl, including breakfast.*

🏠 **Park OK Hotel** (4 suites, 2 apartments) 43 Mazā Nometņu iela; 📞 789 4860; f 789 2702; e parkhotel@okhotel.lv; www.okhotel.lv. Not to be confused with the OK Hotel (see page 77), this is a super-luxurious and super-expensive hotel on the far side of the River Daugava, set in parkland around 4km from the town centre. Included in the lower prices is a welcome drink, half/full board, a butler, a trip to Jūrmala in the summer and an Old Riga tour. *Suites start at Ls270 and go up to Ls650 for the presidential suite.*

First class

🏠 **Ainavas** (22 rooms) 23 Peldu iela; 📞 781 4316; f 781 4317; e reservations@ainavas.lv; www.ainavas.lv. In this hotel, opened in 2001, each room has a different colour scheme and décor based on the browns or greens of Latvia's countryside ('*ainavas*' means landscape). The tone is set in the lobby bar, which is decorated with wood and flowers and where a welcoming fire burns in the hearth. Located in a quiet street in the south of the Old Town, the hotel is suitable for both tourists and business people: each room has a TV with email connection and a dataport. *Sgl Ls60, standard dbl Ls77.*

🏠 **Centra Hotel** (27 rooms) 1 Audēju iela; 📞 722 6441; f 750 3281; e hotel@centra.lv; www.centra.lv. The hotel opened in 2000 and is wonderfully situated near St Peter's. It is decorated in a minimalist style with furniture and fabrics which all come from Latvia.

🏠 **Reval Hotel Ridzene** (95 rooms) 1 Reimersa iela; 📞 732 4433; f 732 2600; e ridzene@revalhotels.com; www.revalhotels.com. Formerly a Soviet hotel, the Ridzene has been elegantly refurbished several times since independence and is now part of the Reval group. It is located opposite the Esplanade Park in the New Town, and beside the American Embassy, which probably makes it the safest address in Riga. From the sauna you can enjoy superb views over the New Town. The Piramida restaurant in the glass pyramid is amongst the best in Riga. *Room prices range from Ls112 for a sgl room to Ls123 for a dbl.*

🏠 **Radisson SAS Daugava Hotel** (361 rooms) 24 Kuģu iela; 📞 706 1111; f 706 1100; e info.riga@radissonsas.com; www.radissonsas.com. This is one of the leading business hotels in the Baltics. It is an international-standard establishment with both rooms and suites, including two floors of 'business class' rooms which have their own lounge for drinks and are fully equipped for business needs, including two telephone lines for internet access. There is security parking, 24-hour room service and cable TV. With 10 air-conditioned conference rooms the hotel can lay on conferences for up to 360 delegates. A business service offers translation, secretarial and other commercial services. The Grill Room restaurant is highly recommended. There is a modern fitness centre, sauna, swimming pool and shops. The Radisson, however, is very much a business hotel. It is a rather unimaginative white block of a building and is on 'the wrong side' of the Daugava away from the main part of the city, but is quiet and has good views over the river. It offers free transfers from the airport and an hourly shuttle bus to the Old Town. *Prices are from Ls76 for a sgl room to L82 for a dbl.*

Although the area nearby can be noisy at night, being the centre for stag parties, the rooms are well soundproofed. Rooms on the higher floors offer unusual views of the Old Town. The hotel is excellent value, with rooms at prices below those in similar hotels in the same area. *A dbl typically costs around Ls60.*

🏠 **Domina Inn Riga** (100 rooms) 11 Pulkveža Brieža iela; 📞 763 1800; f 763 1801; e info@dominahotels.lv; www.dominahotels.com. This is one of the very few hotels to open in Riga during 2005. It is near Albert iela, close to several museums if not quite in the Old Town. With nearly 100 standard rooms, and little sense of design anywhere, it is clearly planned for groups. Domina, an Italian company, already run two successful hotels in Tallinn and hopefully the artistic taste shown there will soon spread south. *Dbl Ls80–100.*

Europa City (150 rooms) 199 Brīvības gatve (contact details not yet available). This hotel will open in late 2006. If the 3km distance from the Old Town is to some extent a disadvantage, the large number of buses that run along Brivibas will make up for this, as will ease of parking for both cars and coaches.

Hotel Gutenbergs (38 rooms) 1 Doma laukums; ☎ 721 1776; f 750 3326; e hotel@gutenbergs.lv; www.gutenbergs.lv. Located in one of the Baltic states' first publishing houses, hence the name, in a quiet street next to the Dome Cathedral, this hotel has proved very popular since its opening in 2001, and often needs to be booked well in advance. It consists of two connected four-storey buildings, one built in the 17th century and one in the 19th, and has a rich, 19th-century décor throughout. An attraction in summer (which the hotel thinks begins in April) is the rooftop terrace, where you can eat, drink and count the 17 churches visible from this wonderful vantage point. Another speciality is musical lunches in the main restaurant: Latvian musicians play every Sun from 13.00 to 15.00. *Prices from Ls60 for a sgl and Ls70 for a dbl.*

Konventenhof or **Konventa Sēta** (80 rooms; 61 apartments) 9–11 Kalēju iela; ☎ 708 7501–5; f 708 7506; e reservation@konventa.lv; www.konventa.lv. The Konventa Sēta stands out from other hotels in Old Riga in that it is housed on the site of the old city walls in a complex of restored buildings, some dating back to the 13th century. The complex includes a good restaurant, Raibais Balodis, and a bar, Melnais Balodis. Although the hotel's position next to St John's Church could hardly be more central, on occasions it can be noisy at night on the Kalēju iela side. *Sgl cost Ls46 per night; dbl and suites from Ls55–70 a night. The hotel also aims at the business market with its 4 conference rooms which can be hired from Ls90–160 a day.*

Man-Tess (10 rooms) 6 Teātra iela; ☎ 721 6056; f 782 1249; e info@mantess.lv; www.mantess.lv. This charming hotel in the centre of Old Riga is an elegant 18th-century house once owned by H Haberland, a Riga architect. Its 10 rooms are each in a different style (the so-called white room is light and modern, the 18th-century room is furnished in the style of the Hanseatic period). The ground-floor restaurant is exotically decorated (marble, a pond with goldfish, and even caged birds) and is one of the best in the Old Town. There is a good restaurant, and a banquet/conference hall on the 5th floor. *Prices range from Ls60 for the sgl room to Ls100 for a suite.*

Maritim Park (240 rooms) 1 Slokas iela; ☎ 706 9000; f 706 9001; e reservations@maritim.lv; www.maritim.com. A large hotel across the river from the Old Town. The location may put off some people,

but it is quiet and you can reach the Old Town in about half an hour on foot or by taking the number 2, 4 or 5 tram. On the positive side, the rooms and the Bellevue restaurant on the 11th floor have wonderful views of the Old Town. If walking into town isn't enough exercise, you can use the hotel's gym. Free transport to and from the airport is offered. *Standard rooms cost between Ls59–101 for a sgl, Ls68–110 for a dbl.*

Metropole (80 rooms) 36–38 Aspāzijas bulvāris; ☎ 722 5411; f 721 6140; e metropole@brovi.lv; www.metropole.lv. The Metropole is suitable for both tourists and business travellers. Built in 1871 the Metropole is the oldest hotel in Riga and has been completely refurbished in an attractive Scandinavian style. It is conveniently located on the edge of the Old Town and only a short walk away from the New Town. All rooms are equipped with satellite phone and cable TV. *Sgl rooms cost from Ls37, dbl from Ls44 and suites about from Ls75, including breakfast.*

Monika (80 rooms) 21 Elizabetes iela; ☎ 703 1900; f 703 1901; e monika@centrumhotels.com; www.centrumhotels.com. This four-star hotel was opened in January 2006 by the Lithuanian Centrum group, who run the Artis and Ratonda hotels in Vilnius. As with the Artis, a solid 19th-century building has been taken over and the interior completely modernised. It is one of the early works of Edmund von Trompowsky (1851–1918), probably Riga's most prolific eclectic architect from that time. Several of his other works are within walking distance of the hotel. Many of the rooms have a bath, and some have a balcony offering views across Elizabetes iela to Kronvalda Park. All have AC. *Sgl cost Ls90 and dbl Ls100.*

Nams 99 (House 99) (8 apartments) 99 Stabu iela; ☎ 731 0762; f 731 3204; e nams-99@delfi.lv; www.nams99.lv. Located in a renovated art nouveau building, the Nams offers apartments and a restaurant. Intended mainly for business users. *Rates range from Ls90–150 for an apartment.*

Reval Hotel Latvija (380 rooms) 55 Elizabetes iela; ☎ 777 2222; f 777 2221; e latvija@revalhotels.com; www.revalhotels.com. This was the hotel in which Intourist put up its customers in the days of the USSR, but it has been totally renovated and reopened in May 2001 as a high-quality international-style hotel. It already offers bars and a restaurant and by April 2006 an extension to the hotel will have opened, increasing the total number of rooms to over 500 as well as offering the largest conference centre in the Baltics. Two advantages are its location in the New Town but just 5 mins from the Old Town and the views from its upper storeys, its two glass-sided lifts and the skyline bar on the 26th floor. All rooms include satellite TV with games and email possibilities, and minibars with drinks, chocolate and condoms. If you fancy a night in, you can also order a Lulu pizza in your room. Underground parking is available, and on the 27th floor there is a sports and leisure club, equipped with a weight room and sauna. *Rooms cost from Ls77 a night for a sgl and Ls88 for a dbl.*

🏠 **Riga Hotel** (280 rooms) 22 Aspāzijas bulvāris; ✆ 704 4222; f 704 4223; e info@hotelriga.lv; www.hotelriga.com. On the edge of the Old Town, the Riga is one of the largest and oldest hotels in central Riga. Fully refurbished in 2002–03, all the rooms are pleasantly decorated and spacious. Some have internet dataports. The hotel offers a sauna, bar, conference facilities and a casino. To see what the staff got up to before 1991, visit the Occupation Museum which displays the bugging devices they used to monitor

phone calls. The building was bought by the Kempinski group in late 2005 and by 2007 will reopen as a 5-star hotel. *Sgl cost around Ls60 and dbl Ls75.*

🏠 **Rolands** (29 rooms) 3a Kaļķu iela; ✆ 722 0011; f 728 1203; e info@hotelrolands.lv; www.hotelrolands.lv. The hotel was closed in late 2004 due to a legal dispute, but is expected to reopen eventually.

🏠 **Vecrīga** (10 rooms) 12–14 Gleznotāju iela; ✆ 721 6037; f 721 45 61; e vecriga@inet.lv. A small hotel in a renovated 18th-century house in a quiet street in the Old Town, next to the Palete restaurant. Spacious bedrooms are fitted out with comfortable antique-style furniture, although the bathrooms tend to be small. The hotel has an intimate atmosphere but all modern facilities, and an elegant restaurant. Dbl rooms cost Ls55–65.

Tourist class

🏠 **Albert** (250 rooms) 33 Dzirnavu iela; ✆ 733 1717; f 733 1718; e info@alberthotel.lv; www.alberthotel.lv. This 11-storey hotel opened in December 2005. It is run by the Estonian Legend group, who operate the Three Sisters in Tallinn and the Georg Ots in Kuressaare. It has around 250 rooms, all with AC and many with good views towards the Old Town. Its Star Lounge bar on the top floor will clearly aim to compete with that at the Reval Latvia for offering the best Old Town view. Tourists interested in Jugendstil will appreciate the location close to Albert iela. *Dbl from Ls90.*

🏠 **Avitar** 127 Valdemāra iela; ✆ 736 4444; f 736 4988; e avitar@apollo.lv; www.avitar.lv. A modern hotel a few kilometres away from the centre but on public transport routes. A shuttle service is also available to the airport and to the train and bus stations. Rooms are clean and spacious, and have cable TV, a telephone and bathroom with shower. *A dbl is Ls36–52.*

🏠 **City Hotel Bruņinieks** (The Knight) Bruņinieku iela 6; ✆ 731 5140; f 731 4310; e hotel@bruninieks.lv. Originally known just as Bruņinieks, the hotel changed its name to City in 2003 as no foreigner could pronounce the name. A suit of armour is displayed in the foyer, but otherwise this is a perfectly normal 3-star hotel. Some may find the location near the theatre of help and it is sufficiently far from the town centre for the neighbouring shops all to offer Latvian rather than Western prices and for peace and quiet to be assured in the evenings. The lack of a restaurant is a bonus in this respect, too. The hotel caters in particular for families, with adjoining rooms available and – for those with smaller children – triple rooms with a roll-up bed. Being just off Brīvības iela, the main road leading to the

Freedom Monument, the hotel has a wide range of buses within walking distance. *Dbl costs Ls50.*

🏠 **Felicia Hotel** 32b Stirnu iela; ✆ 759 9942; f 754 8145; e mail@hotelfelicia.com; www.hotelfelicia.com. Take trolleybus number 11 or 18 from the city centre to the Ūnijas iela stop. The hotel is good value for money if you don't mind the 15-min ride from the town centre. It offers sgl and dbl rooms, and also 'minis', very small singles for tourists watching their budget. In addition to a restaurant, 2 bars and a nightclub, it has billiards, saunas, a swimming pool and even indoor tennis courts. *Dbl from Ls30–40; very small sgl for around Ls8.*

🏠 **Forums** (32 rooms) 45 Vaļņu iela; ✆ 781 4680; f 781 4682; e reservation@hotelforums.lv; www.hotelforums.lv. On the edge of the Old Town, near the train station, the hotel has large rooms, with a bath and satellite TV. Despite the modest exterior, it offers elegantly decorated accommodation. Some of the rooms on the upper floors have good views. Breakfast is served, but there is no bar or restaurant, so evenings are quiet. *Dbl rooms cost Ls37–48.*

🏠 **F-Villa** (30 rooms) 9 Skanstes iela; ✆ 751 9922, 751 9921; e hotel@miests.lv, www.meists.lv. This is a new hotel a few kilometres away from the Old Town. Rooms are comfortable, the environment quiet, green and friendly, and the prices relatively modest. The hotel has a restaurant and bar, and in summer opens a beer terrace. *Dbl rooms cost around Ls24.*

🏠 **Karavella** (80 rooms) 27 Katrīnas dambis; ✆ 732 4597; f 783 0187; e hotel@karavella.lv; www.karavella.lv. This is a fairly large hotel situated about 10 mins by car (2km) from the centre of Riga towards the harbour (it is 1km from the marine passenger terminal). You can also reach the hotel on tram number 5 or 9, alighting at Katrīnas iela. Some rooms overlook the harbour; all have cable TV, a refrigerator and telephone. The hotel has a café, which serves snacks and drinks, and a bar. *Sgl rooms from Ls35 and dbl from Ls41.*

⌂ **Ķeizarmežs** Ezermalas iela; ☎ 755 7576; f 755 7461. Situated on Lake Ķīšezers, near the zoo and Mežaparks, this is a modern complex which may appeal to sports lovers, particularly in summer. There is a well-equipped fitness centre, with a swimming pool, squash court, billiards and sauna. Rooms have satellite TV, phone and a private shower or bath. To get there takes around 25 mins from the Old Town: take trolleybus number 2 to the terminus. *Dbl cost from Ls30–38.*

⌂ **Laine Hotel** (28 rooms) 11 Skolas iela; ☎ 728 8816 or 728 9823; f 728 7658; e info@laine.lv; www.laine.lv. A small hotel, the Laine has the advantage of being centrally located in the New Town, not far from the Reval Hotel Latvija. Situated in an elegant art nouveau building, the Laine is exceptionally good value. Most rooms now have satellite TV and a minibar. Do not be put off by the entrance through an unprepossessing courtyard. *Rooms at prices ranging from Ls30–40 for a sgl to Ls40–60 for a dbl; the cheaper rooms require you to use communal showers.*

⌂ **Best Western Hotel Mara** (24 rooms) 186 Kalnciema iela; ☎ 770 2718; f 770 2708; e mara@mailbox.riga.lv; www.hotelmara.lv. Part of the Best Western chain, it is out of the centre on the way to the airport, and is the only 3-star hotel near it. It operates a shuttle bus to both airport and city centre. More of a business hotel than one for tourists. *Dbl Ls65.*

⌂ **OK Hotel** (34 rooms) 12 Slokas iela; ☎ 786 0050; f 789 2702; e service@okhotel.lv; www.okhotel.lv. The OK opened in 2001 and is modest but good value.

Budget

⌂ **Baltā Kaza** (35 rooms) 2 Ēveles iela; ☎ 737 8135. The name means 'White Goat'. Located some way out of the centre of Riga, this small and simple hotel looks grim but is clean. It also has dormitories and bunk-bed accommodation. To get there take tram number 3 from Barona iela. *Prices start from Ls25 for a dbl or Ls4 in a dormitory (4 beds to a room).*

⌂ **Elias** (7 rooms) 14 Hamburgas iela; ☎ 751 8117. A small hotel near Lake Ķīšezers reached by taking the number 11 tram from Kr Barona iela or the number 9 bus from the station. The location in the Mežaparks is pleasant, and the rooms have private bathrooms and TV. *Rooms are Ls16 a night; breakfast not included.*

⌂ **Lidosta** At the airport; ☎ 720 7149 or 720 7375. A hotel next to the airport (look for the Soviet-style

Rooms are adequately furnished and include telephone and cable TV. The disadvantage is its location, over the river from the Old Town. It is a 30-min walk from the Old Town, but the hotel can also be reached quickly by taking tram number 4 or 5 from the Grēcinieku stop to the Kalnciema stop, just over the river. *Dbl cost Ls40–60.*

⌂ **Radi un Draugi** (Relatives and Friends) (76 rooms) 1–3 Mārstaļu iela; ☎ 782 0200; f 782 0202; e radi.reservations@draugi.lv; www.draugi.lv. This hotel, right in the centre of the Old Town, is comfortable and affordable, as well as being in a superb location. Recently modernised and extended, the hotel has only one drawback: the proximity of many pubs and clubs means it can get noisy late at night. *Sgl cost Ls35 and dbl Ls44.*

⌂ **Viktorija** (42 rooms) 55 A Čaka iela; ☎ 701 4111; f 701 4140; e info@hotel-viktorija.lv. This small hotel in a lovely art nouveau building has been partially renovated. The rooms in the renovated area are comfortable and have cable TV. Although not quite central (about 10 min by car from the central station and a bit further to the Old Town) it is not too far to walk. *Sgl are Ls30 and dls Ls40.*

⌂ **Tia** (50 rooms) 63 Kr Valdemāra iela; ☎ 733 3918, 733 3035 or 733 3396; f 783 0390; e tia@mail.bkv.lv. A clean and comfortable hotel near the centre. *From Ls29 for a sgl to Ls51 for a suite.*

⌂ **Valdemārs** (85 rooms) 23 Kr Valdemāra iela; ☎ 733 2132 or 733 4462; f 733 3001; e reservations@valdemars.lv; www.valdemars.lv. This hotel was completely renovated during 2005 and upgraded from a hostel to a serious hotel, although its elegant, centrally located art nouveau façade makes it look grander than it really is. *Room prices range from Ls45 for a sgl, Ls55 for a dbl.*

building beyond the car park outside the terminal), and therefore unprepossessing in location as well as appearance. It closed in 2005 for renovation. *Rooms from Ls9–23; breakfast not included.*

⌂ **Saulīte** (38 rooms) 12 Merķeļa iela; ☎ 722 4546; f 722 3629; e hotel_saulite@one.lv; www.hotel-saulite.lv. This former hostel was upgraded to a hotel in 2005, with price increases to match. However it offers good value, and the location opposite the railway station and next to the bus station makes it a convenient base for tourists not using Riga Airport. Its currency exchange is competitive and open 7 days a week and it also offers a unisex hairdresser. *Rooms from Ls30–45.*

Eating has been transformed in Riga over the past few years. Whatever your taste and whatever your budget, you should have no difficulty finding something to tempt you. Riga offers an immense selection of restaurants, cafés and bars, many up to the best international standards. In both the Old Town and the New Town Japanese and Chinese restaurants compete for custom with Italian, Russian, Ukrainian and, of course, Latvian restaurants. And if you just want a coffee or a snack, you won't need to walk far to find one of the many new coffee shops or tea houses. Wine is widely available in restaurants but is all imported and therefore not cheap. Beer is good quality and good value for money.

In general you don't need to book in advance, although if you want to make absolutely certain of a table in a particular restaurant at peak times you could do so. Menus are nearly always available in English, so don't be afraid to ask if one doesn't appear automatically. Prices are given to provide a rough indication of what you can expect to pay for a three-course meal excluding wine.

Latvian cuisine, if eaten regularly, is not for the weight-conscious. Once or twice on a weekend trip to Riga, however, it is an enjoyable and fun thing to try.

RESTAURANTS

✕ **Arbat** (named after an area in Moscow) 3 Vāgnera iela; ☎ 721 4056. This is probably the most upmarket Russian restaurant in Riga, although the prices, for the quality of the food, are not at all unreasonable. Caviar, sturgeon and vodka feature prominently on the menu and blend well with the richly ornate interior. The dishes are attractively presented by staff who are unusually keen to please. If you have always wanted to know what it would feel like to be a character in *War and Peace*, a visit here will help you imagine it. *45Ls.*

✕ **Bellevue** Maritim Park Hotel, 1 Slokas iela, ☎ 706 9000; www.maritim.com. The 11th-floor restaurant looks out over the river on to the Old Town and is an ideal place for a sunset dinner in summer. The menu changes every month, so it is difficult to make recommendations. Fish and seafood are often among the highlights, and there are frequently local game dishes, too. The décor, like everything else in this hotel, is modern, airy and elegant. *40Ls.*

✕ **Bergs** Hotel Bergs, in Berga Bazārs, 83–85 Elizabetes iela; ☎ 777 0957; www.hotelbergs.lv. Since the opening of the hotel, this restaurant has established itself as one of the best places to eat in Riga. The atmosphere is relaxed and the food includes a wide range of original dishes. The chef used to work at Vincents restaurant, where he achieved the high recognition he has now brought to Bergs. The Bergs serves lunch and dinner, and there is a breakfast buffet from 07.00–11.00; in the afternoon you can drop in for tea and cakes on the terrace. *35Ls.*

✕ **Coco Loco** 6 Stabu iela; ☎ 731 4265. The only Jamaican bar and restaurant in Riga (although there is now also a branch in Jūrmala), Coco Loco is a colourful and lively venue, offering Jamaican and other Caribbean dishes in generous portions and at very affordable prices. If you like reggae music, this will be paradise: reggae plays every day, but on Fri and Sat nights from 20.00 the restaurant becomes a club with DJs putting on the music. As you might expect, there is also a choice of trendy cocktails. Although slightly out of the centre, this area around Stabu iela is enjoying something of a renaissance. Close to Coco Loco is the Sarkans restaurant, a branch of Zen café and also of Double Coffee. *Ls12.*

✕ **Da Sergio** 65 Tērbatas iela (entrance from Matīsa iela); ☎ 731 2777. A very Italian Italian restaurant, with a chef from Venice, many ingredients imported directly from Italy, Italian music and Italian food and wine. The atmosphere is warm and welcoming and puts you in the mood to enjoy everything from the bread, baked daily on the premises, to the excellent desserts, via an interesting range of pizza, pasta, meat and fish main courses. Prices are very accessible. *Ls14.*

✕ **Dzirnavas** (The Mill) 76 Dzirnavu iela; ☎ 728 6204; www.lido.lv. One of the most popular of Riga's restaurants among locals, this Latvian farmhouse-style restaurant is not the place for a quiet tête-à-tête. The service is buffet style: choose from a vast array of food laid out in several rooms, take it back to your table, across the stream in the centre, and enjoy it to the strains of Latvian country music. The food is decent, the atmosphere fun, and the prices very affordable. If you want a quick initiation into Latvian food and at the same time to observe local life, this is a good place to start. *7Ls.*

✕ **Hongkonga** 61 Valdemāra iela; ☎ 781 2292. What a relief to find a Chinese restaurant in the Baltics where what you see is what you get. The ambience is straightforward but the cooking more elaborate. It is clear that Chinese are in control of the whole operation and are catering for their colleagues; if others wish to come, they are welcome to have a meal that makes no concessions to so-called Western tastes. *Ls12.*

✗ Kamāla 14 Jauniela; ☎ 721 1332. An Indian ambience suffuses the restaurant: you'll notice the incense before you enter, and once inside the colourful table and wall decorations will transport you beyond Riga. The menu too features Indian food fairly strongly, but a range of other dishes is also available. Recommendations are difficult as the menu changes from day to day but you will always find a number of very appealing, and rather different, options, including perhaps tofu shashlik (bean-curd kebab). *Ls11.*

✗ Krievu Sēta/Russkij Dvor (The Russian Courtyard) 3 Ķengaraga iela; ☎ 713 4930; www.lido.lv. This is the Russian equivalent of the Latvian-food Lido restaurant, and owned by the same group. A huge building in an unfashionable part of the city, off Maskavas iela (Moscow Street), the interior resembles a theme park, with its painted wood and traditional matroshka dolls. Like the Lido it offers a self-service restaurant with a massive choice of dishes and a recreational area outside. The food includes Russian favourites such as borscht, blini, solyanka and pork, all at low prices. Tram number 7 or 9 from opposite the Opera will take you there. Alight at the Ķengaraga iela stop. *Ls6.*

✗ Lido Atpūtas Centrs (Lido Recreation Centre) 76 Krasta iela; ☎ 750 4420; www.lido.lv. This is undoubtedly one of Riga's recent success stories in the restaurant world. To take over an out-of-town estate rather than a house in an area barely accessible by public transport required considerable daring but the gamble has paid off as the crowded car park proves every evening. Family groups are the main target, as large play areas are available, and service is cafeteria-style with trays along the counter. More and more foreigners are now coming, too; they enjoy, as the Latvians do, the space, the light and the wooden tables, not to mention the variety and quality of food available in the bistro, express restaurant or beer cellar with its own micro-brewery. They enjoy the broad clientele, too; Latvia mixes here in a way it hardly does elsewhere. The centre also has the largest skating rink in the Baltics. To get there take tram 7 or 9 to the Dzērvju stop. It's then a 10-min walk towards the windmill. Alternatively take a short taxi ride (Ls2–3). *Ls8.*

✗ Livonija 21 Meistaru iela; ☎ 722 7824. There are few restaurants in Riga where an identical review could be written year after year. For the Livonija, this is the case and it has always been positive. Nothing changes,

and why should it? A broad international menu, with a wine list to match, is offered, although there is a good choice of Latvian dishes. Acclaimed dishes include local venison, pork knuckle, smoked eel and lamprey. The service remains unobtrusive and the art nouveau chairs will never be forgotten. The restaurant is in a cellar well underneath the hurly-burly of Livu laukums; this position shelters it not only from noise but also from the climate: it stays cool in summer and warm in winter. *Ls18.*

✗ Melnie Mūki (The Black Monks) 1–2 Jāņa Sēta; ☎ 721 5006. Dark and rather formal, this highly respected restaurant in what used to be a cloister in the Old Town is rapidly gaining popularity for international food at prices that, if high for Riga, are by no means off the scale for the overseas visitor. The cuisine is genuinely international; Turkish kebabs alongside dishes with Asian influences. *Ls11.*

✗ Monterosso 9 Vaļņu; ☎ 722 2017. Perhaps the display of the menus just in Italian puts off the stag groups who otherwise might take advantage of this very central location. Visitors will be pleasantly surprised at the diversity of the menu and the resulting range of ingredients given that 'Italian' is all too often a debased term now.

✗ Otto Schwarz Hotel de Rome, 28 Kaļķu iela; ☎ 708 7623; www.derome.lv. Located on the top floor of the hotel, this is an international restaurant with an emphasis on German cuisine, including even a special asparagus menu in season. It is one of Riga's most established restaurants, but has lost none of its prestige as the number of competing restaurants has grown. A major advantage is the excellent views over the Freedom Monument and the parks. A good choice of vegetarian dishes is always available. *Prices are international, but at lunchtime there is a business menu for Ls8 (2 courses) or Ls10 (3 courses).*

✗ Palete 12–14 Gleznotāju iela; ☎ 721 6037; www.palete.lv. Located in an elegant building in a narrow street in the Old Town, the Palete is worth a visit. Despite its central location, it is often missed by tourists, so even in summer it tends to be uncrowded. Good value, atmospheric and elegant with unobtrusive piano music. Dishes range from pasta to fried shellfish, chicken fillet with fried cheese and melon, and sometimes even rarer finds such as ostrich. The name means 'palette' and comes from its location in Painter Street. *About Ls12 per person for a full meal with wine; much less if you just have a snack.*

✗ Pizza Jazz 15 Raiņa iela; ☎ 721 1237. The pizzas offered by this Lithuanian chain may not be the best you've ever tasted, but they are highly acceptable and eminently affordable. The menu has a large choice of pizzas, available in large or small size (and small really is quite small), as well as pasta and salad. Even large pizzas are only a little over Ls2. The main menu is in English as well as Latvian and Russian. The dessert menu isn't in English but there are enticing pictures. Try the *biezpiena štūdele*, cottage cheese strudel, if you fancy something with a Latvian flavour. Other branches are at 76 Brīvības iela, 19 Šķūņu iela and at the railway station. *6Ls*.

✗ **Planeta Sushi** 16 Šķūņu iela; ☎ 722 385. Owned by the Russian Rostik restaurants group, like TGI Friday and Patio Pizza, and with branches in Moscow and other Russian cities, the pedigree for serving authentic Japanese food may not sound too promising. The quality of the vast range of Japanese dishes, however, comes as a very pleasant surprise. From miso soup to sushi (Japanese and Californian), teppan steaks or shabu shabu, the taste is first rate, and the prices quite reasonable too, with shrimp or squid sushi at only Ls1.20 per portion and teppan steaks at Ls5.00. The paintings of cherry trees on the wall and the Westernised kimonos worn by the waitresses are definitely less authentic, but the overall ambience is pleasant, unhassled and comfortable, and the location, close to Dome Square, makes this a convenient and highly recommendable spot. *16Ls*.

✗ **Pomodoro** 81 Vecpilsēta iela; tel 721 1044. Turn off Audēju iela with its crowds of shoppers into the peace of Vecpilsēta iela and you will shortly find yourself at Pomodoro, a bar, café and restaurant. The restaurant is on the ground floor of a 17th-century warehouse, and the décor is a mixture of traditional and modern, but the mood is definitely contemporary. Pizza and homemade pasta are the specialities, and the Italian owners ensure authenticity. Prices are very reasonable, and a special children's menu is also available. Another branch has recently opened at the Domina shopping centre (2 *Ieriķu iela*; ☎ 787 3648). *16Ls*.

✗ **Raibais Balodis** (Colourful Dove) Konventa Sēta, 9–11 Kalēju iela; ☎ 708 7580. Part of Konventenhof Hotel. Although the name may suggest a Latvian restaurant, the food here is definitely international. Menus change to make use of seasonal produce such as asparagus. The setting in the 13th-century convent is a definite plus, as are the fresh flowers and helpful service. *17Ls*.

✗ **Rolands** Hotel Rolands, 3a Kaļķu iela; ☎ 722 0011. The medieval atmosphere of this cellar restaurant has been reconstructed by murals painted by local artist Lila Dinere, a covered well in the centre, and the heavy oak furniture. A nice touch (literally), particularly in winter, is the warmed table tops. Game dishes are what the restaurant has become known for, but it also serves fish, including eel, pork and other meat dishes. If available, try

the *confit* of duck with vanilla pod potato mash and Cumberland sauce, or one of the dishes with a Japanese influence (shiitake mushrooms, udon, etc). The hotel and restaurant were closed in late 2004 due to a legal dispute, but are expected to reopen eventually.

✗ **Rozengrāls** 1 Rozena iela; ☎ 722 0356; www.rozengrals.lv. Given the success of medieval restaurants in Tallinn, it is perhaps surprising that it took until summer 2005 for a similar one to open in Riga. Abandon any thoughts of electric lighting, cutlery or quick service and descend into the cellar for a long carnivorous lunch or dinner. The long tables here lend themselves to group celebrations, not for quiet dinners *à deux*. *15Ls*.

✗ **Saules Bura** Balasta dambis 1a; ☎ 740 9893. An office block over the river is perhaps an unlikely site for a new restaurant, but not only photographers wanting views of the Old City will find the journey worthwhile. As the building is owned by the Hansapank, the extensive menu bankers demand is of course provided, but fortunately at prices which even their modest private customers can afford. *9Ls*.

✗ **Skonto Zivju Restorāns** (Fish Restaurant) 4 Vāgnera iela; ☎ 721 6713; www.zivjurestorans.lv. Riga's best fish restaurant is commensurately expensive and generally used by expense account diners. When we visited, the president was holding a private reception in a room at the back of the restaurant. There are 4 separate dining rooms, so wherever you are sitting the atmosphere is quiet and intimate. Fish is a mixture of local catch (try, for example, the Baltic Pike Perch Rolls as a starter) and of more exotic origins, and is always a pleasure to look at as well as to eat. *Main courses go up to Ls17*.

✗ **Spotikačs** 12 Antonijas iela; ☎ 750 5955. Unless you visit Ukraine there are not many opportunities to sample the cuisine. This restaurant will give you a good idea of what's eaten in Kiev: straightforward, tasty dishes, with plenty of meat, potatoes and *vareniki* (dumplings). The floral friezes and puppets give the décor a childish feel and, added to the friendly service, should make your visit here a happy experience. If you need any further help, try the chilled homemade vodka. A branch has also opened in Jūrmala. *8Ls*.

✗ **Sue's Indian Raja** 3 Vecpilsētas iela; ☎ 721 2614; www.indianraja.lv. This is one of Riga's few Indian restaurants, but would be likely to be one of the best even if it had lots more competitors. The food is authentically Indian and includes tandoori and tikka dishes as well as curries. Thai dishes are also available. The camel images that feature on the door are possibly a reference to the fact that Indian spices, transported by camel on part of their journey, used to be stored in a warehouse here. Prices are not low, but the quality of food and service is worth paying for. There is also a branch of the restaurant in Jūrmala. *1 1Ls*.

✗ Traktieris 8 Antonijas iela; ☎ 733 2455. Hearing Russian and Ukrainian spoken here by other diners is clearly a good sign. The Russia to which this restaurant wants to link is of course the one that died in 1917, not the later variant that died in 1991. Although in the heart of the art nouveau area, the décor is from rural Russia, as are the costumes worn by the staff. The menu is from aristocratic St Petersburg and includes staples such as *blini* and *borscht* as well as more unusual dishes, but the prices appeal to quite a range of classes. In 2002, a buffet was opened, presumably for architecture fanatics determined to miss nothing in the surrounding neighbourhood, but a stay of at least two hours is recommended in the main restaurant.

✗ Vincents 19 Elizabetes iela; ☎ 733 2634 or 733 2830; f 783 0206; www.vincents.lv. Vincents (the name comes from the van Gogh reproductions which decorate it) is one of Riga's best-known restaurants. Situated in the New Town, it offers a wide variety of dishes based on cuisines from around the world. Like many restaurants it is making increasing use of high-quality local products, for example farm chicken from the Dobele region in western Latvia, but also has an impressive range of meat and fish dishes based on the best imported ingredients. A fairly recent addition is a sushi menu. It also has an attractive terrace for open-air eating in summer. Its reputation as a place where the 'stars' dine has led to very high prices by Riga standards. If you can't afford to go there, you can always try the menus on the website yourself (*www.vincents.lv*). *Ls25*.

✗ Vērmanītis 65 Elizabetes iela; ☎ 728 6289. If Latvians meet each other, this is often the place they will choose. Prices are certainly not 'Old Town' and it manages to bridge the generation gap better than many other restaurants. Probably the self-service elements and the wooden dance floor help to do this. Older folk will be soothed by the stained glass and stone in much of the decoration. It is supposed to recall the first independence period from 1920 to 1940. Pizza and salad are always popular dishes here amongst foreigners but Latvians stick to the dependable local meat dishes. *Ls6*.

QUICK SNACKS

✗ Blinoff 30 Brīvības bulvāris. If you want to replenish your energy between the Old Town and the New Town, call in at Blinoff. This small but welcoming café offers a long list of *blini* for Ls1–2. Choose from sweet or savoury *blini*, with coffee or a soft drink.

✗ Sievasmātes Pīrādziņi (Mother-in-law's piragi) 10 Kaļķu iela. *Piragi* (Latvian pasties) and cakes are baked here on the premises and sold for as little as Ls0.08.

Good quality and very popular. You can afford several, and a juice (no alcohol available) as well, and still have plenty of money left in your pocket.

✗ Pīrādziņi 14 K Barona iela; ☎ 728 7824. A *piragi* (Latvian pasties) shop offering pasties with a wide range of fillings from cabbage to meat. An excellent snack if you're in a hurry in the New Town.

CHEAP AND FILLING

✗ Ham and Cheese 1 Arhitektu iela; ☎ 722 4686; www.ham-cheese.com. With so many Latvians now having visited the US and Britain, it is perhaps surprising that none had seen the need for a specialist sandwich bar for so long. However in summer 2005, this gap was filled, and filled literally. A single sandwich is a meal in itself and the website offers a detailed preview of everything on offer.

✗ Lotoss 7 Skārņu iela; ☎ 721 2665. It is surprising to find good value on the route along which all cruise passengers are frog-marched through Riga, but here it is certainly provided and lucky patrons (or those who come in the off-season) can take advantage of the window seats overlooking St Peter's. Brunch is the speciality here but plenty of visitors are just as happy with eggs and filling soups in the early evening as at midday.

✗ Pelmeņi XL 7 Kaļķu iela; ☎ 722 2728. It's not sophisticated, but it certainly won't leave you either hungry or bankrupt. *Pelmeņi* are rather like ravioli, but their Russian origin means they're more substantial. You can fill up your plate with an XL portion from a choice of 6 different types (chicken, pork, vegetarian etc) and accompany the main dish (Ls1.50) with soup and salad. There is a similar ambience, but bigger choice, at Pelmeņi, 38a Čaka iela.

✗ Olé 1 Audēju iela; ☎ 722 9563. Another buffet-style café, which, despite the name, serves international, not Spanish, food. Take as much as you can eat and you should still have change from Ls3.00.

BREAKFAST ALTERNATIVES If you fancy a change from hotel breakfasts, you won't need to go far to find interesting alternatives. All the options below are open from 08.00 Monday to Saturday. On Sundays you'll have to force yourself to have a late breakfast.

✗ **Ai Karamba!** 2 Pulkveža Brieža iela; ✆ 733 4672. In the New Town, close to the art nouveau area. Cereal, eggs and pancakes. *Sun from 10.00. 6Ls.*

✗ **Dzirnavas** (The Mill) 76 Dzirnavu iela; ✆ 728 6204. Also in the New Town, this restaurant which later in the day offers a Latvian buffet also offers a breakfast buffet with all you could desire, for *Ls2.50. Closed Sun.*

✗ **John Lemon** 21 Peldu iela; ✆ 722 6647. In the Old Town, close to the Ainavas Hotel. A range of breakfast menus, some healthy, some less so, in pleasant surroundings. *Sun from 10.00. 5Ls.*

✗ **I love you** 9 Aldaru iela. For only Ls1.49 you can help yourself from a small breakfast buffet in this Old Town café. *Sun from 10.00.*

CAFES

For internet cafés, see *Internet*, pages 67–8.

🍵 **Café Opera** Aspāzijas bulvāris. A suitably ornate café has been inside the Opera House since it opened in 1995, with plenty of marble and wood. It never advertises, which suits the regulars who prefer the peace and quiet and the absence of tourists even in July and August. A thick soup followed by a light salad makes a good lunch here. The café has an outside terrace, too – with parasols which appear at the first drop of rain.

🍵 **Lidojošā Varde** 31a Elizabetes iela at the corner of Antonijas iela; ✆ 732 1184. 'The Flying Frog' serves simple food (omelettes, pasta, salad, hamburgers) at very affordable prices, as well as drink. Popular both in summer, when you can sit on the terrace, and in winter, when a fire glows in the hearth. Handy when exploring Riga's art nouveau buildings.

Coffee and tea A new generation of coffee and tea houses has arrived in Riga in the last few years. Gone are some of the traditional Viennese-style cafés, to be replaced by an ever-growing choice of cappuccino bars and tea houses. Wherever you are in central Riga, you will never have to go far for a high-quality coffee or a mouth-watering cake. Chains of coffee shops have emerged, but they have not (yet) been joined by the international chains so well known elsewhere. An unusual feature in most coffee shops (although not in Coffee Nation) is that take-away coffee costs a little more than drinking in the café.

Coffee houses

🍵 **Monte Kristo** 18–20 Kalēju iela, close to Konventa Sēta; ✆ 722 7443. Also at 27 Ģertrūdes iela and 10 Elizabetes iela. At once spacious but cosy, this high-class coffee house offers a very wide choice not only of coffee but also of tea. Cakes include an enticing berry tart, excellent warm and with cream.

🍵 **Double Coffee** 11 Vaļņu iela, on the corner of Kaļķu iela; ✆ 712 3522. Also at 40 Brīvības iela, 25 Raiņa iela, 15 Stabu iela and 52 Barona iela. Always busy, with good reason. The cafés offer an immense choice not only of coffee, tea and chocolate, but also of sandwiches, cakes, omelettes and even sushi. The extensive menu is fully illustrated, so it's easy to pick out exactly what you'd like. Prices are very reasonable too, with a single cappuccino available for well under Ls1.

🍵 **Coffee Nation** 4 Tirgoņu iela. Also at 21 Valdemāra iela, 5 Blaumaņa iela, 24–26 Barona iela and Stacijas laukums (Station Square). Another popular coffee-house chain, serving a selection of coffees, as well as some snacks and sandwiches. The chain is owned by Latvians, but is modelled on Starbucks and was the first in Riga to offer American-style coffee-to-go.

🍵 **Franču Maiznīca** (French Bakery) 8 Basteja bulvāris. It would have been easy for standards to slip here, once the novelty of real France penetrating Riga had worn off. Fortunately this is not the case; the croissants and baguettes remain as fresh as ever and nobody will mind French liqueurs rather than wine being a major ingredient in winter warmers or summer coolers. New clients are reassured by *le patron* looking in on most days to check on standards and to greet his regulars. A second café will open in early 2006 at 30 Ģertrūdes iela.

🍵 **Kafijas Veikals** (Coffee shop) 6 Mazā Pils iela; ✆ 722 42 16. Now an exception in Riga, this Viennese-style café is small, popular and one of the best for coffee and cakes. Unfortunately it is closed on Sat and Sun as well as in the evenings.

🍵 **Charlestons Cappuccino Bar** 38–40 Blaumaņa iela; ✆ 777 0573. A popular café with locals, who enjoy the coffee and the range of sandwiches, cakes and salads. If you're in Riga long enough, a loyalty card will make your 7th cup of coffee free.

🍵 **Emihla Gustava Shokolahde** 13/VI Marijas iela (in Berga Bazārs); ✆ 728 3959. Also at 24 Aspāzijas bulvāris (in Valters un Rapa bookstore). Essentially handmade chocolate shops, but you can also have coffee, or chocolate, watch Belgian-style chocolates being made (at the Berga Bazārs) and enjoy a chocolate or two with your coffee. The cappuccinos are large and extremely frothy, the service very friendly, and the prices rather on the high side for Riga.

Tea houses

Aspara Tea Rooms 22 Skārņu iela, ☎ 722 3160. In the historic Ekke's convent built in 1435 as a guesthouse for travellers (page 75), this tea house offers a relaxing ambience in the heart of the Old Town. In the basement you can sit on cushions and choose from a vast array of Japanese, Chinese and Indian teas, while upstairs the décor is European medieval. Another branch is located in a small wooden house in the Vermānes Garden (opposite house number 75 on Elizabetes iela). Other branches also at 10 Šķūņu iela, 77 Valdemāra iela and 2 Tērbatas iela.

Zen 6 Stabu iela; ☎ 731 6521; www.zen.lv. This will definitely not be your cup of tea if you are just looking for a refuelling stop. Enter Zen and you enter a slow-motion world which you will need some time to enjoy. Chinese tea is prepared in ceremonial style and, authentically, takes at least 20 minutes. The décor is oriental too: tatami, cushions, candles and lanterns, though – slightly out of kilter with the rest of the place – waterpipes are also available.

ENTERTAINMENT AND NIGHTLIFE

OPERA AND CONCERTS The **Latvia National Opera** (*3 Aspāzijas bulvāris;* ☎ *722 5803;* f *722 8240;* e *boxoffice@opera.lv; www.opera.lv*) has an extensive programme of opera, ballet and recitals. Ticket prices are extremely reasonable by international standards, tending to range from Ls2–30, although international stars may sometimes dictate higher prices. Tickets can easily be booked from outside Latvia via email, and then collected at the ticket office (slightly behind the main building, towards the park) on arrival in Riga. Even if you do not book in advance, it is often possible to buy tickets once you are in Riga. Performances are normally in the original language but subtitled in English and Latvian where necessary. Programmes are in Latvian and English. An opera festival is held every year in June. This can be booked directly or as part of an opera tour (see page 7). Unfortunately the opera is closed in July and early August. Inside the Opera is Café Opera, a peaceful haven of wood and marble, which offers a pleasant venue for a snack and is open even in July and August when the theatre is closed.

The Latvia National Opera has an extremely high reputation and over the years has attracted a wide variety of well-known musicians and designers. Richard Wagner conducted over 40 operas during his time in Riga (1837–39), although in the forerunner to the current building, which was not built until 1863. He also wrote a large part of *Rienzi* while he was here, and it is said that he conceived some of the motifs for *The Flying Dutchman* on a journey from Riga to Copenhagen. More recently Bruno Walter spent several years conducting at the Opera House. Although many performances are of the classical repertoire, there is a strong tradition of contemporary dance, and the choice of operas is often bold, including for example in 2004 a revival of Anton Rubinstein's little-known *Demons*.

Classical concerts are held in a variety of venues, including the **Wagner Hall** (*Vāgnera Zale*) (*4 R Vāgnera iela;* ☎ *721 0817*), the **Great Guildhall** (*Lielā Ģilde*) (*6 Amatu iela;* ☎ *721 3798*) and the **Small Guildhall** (*Mazā Ģilde*) (*3–5 Amatu iela;* ☎ *722 3772*). Organ and other chamber recitals are given regularly at the **Dome Cathedral** (*Doma laukums*), usually on Wednesdays and Fridays. Tickets can be purchased just inside the porch of the main entrance. In all these cases, there is generally no need to pre-book, unless the artist is extremely well known. Other venues also host occasional performances: if you keep your eyes open when walking around Riga you will see adverts for upcoming events. The *Baltic Times* also gives a selection of concerts with details of time and place. Information on music in Riga generally can be found at www.lmic.lv.

Venues for non-classical music are more varied. For blues, one of the most highly recommended places is **Bites Blūzs Klubs** (*34a Dzirnavu iela;* ✎ *733 3125*), which frequently attracts singers from the USA and elsewhere. **Sapņu Fabrika** (Dream Factory) (*101 Lāčplēša iela;* ✎ *729 1701;* e *info@sapnufabrik.com*) is a large hall which puts on a variety of world music, jazz and rock concerts. The **Hamlet Club** (*5 Jāņa Sēta;* ✎ *722 8838*) hosts jazz concerts, and also serves as a small theatre, putting on plays which often have a strong political content. For a genuine Latvian experience, try **Četri Balti Krekli** (Four White Shirts) (*12 Vecpilsētas iela;* ✎ *721 3885; www.krekli.lv*), which specialises in Latvian musicians, including for example Ainars Mielavs.

Every summer the **Rigas Ritmi** festival (*www.rigasritmi.lv*) is held in Riga in June/July. It attracts well-known musicians from around the world, who not only perform but also give masterclasses. The music is wide-ranging, including reggae, world music, bossa nova, jazz'n'soul and Caribbean. Venues include open-air performances in parks and squares in Riga and even on cruise ships on the Daugava.

FILMS AND THEATRE Riga offers a number of state-of-the-art cinemas, all of which show films in the original, rather than dubbed, so visitors will have no problems viewing missed Hollywood films. Seat prices are low by international standards at an average of Ls2.0–2.70, but even so discounts are offered on weekday showings before 17.00. Information on what's showing can be found at www.filmas.lv (in Latvian but comprehensible to English speakers: click Afiša on the top horizontal for film times and locations), on the individual websites indicated below, by phoning ✎ 722 2222 or checking one of the city guides.

With 14 screens, **Forum Cinemas** (*www.forumcinemas.lv*) is the largest cinema in Riga and the second-largest cinema complex in the whole of northern Europe. It is situated on Janvāra iela, between the bus and railway stations, opposite the end of Aspāzijas bulvāris, and has all the modern facilities you would expect. Other possibilities include **Daile** (*31 Barona iela;* ✎ *728 3843; www.baltcinema.lv*), which shows older films for just Ls1.20 per person; **K Suns** (*83/85 Elizabetes iela;* ✎ *728 5411*), which tends to show European, rather than Hollywood films; **Kinogalerija** (*24 Jauniela;* ✎ *722 9030*) which specialises in classics; and **Riga** (*61 Elizabetes iela;* ✎ *728 11 95*), the first cinema to open in Riga and recently renovated in its original style but with modern equipment.

Riga has a number of theatres but most of these are inaccessible to visitors who do not speak Latvian or Russian. For those who do, the **New Riga Theatre** (*25 Lāčplēša iela;* ✎ *728 0765; www.jrt.lv*) tends to perform avant-garde plays in Latvian, while the Russian Drama Theatre (*16 Kaļķu iela;* ✎ *722 4660*) does what it says. The **National Theatre** (*2 Kronvalda bulvāris;* ✎ *732 2759; www.teatris.lv – Latvian only*), housed in a classical building close to the canal, performs a primarily classical repertoire. It was here that Latvia declared independence on 18 November 1918. A concert is held here every year to commemorate the event. For more information, see www.theatre.lv, which gives information in English as well as Latvian.

Of possible interest is the **State Puppet Theatre**, based at 16 Kr Barona iela (✎ *728 5418;* e *info@puppet.lv; www.puppet.lv*). The puppet theatre is a strong Latvian tradition and performances are generally well acclaimed. They are in Latvian or Russian, but visitors with a particular interest may appreciate the artistry.

BARS AND CLUBS Riga's night scene has blossomed in the last few years. It now offers a huge variety of venues and entertainments to suit all tastes and most pockets. The venues below are only a very small selection of what is on offer. For up-to-date listings in this rapidly changing area, consult *Riga In Your Pocket*.

☆ **Pulkvedim Neviens Neraksta** (Nobody Writes to the Colonel) 26–28 Peldu iela; ↘ 721 3886. One of the longest-established clubs in Riga, this is also one of the city's trendiest venues, regularly crowded with young locals and visitors – but seems to have no connection with the Márquez novel of the same name. The food is generally well liked, although the service can be slow. If you like sitting in a warehouse listening to alternative music, this is for you. If you prefer something more colourful, go down to the Baccardi Lounge in the basement of the same building, and enjoy cocktails to the accompaniment of disco house, but be warned that if you're over 20 you may well be the oldest there.

🗗 **Rigas Balzāms** (Black Balsam) Bdg 1b at 4 Torņa iela in the Jēkaba Kazarmas row of shops near the Powder Tower; ↘ 721 4494. If you'd like to try Riga's distinctive alcoholic drink then the bar named after the drink, Rigas Melnais Balzāms, is a good bar to visit. It is recommended trying it first in a fruit cocktail. The faint-hearted can choose from many better-known drinks. The bar also serves pub-type food, and the pleasant ambience makes it a popular place for Rigans relaxing after work – and well into the evening. The same management have now opened a second bar, Jaunais Rigas Balzāms at 2 Doma Laukums (Dome Square).

🗗 **Skyline Bar** (in Reval Hotel Latvija) 55 Elizabetes iela; ↘ 777 2222. One of the best views in Riga is to be had from the Skyline Bar on the 26th floor of the Reval Hotel Latvija. Take one of the two glass-sided lifts up to the top and enjoy a beer or a cocktail with all Riga spread below you.

🍸**Vairāk Saules** Cocktail Bar (More Sun) 60 Dzirnavua iela; ↘ 728 2878. One of the longest cocktail menus in Riga (around 90) won't prevent you being stunned by the brightness of the décor in this trendy bar. The music is mostly R&B and the service better than in many bars. It is a popular venue with locals, so make sure you arrive early if you want a seat.

🗗 **Paldies Dievam Piektdiena Ir Klāt** (Thank God it's Friday) No 9, 11. Novembra krastmala; ↘ 750 3964. Closed on weekdays until the eponymous Friday, this weekend bar offers a taste of the Caribbean on the banks of the River Daugava. Everything about the bar transports you across the Atlantic: the food, including Cuban black bean soup, the reggae music, the barman in shorts, the flamboyant cocktails and, on Fri and Sat, women dancing on the bar.

☆ **La Habana** 1 Kungu iela; ↘ 722 6014 (entrance from Rātslaukums, Town Hall Square). On the upper floor this is a quiet restaurant serving Tex-Mex dishes. The basement is quite different. From Thu to Sat, it turns into a popular disco hosted by local DJs. The rest of the week Latin music predominates, as you'd guess from the decoration – pictures of Che Guevara, Fidel Castro et al.

☆ **Voodoo** (part of Reval Hotel Latvija) 55 Elizabetes iela; ↘ 777 2355; www.voodoo.lv. Newly revamped club offering several dance floors, quieter areas for drinking and a lively atmosphere. It attracts many Russians, partying in Riga, as well as locals. Admission at Ls3–5 is good value.

GAY RIGA Although the legal restrictions which the Soviet authorities imposed have long since disappeared, the gay scene is not yet well developed in Riga. Open affection in public is rarely seen and may attract hostility. The first gay pride march in Riga took place in July 2005, with many more protestors than participants and with the prime minister expressing open hostility to it. Only two gay clubs are widely advertised:

☆ **Purvs** (The Swamp) 60–62 Matīsa iela; ↘ 731 1717; www.purvs.lv. Generally well reviewed, if you can find it – there is no sign. It offers dance performances, sometimes including transvestite shows. *Open 22.00–24.00; Fri and Sat 22.00–6.00. Closed Tue. Admission Ls1–4.*

☆ **XXL** 4 A Kalniņa iela; ↘ 728 2276; e xxl@xxl.lv; www.xxl.lv. XXL started life as a small bar but has now expanded into a larger club and restaurant, with shows on Fri and Sat at 03.00. Video cabins and dark rooms are also available. *Open 18.00–07.00 every day, but men only on Sun. Admission Ls1–10.*

For further information, contact Gays and Lesbians Online (↘ 727 3890, e gay@gay.lv; *www.gay.lv; in Latvian only*). A new website is also currently under construction (*www.gaybaltics.com*).

SHOPPING

Riga is the most expensive of the three capitals for shopping, probably because of the larger base of local and expat ostentatious consumers there than in Tallinn or Vilnius.

It is also becoming increasingly favoured by rich Russians, who have happy memories of earlier stays during Soviet times. To some extent this is reflected in the higher quality of goods sold and in the type of items offered. Forget the small items of linen or wood that adorn the markets elsewhere and think in terms of amber or silver.

During the summer, shops open every day from 10.00–19.00, sometimes closing a little earlier on Saturday and Sunday. In the winter, some will close on Sundays. Credit cards are widely accepted and bargaining is usually futile.

Unlike in Tallinn, there is no need to avoid the centre to get cheaper prices. There is sufficient competition in the Old Town, and fewer set routes for the cruise groups, so prices are not so varied. There are also fewer street traders. For **jewellery A & E** at Jauniela 17 (note that in this case the suffix 'iela' for street is part of the name whereas normally it is written as a separate word) has reigned supreme ever since Hillary Clinton graced the shop with her presence during her husband's presidential visit in July 1994. Other spouses of world leaders have followed in her footsteps. For tasteful souvenirs in china and glass, **Laipa** (Laipu iela 2–4) can be recommended. They also stock woollen goods wooden toys and some paintings. Those who take an excursion to the **Open Air Museum** on the outskirts of Riga will find an extensive selection of crafts for sale there, with prices set for Latvians rather than for foreign visitors.

Books are an excellent memory from Riga, given the number of English-language ones that have excellent photographs of the architecture. They range in size from pocket-size booklets to massive coffee-table volumes. Prices are usually cheaper for them at the **Tourist Office** on Town Hall Square although the selection at **Valters un Rapa** (Aspazijas iela 24) opposite the Riga Hotel and at **Globuss** (Vaļņu iela 26) just around the corner is usually more extensive. Globuss has a congenial café on its first floor. An extensive selection of second-hand books about Latvia and the Baltics, in English and in German, is always available at **Jumava** (Vāgnera iela 12). The **Occupation Museum** on Town Hall Square has the best selection of books about World War II and the Soviet era. Again, most of these are in English.

AMBER

Amber is formed from the resin which oozed from pine trees some 30 to 90 million years ago and gradually fossilised. It is found in several parts of the world, but the oldest source, some 40–50 million years old, is in countries around the Baltic Sea, including Latvia. The use of Baltic amber goes back a very long way: amber of Baltic origin has been found in Egyptian tombs from around 3200BC, and Baltic amber was regularly traded in Greek and Roman times. Animal figurines made of amber have also been found in Latvia dating back to the 4th millennium BC. After the Teutonic Order conquered Latvian territory, local people were forbidden to collect it on pain of hanging and only in the 19th century could inhabitants of the coast once again begin amber-working.

Traditionally Latvian folk costumes made use of three items made from amber: beads, brooches and *kniepkeni* (fastenings for women's blouses). All of these items, and many others, can be found in shops in Riga. Are they all real natural amber? Definitely not. Unfortunately the only recommended test to establish authenticity is hardly a practical shopping tip: make a solution of water and salt and drop in your amber. Only real amber will float.

Dzintars, the Latvian word for amber, can be seen and heard all over Riga. It is the name of Latvia's main perfume company, a brand name for a cheese spread, the name of a well-known choir, a children's dance group, and is also a common first name (*Dzintars* for men and *Dzintra* for women).

Alcohol is of course easily purchased all over the town, at least until 22.00 when sales in shops have to stop. **Latvijas Balzāms** produce most of the local spirits, so not only Riga Balzāms but also gin and vodka. They have several shops in the Old Town but the largest selection is available at Vaļņu iela 21. The exchange office in this shop usually gives good rates for sterling and US dollars. Prices for alcohol at the airport are close enough to those in town for it not to be worthwhile dragging bottles there, but cigarettes are much cheaper in town so should be bought in advance.

The **Centrs** supermarket (Audēju iela 16) which dates from the 1930s has gone through several metamorphoses since 1991 and another one is underway in 2006. When this is complete, it should probably offer a one-stop shop for those wanting to buy all their souvenirs as quickly as possible under one roof.

WALKING TOURS

The majority of sights are in the Old Town (Vecrīga), the area of the city located between the Daugava River and the city canal (*pilsētas kanāls*). If your time is limited, this is the place to start. If you have more time, you could include a look at the art nouveau area. For visitors with still more time or other interests, a number of other walks in and around the centre are also described.

The Old Town contains a wealth of historic buildings, from the medieval town walls dating back to the 13th century to the grey modernity of the flats and offices built when Latvia was part of the Soviet Union. Between the two extremes there are buildings of almost every period and style, including classical, Gothic, art nouveau and modern. Much of the Old Town suffered neglect when Latvia was part of the USSR, but a great deal of restoration and reconstruction has now been undertaken (the reconstruction of the Blackheads' House and surrounding area being one of the most striking examples).

The best way to see the Old Town is on foot: the area is relatively small, but in any event, large parts of the Old Town have been made traffic-free zones (there is access for vehicles, but you have to buy a pass), while other parts consist of narrow streets, making vehicle access impractical. Many of the streets are cobbled and others suffer from lack of maintenance, so you have to keep your eyes open for holes and uneven road and pavement surfaces. Wear sensible walking shoes.

The main sights of the Old Town are described below by reference to two suggested walking routes covering the Old Town sights on either side of Kaļķu iela.

OLD TOWN WALK I Our first walk starts from the Hotel de Rome at the corner of Kaļķu iela and Aspāzijas bulvāris, not far from the Freedom Monument. Walk down Kaļķu iela away from the Freedom Monument and the parks along the side of the hotel and you will find yourself almost immediately at Vaļņu iela, a pedestrianised street of shops, bars and cafés. Turn right into Vaļņu iela. At the end of the street you will see one of the major landmarks of the Old Town, the **Powder Tower** (*Pulvertornis*, page 106). This sturdy tower is all that remains of the 18 towers which once formed part of the city walls. You may wish to visit the **War Museum** (*Latvijas Kara Muzejs*, page 106), which the Tower now houses. If not, stand on Smilšu iela (Sand Street), one of Riga's oldest streets, with your back to the Powder Tower and look across Basteja bulvāris where you can see the remains of Bastion Hill (*Basteja kalns*), one of the fortification towers dating back to the 17th century.

Behind the Powder Tower is Torņa iela (Tower Street), a well-restored, traffic-free street. Walk along this street and you come to part of the city wall (best seen from the parallel Trokšņu iela). Riga was protected by a wall from the early 13th century. Eventually it extended to a length of over a mile. By the 14th century the walls were 1.83m thick. The arches between the pillars would be filled with stones and sandbags

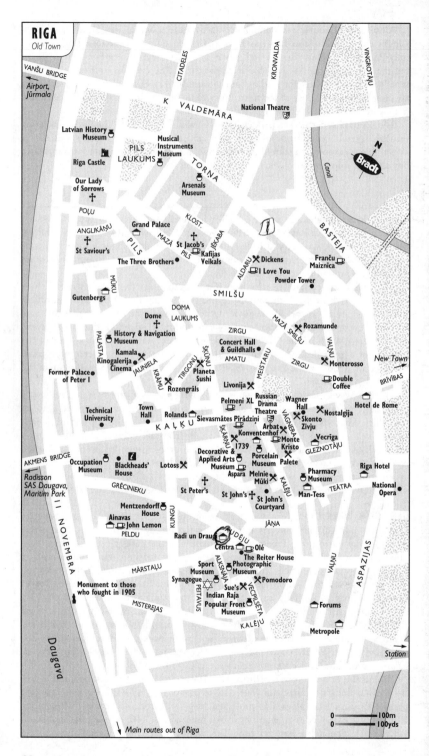

RIGA
Old Town

VANŠU BRIDGE

← Airport, Jūrmala

CITADELES

KRONVALDA

VINGROTĀJU

K VALDEMĀRA

National Theatre

Canal

Bradt

N

Latvian History Museum

PILS LAUKUMS

Musical Instruments Museum

TORŅA

BASTEJA

Riga Castle

Our Lady of Sorrows

Arsenals Museum

POĻU

ANGLIKĀŅU

St Saviour's

Grand Palace

KLOST.

PILS

MAZĀ

St Jacob's

PILS

Kafijas Veikals

Aldaru ✗ Dickens

Franču Maiznīca

MUKU

The Three Brothers

✗ I Love You

Powder Tower

Gutenbergs

SMILŠU

DOMA LAUKUMS

Dome

History & Navigation Museum

ZIRGU

MAZĀ SMILŠU

✗ Rozamunde

PALASTA

Kamala Kinogalerija Cinema

JAUNIELA

ŠĶŪŅU

Concert Hall & Guildhalls

AMATU

MEISTARU

ZIRGU

VALŅU

✗ Monterosso

New Town

Former Palace of Peter I

KRĀMU

TIRGOŅU

Planeta Sushi

Livonija

BRĪVĪBAS

Double Coffee

✗ Rozengrāls

Pelmeni XL

Russian Drama Theatre

Wagner Hall

Hotel de Rome

Technical University

Town Hall

Rolands

ŠĶĀRŅU

KAĻĶU

Sievasmātes Pīrādziņi

VAGNERA

Skonto Zivju

Nostalgija

Vecrīga

GLEZNOTĀJU

Arbat

Konventhof

1739

Monte Kristo

Occupation Museum

Blackheads' House

AKMENS BRIDGE

← Radisson SAS Daugava, Maritim Park

Lotoss ✗

Decorative & Applied Arts Museum

Porcelain Museum

Palete

Aspara

Melnie Mūki

Pharmacy Museum

Riga Hotel

GRĒCINIEKU

St Peter's

St John's ✝

St John's Courtyard

KAĻĒJU

Man-Tess

TEĀTRA

National Opera

VALŅU

Mentzendorff House

KUNGU

Ainavas John Lemon

PELDU

Radi un Draugi

JĀŅA

Centra

Olé

ALKSNĀJA

The Reiter House

Sport Museum

Photographic Museum

Synagogue

✡ Sue's ✝

Pomodoro

II NOVEMBRA

Monument to those who fought in 1905

MISTEREJAS

MĀRSTAĻU

PEITAVAS

Indian Raja

Popular Front Museum

VECPILSĒTA

ASPAZIJAS

Forums

KAĻĒJU

Metropole

Daugava

→ Station

0 ————— 100m
0 ————— 100yds

↙ Main routes out of Riga

to provide reinforcement when the city was under siege; in peacetime they were emptied again and used for storage or as stables or even accommodation. The income derived from letting the arches was used to raise money to pay for the upkeep of the city's defences.

At the corner of Torņa iela and Aldaru iela (Brewer Street) is the **Swedish Gate** (*Zviedru Vārti*), so called because it was built when Riga was under Swedish rule and because it was the gate through which the Swedish king, Gustavus Adolphus, entered the city in 1621 (a stained-glass window in the Dome commemorates this). It is the only city gate still left intact. According to legend, the citizens of Riga abducted a young Latvian woman who had unwisely fallen in love with a Swedish soldier and was meeting him secretly near the gate, and walled her up in the gate as a warning to others. The Swedish Gate is unusual in that it passes through a whole house, number 11 Torņa iela: the first recorded house in private ownership in Riga.

Although it is not possible to visit them, there are several attractively restored historic houses on Torņa iela of which the most notorious is the one now at number 7, a large pink house that was once occupied by the city executioner until the position was abolished in 1863. Number 5 Torņa iela was the site of the prison built in 1685 by Rupert Bindenschu, the architect who also worked on the reconstruction of St Peter's Church.

At the end of Torņa iela you come to Jēkaba iela (Jacob's or James's Street) and to the right **Jēkaba laukums** (Jacob's or James's Square), where concrete barricades were erected during the struggles of January 1991. The square, which was first laid out in the 18th century, was once used for military parades and exercises. On the side of the square closest to Jēkaba iela is a row of low buildings. The middle building, taller than the others, is the former arsenal. Built between 1828–32 to designs by I Lukini and A Nellinger on the site of what was once part of the town wall, the arsenal that stood here was replaced by a customs house. Now the building is a gallery (the **Arsenal Museum of Fine Arts**, *Mākslas Muzejs* or '*Arsenals*') where modern painters exhibit (page 99).

Close to the end of Torņa iela is a green which forms part of **Pils laukums** (Castle Square). The large building on the corner on your right is the Bank of Latvia, built in 1905 to designs by the Latvian architect, Reinbergs. Number 2 Pils laukums was formerly a Red Army museum but is now the **Museum of Writing, Theatre and Music** (Rakstniecibas, Teatra un Muzikas Muzejs, page 107). The main building on Pils laukums, at the other side of the square, is **Riga Castle** (*Rigas pils*), a large cream building with a red roof (page 111), where the president of Latvia now lives.

The castle also houses two museums, the **Latvian History Museum**, *Latvijas Vēstures Muzejs* (page 102), which traces the course of Latvian history from 9000BC to the 20th century; and the **Latvian Museum of Foreign Art**, *Latvijas Ārzemju Mākslas Muzejs* (pages 101–2), the biggest collection of foreign art in Latvia. To the right of the castle, in the direction of Kr Valdemāra iela, is the old stable block, recognisable by horse-head designs on the wall.

Leaving Castle Square (*Pils laukums*) and crossing the cobbled area of the square (the opposite end to the one at which the stables are located, in the direction of Lielā pils iela) you come to a church, the Roman Catholic church of **Our Lady of Sorrows** (*Sāpju Dievmātes baznīca*, page 108). Just beyond the Catholic church is Riga's only Anglican church, **St Saviour's** (page 110), which stands in Anglikāņu iela, just off Lielā pils iela. The church was built for the British community in 1859 and became a discothèque during the Soviet occupation, but is now restored and holds regular Sunday services. On a fine day the outdoor café at the end of Anglikāņu iela offers views over the river and the imposing Vanšu bridge, and makes a pleasant stop. The tall building on the far bank is the Hansapank 26-storey office building.

Returning to Pils iela, go back to the corner of the square and turn right into Mazā pils iela, heading away from the tower of Riga Castle. The three houses at numbers 17, 19 and 21 Mazā pils iela are known collectively as 'the three brothers' (*Trīs brāļi*, page 112). Note also the house at 4 Mazā pils iela where the Baltic historian Johans Kristofs Broce worked from 1742–1823 as rector of what was then Riga's imperial lycée.

Opposite 'the three brothers' is Klostera iela (Monastery Street) which leads to **St Jacob's**, or **St James's**, **Church** (*Jēkaba baznīca*, page 108), the Roman Catholic cathedral of Riga, and the church with the lowest of the three spires which dominate the Old Town.

At the corner of Jēkaba baznīca, if you turn right, you come to a formidable brown building with a coat of arms and a balcony over the main entrance. This is the building where the Supreme Soviet of Latvia used to sit. Between 1919–34 it was the seat of the **Latvian National Parliament**. Now it functions once again as the parliament building, the seat of the Saeima. It was here on 4 May 1989 that parliament passed a resolution on the independence of Latvia. The building itself is in the style of a Florentine palace. Note the decoratively carved double doors and heavy lanterns. In the outbreak of crime which followed independence in the early 1990s, the bronze plaque on the front of the building was stolen.

Turn right into Jēkaba iela and walk along the back of the cathedral. Numbers 6–8 Jēkaba iela form a substantial stone building which houses the **Latvian National Library**. Designs by the Riga-born architect Gunars Birkerts for a new national library, to be known as Gaišmaspils (the 'Castle of Light'), remained for years on the drawing board. However, by late 2005, there seemed to be a genuine determination on the part of the government to build it by November 2008, perhaps because the Bill Gates Foundation expressed an interest in August 2005 in providing some of the necessary funds. Turning left back into Smilšu iela, the house at number 6 has a modern front and is now a bank. The upper storeys are good examples of the art nouveau style of architecture for which Riga is so famous. The buildings at number 2 and number 8 are also worth a look. Next to number 6 is Aldaru iela (Brewer Street) with its view back to the Swedish Gate. The large brown building that dominates the rest of Smilšu iela is occupied by ministries and government offices.

Here the road forks. Take Mazā Smilšu iela (Little Sand Street) and turn right into Meistaru iela (Master Street). On your left is a large yellow building called the **House of the Cat**: perched on each of the building's two pointed towers is an arched cat looking down on the city. The origins of this piece of architectural caprice are uncertain but inevitably there is a story. Apparently a Latvian businessman sought admission to the city guild but was refused. To spite the guild he bought the nearest land he could find to the guildhall, built the house that still stands and had two cats put on top so that each directed its backside towards the guildhall. According to the same story the spurned merchant was eventually forced to move them, hence their present position.

If you continue down Meistaru iela you come to what used to be the Guild Square but is now known as the **Philharmonic Park** (*Filharmonijas Parks*). On a wet day it can look fairly grim but in better weather it is enlivened by kiosks selling ice cream and drinks, and by pavement artists. The **Great Guildhall** (*Lielā Ģilde*, page 83) is the large, dull yellow building at one edge of the square, at the corner of Meistaru iela and Amatu iela (Commercial Street). The **Small Guildhall** (*Mazā Ģilde*) is right next to it on Amatu iela itself. These buildings represent the centres of Riga's former glory as a Hanseatic City. Continue along Amatu iela to Šķūņu iela (Barn Street). On your right there is a camel-coloured building with white decoration, an excellent example of Riga's art nouveau. Note the sculptures of a boy reading (at roof level) and of frogs (by the entrance).

If you turn right out of Amatu iela, past Zirgu iela, you come to the Cathedral

Square, Doma laukums. The square is dominated by the cathedral, the **Dome Church** (*Rīgas Dome* – the word comes from the German *Dom*, meaning cathedral, page 107) or St Mary's Cathedral, as it is sometimes referred to, the largest church in the Baltic states. The church opens from 10.00 to 18.00 daily (*www.doms.lv has full information*), but there are also opportunities to attend concerts there on Wednesdays and Fridays, frequently featuring the cathedral's splendid organ, and services are held (in Latvian) at 08.00 every day and at noon on Sundays. Close to the main entrance and away from the main square is the **Cross-Vaulted Gallery of the Dome** (page 108), the cathedral cloister and courtyard which was finally restored in 2005. This can be visited daily and has good views of the Dome exterior.

Just off Doma laukums, Tirgoņu iela (Traders' Street) has a number of bars and restaurants. Behind the Dome is Jauniela (New Street): the **Pūt, Vējiņ!** is a good place to eat and drink (there is a bar downstairs and a good restaurant upstairs).

The building at 8 Doma laukums is the **Latvia Radio Building**. It and the nearby Finance Ministry recall the architectural style of Nazi Germany and were built during the 1930s at the time of the Latvian president, Kārlis Ulmanis. The Radio Building was one of the buildings that was barricaded in 1991 by demonstrators resisting communist sympathisers; bullet holes in the building offer a grim reminder of the fighting. Doma laukums was heavily guarded and occupied by people lighting bonfires and erecting tents. From time to time radio staff would appear on the balcony of the Radio Building to announce the news to the people gathered in the square below. It was from the same balcony that President Gorbunovs proclaimed independence in August 1991. Opposite the Radio Building is Rigas Fondu Birža, the **Riga Stock Exchange**, a green and brown building with ornate statues. It was built in 1852–55 in Venetian style to a design by the architect Harald Bose, but fell into disuse during the Soviet occupation; during the 1990s it was again occupied by a bank.

If you leave Doma laukums passing the main door of the cathedral with the Radio Building behind you, you come into Herdera laukums, **Herder Square**. This small square is dominated by the statue of the German critic, writer and theologian, Johann Herder, who lived in Riga from 1764–89. Turning out of Herdera laukums you come to Palasta iela (Palace Street). The building that was once the clergy enclosure of the abbey attached to the Dome is now the **Museum of History and Navigation of the City of Riga** (*Rīgas Vēstures un Kuģniecības Muzejs*, page 102). Further on in Palasta iela at number 6 stands a tiny building in which the Russian tsar, Peter I, kept his personal carriage when he visited Riga. Just beyond it at number 9 is what used to be **Peter I's palace**, from which Palasta iela derives its name. In 1745 the palace was rebuilt to designs by Rastrelli, the architect better known in Latvia for his work on the Rundāle Palace (page 119).

OLD TOWN WALK 2 Our second walk in the Old Town starts from the beautifully restored Rātslaukums (Town Hall Square) towards the end of Kaļķu iela near the river.

The distinguished building dominating the square is the **Blackheads' House** (*Melngalvju nams*, pages 100–1), rebuilt in 1999. Although the ornate exterior is the most stunning aspect, the interior can also be visited. Particularly impressive is the assembly hall on the first floor. If you have any questions about Riga, you can visit the Riga tourist information office housed in part of the Blackheads' House. Next to the museum entrance there is a small café, where the brave can sample Vecriga coffee (coffee with Balzāms). While on the square, have a look at the **statue of Roland** (page 113) and also at the newly restored **Town Hall** (*Rātsnams*) opposite the Blackheads' House.

After the medieval atmosphere of the Town Hall Square, the aggressively 20th-century atmosphere of the Riflemen's Square (Strēnieku laukums) next to it towards the river comes as something of a shock. The large statue is the **Riflemen's**

Memorial (page 112) which was erected in 1970 to commemorate the valour of the Latvian Rifle Regiment during the civil war. The ugly black cuboid building behind the memorial was also built in 1970 and used to be a museum devoted to the exploits of the regiment. Now it is the **Museum of the Occupation of Latvia** (*Okupācijas Muzejs*, page 104). The museum offers a detailed and poignant account, with many personal histories, of the various occupations Latvia was subjected to during the 20th century.

The traditional bridge with the large lantern-like lights is the **Akmens tilts** (Stone bridge) which replaced the long pontoon bridge that spanned the river before World War II. A more elegant example of 20th-century architecture is the dramatic modern bridge, the harp-like **Vanšu tilts**, which crosses the river to the north.

Leave the square by turning into Grēcinieku iela (Sinner's Street) and taking Kungu iela (Gentleman's Street). On the corner of Grēcnieku iela and Kungu iela is the **Mentzendorff House** (*Mencendorfa nams*, page 103). The house once belonged to a rich Riga merchant family and is now a museum of life in the 17th and 18th centuries. Walk down Kungu iela past the Mentzendorff House to Mārstaļu iela. Number 21 Mārstaļu iela is (or will be, once restored) a fine example of baroque domestic architecture and was built in 1696 for another wealthy citizen of Riga, Dannenstern and his family. Nearby at number 19 is a plaque to George Armisted (1847–1912), a Scot who was lord mayor of Riga city. (If you are travelling more widely in Latvia, you can see the manor house he built, Jaunmoku Pils, just outside Tukums.) The red house at number 2 Mārstaļu iela is the **Reiter House** (*Reitera nams*), built in 1682 for another wealthy Riga merchant, Johann von Reiter, and now used for conferences and exhibitions.

Turn right into Audēju iela (Weaver Street) and then right again into Vecpilsētas iela (Old Town Street). The buildings at numbers 10 and 11–17 are good examples of some of the 20 or so medieval warehouses of the old town. On the corner opposite the Italian restaurant is the house from which the **Latvian Popular Front** operated in the late 1980s and which is now a small museum (page 105). Return to Audēju iela and continue walking away from Mārstaļu iela. The street is normally packed with shoppers, but if you have chance glance up over the door of number 3. Next to the German motto 'God protect our going in and going out' you will see **storks** on a nest. Storks are a striking feature of rural Latvia, where the 6,000 or 7,000 pairs which arrive annually are welcomed by local people as bringers of good luck. Throughout Latvia, including in the ballroom decoration at Rundāle (page 119), you will find the stork motif.

Turn left into Rīdzene iela, alongside the Centrs shopping centre, then left again into Teātra iela (Theatre Street), which brings you to Kalēju iela. Just off Kalēju iela is a passage leading to the **Konventa Sēta**, an area of beautifully restored historic buildings between Kalēju iela and Skārņu iela. The area, which dates back to the 13th century, now contains a hotel, shops and the **Porcelain Museum** (*Rigas Porcelāna Muzejs*, page 105). Close to the Konventa Sēta at the end of Teātra iela there is a part of the city wall. An archway in Kalēju iela leads to Jāņa Sēta (John's Courtyard), a cobbled courtyard with the city wall on one side and a bar, café and restaurant forming the other sides of the quadrangle.

A second arch leads out of the courtyard to **St John's Church** (*Jāņa baznīca*, page 109), with its wonderful vaulted ceiling inside and intriguing stone faces outside.

Skārņu iela (Butchers' Street) got its name from the shops that were located in this part of Riga in medieval times. Number 22, next door to St John's Church, is a house known as **Ekes konvents** (Ekke's Convent). The building is currently a tea house. Further along Skārņu iela, next to number 10, the old white building with brick-lined windows is **St George's Church** (*Jura baznīca*), possibly the oldest building in Riga and generally dated at 1202 or 1204. In 1989 it became part of the **Museum of**

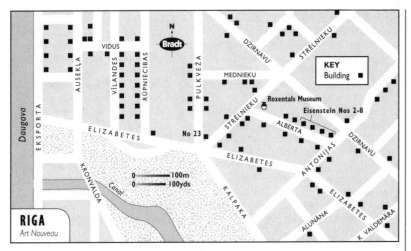

RIGA
Art Nouveau

Decorative and Applied Arts (*Dekoratīvi Lietišķās Mākslas Muzejs*, page 101), which specialises in applied art from Latvia and abroad from the 19th century onwards. Opposite Ekke's Convent in the shadow of St Peter's there is a modern statue of some animals called **The Town Musicians of Bremen**. Based on an old German tale, it is a gift from the city of Bremen to the people of Riga and marks a long association between the two cities.

On the other side of Skārņu iela stands one of Riga's most famous and distinctive churches, **St Peter's** (*Pētera baznīca*, page 109), a large red-brick church with a simple, light interior decorated by coats of arms. St Peter's is the tallest spire in Riga. Except on Mondays you can take a lift up to the viewing platform and have a spectacular view of Riga. On leaving St Peter's, return to Skārņu iela and then turn right into Kaļķu iela. This last part of our walking tour of Old Riga will take you past some of Riga's newest shops and bring you back to the Hotel de Rome and a sign that Riga is now a thoroughly 21st-century consumer-oriented city: opposite the hotel and almost in the shadow of the Freedom Monument is what was Riga's first McDonald's.

ART NOUVEAU WALK Riga has one of the largest collections of art nouveau buildings in the whole of Europe. Around one-third of all the buildings in central Riga were built in this style between around 1896 and 1913. Even if you did not think you were interested in architecture, it is worth having a look at a few of the most striking examples – which may make you change your mind. In this case, you can integrate a quick tour of the art nouveau area within the New Town walk (see pages 95–6). Visitors more interested in buildings could easily spend a half-day exploring the area in more detail and visiting the Jānis Rozentāls and Rūdolfs Blaumanis Memorial Museum (see page 106).

Although art nouveau buildings are to be found throughout the New Town, as well as in certain parts of the Old Town, the area with the most striking buildings is the rectangle bounded by Elizabetes iela, Antonijas iela, Alberta iela and Strēnieku iela. Also of interest are many of the buildings along Brīvības iela, Lāčplēša iela, Ģertrūdes iela, A Čaka iela and Tērbatas iela, all in the main New Town shopping area.

Wandering around these areas, and remembering to look up to the very top of the buildings, gives an idea of the range of styles and the sheer inventiveness of many of the architects. Some of the most memorable buildings are the work of Mikhail Eisenstein (1867–1921), father of film director Sergei of *Battleship Potemkin* fame. These include **10b Elizabetes iela**, with its monumental faces, and the well-restored building at 41Strēnieku iela, now occupied by the School of Economics. Numbers 2,

Within the relatively short time when art nouveau flourished in Riga various substyles can be distinguished: eclectic art nouveau, perpendicular art nouveau and from 1905 the distinctively Latvian National Romanticism.

Art nouveau (or *Jugendstil* as it is known in German) originally developed in Germany and Belgium towards the end of the 19th century and spread rapidly throughout Europe as far as Spain and Hungary. Its original decorative elements – birds, animals, shells and elaborate flower motifs are typical – were in stark contrast to the academic styles of the late 19th century. Philosophically, art nouveau introduced the concept that everything useful should be beautiful; the outside of a building for example should be suited to the function of the building. As the style spread throughout Europe individual countries developed their own variations.

The style which developed in Riga was influenced mainly by German, Austrian and Finnish architects, but the approach also has distinctive elements drawn from Latvian cultural traditions and construction techniques. Most of the architects who designed Riga's art nouveau buildings were trained at the Riga Polytechnical Institute; almost 90% were Baltic Germans, but the 10% or so of native Latvian architects built about 40% of the new buildings.

The most extravagant art nouveau buildings are in Alberta iela. Five of the apartment blocks here (numbers 2, 2a, 4, 6, 8) were designed by Mikhail Eisenstein. Close by, Elizabetes iela is also rich in art nouveau buildings, including the former studio of the painter Jānis Rozentāls, now a museum. The building was designed in 1904 by Konstantīns Pēkšēns (one of the most prolific art nouveau architects, responsible for over 250 buildings). The spectacular murals lining the circular staircase inside the building bear witness to the fact that art nouveau was not limited to building exteriors, but also included interior design, furniture, china, glassware and book design.

After the revolution of 1905 a distinctively Latvian variation of art nouveau developed, known as National Romanticism. Keen to promote national awareness at a time of oppression, architects sought to use traditional Latvian folk art elements and to use the language of the indigenous art of wooden construction. Natural building materials were used, and typical elements were steep roofs, heavy structures and the use of ethnographic ornamental motifs. Some examples include Brīvības iela 47, Terbātas iela 15–17 and Kr Valdemāra iela 67, all built by Eižens Laube (together with K Pēkšēns in the case of the school building at Tērbatas iela 15–17).

2a, 4, 6 and 8 and 13 Alberta iela are also his work. Number 4 is of particular interest. With lions dramatically astride the turrets, it was for several years the home of Eisenstein himself. At number 12 Alberta iela, designed by Konstantīns Pēkšēns, is the **Jānis Rozentāls and Rūdolfs Blaumanis Memorial Museum** (*Jāņa Rozentāla un Rūdolfa Blaumaņa Memoriālis Muzejs*, page 106). The museum is an interesting record of the lives of the painter and the writer, but even if you do not visit the museum, it is worth looking into the entrance and admiring the elaborate staircase. It is hoped in 2007 to open a museum on Alberta Iela dedicated to art nouveau.

Other buildings of note in this area include the block at the corner of Strēlnieku iela and Elizabetes iela (21a) which has a plaque to commemorate the architect and diplomat Mārtiņš Nukša (1878–1942), 23 Elizabetes iela, with the motto 'Labor vinvit omnia' ('Work conquers all'), numbers 3 and 14 Ausekļa iela, and numbers 3 and 4 Vidus iela.

While Eisenstein's buildings are in the eclectic art nouveau style, the buildings in the New Town shopping area reflect a greater diversity of styles. Examples of perpendicular art nouveau can be seen at 49–51 Terbātas iela, the work of Eižens Laube, and at 61 Lāčplēša iela (architect Rudolf Dohnberg). One of the first National Romanticism buildings is at 4 Lāčplēša iela, an apartment block designed by Pēkšēns and built in 1905.

Although the majority of art nouveau buildings are in the New Town, there are some in the Old Town as well. There are examples at Smilšu iela (number 8, the cake shop; number 6, a bank; and number 2, designed by Pēkšēns); Skūņu iela (number 4 and 12–14); there is an imposing doorway opposite the Pūt,Vējiņ! restaurant at 25–29 Jauniela (architect Wilhelm Bockslaff); and a more colourful example at 23 Kalēju iela, the work of Paul Mandelstamm. The attractive Flower House, with paintings of pharmaceutical plants on the outside walls, is at the corner of Mazā Monētu iela and Mazā Jaunava, just behind the Rolands Hotel.

NEW TOWN WALK The Old Town and New Town are separated by the city canal (*pilsētas kanāls*) which runs through a series of parks and gardens. The canal follows the line of part of the old city wall which was demolished in the 19th century. Through the centre of the parks, separating the Old Town from the New Town, is Brīvības bulvāris (Freedom Boulevard), a pedestrianised street that is also the site of the Freedom Monument. This is where the New Town Walk starts.

The **Freedom Monument** (*Brīvības piemineklis*, page 113) dominates the centre of Riga and has played a central and symbolic role in Latvia's chequered history. Close to the Freedom Monument (on the Old Town side of the park) stands the **Laima Clock**, another landmark and a popular meeting point. Laima is the name of a well-known chocolate manufacturer and the Latvian word for happiness or good luck (there was an ancient deity of that name).

Southwest of the Laima clock is a fountain, the Nymph of Riga, which dates back to 1888. It stands in front of the stately **National Opera**, the home of Riga's opera and ballet companies. Originally built as a German theatre, this impressive building (classical on the outside, baroque on the inside) can be seen from anywhere in this central parkland area. Founded in 1919, the National Opera was the focus of Latvian cultural life during the first independence and has resumed an important role in recent years (page 83).

The Opera House is a good starting point for strolls through the parks in the centre of Riga: through **Bastejkalns Park** (pages 113–14) with its memorial to five victims of the events of 1991, through **Kronvalda Park** (page 114) with its monuments to Latvian writers, Riga Congress House (*Rigas kongresu nams*) and the Riga Council Building (*Rigas dome*), or beyond the Freedom Monument towards the New Town, through **Vermānes Park** (page 114) or the **Esplanade Park**.

A number of interesting buildings are scattered in or around the parks. These include **Riga University** on Raiņa bulvāris, a Gothic building with elements of the Romanesque. It stands on the site of the ancient Rīdzene River, long since channelled underground, and was originally used by the Riga Polytechnical Institute. It features a stone staircase divided into three parts, the centre section of which is traditionally used only by graduates. On Merķeļa iela, the street behind the university and alongside Vermānes Park, is the impressive **House of the Riga Latvian Society** (*Rigas Latviešu Biedrība*). The society was founded in 1868 at a time when Latvian was fighting to become a widely acknowledged language but the current building, with paintings on the façade by Jānis Rozentāls, dates from 1910. Just opposite, say hello to the engaging **statue of Kārlis Padegs**, an artist whose scandalous paintings were the talk of Riga in the 1930s (page 112). At the north end of the Esplanade Park on K Valdemāra iela stands the **Academy of Art** (*Mākslas akademija*), a fine example of neo-Gothic architecture. In front of it there is a statue by Burkards Dzenis (1936) of Jāņis Rozentāls, the founder of the Latvian Realist school of painting. Next to the Academy is the **National Museum of Art** (*Nacionālais Mākslas Muzejs*, page 99), built in 1905 by Wilhelm Neumann in German baroque style, which houses a collection of 17,000 paintings. If you are not making a separate trip to examine the **art nouveau area** (pages 93–5) in detail, here would be a good point to make a quick foray into the area. From the State Museum of Art return to Elizabetes iela and proceed a little way north away from the park. Quite soon you will come to 10b Elizabetes iela, a highlight among Mikhail Eisenstein's art nouveau buildings. Make sure you cross the road to look up at it or you will miss the impressive details at the top.

At the south end of the Esplanade Park on Brīvības bulvāris is the **Russian Orthodox Cathedral** (page 108), with its distinctive domes surmounted by Orthodox crosses, built in 1876–84 to designs by Roberts Pflugs. During the Soviet years it was used as a planetarium and for scientific lectures. Now it has been handed back to the Orthodox church, and has been magnificently restored.

Opposite the cathedral, the large government building is the Ministru kabinets, the Cabinet Office.

If you are interested in churches, it is worth continuing up Brīvības iela for two blocks beyond the Hotel Latvija, where you will come to another Russian Orthodox building, the **Alexander Nevsky Church** on the corner of Brīvības iela and Lāčplēša iela. It is named after the 13th-century Russian prince who was canonised by the Russian Orthodox Church in 1547 for his efforts to preserve Orthodoxy in Russia against the Germans whom he defeated at Lake Peipus (now in Estonia) in 1242, a story immortalised in Eisenstein's 1938 film *Alexander Nevsky*. A little further on, down Ģertrūdes iela on the left of Brīvības iela, is St Gertrude's Church, a large red-brick church built in 1863–67 to designs by J D Felsko. The plain interior and pleasing woodwork and gallery are typical of so many Latvian churches.

Wander back towards the parks through the boulevards lined with shops and, increasingly, cafés and restaurants, and admire the many different styles of art nouveau buildings on Terbātas iela, Lāčplēša iela and the surrounding streets.

MOSCOW DISTRICT WALK Depending on how energetic you are feeling, you can either walk to the Maskavas district or take tram number 7 from the stop opposite the National Opera on Aspāzijas bulvāris. Either way, you will start off going round or through the **Central Market** (*Centrāltirgus*). In the 19th century this area was full of what used to be called 'red warehouses' (some still stand), so called after the colour of the bricks used to build them. The modern market buildings consist of five large pavilions, each one originally designed to deal with a different product. Each one is 12m high and covers an area of 75,000m^2, and was built in 1930 to a design intended for Zeppelin hangars. Apart from the formal market, the area around the hangars is full of stalls selling all manner of food, clothing and other goods. Maskavas iela starts at the end of the market, close to the river. Whether on foot or by tram, follow this road away from central Riga, and very shortly you will see on your left an excellent example of Soviet architecture of the Stalin era in the form of the **Academy of Sciences** building. Built in 1957, its nickname, 'Stalin's birthday cake', reflects its ornateness. Similar buildings can be found in Moscow and Warsaw. Though they are now faded and difficult to see, sharp eyes may spot the communist hammer and sickle motifs close to the top. A little further on, also on your left, is the **Evangelical Lutheran Church of Jesus**. Strūgu iela (between Gogoļa iela and Maskavas iela, just before the elevated Lāčplēša iela) reflects the area's Russian past: the name means 'Barge Street' and recalls the days when barges and rafts sailed along the Daugava between Riga and ports in Russia.

Before long the road passes under the elevated approach to Salu bridge and you find yourself in **Maskavas district** (*Maskavas Forštate*), so called because it was a Russian area in earlier times (*Maskva* is Moscow in Russian) and the road to Moscow passed through it. For many years it was inhabited mainly by Russians and Jews and, although this is no longer the case, it continues to attract a high proportion of people of non-Latvian origin. The area is a quiet haven where it is easy to imagine yourself back a hundred years: the streets are still cobbled, many of the houses wooden, trees and parks plentiful and the number of cars typically very low.

If you have come by tram, get off at Mazā Kalna iela (two stops after coming under the elevated road). The area near the junction of Maskavas iela and Mazā Kalna iela used to be known as Krasnaja Gorka (Red Hill) and was where the Russian population of Riga came to celebrate the first Sunday after Easter, a traditional Orthodox feast day. The traditional Russian name is barely remembered now, but the tradition remains alive in the name of the nearby street, Sarkanā iela (Red Street). Walk up Mazā Kalna iela as far as you can go, noting the traditional 'shops' on the left (holes in the wall), and you will come to the **Russian Orthodox Church of St John the Baptist** at the edge of the **Ivan Cemetery** (*Ivana Kapi*). If you are interested in trains, you can turn left when leaving the church and walk along Lielā Kalna iela. Where the road turns you will find a footbridge across a huge swathe of railway lines. From the centre of the bridge is a good view of Riga New Town, including the dominant Reval Hotel Latvija. If trains are of little interest, turn right out of the church and then right along Daugavpils iela. A left turn along Jēkabpils iela leads through two parks, formerly cemeteries, **Klusais dārzs** (Quiet Garden) to the left and **Miera dārzs** (Peace Garden) to the right. Each has a church in its ground: St Francis, a Catholic church in the latter, and All Saints, a Russian Orthodox church in the former. At the edge of the park turn left down Katoļu iela as far as Maskavas iela.

It was in this area that the **Jewish ghetto** was established in 1941. In August 1941 the Rigan citizens who lived in the district were moved to locations closer to the centre of the city, and by October an area of about 750m^2 had been formed taking in Lāčplēša iela, Maskavas iela, Ebreju iela (Jews' Street) and Daugavpils iela. The total Jewish population of the ghetto was about 30,000. The men in the ghetto who were fit to work were put to forced labour; the others were taken to Rumbula Forest on 30 November 1941 and systematically murdered by German guards with the assistance of a significant number of Latvian collaborators. Other Jews were brought in to replace those murdered, only to suffer the same fate in the forests of Biķernieki or in Dreiliņi. The total number of people killed in this way has never been finally ascertained, but estimates indicate it to be around 50,000. On 2 November 1943 the Riga ghetto was closed following the Warsaw ghetto uprising, and the few remaining inhabitants were shot or transported to concentration camps. No trace of the ghetto remains today, although there is a Jewish cemetery (*Ebreju kapi*) not far away between Tējas iela and Lauvas iela.

A left turn along Maskavas iela, followed by a right turn into Grebenščikova iela leads to the **Church of the Old Believers** (page 108), the glittering dome of which you can see from a distance. The area beyond the church and close to the river has seen considerable development in recent years. The large Mols shopping centre now stands on the river bank and its buildings dominate the environs. Before crossing to it, you may like to visit the **Armenian Apostolic Church** (at the time of writing being restored) on Kojusalas iela. From in front of the shopping centre you can take a shuttle bus back to the station, close to the Central Market.

MEŽAPARKS WALK The Mežaparks area in the northeast of Riga lies on Ķīšezers (lake) and includes a park, which houses Riga Zoo as well as the immensely large Lielā Estrāde (large stage), a stadium which can hold up to 20,000 singers and 30,000 spectators and is used for the annual Song Festival. The area also includes a spacious residential sector, which claims to be Europe's first garden city. To visit Mežaparks, take

The only synagogue that now operates in Riga is in Peitavas iela. The site of what used to be the main synagogue (the Choral Synagogue) on the corner of Dzirnavu iela and Gogoļa iela is marked by a memorial (not a very impressive one) consisting of parts of the old synagogue set in a sort of park. A plaque records the destruction of the synagogue on 4 July 1941. Number 29 Dzirnavu iela was also the site of a Jewish school until 1940. It opened again in 1989 as the only recognised Jewish school in the country.

There is a Jewish Museum and community centre (page 102) at 6 Skolas iela, a short walk from the Reval Hotel Latvijā, which deals with the history of Jewish life in Latvia since the 18th century and the revival of Jewish life in the country since independence.

A number of plaques in Riga commemorate influential Jews in Latvia. At 2a Alberta iela a plaque marks the house where Sir Isaiah Berlin, 'the British philosopher', lived between 1909–15. At 6 Blaumaņa iela there is a plaque for Marks Razumnijs (1896–1988), a Jewish poet and playwright.

On Ķīpsala (Kip island) is the house of Jānis Lipke (1900–87), who sheltered 53 Riga Jews in his house on the island during World War II. As their number grew, two large cellars were dug to conceal them, and 43 survived the war.

On the outskirts of Riga are also a number of sites which may be of interest. Rumbala, 10km outside Riga off Maskavas iela, is a site where some 25,000 Jews from the Riga ghetto were murdered in 1941. Biķernieku mežs, also close to Riga, is a similar site. A memorial was recently dedicated to the victims here by the Latvian president. To get there take bus number 14 from Brīvības iela to Biķernieku mežs. Finally, Salaspils, 20km south of Riga, was a Nazi camp where many thousands of people, including Jews, were killed (page 120).

For information on the Jewish ghetto, see page 97.

tram number 11 from Kr Barona iela to the Zooloģ iskais dārzs (Zoological Park) stop, a trip of around 20 minutes. The route takes you past Meža kapi (cemetery, page 116).

The first houses and streets here were built in Kaiser's Park, as it was then called, in 1902 but the area was gradually extended over the next 30 or so years. In its heyday it included art nouveau, functionalist and art deco family houses, all individually designed and all set in spacious green gardens. Between them, the individual gardens boasted around 100 species of trees and shrubs, many of them rare. The majority of owners were Baltic Germans, most of whom left Latvia from 1939 onwards. Under the Soviet occupation the houses, originally intended for one family, were turned into multi-occupancy dwellings and gradually fell into disrepair due to lack of money. Over the last few years, many of the properties have been restored, although some are still in various stages of neglect, and the area is now once again one of the most sought after areas of real estate in Riga.

The best way to see the area is just to wander along some of the streets to the east of Kokneses prospekts. An interesting circular route would take you from the tram stop along Ezermalas iela, right into E Dārziņa iela, right again into V Olava iela, left down Jāņa Poruka iela, right into Vēlmas iela, left into Sigulda iela, left along Kokneses prospekts, a short detour into Visbijas prospekts, returning again to Kokneses prospekts, left along Pēterupes iela, continuing into Hamburgas iela and finally back along Ezermalas iela to the tram stop.

Some houses which may be of interest include the richly decorated Villa Adele at Hamburgas iela 9, now the residence of the German ambassador; the plain house at Jāņa Poruka iela 14, an attempt to create a distinctly Latvian style of functionalism;

Hamburgas iela 25, a decorated art nouveau mansion built on top of what used to be a sand dune; and the mansard roofs, verandas and terraces of houses designed around 1911 by architect Gerhard von Tiesenhausen at 2, 4, 6–8 Visbijas prospekts.

WHAT TO SEE AND DO

MUSEUMS Riga has a huge number of museums, most of them of a high standard. They tend to be closed on Mondays and sometimes Tuesdays, so if you have a particular interest you should plan your trip carefully. The website of the Latvian Association of Museums (*www.muzeji.lv*) is usually fairly up to date on museum opening times but it does not help with information about this for national holidays.

The only museums open on Monday are the State Museum of Art, the Motor Museum, the Open Air Ethnographic Museum, 'Jews in Latvia', the Sports Museum and the Museum of the Occupation (in summer only). In general museums open at 10.00 or 11.00 and close at 17.00. In summer, a few of the museums stay open until 19.00, usually on Wednesday or Thursday. These include the State Museum of Art, the Arsenal Museum of Art, the Museum of Decorative and Applied Art, the Museum of Natural History, the History Museum and the Photographic Museum.

Which, if any, museums you visit, obviously depends on your personal interests. The most commonly visited museums include the Open Air Ethnographic Museum, the Museum of the Occupation, the Motor Museum, the State Museum of Art, the Jānis Rozentāls Memorial Museum and the adjacent art nouveau houses, and the Blackheads' House.

Jaņa Akurāters Museum (*6a O Vāciesa iela, Pārdaugava;* \ *761 9934 (across the Daugava River from the Old Town); open 11.00–17.00 Wed–Sat*) The wooden house was the home of Jānis Akurāters (1876–1937), the popular Latvian writer, rifleman and later director of the Radio Service in Riga. Right up to his death, he wrote poetry and novels, his best known being *Kalpa zena vasara* (*The Young Farmhand's Summer*) and *Degosa sala* (*The Burning Island*). The fact that the house was not large meant it was not nationalised under the Soviet occupation, and Akurāters' family continued to live there, with his original furniture and other belongings, until 1987.

Arsenal Museum of Art (Mākslas Muzejs Arsenals) (*1 Torņa iela;* \ *721 3695; open 11.00–17.00; closed Mon 1 May to 1 Oct; open until 19.00 on Thu*) The museum has a reserve of 12,500 pictures, sculptures etc by Latvian artists who emigrated after 1945. Exhibitions are held on the ground floor and paintings by children displayed on the first floor.

National Museum of Art (Nacionālais Mākslas Muzejs) (*10a Kr Valdemāra iela;* \ *732 4461; www.lnmm.lv; open 11.00–17.00 every day except Tue; 1 May to 1 Oct open Thu 11.00–19.00; admission Ls1.20; tours in English Ls5*) The museum, built in 1905 by Wilhelm Neumann in German baroque style, houses a collection of 32,000 works of art and is a must for anyone interested in 19th- and early 20th-century Latvian art. Inevitably, there is a great deal of work by Rozentāls (his portrait of the singer Malvine Vignère-Grīnberga painted in the last year of his life is particularly well known). Other names, less well known outside Latvia, are also of interest: Vilhelms Purvītis (1872–1945), whose Impressionist landscapes depict Latvia's forest and lakes; Jūlijs Feders (1838–1909), who painted a vast and imposing landscape of the Gauja valley north of Riga; and many others. Also of interest may be a portrait of the Russian writer Turgenev (painted in 1869) by A Gruzdins (1825–91), a bust of the Russian composer Mussorgsky by Teodors Zaļnkalns (1876–1928), a portrait of Kārlis Zāle (the designer of the Freedom Monument) by Ludolfs Liberits (1895–1959) painted in

1934 and showing a relaxed Zāle smoking a cigarette, and a picture of the old harbour when it was located closer to the Old Town, by Jānis Roberts Tilbergs (1880–1972). Latvia's best-known woman painter is Alexandra Belcova (1892–1981). Several of her portraits are on show. Art by non-Latvian artists is less prominent, but the museum does have a notable collection of paintings of the Himalayas by the Russian artist and explorer Nicholas Roerich (1874–1947). In addition to the permanent collection, the museum also holds frequent exhibitions of works by more modern or contemporary artists. At the entrance is a small area selling postcards of some of the paintings and greetings cards of Old Riga.

The museum is beautifully located in the Esplanade Park. When leaving have a look at the sculpture of Jānis Rainis, one of Latvia's most famous writers and translators, and admire too the building next door, the Latvian Academy of Art, a fine example of neo-Gothic brickwork.

Aviation Museum (*Riga Airport – to the right of the terminal;* ☏ *720 7482; allegedly open 10.00–17.00; closed Sat and Sun, but phone to check before visiting*) The museum is not well known by the general public but has achieved cult status among people interested in the Soviet era. The museum contains Soviet helicopters and planes of various ages, including almost all the models of the Soviet MiGs, which can be viewed in detail when the museum is open, or over the wall if it is closed.

Krisjānis Barons Memorial Museum (Krisjāņa Barona Memoriālais Muzejs)

(*3–5 Kr Barona iela;* ☏ *728 4265; open 11.00–18.00 except Mon and Tue; admission Ls0.40*) The museum is the flat (number 5) occupied by Krisjānis Barons (1835–1923), the Latvian poet and folklorist who is best remembered as the collector of Latvian oral literature; *dainas*, traditional four-line songs. Fearing that traditional Latvian culture would be lost, Barons travelled around the country collecting songs. He also advertised in newspapers and was sent tens of thousands of examples of dainas which he then catalogued. He began to publish his collections of dainas in 1894 and the project eventually ran to six large volumes containing around one and a half million songs. The museum recreates his life and work through documents and photographs. Information is available in English; examples of folk music and videos can also be purchased.

The Blackheads' House (Melngalvju nams)

(*7 Rātslaukums;* ☏ *704 4300; www.nami.riga.lv; open 10.00–17.00 except Mon; admission Ls1.0*) The Blackheads' House, one of Riga's most important monuments, was restored in 1999. The wonderful façade is one of Riga's highlights, both during the day and when floodlit at night. This magnificent house (really a building made up of two houses connected by an enclosed courtyard), with its Dutch Renaissance façade (1620), dated back to 1334 but was badly damaged in World War II and finally destroyed by the Soviets in 1948. The 'Blackheads', first mentioned in 1413, were an association of unmarried merchants who lived in Riga and Reval (Tallinn). Originally a loose association, they grew to become a powerful force. It is believed that they got their unusual name from their black patron saint, St Maurice. The first floor of the building was used for shops and businesses; the guildhall of the association occupied the second floor; the upper floors were used for storage and warehousing.

The huge step-gable is 28m high and highly decorated with statues of people and other animals. The building is topped by a large figure of St George which acts as a weathervane. A statue of Roland stands in front of the building. A popular figure in the Middle Ages, and especially in Germany, the Roland statue was originally erected in 1897 but damaged in World War II. A replica has now replaced it (see page 113).

The interior is now a museum. Particularly impressive is the assembly hall on the first floor. Although none of the paintings here are original, they are faithful copies. Note the Swedish and Russian royal families looking across the floor at each other. Much of the silver collection which used to be here is now in Bremen, taken by Baltic Germans who left Riga in the 1930s, and some in St Petersburg, although some families have been helping to rebuild the collection in Riga. You can also visit restored rooms on the ground floor and tour the old foundations in the basement.

Cinema Museum (Rigas Kino Muzejs) (Krāslavas iela 22; ☎ 722 0282; open 12.00–17.00 every day except Mon) The building, which is in the old Russian working-class district of Riga (Maskavas Forštate), used to house the secret printing press used by the communist newspaper, Cīņa ('Battle'). You can still visit the secret passages underneath the building and view the model printing presses.

The Cross-Vaulted Gallery of the Dome (see page 108)

'Dauderi' Latvian Cultural Museum (Latvijas Kultūras Muzejs) (30 Sarkandaugavas iela; ☎ 739 2229; take tram 9 from the centre north to Aldaris; open 11.00–17.00 every day except Mon and Tue) This museum is housed in an elegant red-brick house and was built between 1897–98. During the first independence it was the summer residence of the Latvian president, Kārlis Ulmanis, before he was deported. It contains a vast collection of memorabilia related to the recent history of the country brought together by Gaidis Graundiņš, a Latvian living in Germany. There are also mementoes of Latvia's first period of independence, such as banknotes, stamps, photographs and so on, all collected from Latvian exiles.

Museum of Decorative and Applied Art (Dekoratīvi Lietišķās Mākslas Muzejs) (10–20 Skārņu iela; ☎ 722 2235; www.dlmm.lv; open 11.00–17.00 every day except Mon; Wed 11.00–19.00) The Museum of Decorative and Applied Art opened in 1989 in the restored Jura baznīca (St George's Church) in the Old Town, generally acknowledged as the oldest stone-built religious building surviving in Riga. The exhibition hall still has a church-like feel about it, although it has not been used for church services for almost five hundred years. The exhibits include tapestries, pottery, glasswork and sculpture, and the old churchyard has been transformed into a sculpture garden. The building itself has been very well restored, and is sometimes used for state occasions: in 1998 a summit of European prime ministers was held here.

Museum of Fire-Fighting (Ugunsdzēsības Muzejs) (5 Hanzas iela; ☎ 733 1334; open 10.00–16.30 every day except Mon and Tue; admission L0.20) This unusual museum is housed in an art nouveau fire station built in 1912 just north of the art nouveau district and contains displays depicting the history of fire-fighting in Riga. The engines displayed go back to 1899 and include a Chevrolet from America. Whatever the nature of the regime, many fire crews in Latvia have been voluntary, and there are photographs of them in action and posing formally. Foreign fires are covered too, from Moscow in 1812 to New York in 2001. A major feature is a fire engine built during the first period of independence.

Latvian Museum of Foreign Art (Latvijas Ārzemju Mākslas Muzejs) (3 Pils laukums; ☎ 722 6467; www.amm.lv; open 11.00–17.00 every day except Mon; admission L1.20) Housed in part of Riga Castle, the museum consists of three floors of paintings, sculptures, drawings and ceramics by artists from Germany, Holland, France and Belgium. It is a rather odd museum: many of the oldest exhibits (sculptures from Greece and Rome and artefacts from ancient Egypt) are mixed up with modern works; the more conventional galleries exhibit paintings by 17th-century Dutch

artists, German works dating from the 16th–19th century and Belgian painting of the 20th century. There are almost no works of great distinction.

Latvian History Museum (Latvijas Vēstures Muzejs) (*3 Pils laukums;* ☎ *722 1357; open 11.00–17.00 every day except Mon and Tue; Thu 11.00–19.00; admission Ls0.70, free on Wed*)

This museum, part of the castle complex, traces the history of Latvia and Latvian culture from 9000BC to the present. Each room takes a different and unrelated theme. It is good to see a museum in Latvia that is keeping up to date and where care is taken over presentation and lighting. Do not judge the museum by the gloomy entrance to the building or by the torn signs on the stairs. One room concentrates on archaeology but sadly the labels are only in Latvian; another covers religious statues in both stone and wood which have been rescued from churches all over the country. Turning to more modern history, there are models and original tools to display 19th-century farming, a school room from the 1930s and a costume room from the same period. When the EBRD (European Bank for Reconstruction and Development) met in Riga in May 2000, a permanent coin room was set up in the museum. The coins on display go back to the 9th century but of most interest, perhaps, are those from the 1914–20 period when German and Russian ones circulated side by side. A hat exhibition opened in 2002.

'Jews in Latvia' Museum (*3rd floor, 6 Skolas iela;* ☎ *738 3484; open 12.00–17.00 Sun–Thu; admission free*)

The museum is in the New Town in a street close to the Reval Hotel Latvija. This small but moving museum is devoted to the history of Jews in Latvia, from the first records of Jewish families living with full civil rights in Piltene in the mid 16th century, through growing discrimination in the 19th and early 20th century to the destruction of the synagogues in Riga, Jelgava and Liepāja in 1941 and the terrible sufferings subsequently imposed by both the Nazis and the Soviets. The exhibits, in English as well as Latvian, illustrate the many fields in which Jews contributed to Latvian life in the past, and continue to do so today. On the staircase going up to the museum are photographs and descriptions of some of the Latvians who saved Jews from persecution during World War II, sometimes at the cost of their own lives.

Museum of Riga's History and Navigation (Rigas Vēstures un Kuģniecības Muzejs) (*4 Palasta iela;* ☎ *735 66 76; www.vip.latnet.lv/museums/riga; open 11.00–17.00; closed Mon and Tue; admission Ls1*)

Founded in 1773, this is the oldest museum in Latvia. It was originally set up to house items from the private collection of Nicolaus von Himsel (1729–64) whose portrait by an unknown artist hangs in the ground-floor exhibition hall. The main permanent exhibition traces the development of Riga from its beginnings to 1940. It does so by reference to maps, plans, pictures and objects of all kinds from the everyday life of the city's inhabitants.

The collection is weak on the medieval period but particularly strong on 1920–40, showing how affluent and diverse life was for a reasonable number of people at that time. The display covers magazines published in several languages, fans, pottery, glasswork and clothes. In 2002 the impressive Colonnade Hall reopened; it was originally built between 1778 and 1783 but was closed for renovation in 1984 and this has only now been completed. Some of the original brickwork can be seen. It houses a large portrait of Peter the Great arriving in Riga in 1710.

The second main permanent exhibition is devoted to the history of navigation from ancient times to the present day. One room is dedicated to the work of Krišjānis Valdemārs (1825–91), a pioneer in naval education in Latvia. What is displayed here would be more than enough work for most people, but Valdemārs was also active as a short-story writer, a newspaper editor and as a constant political campaigner in the National Awakening Movement. The exhibition also includes many models of ships which have been connected with Riga from the 10th century to the present day.

Mentzendorff House (Mencendorfa nams) (*18 Grēcinieku iela;* ↘ *721 2951; open 10.00–17.00 every day except Mon and Tue; open by prior arrangement for groups on Mon and Tue; admission Ls1.20; guided tours in English Ls3*) The former residence of a wealthy Riga merchant family, this house is now a museum devoted to life in Riga in the 17th and 18th centuries. The building dates from the 1720s when it replaced an earlier one destroyed in the Riga fire of 1677. Wall paintings from that time have only recently been discovered; in some rooms there were as many as five layers of paintings and then 20 layers of wallpaper from the 19th and 20th centuries. Some of the early paintings were modelled on the work of the French artist Antoine Watteau (1684–1721). The house now carries the name of the last Baltic-German family to live here until 1940, though it is sometimes still called the 'Merchant's House' in view of the number of trades carried out here. The outlines of the grocery store that the Mentzendorff family ran can be seen on the ground floor, although not all the articles displayed are originals from this house. Note the raised edge of the long wooden table, which prevented coins slipping to the floor. In winter, the kitchen stove was the centre of the household: it was used to cook the food, smoke the meat and heat the whole house. The basement is used for temporary art exhibitions, but the higher floors display furniture, clothes, clocks, playing cards and musical instruments which the Baltic Germans would have enjoyed in the 18th and 19th centuries. In Soviet times 15 different families lived in the building and they were only moved out in 1981 for restoration to begin. It was completed in 1992.

Motor Museum (Rigas Motormuzejs) (*6 S Eizenšteina iela;* ↘ *709 7170; open 10.00–18.00 Tue–Sun, 10.00–15.00 Mon*) The museum is around 8km from the Old Town. The best way to go by public transport is to take a number 14 trolleybus from Brīvības iela or a number 18 from Čaka iela and get off at Gaiļezers hospital, about 500m from the museum. The museum is not easy to spot: look out for what appears to be a large Audi dealership and showroom; it is a modern red-brick and glass building. The entrance is reached via a bridge from the car park.

The collection was started by enthusiasts for old cars in 1972 and the museum opened in 1989 at the end of the Soviet era. It houses an acclaimed collection of over 100 motor vehicles, including cars which once belonged to the Soviet leaders, Stalin, Khrushchev and Brezhnev, and Erich Honecker, the leader of the former German Democratic Republic. Wax figures of some of these former politicians and motor enthusiasts help to liven up the displays: Stalin sits in his armoured ZIS 115 (said to have done 2.5km to the litre), Brezhnev at the wheel of his crashed Rolls-Royce; Gorky stands next to his 1934 Lincoln.

The first car assembly plant in Tsarist Russia was established in Riga in 1909 and this was followed by no fewer than 30 bicycle factories during the first independence period. Their products are also exhibited here, as are later Soviet motorbikes. A lot of the cars that form the backbone of the collection were abandoned in 1939–40, firstly by the Baltic Germans recalled 'home' by Hitler, and secondly by the embassies closed after the Soviet occupation. Others are German cars abandoned during the long retreat towards the end of World War II. One is a Rolls-Royce which had been built under licence in Germany. Although the museum is famous for displaying the car that Brezhnev crashed, another one of the 40 or so that he owned is also on display – a 1974 Continental presented by the American government.

Latvian Museum of Natural History (Latvijas Dabas Muzejs) (*4 Kr Barona iela;* ↘ *722 6078; open 10.00–17.00 except Mon and Tue; Thu 12.00–19.00; admission Ls0.60*) The museum has permanent exhibitions of geology, zoology, entomology, anthropology and environmental protection. It also has an exhibition concentrating on the Daugava River and the effect of the construction of the hydro-electric power station on the river basin. Note the herbarium display, the work of the botanist J Ilsters. Most information is in Latvian and Russian only but an interactive computer programme for children on the top floor is in English.

Museum of the Occupation of Latvia (Okupācijas Muzejs) (*1 Strēlnieku laukums;* ✆ *721 2715; www.occupationmuseum.lv; open 11.00–18.00, closed Mon from 1 Oct to 1 May; admission free*) This museum, housed in an exceptionally ugly cuboid building, contains a permanent exhibition devoted to the history of Latvia during the Soviet and Nazi occupations of 1940–91. The displays are on the first floor and exhibit photographs and documents, maps and artefacts dealing with the period and also contain a replica of a barracks room from a Soviet gulag. One display covers the life Latvians led in Siberia after release from the camps but while they were still exiled. Another shows the struggle of Latvians in the West to keep the memory of their country alive during the Soviet occupation. Extensive collections of letters, photographs and everyday articles depict the horror of life for those jailed or deported. The renovation of the Hotel Riga provided a new exhibit for the museum – the bugging equipment with which the hotel staff monitored phone calls during the Soviet era. There is excellent background material in English to all the exhibits and a bookshop which sells most of the publications available in English on the two occupations.

The long-term future of the building is a subject of great controversy. Some Latvians feel that the theme of the museum is so important that even if another building were found elsewhere (unlikely under current financial circumstances) it would suggest a loss of interest in the topic on the part of the city administration. Others feel that a Soviet building, whatever its current contents, should no longer be allowed to disfigure the heart of Latvia's capital. The Latvian-born architect Gunars Birkerts, who now practises in America, has suggested alterations to the building which might provide an appropriate compromise and which would certainly make it aesthetically acceptable. No decision has yet (in 2006) been made.

Open Air Ethnographic Museum (Latvijas Etnogrāfiskais Brīvdabas Muzejs) (*Brīvības gatve 440;* ✆ *799 4515; www.virmus.com; open daily 10.00–17.00; admission Ls1*) On the northeastern outskirts of the city close to Lake Jugla, about half an hour by bus number 1. Get on at the corner of Merķeļa iela and Tērbatas iela and get off at the Brīvdabas Muzejs stop.

Although modern Riga has much in common with other European capitals, a visit to the beautifully constructed Open Air Ethnographic Museum will help you understand some of the more distinctive elements of Latvian history and tradition. It will certainly make you appreciate too how close nature lies to the heart of every Latvian and just how attractive Latvian nature can be.

'Museum' is something of a misnomer for this 100ha site, which contains farms, churches, windmills, houses, fishermen's villages and many other buildings, set in a huge pine forest next to Lake Jugla. Brought together from all parts of Latvia, some buildings date back to the 16th century. Most constructions are wooden and blend beautifully with the surrounding trees. It is a pleasure just to walk among them, as well as to learn more about traditional Latvian life from the many exhibits. At the weekends it is usually possible to watch craftsmen at work: a blacksmith forging a hunting knife, a woman weaving traditional clothes.

Some favourites are the strange traditional *dore*, hollowed tree-trunks standing on stone bases and used for beekeeping; wooden *pirts*, traditional baths; the wooden Usma church, which is still used for church services and weddings; and the 18th-century *krogs* (pub) which serves traditional food and drinks including barley beer. You should allow at least two hours for a visit, and you could easily spend a half or even a whole day here.

Museum of the Popular Front (Latvijas Tautas Frontes Muzejs) (*Vecpilsētas iela 13–15;* ↘ *722 4502; open Tue 14.00–19.00, Wed–Fri 12.00–17.00, Sat 12.00–16.00; admission free*) This is a small, recently opened museum in the former offices of the popular movement which contributed so much to the regaining of Latvian independence. It displays pictures of the movement's leaders and the demonstrations leading up to independence and also shows how the office looked in its period of struggle.

Pharmaceutical Museum (Farmācijas Muzejs) (*13–15 Riharda Vāgnera iela;* ↘ *721 6828; open 10.00–16.00 Tue–Sat; admission Ls0.20*) Part of the Paul Stradin Museum of the History of Medicine, this branch is housed in a beautifully renovated 18th-century house in the Old Town. It has an extensive collection of documents, samples of medicine manufactured in Latvia and many other pharmacy-related items which non-visitors would be hard-pushed to imagine. The interior of a 19th-century chemist's brings it all to life.

Latvian Photographic Museum (Latvijas Foto Muzejs) (*8 Mārstaļu iela;* ↘ *722 7231; www.culture.lv/photomuseum; open 10.00–17.00 Tue, Fri, Sat; 12.00–19.00 Wed and Thu; closed Sun, Mon. Admission Ls1*) The basic exhibition is of cameras and pictures from 1839 to 1941, including many of historic events such as the 1905 Revolution and World War I. A studio from 1900 has also been set up, where it is possible for visitors to take a photo using the technology of that time. An interesting exhibit is dedicated to the Minox 'spy camera', invented by Walter Zapp, who was born in Riga in 1905. The cameras were made in Riga between 1938 and 1943 and have been used ever since. The museum is now gradually being extended to cover World War II.

Rigas Porcelain Museum (Rigas Porcelāna Muzejs) (*Kalēju iela 9–11, in Konventa Sēta courtyard;* ↘ *750 3769; open 11.00–18.00, closed Mon; admission Ls0.50*) The museum opened to acclaim in 2001 and is the only porcelain museum in the Baltic states. Riga has a long history of making porcelain, starting with the opening of the Kuznetzov factory in the first half of the 19th century, and the 6,000 exhibits reflect the many types of porcelain, from prestigious tea sets to crockery for everyday use, which have been made in the city from the mid 19th century to the present day. One room is devoted to items from the Soviet era, including vases and statues of Lenin, Stalin and other leaders. By far the most dominant item is a 2m-high red and gold vase made to celebrate Riga's 700th anniversary in 1901. Visitors can see demonstrations of porcelain manufacturing and for Ls3 can take part and decorate mugs themselves.

Latvian Railway Museum (Latvijas Dzelzcela Muzejs) (*2–4 Uzvaras bulvāris;* ↘ *583 2849; www.railwaymuseum.lv (just across the river from the Old Town, five minutes beyond the Akmens bridge); open 10.00–17.00 Wed–Sat; admission Ls0.50*) The museum dates from 1994 and is run by Latvian Railways. The building was previously an engine repair shop. During its short life it has accumulated a wide range of materials going back about 100 years, including signals, timetables, track and above all, steam engines. There are constant additions to the collection. One German engine from World War II is fitted out as a snowplough. As late as April 1944, the Germans produced a timetable for the whole Baltics area. It is displayed here and it remains the last one to have appeared. The Soviets regarded such information as too dangerous to impart and the three Baltic railway administrations have been unable to co-ordinate a similar publication. Railway enthusiasts may be interested to know there is another branch of the museum at Jelgava (one hour by bus from Riga), which concentrates on railway safety and training.

Jānis Rozentāls and Rūdolfs Blaumanis Memorial Museum (Jāṇa Rozentāla un Rūdolfa Blaumaṇa Memoriālais Muzejs) (*12–19 Alberta iela;* ☏ *733 1641; open 11.00–18.00 except Mon and Tue; admission Ls0.60*) The entrance to this museum is on Strēlnieku iela. It commemorates the life and work of two well-known Latvians: Rozentāls, the painter, lived here between 1904 and 1915; Blaumanis only for two years. Take the elaborate staircase in the rather neglected hallway to the top floor and ring to gain admission. The ironwork, the tiling and the paintings on the ceiling are all original but the windows are of a later date. The architect for the building was Konstantīns Pēkšēns (1859–1928). He designed it for his own use, but then gave the top floor to Jāṇis Rozentāls in 1904.

Rozentāls and his wife Elija, a renowned mezzo-soprano, lived here with their three children. The writer Rūdolfs Blaumanis rented a room in the flat and lived here in 1906–08. The living rooms contain pictures, photographs and artefacts connected with the life of the artists. The studio and other rooms on the top floor are an art school and are used to exhibit works by the students who range from young children to mature painters. Good photographs of Alberta iela can be taken from the top floor.

Latvian Sport Museum (Latvijas Sporta Muzejs) (*9 Alksnāja iela;* ☏ *721 5127; open 11.00–17.00 Mon–Fri, 11.00–17.00 Sat*) This has a unique collection of bicycles, including a collapsible Peugeot built in 1915 and used during World War I and an English Raleigh lady's bicycle dating from 1895, as well as more conventional exhibits. It is housed in an attractive 17th-century warehouse.

Paul Stradin Museum of the History of Medicine (P Stradiṇa Medicīnas Vēstures Muzejs) (*1 Antonijas iela;* ☏ *722 2656; www.mvm.lv; open 11.00–17.00 every day except Sun and Mon and last Fri of each month*) Located in the New Town on the corner of Antonijas iela and Kalpaka iela. This museum is the creation of the Latvian doctor and surgeon, Paul Stradin (1896–1958), who collected the majority of the exhibits over a period of 30 years and presented them to the city of Riga. The exhibits, which include medical instruments, books and papers, cover a wide range of topics, from Riga during successive plague epidemics to how the human body copes with eating in outer space.

Latvian War Museum (Latvijas Kara Muzejs) (*20 Smilšu iela (in the Powder Tower);* ☏ *722 8147; www.karamuzejs.lv; open 10.00–18.00 every day except Mon and Tue; admission Ls0.50*) During the Soviet occupation this museum was devoted to demonstrating how Latvia became a revolutionary Soviet state. Now it is a mainstream war museum with collections of army uniforms and other exhibits devoted to the military history of Latvia. Exhibits cover the period from the 15th to the 20th century but the main part of the collection focuses on the traumatic events of the 20th century. Of particular interest are the exhibitions devoted to the Latvian Riflemen's Regiment, and a recent addition, the development of the Latvian army from World War I to 1940.

Theatre Museum (Eduarda Smilģa Teatra Muzejs)
(*37–39 Smilģa iela, in Pārdaugava;* ☏ *611893; open 11.00–18.00 every day except Mon and Tue; 12.00–19.00 Wed*) This museum is housed in the building where theatre director and actor Eduards Smilģa (1886–1966) lived for all but five years of his life. It was empty for five years after his death before being converted into a museum that opened in 1974. Although his personal theatre here could have accommodated an audience, he always rehearsed in strict privacy, totally on his own. This theatre was modelled on the Daile Theatre in central Riga. He played every major role in the plays of Jānis Rainis and of Shakespeare, and when he gave up acting in 1940, he continued

to direct. Both his sons were killed fighting, one in the German army and one in the Russian army. The collections comprehensively cover the history of the Latvian theatre, not only in Riga but also in Ventspils and in Liepāja. No famous actor is missed, nor any famous stage-set. The private rooms and offices have been left just as Smiļģis would have known and used them.

Literature, Theatre and Music Museum (Rakstniecības, Teātra un Mūzikas Muzejs) (*2 Pils laukums;* ↘ *721 1956; open 10.00–17.00 every day except Mon and Tue; admission Ls0.40*) The former Rainis Museum, founded in 1925 and devoted to Latvian literature, has recently been rebranded as the Museum of Writing, Theatre and Music. Permanent exhibits include photographs, manuscripts and texts relating to the history of Latvian literature from its earliest times right up to the 20th century. Recent additions are two exhibitions devoted to Gunārs Freimanis (1927–93) and Voldemārs Zariņš (1917–81), both of whom were persecuted by the Soviet authorities. Freimanis spent ten years in the Russian gulags; Zariņš was sent to forced labour in the coal mines of Tula. Other exhibitions are changed periodically. Unfortunately, all the information (except for a short pamphlet) is in Latvian.

CHURCHES Churches are one of the highlights of a visit to Riga. Three spires dominate the Old Town skyline – St Peter's, the highest, the Dome and St Jakob's – but other churches are also well worth a visit, including St John's, the Orthodox Cathedral and the Grebenshchikova Church of the Old Believers.

Like museums, several churches close on Mondays and/or at weekends, including the Dome, St John's and St Peter's, so check opening hours when planning your visit.

Dome Cathedral (Doma baznīca) (*Doma laukums (Dome Square);* ↘ *721 34 98; open Tue–Fri 13.00–17.00, Sat 10.00–14.00, closed Sun, Mon; admission Ls0.50*) Although size alone does not justify a visit, there is no denying the huge dimensions of this, the largest church in the Baltics. The solid brick walls and 90m tower dominate not only the Cathedral Square but much of the Old Town, and have done so for almost 800 years. Commonly known as the Dome Cathedral (a tautology, as Dome comes from the German *Dom* meaning cathedral), the church was built at the instigation of Albert, Bishop of Riga, now buried in the cathedral. The foundations of the church were laid in 1211 and the building consecrated in 1226. Over the years, the church has been modified and reconstructed a number of times, with the result that it is now a mixture of various styles, although it retains a strong Teutonic flavour.

Originally the church was built on a hill but today visitors walk downhill from Dome Square to enter via the main door. This is because earth has gradually been built up around the cathedral to try and avoid the floods which used to occur frequently in Riga. On one occasion in 1709 it is even reported that fish were caught inside the church.

After it became a Protestant church in the Reformation, much of the cathedral's elaborate interior decoration was destroyed. A striking feature which remains is the large number of coats of arms of merchants from Riga fixed on the sides of the immense pillars, all of which were donated by rich mercantile families in search of immortality. Of interest too are the stained-glass windows. Two towards the front on the north side illustrate important moments in Riga's history: one depicts Walter von Plettenberg reading the edict proclaiming religious freedom and pledging protection from the Catholic bishops (1525) and another the welcome of the Swedish king, Gustavus Adolphus, in Riga on 25 September 1621. The impressive wooden pulpit, in the middle of the church in accordance with Lutheran tradition, dates from 1641.

What the Dome Cathedral is most famous for, however, is its organ, a huge instrument with four manuals and a pedal board, 124 stops and 6,718 pipes. When it was built in 1884 by the firm of Walcker & Co of Ludwigsburg it was the largest organ in the world.

The Cross-Vaulted Gallery of the Dome, the cathedral cloister and courtyard

(*Next to the main cathedral entrance; open daily in summer 10.00–17.00; small admission charge*) The cloister itself is a remarkable Romanesque masterpiece, with impressive ornamentation of twining flowers and leaves. Restoration has been in progress since the mid 1980s but is not yet complete. Displayed within the cloister is an assortment of items, including the original weathervane from the Dome spire, a cockerel some 6ft tall, originally constructed in 1595 but replaced by a replica in December 1985; a plaster copy of the statue of Peter I, the original of which stood between 1910 and 1914 where the Freedom Monument now is; and a 3ft-high stone head, unearthed in the cloister in 2000. This last exhibit is still something of a mystery. Originally found in 1851 near Salaspils (just outside Riga), the stone was then lost for almost 150 years. It is possible that the head served as an idol for the Livs, the group of people who have lived on what is now Latvian territory for over 20 centuries. Records exist of the worship and making of idols in Latvia as late as the 16th to 18th centuries, but to date no other idol has been found with such strange and expressive features.

Grebenshchikova Church (Grebenščikova baznīca) (*Krasta iela 72 at the end of Grebenščikova iela; ☏ 711 3083; tram 7 or 9 from opposite the National Opera to the Daugavpils stop, approx 10 minutes*) This is a church used by Orthodox Old Believers, a sect which fled from persecution in Russia in the 18th century. Their first church was erected on this site in 1760 but was burnt down and replaced by the current one in 1814. The steeple was added later, in 1906, and has traces of art nouveau in its design. It is surmounted by the only golden dome in Riga and can easily be spotted from any high building in the city centre. The interior contains icons dating back to the 15th century.

Orthodox Cathedral (Pareizticīgo Katedrāle) (*Brīvības bulvāris, in the Esplanade Park; ☏ 721 1216*) The Russian Orthodox Cathedral with its five imposing cupolas offers an insight into another aspect of multi-sided Riga: traditional Russian culture. Built between 1876 and 1884 to designs by Roberts Pflugs, the cathedral was used as a lecture hall and then as a planetarium in Soviet times, and even today Rigans often refer to it as the *planetārijs* – the planetarium. It now functions again as a place of worship and has been beautifully restored. The final touches were in early 2006 still being made, and there are plenty of opportunities to donate to the restoration fund. The interior now sparkles with newly gilded coffins, iconostases (screens containing icons) and wall and ceiling paintings. During the Soviet occupation the crosses were removed from the building. Those now in the cathedral were made in Würzburg in Germany, consecrated in 1990 and given to the cathedral by a Latvian living in Germany.

Our Lady of Sorrows (Sāpju Dievmātes baznīca) (*Lielā pils iela*) The Roman Catholic Church of Our Lady of Sorrows dates from 1784–85, although a humbler church was located on the site before the Russian tsar Paul I and the king of Poland, Stanislav August, were persuaded by the Austrian emperor, Joseph II, to donate money for the construction of the present church. For many years it was the only Roman Catholic church in Riga and the surrounding area. The statue of the Sorrowful Virgin above the outside door originally belonged in St Jacob's Church, but was left there by the Jesuits, later found by the Lutherans and given to this congregation.

St Jacob's or St James' (Jēkaba baznīca) (*Klostera iela 2; ☏ 732 6419; open for visits 07.00–20.00; closed Sat*) Note: Jacob and James are alternative translations of the Latvian Jēkabs. Now the Roman Catholic Cathedral of Riga, the church was originally built in 1225–26. It has subsequently been rebuilt several times, although the sanctuary and the tall, whitewashed brick naves are original. The 73m spire is the lowest of the

three spires which dominate the Old Town. The church has changed hands on several occasions: in 1522 it was the first church in Latvia to hold a Lutheran service, but only 60 years later it was handed over to the Jesuits. In 1621 it became a Swedish garrison church before finally returning to the Roman Catholic Church in 1922.

The brick walls have held a number of unexpected items. In 1656 the Russian tsar Alexis Mikhailovich was attacking Riga. During the battle, several grenades hit the church and two of them were later immured above the altar. Then in 1774, during renovation work, the body of a man was found immured in the north wall. His silk garments indicated he was a man of some wealth, but his identity has never been discovered.

St John's (Jāņa baznīca) *(Jāņa iela 7; ℡ 722 4028; open Tue–Fri 10.00–17.00)* St John's Church was built for the Dominicans in 1234 but has since been much extended. The stunning high nave with a meshed vaulted ceiling dates from the 15th century and the ornate baroque altar, with sculptures depicting the crucifixion and SS Peter and Paul, from the 18th. The altar painting, *The Resurrection*, is by the 18th-century Rigan artist August Stiling, while the painting *Christ on the Cross* in the sacristy is by one of Latvia's best-known artists, Jānis Rozentāls (page 107).

The history of the church again reflects Riga's turbulent past. The Dominicans were ousted in the Reformation, and for some time after 1523 the church was used as stables by the mayor of Riga, then as an arsenal, until in 1582 the Polish king, Stephen Batory, seized it and handed it over to the Jesuits. In due course it was returned to the Lutheran Church.

The outside of the church is also worth a good look. Behind the church on Jāņa iela are two life-sized statues, one of St John the Baptist, the patron saint of the church, and the other of Salome, who persuaded Herodias to give her John's head on a platter as a reward for her dancing. Round the corner, on the wall facing Skārņu iela, are two stone faces with open mouths. Some sources say they were an early elocution aid – to show monks how to open their mouths to project their voices. Others say they were used to somehow indicate that a sermon was about to begin inside the church. Also on that wall is a covered cross-shaped opening. Legend suggests that in the 15th century two monks voluntarily immured themselves in the wall in the hope of becoming saints. Until their death, passers-by gave them food and water through this hole. Unfortunately their plan did not succeed, as the pope refused to canonise them on the grounds that their motives were callow.

St Peter's Church (Pētera baznīca) *(19 Skārņu iela; ℡ 735 6699; open 10.00–17.00; 10.00–18.00 in summer, closed Mon)* St Peter's tower is the tallest and arguably the most beautiful church tower in Riga. The gracefully tiered steeple rises to a height of 123.5m and, along with the plainer and shorter towers of the Dome Cathedral and St Jacob's, dominates the Old City skyline. If you like bird's-eye views of cities, you can buy a ticket in the church entrance (Ls1.50) and take the lift up to the observation platform.

As you ascend, you may like to consider the tower's rather chequered career. A wooden tower was originally erected in 1491 but collapsed in 1666, killing the inhabitants of a neighbouring building. The replacement tower, completed in 1690, was badly damaged by lightning in 1721 and had to be reconstructed. When reconstruction was completed in 1746, it is said that the builder climbed to the top, drank a goblet of wine and then threw down the goblet: the number of pieces it shattered into would indicate the number of years the building would stand. Unfortunately, the goblet fell into a passing hay cart and suffered only a minor crack, as you can see for yourself if you visit the Museum of History and Navigation. Disaster struck for the third time, ironically on the feast of St Peter (29 June), in 1941 when

German mortar fire destroyed both the tower and most of the church. Rebuilding took until 1973. Again a glass was thrown down from the top, but this time it shattered into many pieces. Since then, the only threat to the tower occurred in 2000, when a group of National Bolsheviks from Moscow took over the tower in a bid to reassert Soviet dominance after Latvia had regained its independence. Bearing the good omen in mind, visitors can ascend the tower with complete confidence and enjoy a 360° view from the recently renovated observation platform.

The church itself is an excellent example of Gothic architecture. Although first mentioned in records in 1209, only a few sections of the outer walls and some inside pillars remain from the 13th century. The interior style dates mainly from the 15th century, and is impressive in its sheer size and clarity of line. Before 1941 the church housed many religious and art treasures, including a marble pulpit, an oak altar and a magnificent organ. All were destroyed during the war. To commemorate Riga's 800th anniversary in 2001, seven local students made a reconstruction of the oak altar, based on old photographs, and presented it to the church.

St Saviour's (Anglikāņu baznīca) (*Anglikāņu iela 21;* Vf *722 2259; open only for services and concerts*) St Saviour's is Riga's only Anglican church and was built in 1857–59 to serve the English seamen and merchants who came to Riga. The bricks used to build the church were imported from England, as was the layer of soil on which the church was built, although a Riga architect, Johann Felsko, supervised the construction. During Soviet times, the church was used as a discothèque, but was given back to the Church of England when the Archbishop of Canterbury visited Riga in 1994 (see page 111 for a first-hand account of the church in the early days of independence).

BUILDINGS

Guildhalls At the end of Meistaru iela is what used to be the Guild Square but is now known as the Philharmonic Park (*Filharmonijas Parks*). The Great Guildhall (*Lielā Ģilde*) is the large, dull yellow building at one edge of the square, at the corner of Meistaru iela and Amatu iela (Commercial Street). The Small Guildhall (*Mazā Ģilde*) is right next to it on Amatu iela itself. These buildings represent the centres of Riga's former glory as a Hanseatic City. The Great Guildhall was the council chamber of the merchants; the smaller one housed the council of the less influential craftsmen's guilds. The Great Guildhall was originally established in the 14th century, but has undergone substantial changes over the years. Between 1853–60 it was reconstructed in English Tudor style according to designs by Beine and Scheu. The Old Guild Chamber dates back to the 16th century and is decorated with the emblems of the 45 Hanseatic towns. The so-called 'Brides' Chamber' dates back to 1521: until the 19th century it was still used on the wedding night of children of members of the guild or members themselves. However, a great deal of damage was done by a fire in 1963. Now the building is used as a concert hall. The smaller hall was built (in its present form) between 1864–66. It is also sometimes called the St John's Guildhall – notice the statue of St John with a lamb in one corner of the façade under the tower. Now it is used as offices.

Powder Tower The Powder Tower (*Pulvertornis*) is one of the oldest buildings in Riga. Its name is derived from the fact that it was once used to store gunpowder, although at times it was also referred to as the Sand Tower after Smilšu iela (Sand Street), the road that leads past the tower and which was once the main road to Pskov in Russia. Records of the tower can be traced back to 1330. The tower is the sole survivor of what used to be 18 towers that formed part of the city fortifications. Because it was used to store gunpowder it had to be dry, well ventilated and secure,

Frances Samuel

The English Church of St Saviour's, built for the British community in Riga in 1859, had been used in Soviet times as a disco, painted a depressing purple, and was now closed up and empty. A visiting Anglican clergyman, a friend of the then US Ambassador in Riga, offered to hold a communion service in the derelict building. Ten or so of us joined in the first such celebration for 50 years or more, standing in a semicircle in front of a plain wooden table which served as an altar, with a cross made from two wooden poles tied together propped up in a camera tripod, and bread from a local baker's shop. The chalice was an ordinary wineglass we borrowed from the hotel bar. Our vicar had a fine actor's voice, which swept us along as we gave our hesitant and emotional responses; it was an extremely moving experience. Some months later a young American Lutheran minister began to hold regular services. The church in those early days was a lifeline for the tiny group of foreign diplomats, traders, students and others, as well as a few brave Latvians, and one splendid old Russian lady. We would gather after a stressful week, stand in a comforting circle for communion and say the Lord's Prayer together, each in her or his own language. Before we left Riga we got a young Latvian silversmith to put a silver collar on the humble wineglass. It is still sometimes used by the now thriving congregation of the fully re-established Anglican church.

Richard and Frances Samuel reopened the British Embassy in Riga in 1991

hence the walls which are 2.5m thick. They were relatively effective: nine cannonballs are said to be embedded in the walls, relics of the Russian invasions of 1656 and 1710. Only the lower parts of the tower are original. The tower was substantially destroyed by Swedish forces in 1621 and restored in 1650.

Since it ceased to have any military significance, the Powder Tower has been put to various uses. In 1892 it was used as the headquarters of a German student fraternity called Rubonia. After World War I it was turned into a war museum. In 1957 it became the Latvian Museum of the Revolution and functioned as such until independence. Now it houses the War Museum (see page 107).

Reiter House The house at number 2 Mārstaļu iela is the Reiter House (*Reitera nams*), a building that derives its name from another wealthy Riga merchant, Johann von Reiter. The house was built in 1682. Note the six pillars that decorate what appears to be the front of the house but is, in fact, the side. As with the Mentzendorff House, restoration that started around 1980 revealed a large number of wall and ceiling paintings. It is now mainly used for lectures and conferences, but the public are able to see the entrance hall and the balustrade leading to the first floor.

Riga Castle The main building on Pils laukums is Riga Castle (*Rigas pils*), a large cream building with a red roof. The present structure is the last of three which have stood here. Its predecessors were two Livonian castles, the first of which was built in 1330, the second in 1515. The leader of the Livonian Order lived in Riga Castle up to 1470 when his residence was moved, eventually to Cēsis. The people of Riga destroyed the castle in 1487 but were forced to build a replacement by Walter von Plettenberg, the last head of the Livonian Order. It was completed in 1515 and included the so-called Lead Tower (*Svina tornis*) which still stands. The castle was extended in the 18th century by the addition of a new wing which became the residence of the Russian governor, and between 1918–40 that of the President of

Riga **WHAT TO SEE AND DO**

3

Latvia. It also underwent substantial restoration in 1938 which included construction of the 'three stars tower', easily recognised by the three stars on its top. In the early part of the 19th century Wilhelm von Kester built an observatory on the main tower from which Alexander I of Russia observed the solar eclipse of 23 April 1818. Today the castle is once again the residence of the president. It also houses two museums.

The Three Brothers Returning to Lielā pils iela, turn right into Mazā pils iela, heading away from the tower of Riga Castle. The three houses at numbers 17, 19 and 21 Mazā pils iela are known collectively as 'the three brothers' (*Trīs brāļi*). The oldest is the right-hand house with the Germanic step-gable and dates back to the 15th century. It is claimed that it is the oldest domestic building in Riga. Little is known about its history except that in 1687 it is recorded that it was used as a bakery. Numbers 19 and 21 were built later in the 17th and 18th centuries respectively. In 1966 repair work began with a view to restoring the buildings after years of neglect. Number 17 is set back from the street: when it was built there was less pressure on building land in Riga so a small area was left for stone benches to be installed by the main entrance; but by the time the other houses were built land had become more expensive, so they were built closer to the road and with more storeys so as to maximise land use.

MONUMENTS AND STATUES
Riflemen's Memorial (Strēlnieku piemineklis)
The Memorial to the Latvian Riflemen was erected in 1971 to commemorate the valour of the Latvian Rifle Regiment during the civil war. The Riflemen were first known for their courage in fighting on the front near Riga in 1915. Some of the Riflemen also formed Lenin's bodyguard during the 1917 Revolution. During 1917 the Riflemen split into white and red divisions and were caught up on different sides in the struggles of 1918–19: some reds later rejoined the whites and fought against the Germans, but a Latvian Rifleman became the first commander of the Red Army and some reds stayed in Russia and were eventually shot on Stalin's orders in the purges of 1937–38. The statue has long been a subject of strong disagreement. Some see it as an acknowledgement of the bravery of Latvians at the beginning of the civil war, 'a monument to the beginning of the Latvian nation'. Others feel it is too closely allied to the Soviet era and would like it removed and replaced by something more politically neutral.

Monument to the Repressed (Represēto piemineklis)
The work of Latvian sculptor Pēteris Jaunzems and the architect Juris Poga, this monument was unveiled on 14 June 2001 to commemorate the 60th anniversary of one of the largest deportations of Latvians to Siberia. In 1941, over 14,000 Latvians were rounded up and loaded into trains at stations around Latvia, including Torņakalns. Families were split up. Women and children were mainly sent to camps in Siberia, men as slave labour to coal mines in the Arctic Circle or uranium mines in Turkmenistan. The modern monument, which has received criticism as well as praise, stands just outside Torņakalns railway station, south of Uzvaras Park, and can be reached by taking a train heading for Jūrmala or Jelgava from the central station; Torņakalns is the first stop.

Statue of Kārlis Padegs
As you walk along Merķeļa iela opposite the House of the Riga Latvian Society, have a look at the artist who will be lolling stylishly against a railing, most probably adorned by flowers from his admirers. The work of Andris Vārpa, this delightfully informal statue, unusual in Riga, commemorates Kārlis Padegs (born in 1911 and died in 1940 in Riga), an idiosyncratic personality in Riga in the 1930s. Padegs broke with the traditional themes of Latvian painting of his time, preferring instead shocking topics, freely expressed. His anti-war paintings and

frequently ironic approach were frowned on during the Soviet occupation and his work was rarely seen. The monument was presented as a gift in 1998 by Rita Červenaka-Virkavs, a Latvian artist living in Germany. It has been erected on the spot where Padegs once held an open-air exhibition of his works (see page 96).

Freedom Monument (Brīvības piemineklis) The Freedom Monument dominates the centre of Riga. Known locally as 'Milda', it was erected in 1935 and paid for by public subscription. It stands over 350m and is the tallest monument of its kind in Europe. It was designed by the Latvian architect Kārlis Zāle and consists of a tall granite column surmounted by a 9m-high figure of a woman holding three golden stars above her head. The three stars represent the three cultural regions of Latvia – Kurzeme, Vidzeme and Latgale. Engraved in gold letters on the base are the words 'Tevzēmei un brīvībai' ('for fatherland and freedom'). Also decorating the monument is a sculpture of Lāčplēsis, the legendary Latvian bear-slayer, who has long been a symbol of freedom in the country. The monument was dedicated on 18 November 1935, the 17th anniversary of the declaration of independence.

Nowadays the base is often surrounded by flowers, frequently red and white, the colours of the Latvian national flag. Flowers were forbidden during the Soviet era; indeed the Soviet authorities had contemplated removing the monument altogether, since it served as a focus of Latvian nationalistic aspirations, but thought better of the idea, fearing demonstrations and reprisals. Instead they erected a statue of Lenin. The two monuments stood back to back for decades, Lenin facing east towards Moscow, the Freedom Monument facing west. Lenin has now disappeared, but the Freedom Monument remains. The guards who now stand at the monument change every hour on the hour between 9.00 and 18.00.

Monument to the 1905 Demonstrators In the 1905 park in Grīziņkalns, northeast of the New Town, is a monument to commemorate the meeting place of the 1905 demonstrators. It was erected there in 1975 in a park which also includes a stage for musical shows built in 1911. Trolleybus 13 takes you to Pērnavas iela in front of the park.

Statue of Roland Statues of the knight Roland appeared in Hanseatic towns during the 14th and 15th centuries. Erected as symbols of liberty and independence, they were normally displayed prominently in the main square. Riga was no exception: a wooden statue was made and frequently used as a target during jousting matches and tournaments. Not surprisingly, the wooden statue was frequently damaged and then repaired, so in 1896 a stone statue, designed by Wilhelm Neumann and August Volz, replaced it. The knight rests his left hand on a shield bearing the coat of arms of Riga, while in his right hand he holds a sword. It was from the point of this sword that distances from Riga to other places in Latvia were traditionally measured. The statue was damaged in World War II and for many years was not seen in Riga. The original can now be seen in St Peter's Church, while a replica has been placed in the Town Hall Square outside the Blackheads' House.

PARKS AND GARDENS One of the most attractive aspects of Riga is the large amount of green space in the centre. Almost the whole of the area separating the Old Town and the New Town consists of well-tended parks and gardens which are a delight to stroll through whatever the season. In Riga as a whole, parks make up 19% of the total city area, and lake, rivers and canals a further 16%.

Bastejkalns Park The parks on either side of the Freedom Monument were laid out in 1853–63. The one through which Brīvības bulvāris runs is the Bastejkalns Park, named after the 17th-century bastion that once stood here and formed a vital part of Riga's defences. If you walk through Bastejkalns Park you will come across a set of engraved stones near the bridge that crosses the canal (most are on the New Town side, one is on the Old Town side of the canal). On the night of 20 January 1991 Black Beret forces loyal to Moscow attempted to capture a number of government buildings including the Ministry of the Interior on Raiņa bulvāris, the street running alongside the canal on the New Town side. Several Latvians were shot, some say by sniper fire from the rooftops. The stones preserve the memory of five victims: Gvīdo Zvaigne, a cameraman who was filming events; Andris Slapiņš, a cinema director and cameraman; two militiamen, Sergejs Kononenko and Vladimirs Gomanovics; and Edijs Riekstiņš, a student.

The park also contains monuments to the composer Alfrēds Kalniņš and the researcher Keldys.

Kronvalda Park Next to Bastejkalns Park is Kronvalda Park with its monuments to the Latvian writers Edžus and Upīts. Also set in this park are the Riga Congress House (*Rigas kongresu nams*) and a monument to Rūdolfs Blaumanis. A canal runs all the way through Kronvalda Park and behind the National Opera, extending in total for 3km, both starting and finishing in the Daugava, thus ensuring a steady flow of water. In summer a popular pastime is hiring pedal boats and drifting along the canal.

Vērmanes Gardens Bounded by Elizabetes iela, Kr Barona, Merķeļa and Tērbatas iela, the Vērmanes dārzs (as the gardens are called in Latvian) is the most popular of Riga's central parks. Opened in 1817, it was named in honour of the woman who donated the land to the city. Originally it was a refuge for residents of Riga who could not get out to the countryside. It soon acquired attractions, including a bronze fountain cast in Berlin, a playground, an ice rink, a sundial and the first rose garden in Riga. It has an open-air theatre and a statue of Krišjāņis Barons, the writer and poet.

Uzvaras Park (*Walk across Akmens bridge (Akmens tilts) or take the number 2, 4 or 5 tram from 11. Novembra krastmala to the second stop after the bridge across the river*) Uzvaras bulvāris (Victory Boulevard), which leads on from the bridge, heads directly to Uzvaras Park (Victory Park), the largest park in Riga. The plan for the park was made by Georg Kuphaldt in 1909 and, to commemorate 200 years since the incorporation of Riga into the Russian Empire, the park was called after Tsar Peter I. In 1915, while the park was still being completed, Kuphaldt, a German, was expelled from the country along with all his compatriots. A few years later, in 1923, the park was renamed Victory Park (Uzvaras Parks) to commemorate Latvia's liberation from German occupation – somewhat ironically given the fact that the park was so much the work of a German. Today the park is dominated by the Soviet War Memorial, more correctly the monument to the Fallen Soldiers of the Army of the USSR, Liberators of Riga, and the Latvian SSR from the German Fascist Conquerors. Erected in 1985, the monument was paid for by contributions automatically deducted from the pay packets of workers in Riga. Since the restoration of independence, the monument has become something of a rallying point for communists who meet here on former Soviet holidays. In 1996 some men from an extreme right-wing group tried to retaliate by blowing up the monument but succeeded only in killing themselves.

Arcadia Park The smaller Arkādijas Parks (Arcadia Park), which directly adjoins it to the south, was created in 1852 by the Prussian consul general, Wehrmann

(Vērmans), and acquired by the city in 1896. Next to it, Māras dīķis (Mary's Pond) is a popular place of recreation. It derives its name from the mill attached to St Mary's Church which was acquired by the city of Riga in 1573. The pond is probably the old mill-pond and is sometimes referred to as Mary's mill-pond (Māras sudmalu dīķis).

Riga National Zoo (*Meža prospekts 1;* ☏ *751 8669; www.rigazoo.lv; take tram number 11 from Barona iela to the Zooloģiskais dārzs (Zoological Park); takes around 20 minutes; open every day 10.00–18.00*) The zoo, the Baltics' oldest and largest though by no means one of the world's largest, has expanded and improved greatly in recent years and makes a pleasant visit, particularly on a summer day. It is set in the pine forest of the Mežaparks, close to the Ķīšezers lake and next to the Mežaparks garden city. Allow at least two hours to see some of the almost 500 species and over 3,000 animals. Attractions include elephants, camels, bears and ostriches. There are pony rides and other entertainment for children too.

Song Festival Park (Viestura dārzs) (*North of the Old Town, on the corner of Eksporta iela and Hanzas iela*) This was once a much larger park owned by Tsar Peter I and containing plants brought from all parts of Europe. Although it has been remodelled since then, it is a scenic and well-maintained park with the attraction of being well off the beaten track. It has a playground for children and also a decorative feature to commemorate the centenary of the First Latvian Song Festival which was held here in 1873. The memorial consists of several fountains, a wall with portraits of seven Latvian composers and a large memorial stone. The annual Song Festival is no longer held here, but in the large open-air auditorium in the Mežaparks (the Mežaparka estrade).

CEMETERIES Riga has a number of cemeteries that are worth visiting, if time permits, since they reflect something of the history of Latvia and present a number of architectural styles. Three (the Brothers' Cemetery, Rainis Cemetery and Woodlands Cemetery) are close together in an area directly south of Mežaparks. Another two are next to each other, in the same direction but closer to the town centre (the Great Cemetery and Pokrov Cemetery). All can be reached by taking tram number 11 from Barona iela towards Mežaparks. For the Brothers' Cemetery, Rainis Cemetery and Woodland Cemetery alight at the Brāļu Kapi stop. For the Great Cemetery get off at Kazarmu iela. For Pokrov Cemetery alight at the Mēness stop.

The Brothers' Cemetery (Brāļu Kapi) (*Aizsaules iela*) The Brothers' Cemetery or the Cemetery of Heroes is a fascinating ensemble of architecture and sculpture in attractive natural surroundings. It was planned in 1915 when thousands of Latvians were dying in the fight against the Germans in Kurzeme, and the same year the first fallen soldiers were buried here. It took 12 years to complete the cemetery, the overwhelming part of the work being done between 1924 and 1936. There are approximately 2,000 graves in Brāļu Kapi, 300 of them simply marked '*nezinams*' ('unknown'). On 25 March 1988 a memorial service for the victims of the years of the Stalin terror was held here, organised by the Latvian Writers' Association, and 10,000 people attended.

In Latvian folklore the oak symbolises masculine strength, while the lime tree symbolises feminine love; both of these powerful symbols are used extensively in the cemetery. The Latvian coat of arms appears over the entrance gate, while on both sides there are sculpted groups of cavalrymen. An avenue of lime trees leads to the main terrace. In the centre an eternal flame burns, flanked by oak trees. Beyond it is the cemetery itself, bordered by trees, shrubs, bushes and walls decorated with the coats of arms of all the Latvian regions and towns.

Especially moving are the *Levainotais Jatnieks* ('The Wounded Horseman') and *Divi brāļi* ('Two Brothers') sculptures. At one end of the cemetery stands the figure of *Māte Latvijā* ('Mother Latvia') who looks down in sorrow at her dead, a wreath to honour her fallen sons in one hand, in the other the national flag. The sculptures are the work of Kārlis Zāle who is himself buried here.

The cemetery was allowed to fall into neglect during the Soviet period, but was restored in 1993 and has since then become a focus of Latvian national feeling.

Rainis Cemetery (Raiņa Kapi) *(Aizsaules iela)* Latvia's best-loved writer, Jānis Rainis, died on 12 September 1929 and was buried here three days later. The cemetery was renamed in his honour. An avenue of silver birch leads to his grave which is marked by a red granite sculpture. Around the monument there is a semi-circular colonnade entwined with ivy.

Alongside Rainis lies his wife, the poet Aspāzija (Elza Rozenberg who died in 1943). The cemetery is also the resting place for a great number of Latvian writers, artists and musicians, many of whose graves are decorated with a creativity to match the lives they were designed to commemorate.

Woodlands Cemetery (Meža Kapi) *(Aizsaules iela)* Woodlands Cemetery was designed by G Kuphaldt, the director of Riga's parks, in 1913. Numerous political and government figures from the period of Latvia's first independence are buried here, including the former president, Jānis Čakste, and the government ministers, Zigfrids Meierovics and Vilhelms Munters. In addition, a number of Latvian artists, writers, poets and scientists lie here, among them Jānis Rozentāls, Anna Brigadere and Paul Stradin. In April 1988 Latvia's leading human rights activist, Gunārs Astra, was buried here. Astra was sentenced to seven years' imprisonment followed by five years' internal exile by the Soviet regime in December 1983 for the crimes of possessing recordings of radio programmes, photo negatives and subversive books and for writing a manuscript of a personal nature. In his final words to the court he delivered an impassioned speech against the Soviet regime including these words: 'I fervently believe that these nightmare times will end one day. This belief gives me the strength to stand before you. Our people have suffered a great deal but have learned to survive. They will outlive this dark period in their history.'

The Great Cemetery (Lielie Kapi) *(Miera and Senču iela)* The cemetery has lost much of its former glory, many monuments having been removed or badly vandalised in the Soviet era and also in the early 1990s, but it still contains the graves of many of Latvia's best-known citizens, including artists, politicians, scientists and business people. Close to the entrance near Klusā iela is the Green Chapel, the oldest building in the cemetery (1776). Confusingly, it is now a red-brick building, although originally it was a wooden construction painted green and the name has stuck. Graves which may be of interest include a monument to Andrejs Pumpurs (1841–1902), author of the *Lāčplēsis*, the epic poem of Latvia's hero bear-slayer; a large granite pyramid to Patrick Cumming, a Scot who came to Riga in 1777 and later became president of the Riga Stock Exchange; the graves of Krišjānis Barons and Krišjānis Valdemārs; and a memorial, erected in 2001 as part of Riga's 800 years' anniversary celebrations, to the Scot who was mayor of Riga from 1901 to 1912, George Armisted.

Pokrov Cemetery (Pokrova Kapi) *(Mēness, Miera and Senču iela)* Across the road from the Great Cemetery, this Russian cemetery is in even greater need of care and attention. Many of the gravestones are from the 19th century and commemorate Russians who died in Riga while working for the Tsarist government. There is also a large monument dedicated to communist soldiers who fell during and after World War II.

If you are in Riga for only two days, you probably will not want to leave the city itself unless you have a particular interest in other parts of Latvia. If you are there for three days or longer, however, you may well like to take one or more half-day trips, enjoy some of the other attractions of Latvia and gain a broader perspective of the country. Latvia is a small country: everywhere can be reached within a few hours, so in a sense the whole of Latvia is your oyster. The most obvious choices, depending on your interests, are Jūrmala (the seaside area close to Riga), Rundāle (a beautifully restored 18th-century palace close to the Lithuanian border), and a visit to the memorial site of the Salaspils concentration camp.

JŪRMALA Jūrmala is not really a place at all but a name: Jūrmala is the Latvian for 'seaside' or 'by the sea' and is in reality the collective name given to a number of small towns and villages along the Baltic coast about 25km from Riga. The beautiful 30-odd kilometre stretch of beach is virtually unspoilt and is the major attraction of Jūrmala. The Gulf waters are clean enough to swim in (the EU blue flag was awarded in 2000), though not always warm enough, and the beaches and woods are ideal for long walks. Sometimes pieces of amber are washed up on the beach, particularly after a storm. Eating and drinking possibilities are good, and if you don't feel healthy enough to enjoy all this, many of the hotels offer spa treatments and massages. Only one word of warning: in hot weather there are often mosquitoes so be sure to carry around a good insect repellent.

The Jūrmala area first became popular in the late 18th and early 19th centuries, when families began to leave Riga for the summer in search of fresh sea air. Wooden summer houses quickly began to appear just behind the coastline. The first hotel in the area was built in 1834 in Dubulti; in 1870 the first sanatorium (the Marienbāde in Majori) was constructed; and in 1877 the railway line to Tukums was completed, opening the area up to greater numbers than ever. Mixed bathing was permitted in 1881. The sea air, mild climate, spa water and medicinal mud also made the small, growing towns along the coast a favourite with convalescents, so Jūrmala also gained a reputation as a health resort. The resort was developed even further under the Soviet occupation: hotels, convalescent homes, sanatoria and pioneer camps were built from 1945 onwards, transforming Jūrmala into one of the most important holiday resorts in the Soviet Union, attracting over 250,000 visitors a year. Since the restoration of independence, much work has been done to redecorate the many summer houses that give the town its distinctive feel. In 1997 the government declared the area around Ķemeri, at the far end of Jūrmala, to be a national park. The most popular spots are Lielupe (named after the river which in turn means 'big river'), Dzintari ('pieces of amber') and Majori.

Getting there and away You can get to Jūrmala from Riga by train, bus, taxi or car. On summer weekends it can also be reached by boat.

Frequent **trains** depart from platforms 3 and 4 of the central railway station in Riga. It takes about 20 minutes from Riga to the first stop at Lielupe, although not all trains stop there. However, all trains do stop at Majori (about 40 minutes from Riga). Trains are most frequent between May and October (one every 10–20 minutes) and run from about 05.00–23.00. The price is Ls0.20 each way. Note that there is no one station called Jūrmala – it is probably best (unless you have a specific goal) to get out at Majori.

During the summer there are frequent **buses** from the bus station. **Taxis** leave Riga from a special taxi rank just outside the station. There is also a comfortable **minibus** connection between Jūrmala and Riga, running every 20–30 minutes.

Jūrmala is only a 20–30-minute **drive** from Riga. However, as you approach Jūrmala you must pull into the lay-by at the toll point and buy a special ticket to gain access to the area by car. Tickets cost Ls1 a day.

The **boat trip** takes two hours and costs Ls3 one-way for adults and Ls1 one-way for children between six and 12 years old. On Saturdays and Sundays in summer the *Jūrmala* leaves from 11. Novembra krastmala, just next to Vanšu bridge, at 11.00, arriving in Jūrmala at 13.00. The return trip leaves Majori at 17.00, arriving in Riga two hours later. (*For further information,* ☎ *957 8329;* f *734 6515.*)

Museums, churches and buildings

The most popular museum in Jūrmala is probably the **Rainis and Aspāzijas Memorial Summer House** (☎ *776 4295; open Wed–Sun 11.00–18.00; admission Ls0.50*) in Majori. It was here that the writer, Jānis Rainis (1865–1929) had his summer house (at 5–7 J Pliekšāna iela) in which he lived with his wife, the poet Aspāzija, from 1927 until his death on 12 September 1929. The room in which Rainis worked has been left intact: his books, papers and even the woven blanket which his mother made for him all remain; a similar room contains the remaining effects of his wife. The third room was used by their housekeeper. Note too the monument to Rainis and Aspāzija on Jomas iela next to the Jūrmala culture centre; erected in 1990 it is the work of the sculptors Z Fernava-Tiščenko and J Tiščenko.

Also nearby is the **Aspāzija House** (*18/20 Meierovica prospekts, Dubulti;* ☎ *776 9445; open Mon 14.00–19.00; Tue, Wed, Thu, Sat 11.00–16.00; admission Ls0.30*), where Aspāzija (1865–1943) lived the last ten years of her life. It is a small summer cottage, typical of wooden seaside architecture of the early 20th century.

If you are interested in traditional Latvian life, you can visit the **Jūraslīcis Open Air Fishery Museum** (*Jūraslīcis brīvdabas muzejs*) at Buļļuciems, a modest complex of 19th-century wooden buildings at 1 Tīklu iela (☎ *775 1121*). To find the museum watch out for the black anchor on a small pillar of stones, just beyond the Kulturnams in the centre of the village. Tīklu iela takes you to the museum. (*Open 10.00–18.00; admission Ls0.50.*)

Luckily the **Exhibition of Old Machinery** (*11 Turaidas iela, Dzintari,* ☎ *926 3329; open 1 Jun to 31 Aug daily 13.00–19.00*) is more interesting than its name implies. It is mainly a collection of old transport (cars, bicycles etc), although there are also some radio sets. One of the exhibits, a motor carriage called 'Victoria', was owned by the Russian tsar Nikolai II and dates from 1907.

The **Lutheran church at Dubulti**, with its art nouveau elements, plain interior and wooden gallery, used as the Jūrmala Museum of History and Art during the Soviet era, is one of the largest churches in Latvia and its spire is a well-known landmark, visible from the Daugava River. The **Dubulti Orthodox church** (Sv Kņaza Vladimira pareizticigā baznīca) at 26 Strēlnieku prospekts dates back to 1896 and contains some pleasing icons.

In the early 20th century, **Ķemeri** was famous for its medicinal mud cures and attracted people from many parts of northern Europe. Like the spa building itself, the **Ķemeri Hotel** is in the classical style. Built between 1933 and 1936 it is known as the 'white castle' or the 'white ship'. The interior is elegant and spacious, the exterior simple yet imposing. The work of E Laube, it ranks as one of the finest examples of architecture from the first period of Latvian independence. The hotel will reopen in 2007 as the Kempinski Kemeri Palace.

Ķemeri National Park

Ķemeri was established as a national park only in 1997. It covers an area of some 40,000ha, about 50% of it forest, 30% bog or marshland, 10% water and 10% agricultural land. About a quarter of all recorded fauna in Latvia can be found here and over half of Latvia's bird species, including the rare sea eagle and black stork. Also to be found here are beavers, which play an important part in the ecology of the area. The park is accessible to the public only by personal application. (*For further information contact the Information Centre of Ķemeri National Park, Meža Maja, Ķemeri;* \ *773 0078;* f *773 0207;* e *nationalparks@kemeri.gov.lv; www.kemeri.gov.lv.*) To get there take a train to Ķemeri station (see page 70). Alternatively you can take bus number 6 from Sloka or bus number 11 from Lielupe. If you go by car, follow the signs to Jūrmala and continue on the A10 towards Ķemeri.

RUNDĀLE PALACE (\ *396 2197;* f *392 2274;* e *rpm@eila.lv; www.rpm.apollo.lv. Open daily 10.00–17.00 Nov–Apr, 10.00–18.00 May–Sep, and 10.00–19.00 Jun–Aug*) is about 77km south of Riga to the west of Bauska and can easily be visited by car or by coach. Consult your hotel or one of the tour organisers mentioned on page 7 for details of coach trips. If you are travelling by car, the road to Rundāle and Pilsrundāle (P103) is signposted on the right after you cross the bridge travelling south over the River Mūsa, leaving Bauska Castle behind you.

If you visit only the palace, a long half-day (four or five hours) would be sufficient. If you combine it with a visit to Mežotne and/or Jelgava, you would need more or less a full day. There is no need to stay in the area, as you can return to Riga easily. If you wanted to sample life in a Latvian manor house, however, you could overnight at Mežotne.

Rundāle is often billed as the most significant palace in the Baltics. Certainly most visitors will be impressed by its grand exterior, dominating the surrounding flat farmland leading down to the Lielupe River, and the 40 or so sumptuously decorated rooms which have been restored.

Rundāle Palace (*Rundāles Pils*) was built in the 18th century as a summer palace for Ernst Johann von Bühren (Biron in Latvian) by the Italian architect Francesco Bartolomeo Rastrelli. Rastrelli, already established as the architect of the Winter Palace in St Petersburg, began work in 1736 and took five years to finish the task. The interiors were mostly completed later, between 1763 and 1768. Among those who worked on them were Italian painters from St Petersburg and Johann Michael Graff from Berlin, whose work includes the artificial marble wall panelling and the decorative moulding in many rooms.

Why was such a lavish palace built by Rastrelli beyond the Russian borders? The link with Russia was Anna Ioannovna, a niece of Tsar Peter I who, in 1710, married Frederick, Duke of Kurland. During the 1720s Ernst Johann von Bühren, a Baltic-German baron, became her chief adviser, and some say lover also. In 1730, on the death of Peter, Anna became Empress of Russia and delegated much of the management of the empire to a group of German advisers, von Bühren among them. When von Bühren expressed the wish for a summer palace, Anna complied by sending Rastrelli to Kurland and providing all the necessary money and craftsmen, too; nearly everyone involved in the construction – a total of 1,500 craftsmen, artists and labourers – was sent from St Petersburg. Before the palace could be finished, however, Rastrelli began work on another major project, a palace at Jelgava, seat of the Duchy of Kurland. Many of the workmen and the materials needed for Rundāle were transported to Jelgava instead. In 1740, just before Rundāle was completed, Anna died, von Bühren was forced into exile, and the building of the palaces halted. Only in 1763 when the Russian empress Catherine II restored von Bühren to favour, did he return to Kurland and finish the work on Rundāle. The palace was finally completed in 1767, but von Bühren was able to enjoy it for only a short time until his death in 1772. When Russia annexed the Duchy of Kurland in 1795, von Bühren's son, Peter, agreed to leave, taking with him some of the splendid interior items from Rundāle and installing them instead in his properties in Germany. Rundāle itself was given to another favourite of Catherine II, Subov.

Since the incorporation of Kurland into Russia in 1795, the palace has had many uses and owners. Although damaged in the Napoleonic Wars and again during World

War II, the exterior has been repaired and remains fundamentally unaltered from its original design. The interior has not survived so well. Parts of the castle were used as a granary after 1945, and other areas fell into severe disrepair. In 1972, however, the Rundāle Palace Museum was established and major restoration work began. Artists in Leningrad began the restoration of works of art, and they were subsequently joined by experts from Riga, Moscow and Belarus. As a result the 40 or so rooms (out of 138) restored contain many impressive, but few original, works of art. Particularly interesting are the Golden Hall (the throne room), with beautiful ceiling decoration and chandeliers, the Grand Gallery (the banquet room) and the aptly named White Hall (the ballroom), with its intricate stucco. Look out here for the storks! The palace also houses some permanent exhibitions: 'Treasures of the Rundāle Palace', with furniture, porcelain, silverware and paintings, and 'The Time of Misery', an exhibition about Lutheran churches in Latvia during the years of Soviet power.

Behind the palace, the French-style formal garden has been largely reconstructed. It is surrounded by a canal, beyond which are hunting grounds.

On the south side of the palace is a formal baroque garden, still being reconstructed. A restaurant in the palace is used for formal receptions, and is a favourite place for weddings.

SALASPILS To reach Salaspils by car take the A6 south towards Ogre and look out for the large granite sign 'Salaspils 1941–44'. Take a train heading southeast for Ogre, Lielvārde or Aizkraukle and alight at the Dārziņa stop. A single ticket costs Ls0.28. Then follow the footpath for about 15 minutes. The tourist office advises that visitors should not walk this footpath alone.

First mentioned as a settlement in 1186 it is a place associated with war, death and destruction. The battle of Salaspils of 1605 delayed the Swedes from gaining a foothold in Latvia. Some 12,000 Swedes under the leadership of Charles IX attacked a Lithuanian unit of about 4,000 men but were repulsed: only about a quarter of the Swedish army managed to retreat to their ships in Riga.

Now, however, it is remembered largely as the site of the Nazi concentration camp, Kurtenhof. Built in 1941 during the Nazi occupation of Latvia in World War II, the camp operated for three years. In 1944, as the Red Army approached Riga, the camp guards and administrators ordered the inmates to exhume and burn the thousands of bodies buried at the camp; it then was burnt to the ground by the retreating Nazis in an attempt to hide the atrocities committed there. Over 100,000 men, women and children, most of them Jews, were put to death here, among them Austrians, Belgians, Czechs, Dutch, French, Latvian, Polish and Soviet citizens. Today, lines of white stones mark the perimeter of the camp.

The Salaspils memorial, which now dominates the site of the former camp, was erected in 1967 to honour those who died there. A huge concrete wall in the shape of a long beam marks the position of the former entrance; symbolising the border between life and death, it bears the words of the Latvian writer, Eižēns Vēveris (a prisoner at Salaspils): '*Aiz šiem vārtiem vaid zeme*' ('Beyond these gates the earth moans'). You can actually walk the length of the wall inside it – there is a door at each end. A series of steps takes you through a number of gloomy rooms, giving the impression of a mausoleum. There is also a small exhibition with photographs of the camp. The seven sculptures which stand in the grounds behind the wall evoke the suffering but also the spirit of defiance and resistance of those imprisoned and killed.

The stillness of Salaspils is broken only by the ticking of an underground metronome beneath the altar-like structure located to the left as you enter the grounds. The noise of the ticking is a reminder of the lives spent and ended here. A narrow path leads through the woods to the place where the prisoners were executed.

4

Vilnius

Lithuania is a Baltic state and Vilnius is its capital. Yet Vilnius is unlike the other 'Baltic capitals' in a number of ways. It is 200 miles from the Baltic Sea and its true links have always been south and west. Links to the north and east have always been imposed, and never voluntarily undertaken. It has in its past been the capital of much more than what is now Lithuania; in the 15th century its boundaries stretched to the Black Sea and the country was 18 times as large as that within its current borders. In later centuries it has suffered as much as Riga and Tallinn, but usually under different occupiers and at different times. Only World War II and the subsequent occupation forced an artificial bond over the three capitals.

If you catch Vilnius on a hot summer's day, you may feel as though you are in southern Europe rather than in the north, with light pastel colours on most façades in the Old Town and an exuberant baroque church staring out from every corner. Shade can be as important as sunshine. Wine is as perfectly natural to drink here as beer, and it is not essential to race back to work after lunch.

The Tsarist and then Soviet rulers from Russia have left an architectural legacy, but it is fortunately far less obvious in the town centre than in Warsaw, Riga, Tallinn or in the other major Lithuanian cities. Like the people, the architecture is sedate.

The 19th- and 20th-century political, religious and military history of Vilnius has been well concealed and perhaps this is just as well; only since 1990 have the population been aware of it. In 1985 three researchers rediscovered the Vilnius Cathedral Treasury that had been hidden since 1939. So frightened were they that the treasures would be taken to Moscow, that only in 1998, when they felt absolutely certain of Lithuanian independence, did they reveal their discovery.

Preliminary work for a new bridge across the Neris which was started in 2000 revealed a hoard of coins that had been hidden from the Swedes before their occupation of Vilnius in 1702. In 2001 two different mounds of bones were discovered; one was from the French soldiers who died in Vilnius during the retreat from Moscow in 1812 and the other from Russian soldiers killed in the recapture of the city from the Germans in 1944. By 2003, excavations revealed the execution chambers at the KGB headquarters where hundreds of Lithuanian patriots were secretly killed in the late 1940s. A few years earlier the Nazis had carried out their executions in the forest at Paneriai, sufficiently far from the town not to be seen and where the evidence could be more easily concealed.

The most recent tragedy to take place in Vilnius was on 13 January 1991 when the Soviet army killed unarmed civilians guarding the Television Tower. This was in front of the world's media and the exposure has probably ensured that Lithuanian independence will never be threatened again. Contemporary Vilnius fights its internal political battles through the media and no longer on the streets. A whole generation has now grown up with no recollection of this past, or of queues, censorship or military service in distant parts of the USSR. Tourists can ignore this past if they wish, but will probably be able to appreciate the present more if they realise the background against which it has arisen.

Fortunately contemporary Vilnius now shows off rather than hides. Tourists may wear torn jeans at an opera or be happy to drive a car 20 years old. Do not expect such behaviour from local people. At 15.00 in an office or at 03.00 in a nightclub, expect them to take care about their appearance and similar care about their surroundings. If you witness raucous behaviour late at night, it will be from tourists taking advantage of the cheap beer, not locals on a regular weekend binge.

In early 2005, Vilnius was awarded the accolade of European Capital of Culture for 2009, which it will share with Linz as the award will by then be shared between a city in 'old' Europe and one in the 'accession' states. Yet Vilnius is as 'old' and as 'European' as any other contenders for this award, in fact in many respects more so. Younger visitors will find it hard to believe that from 1945 until 1990, the only way to travel abroad from Vilnius was by plane via Moscow and that this was a privilege granted to very few local people indeed. The few foreigners who came in the other direction were allowed only three nights there, in case they stayed long enough to 'contaminate' the local population with counter-revolutionary thoughts. Travel outside the city was forbidden.

Now Vilnius is firmly back where it belongs. There are four flights a day to London, but only one a day to Moscow. Dozens of coaches a day drive tourists, students and labourers to Poland and Germany. Very few bother to drive the 100 miles east to Minsk, or the rather longer distances to Kaliningrad or St Petersburg. It is almost impossible to find goods produced in Russia in the shops.

Visitors who delay their visit to Vilnius until the end of the decade will see some of the few aspects of Western life which were still missing in 2005. In the outskirts, garden cities will slowly replace blocks of flats. Skyscrapers there will certainly be, and some were completed as early as 2004, including the shiny new town hall over the river from the Old Town. It will soon just be one of many, as a former sleazy area of town becomes the business centre of the whole country. Stricter parking regulations in the Old Town will give more space to pedestrians. Commuters will come in on smooth-running trams rather than on bumpy trolleybuses. A town bypass will have removed unnecessary lorries from the suburbs and some of the smart Old Town restaurants will have moved to the shopping malls which cater to the burgeoning middle classes. What visitors really want, however, is going to remain – a different walk on their doorstep whenever they leave a hotel, cuisine from any country in Europe that can claim to have one, a choice of music every night from the most reverential to the most outrageous and an artistic legacy as strong in the façades of its buildings as what they display inside.

Visitors are unlikely to see any signs in Polish or Russian. Lithuanian has finally become the dominant language, which shows how far in the past the role of these former masters is. When the local shops start to take the euro, likely to be in 2008, the country's policy of closer integration with its Western neighbours will, for the first time in centuries, have been decided in Vilnius, and not in Moscow, Warsaw, Paris or Berlin.

HISTORY

The main avenue in Vilnius has had several names over the past 100 years – Stalin Avenue, Lenin Avenue and, under the tsars, St George's Avenue, to name but three. The current name, Gedimino Avenue, is, of course, the only appropriate one, being in honour of the man considered to be the founder of the city, Grand Duke Gediminas. The place where the bubbling little River Vilnia meets the broad River Neris is known to have been inhabited since at least the Bronze Age. We know that in the 11th century a castle made of wood stood where the Higher Castle now stands. But it was Gediminas who provided the first known written record of the city, in a letter dated

1323 inviting German merchants, craftsmen and farmers to settle in and around his city, which he had raised to the status of capital, offering them exemption from taxes and freedom of worship.

A popular local legend about the birth of Vilnius tells how Gediminas was on a hunting trip with his entourage around these heavily wooded hills when he decided to set up camp rather than return to his castle at Trakai. During the night he dreamed of a huge iron wolf standing on the hill, howling the howl of a hundred wolves. He consulted a pagan priest about the dream, who told him that it was a sign to build a great fortress and city there. The howling meant that the future city's fame would spread far and wide.

In truth, it was certainly Gediminas who transferred the court from Trakai to Vilnius around the year 1320. At the time Vilnius was already a bustling trading centre with German and Russian communities who had their own churches, even though the country itself remained pagan. The Teutonic Order made frequent and bloody raids on the country, but Gediminas managed to put off any major incursions by promising repeatedly to convert to Christianity – which he never did. While he procrastinated with the West, he expanded the emerging Lithuanian empire to the south and east as far as Ukraine.

In time the threat from the Crusaders became more acute; Vilnius was attacked seven times between 1365 and 1402. More protective fortifications and two more castles were built. The pagan state finally succumbed to Christian conversion when Grand Duke Jogaila initiated a 400-year common history between Lithuania and Poland through marriage. This failed to stop the relentless assaults of Teutonic Knights, however, and it was not until the Battle of Žalgiris in 1410 that Grand Duke Vytautas dealt them a blow from which they never recovered. Vytautas also annexed many Ukrainian and Russian lands, pushing the Lithuanian empire all the way to shores of the Black Sea.

Vilnius flourished for the next 200 years, in a period of growth and prosperity it has never seen since. New roads extended the city in all directions, while Slavs, Jews and Tatars settled in large numbers. The city's first synagogue was built in the 16th century. The Union of Lublin in 1569 further strengthened the bond with Poland, creating a huge unified state, or commonwealth. Vilnius lost its administrative role and Polish dominated as the official language, but the arrival of the Jesuits that same year resulted in a construction boom in the new baroque style of architecture, much of it sponsored by a small number of powerful noble families. A college that the Jesuits founded became a university in 1579, which soon earned itself a reputation as one of Europe's great academic institutions. Meanwhile, the role played by the Roman Catholic Church in the life of the city strengthened.

War and plague followed, however, bringing destruction and decline to this city of 30,000. As the might of Muscovy grew, the commonwealth failed to hold off a powerful invasion in 1655. Cossacks plundered Vilnius for weeks, destroying Catholic and Jewish buildings, wreaking anarchy and terrorising inhabitants. Almost half of the city's population was lost to plague which hit the city in 1657–58, while the rampaging Russians were not driven out until 1660. But, surprisingly, Vilnius recovered quickly. Magnificent baroque churches, chapels, mansions and palaces were built over the coming decades and, despite the city being attacked and occupied by both Russian and Swedish armies in the early 18th century, as well as being devastated by more fires and plague, many have survived to this day.

The long, steady decline of the Polish–Lithuanian Commonwealth resulted in a third and final partition in 1795, in which Vilnius, now a city of 20,000, and most of Lithuania became part of Tsarist Russia. Hopes for independence were briefly revived when Napoleon stormed through Europe and captured Vilnius in 1812 and in the 19 days he spent in the city he set up a provisional national government. But, six

A MacCullum Scott

Late in the evening of 21 June 1924 I arrived in Vilna. It was the eve of St John's Day, the great pagan midsummer festival throughout the Baltics. Fires were lit beside the river, small boats decorated with lanterns and bearing festive parties were rowed up and down stream. The sound of music and singing floated over the water. From the midst of the city, outlined against the pale northern sky, rose abruptly the Hill of Gedimin like an altar to the ancient gods of the Lithuanian race.

Vilna is now, by the turn of the international kaleidoscope, part of the Republic of Poland, but there has been no revolutionary change in social manners. The old formalities of address still continue. The hotel porter and the barefooted chambermaid both addressed me as 'Barin' or lord. 'Would the Barin like some hot water? Will the Barin be wearing his coat?' It is an old, old work in Vilna.

My hotel was in Adam Michevicius Street, named after the national poet of Poland who was a native of Lithuania and a student at the University of Vilna. The next street on the right was Jagellon Street, named after the Grand Duke who united the thrones of Lithuania and Poland. I passed a 'Kultur' shop, in the window of which was displayed a large map showing the extent of the former territories of Poland and Lithuania, stretching from the Baltic to the Black Sea. The new generation in Vilna feeds its soul upon dreams of the past.

Some day Europe will rediscover Vilna. At present few people in western Europe know that this is a bone of contention between Poland and Lithuania and that it is impossible to make out whether it is inhabited by Poles, Lithuanians, Russians or Jews. To discover Vilna is to revisit an ancient civilisation which has for centuries been buried under the debris of later and barbarous regimes. However, the Vilna that now emerges is no city of the dead. It fills its lungs with the exhilarating air of freedom. It is full of energy, zeal and effort as if it were determined to make up for the years which have been lost. Europe must learn that Vilna has a personality and that it is a very vivid one.

From 'Beyond the Baltic' by A MacCullum Scott, published in 1925

months later, a decrepit Grand Armée, beaten at Berezina and frozen by the Russian winter, staggered back to Vilnius with mounted Cossacks hot on their heels. Some 40,000 of Napoleon's soldiers died in Vilnius from starvation, cold or under the Cossacks' swords, most of them bundled into mass graves and church crypts.

The people of Vilnius continued to struggle for independence. Resistance was especially rife at Vilnius University, which paid a harsh penalty for its participation in a rebellion in 1831. It was closed the following year, a measure that would stay in effect right up until Lithuania finally won back its freedom 90 years later. Catholic churches were closed or converted to the Russian Orthodox faith. The Russian authorities even considered changing the name of the city to Chortovgorod ('city of devils'). After hanging the rebels of a second rebellion in 1864 on Lukiškių Square, a ban was imposed on written Lithuanian and street names were changed to Russian ones.

Like other European cities, Vilnius now thrived as a zone of industry. Its population swelled to more than 150,000 by the end of the 19th century, with Russians arriving in large numbers. The city also thrived as a centre of Jewish culture and learning in Yiddish, becoming known as the 'Jerusalem of the North', though the community remained very much cut off from the rest of society. The proportion of Lithuanians shrank, so that by 1904 the authorities could see no danger in lifting the ban on their language. Books, newspapers and cultural organisations quickly encouraged national awareness at a time when feelings of national identity were on the rise throughout Europe. In December 1905, a 'Great Seimas' of 2,000 Lithuanians demanded greater autonomy and the use of Lithuanian in schools. The latter demand was granted.

Nine years later war was once again unleashed on Europe. The mighty German army stormed eastwards and in late 1915 the Russians abandoned Vilnius, which now had a population of 235,000. A new Lithuanian Council was formed, which began negotiations with the Germans for full independence, a goal that was reached in a declaration on 16 February 1918. Chaos reigned, however, and in the scuffles at the end of the war the Bolshevik army and the Polish army each held the city twice and Lithuania once. Lithuania's possession of the city was agreed to on all sides on 7 October 1920, but two days later the Polish army marched north and retook it, an action secretly backed by the Polish leader Jozef Pilsudski, who had been born near Vilnius. When Pilsudski died 15 years later, his wishes were that his body should be buried in Warsaw, but that his heart should be cut out and buried in Vilnius. His heart lies today encased in his mother's tomb in Rasų Cemetery.

After a period of lacklustre international mediation, the League of Nations put Vilnius on the Polish side of a demarcation line in 1922. Lithuania protested by stressing the city's historic role as its former capital, but its appeals fell on deaf ears. In a characteristic display of persistence, the newly independent nation retaliated early in 1923 by seizing Memel (Klaipėda), then under League of Nations supervision, giving it a vitally needed port on the Baltic Sea. Under Polish control, Vilnius's economy and importance declined while Kanuas developed quickly as the new Lithuanian capital. Lithuanian cultural activities in Vilnius were curbed, mass was allowed only in Polish and many ethnic Lithuanians moved to Kaunas.

In March 1939, Hitler was given his last bloodless conquest when Nazi Germany took Klaipėda. The carve-up of eastern Europe that resulted from the Molotov–Ribbentrop Pact of 23 August 1939 initially consigned a helpless Lithuania to the German sphere of influence. But when Lithuania refused to attack Poland as a German ally, a second secret pact signed in Moscow on 27 September transferred it to the Soviet sphere. On 10 October, while Soviet military bases were being established within the country, Vilnius was returned to Lithuania. Occupation, then annexation, followed in June 1940. On 14 June 1941 the first Soviet deportations were carried out and 35,000 people were sent to the frozen wastes of Siberia. Most did not survive the first winter.

On 22 June the Nazis surprised Stalin by launching Operation Barbarossa. Within two days they were in Vilnius. With the Nazi occupation of 1941–44 came the murder of 95% of the country's pre-war Jewish population of 300,000 people. Since Jews made up 40% of the population of Vilnius, this meant that virtually half the city was systematically eliminated, mostly in the Paneriai Forest close to the city. Only one German officer rebelled against this policy, Major Karl Plagge, who probably saved about 1,000 Jews during this time. In April 2005 he was posthumously awarded Israel's 'Righteous Amongst the Nations' honour for his courage.

The war ended with a second Soviet occupation of Vilnius, one that was to last almost 50 years. Demographic changes continued. Tens of thousands of Lithuanians had fled westwards to escape the clutches of the Soviets. With Vilnius now in the Soviet Union, many Poles moved west and there were further deportations to Siberia – about 130,000 between 1944 and 1953, including a third of the clergy. Armed resistance and guerilla warfare took place against Soviet rule throughout the Baltic countries, but by Stalin's death in 1953 this had been brutally crushed. However, as more Russians and migrant Lithuanians arrived in Vilnius, the city's population started to grow again.

Vilnius remained the capital of occupied Lithuania. Churches were closed to become warehouses and car repair garages, then later, during the Khrushchev era, some became art galleries and museums. Grey suburbs of factory-made housing blocks

THE END OF AN ERA

Vytautas Landsbergis

The Soviets had decided to act without delay, and a terrible slaughter took place on the streets of Vilnius that night. The disturbance began just after midnight when Soviet tanks and armoured troop carriers loaded with special KGB riot troops came roaring through our streets. They drove straight to predetermined destinations; their orders were to seize the radio and television studios as well as the television tower which stands on the outskirts of Vilnius. As they followed their instructions, the people responded to their manoeuvres and a sequence of events followed which stirred the conscience of the world. Some people had already kept vigil at the television facilities for several days and nights, and now others hurried through darkened streets, often passing the cumbersome tanks as they lurched slowly forward. When they reached the threatened buildings, they linked hands and began to sing the old folk songs of Lithuania or shouted slogans such as 'Lithuania will be free'. Soon they heard bullets passing over their heads as automatic rifles and machine guns swung into action. According to standard Soviet calculations, the crowd should have been scattered under this onslaught, but they did not move and so the strategy was changed with shots being direct at people's legs and then at their bodies. Back at the Supreme Council, I learned what was going on and immediately summoned the deputies to a rally in Parliament. Most responded without delay, and as they assembled, they witnessed the volunteer defenders inside the building gathering together to take the oath of allegiance afresh. Many of them went on to make their confessions, in grim recognition of what we might all soon be facing. Our defenders had no other weapons than a few pistols and rifles, sticks and petrol bombs.

The most difficult hours still lay ahead of us. Long before dawn on 13 January, the local hospitals began to overflow with the dead and injured. Because Vilnius TV was now in Soviet hands, the Kaunas station replaced it as our chief means of disseminating information. We remained in Parliament awaiting an onslaught. I asked the women to leave us, but they all refused. I then addressed the crowd surrounding the Parliament buildings, imploring them to move away to avoid casualties, but I received the same response. Everyone then knew exactly what to expect, but they all refused to move. Their heroism was unflinching, and later I was told that some had even been angry that I had urged them to leave. I had prepared a videoed speech, which could be transmitted if we were killed. In it, I gave careful directions for a campaign of passive resistance and suggestions about how life could be made difficult for our enemy under a new occupation. Fortunately this did not come about, because the assault ended at daybreak, and although the threat was not over, it was never repeated on that scale. It was a people's victory in the best sense. Indeed, a cynical KGB officer was later overheard to say: 'We did not attack the Parliament because of the excess flesh surrounding it.'

From 'Lithuania, Independent Again' by Vytautas Landsbergis. The author, who would subsequently become President and then Speaker, describes the night of 12–13 January 1991 in Vilnius.

were constructed for the growing numbers of workers. Most Lithuanians managed to find work within the system, whether in collective farming on nationalised land or in the industrialised city. Initially, the institutions of power such as the Communist Party, the government and the KGB were in Russian hands, but gradually, as the years passed, more and more college graduates joined the Party knowing that this would further their careers. However, underground publications also began to appear, particularly in the 1970s, the most significant being the *Chronicle of the Catholic Church in Lithuania*. It was smuggled abroad under the noses of the KGB for 20 years and was never discovered.

When Mikhail Gorbachev tried to stop the stagnation of the Brezhnev years by introducing greater openness, a group of Lithuanian cultural figures and academics set up the Sajūdis national movement in 1988 to push for further discussion about the past. As popular support quickly grew, its leaders began to speak of independence, a full declaration of which came on 11 March 1990. Lithuania was the first Soviet republic to do so.

The move was met by Moscow imposing a tense economic blockade. Then, while the attention of the world was focused on the Gulf, came a night of orchestrated violence as Soviet tanks ran through a crowd of unarmed Lithuanian civilians protecting the Vilnius Television Tower on 13 January 1991, resulting in 14 deaths.

Three weeks later, Iceland became the first country of many to recognise Lithuanian independence. The crumbling Soviet empire fell that August.

Once again Vilnius is the proud capital of an independent country that is today part of the European Union and NATO. Since independence, a succession of dynamic, at times controversial mayors has generated local, national and international funds to restore the Old Town, which was declared a UNESCO World Heritage Site in 1994. Since 2003 a new city of glass-fronted skyscrapers has risen over the river. Whilst friends of Vilnius would argue that the city's selection for the coveted European Capital of Culture award for 2009 was an obvious choice, this did not come about without the serious and long-term planning put into the town's submission by the municipal authorities. The private sector too has shown its confidence in Vilnius. Hardly any major Western company does not have representation there and the number of outside investors in the hotel and construction businesses shows a long-term worldwide commitment to its continuing success.

SUGGESTED ITINERARIES

DAY ONE Start with half a day beside the cathedral (page 163). A visit here, and then to the National Museum (page 152) and the Applied Arts Museum (page 159), will immediately show how close the town's links have been with cultures to the south rather than with those to the north, above all with the Catholic Church. By 2009, there will be another attraction here, immediately behind the cathedral, and this is the rebuilt Royal Palace where work started in 2003. Weather permitting, the journey on the funicular railway to the top of the castle will give a view of Vilnius that reflects each of its conquerors and now the planning policies of a totally independent Lithuania. Note Gedimino Avenue which starts at the cathedral and which is now a pedestrian precinct during the evening. Perhaps take lunch on the corner at Literata, no longer a dissident intellectual café, but more a substantial Nordic restaurant.

After lunch, walk along Universiteto to, of course, the university (page 129) and wander in its courtyards and St John's Church (page 166), now fully recovered from its 40 years of Soviet desecration. Do not forget to visit the bookshop, Littera. The book selection (in English) is fine but even finer is the artistry on its ceiling. Finish at the Picture Gallery (page 163) and see how extensively Lithuanian artists were able to travel in the 19th century and also how they portrayed Vilnius itself. Many of the local buildings shown are still perfectly recognisable today.

Be sure to take in an early evening concert (page 147), preferably in a church so that the music can be enjoyed in the environment for which it was probably written.

DAY TWO The KGB Museum (page 161) probably deserves a half-day to itself, as some time is needed for reflection afterwards. Perhaps it is just as well that it is situated a few

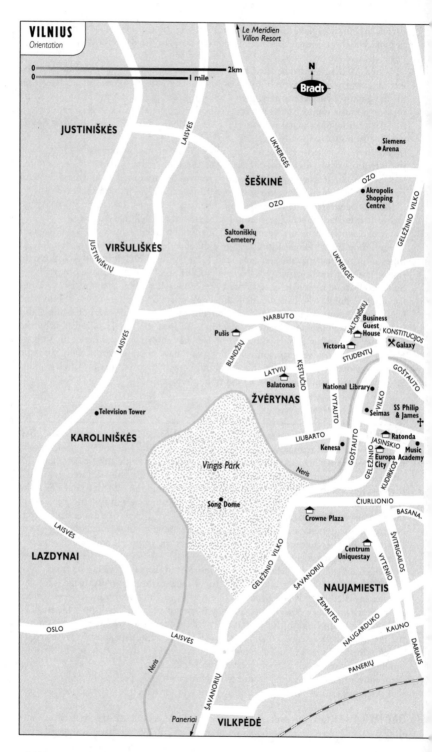

VILNIUS
Orientation

0 ─────────────── 2km
0 ─────────────── 1 mile

Le Meridien
Villon Resort

N
Bradt

JUSTINIŠKĖS

LAISVĖS

UKMERGĖS

ŠEŠKINĖ

OZO

Siemens
Arena

OZO

Akropolis
Shopping
Centre

GELEŽINIO VILKO

JUSTINIŠKIŲ

VIRŠULIŠKĖS

Saltoniškių
Cemetery

UKMERGĖS

LAISVĖS

NARBUTO

SALTONIŠKIŲ

Business
Guest
House

KONSTITUCIJOS

Pušis

BLINDŽIŲ

KĘSTUČIO

Victoria

STUDENTŲ

Galaxy

LATVIŲ

Balatonas

ŽVĖRYNAS

VYTAUTO

National Library

VILKO

Seimas

GOŠTAUTO

SS Philip
& James

Television Tower

KAROLINIŠKĖS

Vingis Park

LIUBARTO

Kenesa

GOŠTAUTO

JASINSKIO

GELEŽINIO

Europa
City

Ratonda

Music
Academy

KUDIRKOS

Neris

ČIURLIONIO

BASANA.

Song Dome

Crowne Plaza

ŠVITRIGAILOS

LAISVĖS

GELEŽINIO VILKO

Centrum
Uniquestay

VYTENIO

ŠAVANORIŲ

LAZDYNAI

ŽEMAITĖS

NAUJAMIESTIS

OSLO

LAISVĖS

NAUGARDUKO

KAUNO

DARIAUS

Neris

ŠAVANORIŲ

PANERIŲ

Paneriai

VILKPĖDĖ

128

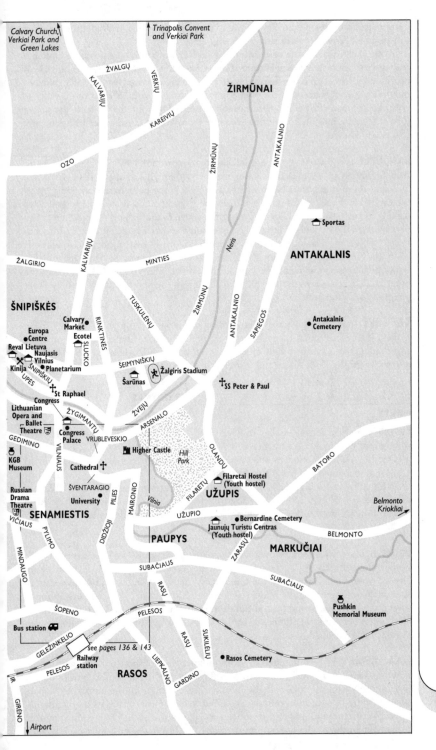

Calvary Church,
Verkiai Park and
Green Lakes

↑ Trinapolis Convent
and Verkiai Park

ŽVALGŲ

VERKIŲ

KALVARIJŲ

ŽIRMŪNAI

KAREIVIŲ

OZO

ANTAKALNIO

Neris

□ Sportas

ŽALGIRIO

KALVARIJŲ

MINTIES

ANTAKALNIS

ŠNIPIŠKĖS

TUSKULĖNŲ

ŽIRMŪNŲ

RINKTINĖS

Calvary
Market ●

● Antakalnis
Cemetery

Europa
● Centre
Reval Lietuva
● Naujasis
Vilnius

Ecotel

SLUCKO

ANTAKALNIO

SAPIEGOS

ŠEIMYNIŠKIŲ

Kinija
SNIPIŠKIŲ
● Planetarium

† Žalgiris Stadium

UPĖS

† St Raphael

⛪ Šarūnas

† SS Peter & Paul

ŽVEJŲ

Congress
Lithuanian
Opera and
Ballet
Theatre

ŽYGIMANTŲ

● Congress
Palace

ARSENALO

OLANDŲ

BATORO

GEDIMINO

VILNIAUS

VRUBLEVESKIO

🏰 Higher Castle

Hill
Park

☕ KGB
Museum

Cathedral †

□ Filaretai Hostel
(Youth hostel)

Belmonto
Kriokliai ↘

Russian
Drama
Theatre

ŠVENTARAGIO

FILARETŲ

UŽUPIS

● University

MAIRONIO

PILIES

Vilnia

BELMONTO

VIČIAUS

SENAMIESTIS

DIDŽIOJI

UŽUPIO

● Bernardine Cemetery

PYLIMO

PAUPYS

ZARASŲ

Jaunujų Turistų Centras
(Youth hostel)

MARKUČIAI

SUBAČIAUS

MINDAUGO

SUBAČIAUS

ŠOPENO

SUBAČIAUS

RASŲ

Pushkin
Memorial Museum

Bus station 🚌

PELESOS

GELEŽINKELIO

RASŲ

SUKILĖLIŲ

See pages 136 & 143

LIEPKALNO

Railway
station

RASOS

● Rasos Cemetery

PELESOS

GARDINO

IR

GRĖNO

↓ Airport

hundred yards from anywhere else likely to be of interest. During 2006 it is expanding to exhibit all facets of life during the Soviet era.

Town Hall Square is the base for enjoying several of Vilnius' best-known churches and is also where the Kazys Varnelis House Museum (page 162) is situated. He is probably Lithuania's most generous benefactor, having returned from his US exile not only with a wide variety of his own paintings but also with an even more valuable collection of maps, first editions, furniture and china. Do not forget to leave the square for a short walk into the former Jewish quarter where each passing year brings further restoration and colour.

DAY THREE It is time now to be outdoors some more. See why Napoleon fell for St Anne's Church (page 165) on his hurried forays through Vilnius in 1812. Cross the bubbling River Vilnia into Užupis (page 157) where the poor have been replaced by the capital's most successful people and also by its most amusing (1 April is the day to see it at its best). Read the Užupis constitution nailed to the wall on Paupio Street, then visit some of the 'republic's' little galleries. Finish the morning at the Amber Museum (page 159) before relaxing over lunch at one of the many tasteful cafés along Pilies.

In the afternoon, walk along the river to St Peter and St Paul (page 167), undoubtedly the most flamboyant of all the churches in Vilnius. Return along the other bank to see New Vilnius arising, literally, given the number of skyscrapers either complete or being built.

DAY FOUR It is a pity to leave Vilnius, but a day around the Island Castle in Trakai (page 175), or in Kaunas (page 171) should not be missed. The architecture and the surrounding nature are so totally different, as is the pace of life. History has maintained a stronger grip in both places and it should be enjoyed.

PRACTICALITIES

MONEY

Currency In 1993 Lithuania re-introduced its pre-war currency, the litas (abbreviated throughout this book as Lt), which is divided into 100 centas.

On the re-introduction of the currency, the exchange rate was fixed at 4Lt to US$1, and remained pegged at that level until 2002, when it was replaced by a similar fixed link, that of 3.45Lt to €1. In 2006 the UK pound was worth around 5.00Lt and the US dollar around 2.80Lt. This fixed exchange rate to the euro is scheduled to remain in place until Lithuania formally joins the single European currency, probably in 2008.

Banks Banks throughout Estonia and Latvia, and also those in Poland near to the border, also sell litas. An exchange office, with good rates, is always open at Vilnius airport when flights arrive and the one situated between the bus and railway stations is open 24 hours a day. Those in the town centre tend to keep to office hours, although several do open on Saturdays and Sundays. Unlike in Estonia and Latvia, rates vary very little between the different banks and exchange offices, no matter which currency is exchanged.

LOCAL MEDIA Visitors interested in recent political news from the Baltic area should buy the *Baltic Times*, which is published in Riga every Thursday and is usually on sale in Vilnius the same afternoon. It also lists concerts and films for the next week. *Vilnius Monthly* started publication only in 2005, but it has quickly made its mark amongst the expat community. However, its articles on culture and history lack context and are really only for those who live in Vilnius. *VilniusNOW!* also started publication in 2005, following the success of a similar monthly magazine in Riga. It is distributed in hotels and concentrates on dining and entertainment. It also has informative business features. The opening of an office for it in Vilnius should ensure that all major hotels will stock copies.

The bi-monthly *Vilnius In Your Pocket* has built up for itself a legendary status since it started in 1992; it became immediately notorious for the sharpness of its pen in the face of bland service, unimaginative décor and tepid food. As standards have improved so much since then, it can usually adopt a more positive tone, but it remains as harsh as ever about the places that still deserve it.

Travellers also planning to visit Riga or Tallinn should try to find the bi-monthly *City Paper*. Its reviews of hotels and restaurants are detailed and in a part of the world not known for lively political and artistic writing, it provides the perfect one-stop shop for English-speaking readers wanting an instant briefing on all the major local issues and attractions.

A few copies of the European editions of British and American daily newspapers are on sale in hotels that cater for business travellers but visitors should not rely on this. No local daily newspaper appears in English nor do local TV stations transmit in English but hotel televisions can nearly always receive BBC World and CNN.

COMMUNICATIONS

Telephone To reach a landline within Vilnius, just dial the seven-digit number. If phoning from elsewhere in Lithuania, use first the prefix 8 which is used for all out-of-town numbers and then the Vilnius code 5 before the seven-digit number. All mobile numbers have nine digits and these are prefixed with 8, wherever the call is made. Phoning Lithuania from abroad, remember the country prefix of 370 which is followed by the city code and then the local number. For mobiles, the 370 country prefix is followed by 8.

Costs for phone calls made from hotel rooms vary enormously. Some hotels have deliberately reduced their charges to try to persuade guests not to use their mobiles. Others have left them at the absurdly high rates of the 1990s. Phone boxes take only cards which can be bought at any kiosk. They are issued in sums of 9Lt, 13Lt and 30Lt. Expect to pay about 2Lt a minute to phone Britain or the USA from these boxes, which are increasingly rare in Vilnius as mobiles take over the communications market.

Mobile phone users wanting to avoid roaming costs can of course buy a SIM card for use within their phone. Prices change in this field all the time but local calls should cost only the equivalent of a few pence and international ones about 40p/US$0.75 a minute, so similar to the charges payable in a public phone box.

Useful telephone numbers

Fire	01	Directory enquiries	118
Police	02	International calls	1573
Ambulance	03		

Post The main post office is at Gedimino 7 and is open 07.00–19.00 Mon–Fri and 09.00–16.00 on Sat. It sells a wide range of postcards and packing materials for those who need to send parcels. It also sells sets of all the stamps that have been issued in Lithuania since the re-establishment of independence in 1991. Its website (*www.post.lt*) gives full information on current tariffs.

Internet At the time of writing only two hotels, the Artis and the Centrum Uniquestay, provided computers free of charge in each room. Most others provide connections for those who wish to use their laptops, but do check charges before settling down to a few hours of emailing. Some provide computers in a business centre for guests, which may be free of charge (as at the Novotel) or may have a cost. With WiFi spreading so quickly, it is impossible to give up-to-date guidance for reception, except to say that all hotels with conference facilities are bound to have it. To check the current situation, refer to www.wifi.lt.

There are not many internet cafés in Vilnius, perhaps because so many local people can now afford to have computers at home, or the use of them in their offices. As the Reval Hotel Lietuva charges 20Lt an hour for its computers, some guests walk across the river to the Old Town where Collegium at Pilies 22 offers congenial surroundings and internet access for 8Lt an hour. Unlike the city's other internet cafés, there might even be people as old as 25 working there. It opens at 08.00 and closes at 24.00.

EMBASSIES IN VILNIUS The number of foreign embassies in Vilnius increases every year, as more countries feel the need for direct representation there rather than treating Lithuania as a sideline from an embassy in Riga, Stockholm or Warsaw. The website of the Lithuanian Foreign Ministry (*www.urm.lt*) gives a full list together with all contact details. The main ones likely to be of interest to readers of this book are listed below. Whilst the phone numbers given will probably be answered in office hours only, there will be a recorded message at other times with the mobile phone number of the duty officer should urgent contact be needed.

Ⓔ **Belarus** Mindaugo 13; ↘ (5) 266 2200; f (5) 266 2212; e lithuania@belembassy.org; www.belarus.lt

Ⓔ **Canada** Jogailos 4; ↘ (5) 249 0950; f (5) 249 7865; e vilnius@canada.lt; www.canada.lt

Ⓔ **France** Švarco 1; ↘ (5) 212 2979; f (5) 212 4211; e ambafrance.vilnius@diplomatie.gouv.fr; www.ambafrance-lit.org

Ⓔ **Russia** Latvių 53/54; ↘ (5) 272 1763; f (5) 272 3877; e rusemb@rusemb.lt; www.lithuania.mid.ru

Ⓔ **UK** Antakalnio 2; ↘ (5) 246 2900; f (5) 246 2901; e be-vilnius@britain.lt; www.britain.lt

Ⓔ **USA** Akmenų 6; ↘ (5) 266 5500; f (5) 266 5510; e mail@usembassy.lt; www.usembassy.lt

HOSPITALS AND PHARMACIES You can find a pharmacy (*vaistinė*) on virtually every street in Vilnius, but only one is open 24 hours: **Gedimino Vaistinė** (*Gedimino 27;* ↘ *(5) 261 0135*). Professional medical care that reaches the sort of standards found in private hospitals in Western countries is available at two locations. If you have private health insurance in your home country you may be exempt from payment, so if possible ask about this beforehand.

✚ **Baltic-American Medical & Surgical Clinic** Nemenčinės pl 54a; ↘ (5) 234 2020; f (5) 276 79 42; e bak@takas.lt; www.bak.lt

✚ **Medical Diagnostic Centre** Grybo 32/10; ↘ (5) 270 9120; f (5) 270 9127; e mdc@medcentras.lt; www.medcentras.lt

Professional medical check–ups in English are also provided by appointment at a small clinic right next door to the cathedral: **Medicine General Private Clinic** (*Gedimino 1a (2nd floor);* ↘ *(5) 261 3534;* f *(8) 684 33100;* e *medgen@takas.lt; www.clinic.lt. Open Mon-Fri, 09.00–17.00*).

ENGLISH-LANGUAGE CHURCH SERVICES

† **Grace International Baptist Church** Verkių 22; www.church.lt. Services every Sun at 11.00.

† **International Church of Vilnius** Vokiečių 20; www.icvilnius.org. An ecumenical service is held in the

Lutheran church every Sun at 09.30.

† **SS Philip and James** Lukiškių aikštė 10; Roman Catholic mass every Sun at 09.00 with confessions beforehand on request.

TOURIST INFORMATION There are two offices in the Old Town (at Vilniaus 22 and at Didžioji 31) and one at the railway station which therefore also serves the bus station, as they are side by side. There isn't one at the airport. Although they are called 'Municipal Tourist Offices', all three can also provide information on other places in Lithuania. The one with the address in Didžioji is in fact in the Old Town Hall in the centre of the Square.

Opening hours vary on a seasonal basis but they are all open at weekends during the summer and sometimes on Saturdays during the winter. Minimum hours at all offices during the week in winter are 10.00–17.00 (↘ *(5) 262 9660;* e *tic@vilnius.lt; www.turizmas.vilnius.lt).*

TRANSPORT

AIRPORT TRANSFER Two buses and several minibuses operate from the airport into town. Bus tickets should be bought on arrival from the kiosk at the airport where they cost 1.10Lt, or 1.40Lt if bought from the driver. The number 1 runs to the bus/train station and the number 2 runs along Švitrigailos across Gedimino and then crosses the river to the Lietuva and Holiday Inn hotels. Unfortunately no buses pass any of the hotels in the Old Town but none is more than a few hundred yards from a bus stop.

Microbuses operate along these routes as well and also on others. They usually charge 2.00Lt and payment is always made to the driver. They stop at all bus stops but will also stop elsewhere. They do not operate within the Old Town. Services by both means of transport operate from early in the morning until fairly late at night so there is almost always public transport, no matter when a flight leaves or arrives.

TAXIS Vilnius taxi drivers had a very bad reputation amongst foreigners in the early '90s, but now problems are few and far between. As anywhere else, enter only a clearly marked car, and check that the meter is turned on immediately. On this basis a journey within the city should not cost more than about £2/US$4 and one to the airport about £4/US$8. At the airport, charges are clearly marked in English on a board beside the taxi rank outside the terminal.

Taxis ordered by phone are a little cheaper than those hailed on the street so if you can get a Lithuanian speaker to do this, take advantage of it. Tip 10% if the driver is polite, does not smoke and turns the radio off when you enter. Reputable companies of several years' standing include:

Denvila ↘ (5) 244 4444	**Martonas** ↘ (5) 240 0004
Ekipažas ↘ (5) 239 5540	**Vilniaus** ↘ (5) 212 8888

BUSES AND TROLLEYBUSES There are a wide number of routes except into the Old Town, where only one bus, the number 11, operates and that only on a half-hourly basis. However a bus stop is never far away wherever you are in the Old Town. Some bus stops have maps showing all the routes and all buses have the main streets along which they travel marked on a side window. Stotis is the railway/bus station where many routes start and finish. Tickets cost 1.10Lt if bought in a kiosk and 1.40Lt if bought from the driver on the bus. In either case, remember to punch them at the start of your journey. There is no reducton for buying a larger quantity as there is in Tallinn.

Full timetables and routes are given on www.vilnius.transport.lt. Much of the fleet, it has to be admitted, is quite elderly but since 2004 serious efforts have been made to replace the entire rolling stock so travellers should be sure of a comfortable ride on many routes.

CAR HIRE There is no point in hiring a car within Vilnius but there are several places on the outskirts of the town for which it would be useful, such as the Television Tower,

Europe Park and the Antakalnis Cemetery. It could also be useful for visiting Kaunas and Trakai where some of the sites are a distance from public transport. In the summer, cars are often booked well in advance so this should be arranged through travel agents abroad at the same time as hotels and flights are booked. However, the firms listed below may be able to help at short notice. Apart from Aunela, they all have offices at the airport and can deliver cars there or to a hotel in town.

🚗 **Aunela** ↘ (8) 686 63444; e aunela@takas.lt; www.aunela.lt
🚗 **Avis** ↘/f (5) 232 9316; e apo@avis.lt; www.avis.lt
🚗 **Budget** ↘ (5) 230 6708; f (5) 230 6709; e budget@budget.lt; www.budget.lt
🚗 **Hertz** ↘ (5) 272 6940; f (5) 272 6970

e hertz@hertz.lt; www.hertz.lt
🚗 **Litinterp** ↘ (5) 212 3850; f (5) 212 3559; e vilnius@litinterp.com
🚗 **Sixt** ↘ (5) 239 5636; f (5) 239 5635; e rent@sixt.lt; www.sixt.lt

CYCLING The streets of Vilnius are a little more cyclist-friendly than other eastern European cities, but drivers can be aggressive and impatient, especially at peak hours. So nobody's going to stop you if you cycle your velocipede on the pavements.

In summer 2001, Mayor Artūras Zuokas introduced 1,000 distinctive orange bikes to Vilnius for public use. Cycle paths were painted and metal racks installed at strategic points throughout the city centre, the idea being that you could jump on a bike and cycle to your chosen destination for free, leaving the bicycle at the nearest rack. Needless to say, every single bike was stolen within hours. But the cycle paths still exist, making pedalling through the Old Town a pleasurable experience.

You can rent a bicycle, and also find out more about biking through the Baltics, at Lithuanian Cyclists Community (*PO Box 61, LT 01002 Vilnius;* ↘ *(8) 699 56009;* f *(5) 278 4330;* e *BaltiCCycle@bicycle.lt; www.bicycle.lt*).

🏠 ACCOMMODATION

There is a wide choice of accommodation in Vilnius, ranging from dorm beds in hostels to luxury hotels. Prices are similarly variable, and are usually a fairly reliable indicator of the quality of any particular establishment.

The years 2003–04 saw a sudden burst of activity in hotel construction, with about 20 new locations opening in that short space of time, in a wide variety of locations and catering to an equally wide variety of clientele. The de-luxe traveller can now rely on the chains that prevail elsewhere, whilst budget travellers are no longer dependent on a haphazard range of guesthouses. There will be further increases in 2007; amongst other hotels due to open then is a Kempinski opposite the cathedral. Many tourists automatically choose the Old Town but regular visitors to Vilnius are now increasingly turning to the larger hotels over the river and in the New Town where rooms are bigger, views more extensive and driving less problematical. Short periods of intense heat in the summers of 2002 and 2003 persuaded most hotels in the four- and five-star category to install air conditioning, even though it only needs to be used for about four to five weeks in most years. Because supply nearly always exceeds demand in Vilnius (unlike in Riga and Tallinn), hotel prices are reasonable on a year-round basis and many agents can offer considerable reductions on the rates advertised by the hotels directly. The published rates are those quoted in the listings.

Independent travellers, however, are unlikely to be offered discounts in summer, even if they stay for several nights, but do ask about weekend rates, which some hotels provide. Prices are generally lower in winter, when you are likely to find a room in most hotels just by turning up on the day. In summer, independent travellers are advised to book ahead. Breakfast is frequently included in the price.

Accommodation is available at the airport but it is not of high quality and as the drive from town takes only 20 minutes by bus and 15 minutes by car, there is no need to use it. Hotels at the airport have therefore not been included here. There are rumours of improvements taking place in 2006 so perhaps such hotels can feature in the next edition of the book.

Luxury hotels

⌂ **Crowne Plaza** Čiurlionio 84; ☏ (5) 274 3400; f (5) 274 3411; e reservation@cpvilnius.com; www.cpvilnius.com. This huge tower block is a longish walk from the Old Town, though it profits from a pleasantly leafy location at the edge of Vingis Park. It is one of the very few hotels that functioned in communist times, but it was completely rebuilt in 2003; all the bedrooms are now equipped to state-of-the-art business and conference standards. In the basement are a swimming pool, sauna and gym. Fine views over the city can be enjoyed from the 16th floor Horizon bar, while the restaurant, The Seasons, presents an international menu, including a choice of vegetarian dishes. *Sgl 304–342Lt, dbl 304–376Lt, suites 328–532Lt, apartments 449–656Lt.*

⌂ **Grotthuss** Ligoninės 7; ☏ (5) 266 0322; f (5) 266 0323; e info@grotthusshotel.com; www.grotthusshotel.com. The hotel advertises that it is a 5-min walk from the President's Office, which suggests the sort of clientele to which it aims to appeal. Although situated on a small street in the Old Town, the rooms are all large enough to work in and the choice of flowers and pictures that abound make work here much more congenial than it otherwise might be. Hopefully its neighbours around the rear courtyard will gradually adopt its aesthetic sense as well. An atrium in this courtyard is the location for its well-known restaurant La Pergola. Exclusivity here is ensured by restricting the number of tables to five, but somehow the dishes on its extensive menu always seem to be available. *Sgl 420Lt, dbl 550Lt, suites 700Lt.*

⌂ **Kempinski Hotel AAA** e info.project.vilnius@kempinski.com. Due to open in 2007, the 107-room Kempinski will be on the edge of the Old Town directly facing the castle, cathedral and bell tower. The 19th-century façade of this former telegraph building is being preserved while the interior will be renovated to offer elegant facilities, such as international restaurants, business centre and health club. Two extension wings are being built.

⌂ **Le Meridien Villon** A2 highway; ☏ (5) 273 9700; f (5) 273 9730; e info@lemeridien.lt; www.lemeridien.lt. This is a huge motel and conference centre, located 19km from the centre of Vilnius, beside the main highway to Panevėžys and Riga. It lays on free shuttle buses to the city, and offers the services of a full holiday complex, including tennis courts, a fitness club, swimming pool and 3 saunas. Despite its distance from town the restaurant, Le Paysage, specialising in Gallic-influenced cuisine, has such a reputation that many people are happy to make the journey. *Sgl 550–690Lt, dbl 600–730Lt, suites 1,000Lt, apartments 2,900Lt.*

⌂ **Narutis** Pilies 24; ☏ (5) 212 2894; f (5) 262 2882; e info@narutis.com; www.narutis.com. With tasteful French furniture and even frescoes in some of the rooms, the elegant Narutis is set in a 16th-century building on the Old Town's partly pedestrianised main street. Guests reach their rooms from a central plush lounge with its own glass elevator. Ask for the upper floors where the views of the Pilies Street market are best. The cosy Kristupo Café serves excellent food on the ground floor and dining is available in an atmospheric vaulted cellar. Now a member of the Summit Hotels & Resorts chain, the Narutis retains its own unique charm. *Sgl 450Lt, dbl 600–800Lt, suites 900Lt.*

⌂ **Radisson SAS Astorija** Didžioji 35/2; ☏ (5) 212 0110; f (5) 212 1762; e reservations.vilnius@radissonsas.com; www.radissonsas.com. This grand early 20th-century hotel in the heart of the Old Town has been refurbished by the Radisson SAS chain, and has a recently opened (2004) health centre prominent among its facilities. All rooms have hairdryer, trouser press, telephone, cable TV, safe. Business-class rooms are larger, have tea/coffee/kettle in them and guests have free access to the health centre. A 'grab and run' breakfast is available in the lobby, but it is a great pity to take it when the alternative is to enjoy a leisurely and lavish buffet breakfast overlooking part of Town Hall Square. *Sgl 550Lt, dbl 580Lt, suite 1,725Lt.*

⌂ **Stikliai** Gaono 7; ☏ (5) 264 9595; f (5) 212 3870; e sales@stikliaihotel.lt; www.stikliaihotel.lt. At an unbeatable location on a narrow cobblestone street in the Old Town, the richly decorated, 5-star Stikliai has stubbornly held on to its reputation as the city's most exclusive hotel since it opened shortly before Lithuania's independence. Royals and celebrities from Western Europe have slept in its four-poster beds, reclined on its sofas and dined in the restaurant on expensive French cuisine. They may also have used its sauna, swimming pool and fitness room. *Sgl 570–775Lt, dbl 690–775Lt, suites 890–1,240Lt, apartments 3,800Lt.*

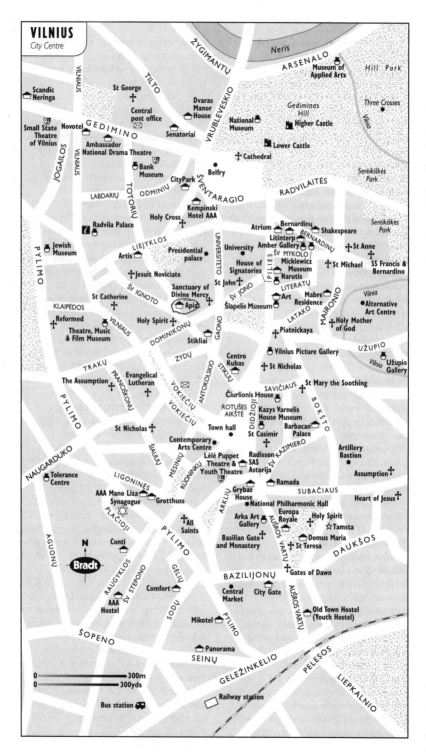

VILNIUS
City Centre

Neris

ŽYGIMANTŲ

ARSENALO

Museum of Applied Arts

Hill Park

Three Crosses

Scandic Neringa

VILNIAUS

St George

TILTO

Dvaras Manor House

VRUBLEVSKIO

Gediminas Hill

Higher Castle

Vilnia

Central post office

National Museum

Small State Theatre of Vilnius

Novotel

GEDIMINO

Senatoriai

Lower Castle

Ambassador National Drama Theatre

Bank Museum

CityPark

Cathedral

JOGAILOS

VILNIAUS

Belfry

Sereikiškės Park

LABDARIŲ

TOTORIŲ

ODMINIŲ

ŠVENTARAGIO

RADVILAITĖS

Holy Cross

Kempinski Hotel AAA

Sereikiškės Park

Radvila Palace

Atrium

Bernardinų

BERNARDINŲ

Shakespeare

PYLIMO

Jewish Museum

LIEJYKLOS

University

Litinterp

Amber Gallery

St Anne

Artis

Presidential palace

UNIVERSITETO

ŠV MYKOLO

Mickiewicz Museum

St Michael

SS Francis & Bernardino

Jesuit Noviciate

ŠV IGNOTO

House of Signatories

PILIES

Narutis

LITERATŲ

Vilnia

Alternative Art Centre

St Catherine

Sanctuary of Divine Mercy

St John

ŠV JONO

Art

Mabre Residence

KLAIPĖDOS

Apia

Šlapelis Museum

LATAKO

MAIRONIO

Reformed

VILNIAUS

Holy Spirit

GAONO

Piatnickaya

Holy Mother of God

Theatre, Music & Film Museum

DOMINIKONŲ

Stikliai

ZYDŲ

UŽUPIO

TRAKŲ

Vilnius Picture Gallery

Vilnia

Užupio Gallery

The Assumption

PRANCIŠKONŲ

Evangelical Lutheran

VOKIEČIŲ

ANTOKOLSKIO

STIKLIŲ

Centro Kubas

St Nicholas

SAVIČIAUS

St Mary the Soothing

Čiurlionis House

BOKŠTO

ŠIAULIŲ

VOKIEČIŲ

ROTUŠĖS AIKŠTĖ

DIDŽIOJI

Kazys Varnelis House Museum

St Nicholas

Town hall

St Casimir

Barbacan Palace

Artillery Bastion

Contemporary Arts Centre

MĖSINIŲ

RŪDNINKŲ

Lėlė Puppet Theatre & Youth Theatre

Radisson SAS Astorija

ŠV KAZIMIERO

Assumption

NAUGARDUKO

Tolerance Centre

LIGONINĖS

Ramada

SUBAČIAUS

AAA Mano Liza Synagogue

Grotthuss

Grybas House

National Philharmonic Hall

Heart of Jesus

PLAČIOJI

PYLIMO

All Saints

ARKLIŲ

Arka Art Gallery

AUŠROS VARTŲ

Europa Royale

Holy Spirit

Tamsta

AGUONŲ

Conti

Basilian Gate and Monastery

Domus Maria

St Teresa

DAUKŠOS

Bradt

RAUGYKLOS

ŠV STEPONO

Comfort

GĖLIŲ

Gates of Dawn

AAA Hostel

BAZILIJONŲ

Central Market

City Gate

AUŠROS VARTŲ

Mikotel

PYLIMO

Old Town Hostel (Youth Hostel)

ŠOPENO

Panorama

SEINŲ

GELEŽINKELIO

PELESOS

LIEPKALNIO

0 ——— 300m
0 ——— 300yds

Bus station

Railway station

⌂ **Art Hotel** Pilies 34; ☏ (5) 266 1626; f (5) 266 1627. At the time of writing in early 2006, this hotel was closed for a complete refurbishment. All the rooms except for one suite will be named after artists whose works will adorn the walls. The paintings will apparently not be mere reproductions; they will be 'near-originals'. Most artists will be impressionists, but guests with an earlier taste can go for the Leonardo room. Those not bothered with privacy will presumably take the suite, called Nude, which has a balcony over Pilies, one of the busiest streets in the Old Town. *Sgl 350Lt, dbl 420Lt.*

⌂ **Artis** Liejykos 11/23; ☏ (5) 266 0363 or 266 0366; f (5) 266 0377; e artis@centrum.lt; www.centrum.lt. The latest addition to Vilnius's Centrum group of hotels occupies a refurbished Old Town mansion overlooking the President's Office garden, so in a very quiet location. All twin/dbl rooms have baths and fabric paintings on the walls. Singles are on the small side here and have conventional paintings. A recent expansion has seen the opening of a swimming pool and gym to which hotel guests have access free of charge. The restaurant is very reasonably priced for a hotel of this standard. *Sgl 430Lt, dbl 500Lt, suites 690Lt.*

⌂ **Atrium** Pilies 10; ☏ (5) 210 7773; f (5) 210 7770; e hotel@atrim.lt; www.atrium.lt. Situated in a peaceful courtyard just off one of the busiest streets in the heart of the Old Town, this hotel boasts large and well-appointed bedrooms. It has an excellent Argentinian restaurant, El Gaucho, which naturally specialises in steaks. *Sgl 300–550Lt, dbl 390–550Lt, suites 700–800Lt.*

⌂ **Barbacan Palace** Bokšto 19; ☏ (5) 266 0840; f (5) 266 0841; e barbacan@centrokubas.lt; www.centrokubas.lt. The hotel is under the same management as the Centro Kubas listed below but they could not be more different. The Barbacan is larger, and is one of the many hotels that opened in 2003. It has conventional décor throughout and is on a quiet side street at the edge of the Old Town. Many rooms have a view of the Artillery Bastion and the restaurant/café has prices well below those normally to be expected in the Old Town. Its original features are a basement bowling alley and billiards table, with reduced prices for hotel guests. *Sgl 360Lt, dbl 385Lt, suites 450Lt.*

⌂ **Best Western Naujasis Vilnius** Konstitucijos 14; ☏ (5) 273 9595; f (5) 273 9500; e office@hotelnv.lt; www.hotelnv.lt. With 114 rooms, this hotel used to be considered large but, with the refurbished Reval Lietuva now towering over it, suddenly it seems small. Every two years it is updated so perhaps is typical of any go-ahead Lithuanian organisation. Finally the surroundings are getting updated too, so there is no need to flee into the Old Town for shopping or different restaurants.

Soon it should be an integral part of 'business Vilnius' which is taking over this side of the river. *Sgl 340Lt, dbl 400Lt, suites 500–560Lt, apartments 600–66Lt.*

⌂ **Centro Kubas** Stiklių 3; ☏ (5) 266 0860; f (5) 266 0863; e hotel@centrokubas.lt; www.centrokubas.lt. A designer-style hotel decked out with old agricultural tools in all the public areas and in the rooms too. A windmill dominates the lobby. There are only 14 rooms, spread across four floors and linked by a glass lift. A peephole in each room is part of the security arrangements. Use of laptop computers is free of charge. *Sgl 320Lt, dbl 360Lt.*

⌂ **Centrum Uniquestay** Vytenio 9/24; ☏ (5) 268 3300; f (5) 213 2760; e hotel@centrum.lt; www.uniquestay.com. The Tallinn-based, British-run Uniquestay group took over the management of this hotel in 2003, so computers were placed in every room at once, as were tea- and coffee-making facilities. Being a 10-min walk from the Old Town, it has taken advantage of the location to offer enormous space in the public areas and larger rooms than might otherwise be expected. Most of these therefore have baths, and not just showers. It used to be seen as purely a business hotel, but has recently been successful in attracting tourists. The 4th floor has cheaper, smaller rooms with showers only. Easy parking for coaches and cars obviously helps access and departures. The location beside the Belarus Embassy ensures peace and quiet around the clock. *Sgl 265–340Lt, dbl 390Lt, suites 490Lt.*

⌂ **CityPark** Stuokos-Gucevičiaus 3; ☏ (5) 212 3515; f (5) 210 7460; e citypark@citypark.lt; www.citypark.lt. Architectural controversy surrounded the unabashedly modern extension added to the original hotel located in a refurbished building with a central courtyard diagonally opposite the cathedral. The fountains and gardens that were added in front of the hotel in 2004 have made its situation particularly attractive, and this has increased the popularity of its Italian restaurant, Rossini. There is also the rare facility of its own underground car park. *Sgl 360–390Lt, dbl 480–560Lt, suites 660–700Lt.*

⌂ **Congress** Vilniaus 2/15; ☏ (5) 269 1919; f (5) 251 4280; e info@congress.lt; www.congress.lt. Housed in a fine old building overlooking the River Neris, this used to be a budget hotel, but it has been totally refurbished to business-class standards and given a new name so has gone through a similar metamorphosis to the Grand in Tallinn. The name perhaps puts off tourists, which is a pity given its convenient location, but this greatly reduces prices at the weekend. Car parking and internet connections are free of charge. *Sgl 300Lt, dbl 400–440Lt, suites 560Lt.*

Conti Raugyklos 7/2; ☎ (5) 251 4111; f 251 4100; e info@contihotel.lt; www.contihotel.lt. The opening of this hotel in 2003 marked the beginning of the regeneration of the rundown area to the rear of the synagogue. It incorporates a host of modern design features including full disabled access, a welcoming lobby with waterfall and well-appointed bedrooms with en-suite facilities and internet access. All bedrooms have prints showing Vilnius as it was about 100 years ago. Try to get rooms 506, 507 or 508 for the best views of contemporary Vilnius. The kitchens are equipped to allow Jewish groups to prepare kosher food. *Sgl 350Lt, dbl 530Lt.*

Dvaras Manor House Tilto 3; ☎ (5) 210 7370; f (5) 261 8783; e hotel@dvaras.lt; www.dvaras.lt. This is a very select hotel, with just 8 bedrooms, and as its name and its décor suggest, it is eager to promote its grand background. All rooms have AC, and internet access free of charge. There is a similarly classy restaurant, which serves a wide international menu and has a notable wine list. *Sgl 340Lt, dbl 400Lt.*

Europa Royale Aušros Vartų 6; ☎ (5) 266 0770; f (5) 261 2000; e reservation@hoteleuropa.lt; www.hoteleuropa.lt. A stylish, modern, luxury hotel in a beautifully renovated Old Town building. Heated bathroom tiles are a novelty in the en suites and most have baths rather than just showers. The nicest rooms are on the 4th floor as they have a view over the Gates of Dawn as well as over the Old Town. *Sgl 432–570Lt, dbl 518–656Lt, apartments 760–1,381Lt.*

Grybas House Aušros Vartų 3a; ☎ (5) 261 9695 or 264 7474; f (5) 212 2416; e info@grybashouse.com; www.grybashouse.com. A delightful small hotel (there are only 9 rooms) in a refurbished baroque house set in a quiet courtyard at the northern end of the Old Town. The décor includes sculptures from the Congo and the former pier in Palanga. Water filters in every room and heated floors are what all guests remember here, and the gratis airport transfer is a nice gesture too. The Grybas family have run this hotel since it opened in 1992, but have modernised it twice since then. There is a fine basement restaurant, with live classical music on Wed evenings. *Sgl 280Lt, dbl 295Lt, suites 330Lt.*

Holiday Inn Šeimyniškių 1; ☎ (5) 210 3000; f (5) 210 3001; e holiday-inn@ibc.lt; www.holidayinnvilnius.lt. Surprisingly, it took until 2002 for this well-known chain to open a hotel in Vilnius, its first venture into the Baltic states and in 2005 this was still its only property in the region. The location, immediately east of the new business district, was a gamble when they first arrived but it has certainly now paid off. Novel then were baths, AC and proper soundproofing in every room and competitors are now trying to catch up. The easy walk over the river to the Old Town ensures that when business clients leave for the weekend or for the summer, tourists always replace them. *Sgl 420–470Lt, dbl 483–587Lt, suites 656–760Lt, apartments 967Lt.*

Mabre Residence Maironio 13; ☎ (5) 212 2087 or 212 2195; f (5) 212 2240; e mabre@mabre.lt; www.mabre.lt. Occupies the grand neo-classical courtyard buildings of a former Russian Orthodox monastery in the quiet eastern part of the Old Town. High walls give it a very exclusive feel, perhaps rather necessary as it is so close to many of the tourist sites, such as St Anne's Church. Facilities for guests include a sauna and fitness centre and a small pool. There is no charge for internet access in the rooms. The hotel is well known to Vilnius residents for its Steakhouse Hazienda, one of the first to open and still one of the best known. *Sgl 320–380Lt, dbl 460–520Lt, suites 580–640Lt, apartments 780–880Lt.*

Mano Liza Ligoninės 5; ☎ (5) 212 2225; f (5) 212 2608; e hotel@aaa.lt; www.hotelinvilnius.lt. This hotel is next door to the grander Grotthuss and both share a passion for good art, but in other respects the Mano Liza is rather simpler, having only 8 rooms and many guests are regulars from the USA. *Sgl 280Lt, dbl 300Lt, suites 360Lt, apartments 470Lt.*

Novotel Gedimino 16; ☎ 266 6200; f 266 6201; e H5209@accor.com; www.novotel.com. This tall hotel became so popular amongst tourists and business visitors as soon as it opened in 2003 that it is hard to believe that it has not always been part of the post-independence scene. It has had its fair (perhaps unfair) share of local critics who feel that such a tall new building has no place so near to the Old Town and that it should have been built on the other side of the river. Gedimino now being a pedestrian precinct for much of the day has made a formerly busy location a quieter one, despite all the attractions and offices nearby. All rooms have baths and these are so placed that the TV can be watched at the same time. The rooms also have separate showers and all provide tea/coffee-making facilities. As the gym is on the 7th floor, it is possible to keep fit here with a view. Even though the restaurant is on the second floor, the view of the activity on Gedimino makes it an attractive location and its prices have been set to bring in local custom as well as hotel guests. Its choice of fish dishes is unusual for Vilnius and puts many restaurants in ports to shame. The hotel stresses its family orientation, organising amongst other things a supervised Sun brunch and offering a children's menu in the restaurant. *Sgl 350–450Lt, apartments 620Lt.*

Ramada Subačiaus 2; ☎ 255 3355; f (5) 255 3311; e hotel@ramadavilnius.lt; www.ramadavilnius.lt.

Emerging late in 2005, the Ramada was the first hotel to open its doors in Vilnius in 2 years. It is comfortable enough, with the unusual feature of TVs and DVD players in each of the rooms. It benefits from an Old Town location close to the Lithuanian Philharmonic – ask for a room at the front for a busy view, or the back if you want to sleep. There's wireless internet access in the lobby, but not in the rooms, which tend to be fairly small. No parking available. Lower prices are available for weekend stays. *Sgl 280–330Lt, dbl 350–410Lt, suites 410–790Lt.*

🏠 **Ratonda** Gedimino 52/1; ☎ (5) 212 0670; f (5) 212 0669; e ratonda@centrum.lt; www.centrumhotels.com. This hotel is under the same management, the Centrum Company, which runs the Artis Hotel. It is not as grand, and the rooms are smaller, but it is convenient for Parliament and government ministries situated near to it. The use of glass in the roof and walls was very special in the mid-1990s when the hotel opened, although is more common now. A sauna and fitness centre were added early in 2005. *Sgl 295–360Lt, dbl 390Lt, suites 490Lt.*

🏠 **Reval Hotel Lietuva** Konstitucijos 20; ☎ (5) 272 6200; f (5) 272 6210; e lietuva.sales@revalhotels.com; www.revalhotels.com. The former Intourist hotel is much the largest and most prominent in Vilnius, with nearly 300 rooms, and is now the main conference centre in the city. It is quite common in winter for conference guests never to leave the building from one day to the next. In 2000 the hotel was acquired by the Reval chain, which eliminated all Soviet features in a radical Scandinavian-style makeover. The even-numbered rooms offer grandstand views over the Old Town, as does the bar on the 22nd floor, which is at its best around sunset. The number 2 bus from the airport passes the entrance and a pedestrian bridge is the best way to get to the Old Town over the river. The Reval chain runs the equally large Latvia Hotel in Riga, the Ridzene there, four hotels in Tallinn and a hotel in Kaunas due in 2007. More hotels will probably follow. Travel agents can often obtain lower rates if clients book more than one Reval hotel on the same tour. *Sgl 380Lt, dbl 450–625Lt, suites 790Lt, apartments 1,210Lt.*

Tourist class

🏠 **Ambassador** Gedimino 12; ☎ (5) 261 5450; f (5) 212 1716; e info@ambassador.lt; www.ambassador.lt. Handily located on the city's main street, this hotel has recently (2004) completed a modernisation that slowly started years before. Unusually for a hotel in this category, several rooms have baths, rather than just showers. Its location combined with its price make it very sought after in the summer, when it is often fully

🏠 **Šarūnas** Raitininkų 4; ☎ (5) 272 3666 or 724 888; f (5) 724 355; e info@hotelsarunas.lt; www.hotelsarunas.lt. Not Vilnius's best-located hotel, a good 20-min walk from the Old Town past a football stadium, the Šarūnas is nevertheless a stylish, modern business hotel owned by NBA basketball star and local hero Šarūnas Marčiulionis. Airport transfer and 24-hour laundry are among the services, together with a well-equipped fitness room and sauna. *Sgl 280–320Lt, dbl 300–340Lt, suites 410–450Lt, apartments 480–600Lt.*

🏠 **Scandic Neringa** Gedimino 23; ☎ (5) 268 1910; f (5) 261 4160; e neringa@scandic-hotels.com; www.scandic-hotels.com. Certainly the most pleasant of the Baltic countries' Scandic hotels, the Neringa benefited from a Scandinavian-style facelift that now perfectly complements Gedimino Avenue's recent overall makeover. Two original features stand out: firstly the library with its deep sofas and armchairs and current editions of foreign newspapers and magazines, and secondly the alcoves on every floor that overlook Gedimino, each with armchairs and fresh flowers. The ground-floor Neringa restaurant, which used to hum with the city's artistic elite in the late Soviet years, is worth visiting for its bizarre Socialist Realist murals, though these days the pizza restaurant next door is far more popular. *Sgl 500–600Lt, dbl 700–860Lt, suites 920–1,000Lt.*

🏠 **Shakespeare** Bernardinų 8/8; ☎ (5) 266 5885; f (5) 266 5886; e info@shakespeare.lt; www.shakespeare.lt. This English-style country hotel on an Old Town backstreet adopts a literary theme, with most of the rooms named after famous writers and containing reading material linked to each. Many offer imposing views of nearby landmarks, such as St Anne's Church; all have safes, internet connections and underfloor bathroom heating, while the more expensive have AC. The Sonnets restaurant is one of the classiest and most expensive in Vilnius. The bar is of course called The Globe, where the drinks are pricey but the sofas so soft you'll have to concentrate while in company to prevent yourself nodding off. Try one of the Gothic-style desserts on the opulent menu. *Sgl 360–720Lt, dbl 600–760Lt.*

booked months in advance. The café/restaurant on the ground floor keeps busy throughout the day and evening. Like the hotel, it is straightforward and functional, without any pretensions. *Sgl 240Lt, dbl 280Lt, trpls 340Lt, suites 360Lt.*

🏠 **Apia** Šv Ignoto 12; ☎ (5) 212 3426; f (5) 212 3618; e apia@apia.lt; www.apia.lt. Wafer-thin and reasonably priced, the Apia allows you to squeeze into the very centre of the Old Town at no great expense to your wallet. If you're not bothered about a minibar, but need the option of satellite TV, this is for you. *Dbl 28Lt, suites 330Lt.*

⌂ **Balatonas** Latvių 38; ☎ (5) 272 2250; f (5) 272 2134; e info@balatonas.lt; www.balatonas.lt. A small, easy-going favourite with visiting middle-class eastern European businessmen, the Hungarian-owned Balatonas is a pearly white villa located in the leafy Žvėrynas district, close to several embassies. *Sgl 160–205Lt, dbl 195–260Lt, suites 260–340Lt, apartments 340–405Lt.*

⌂ **Baltpark** Ukmergės 363; ☎ (5) 238 800; f (5) 238 8555; e vilnius@baltpark.com; www.baltpark.com. You can't miss this 83-room hotel, a bright-blue building on the road to Riga that stands out against the surrounding Soviet-era high-rises. If you don't mind staying right at the far edge of the city, the Baltpark boasts unpretentious, friendly service and spotlessly clean rooms. Most bizarre is the special 'Trio Lux' lighting in every room, which 'creates your own mood'. Choose from a combination of reds, greens and blues to make shades of calming colours. *Dbl 229Lt, suites 349Lt.*

⌂ **Business Guest House** Saltoniškių 44; ☎ (5) 272 2298; f (5) 275 3761; e info@bgh.lt; www.bgh.lt. Set on the bustling northern edge of Žvėrynas close to a main road, the atmosphere inside is Scandinavian and efficient, with business services, sauna, swimming pool, even a commercial art gallery. *Sgl 224Lt, dbl 260Lt, suites 345Lt.*

⌂ **Comfort** Gėlių 5; ☎ (5) 264 8833; f (5) 264 8832; e reservation@takas.lt; www.comfort.lt. With 57 rooms and a location about a 10-min walk from the Old Town, this hotel will suit groups and individuals wanting low prices but reasonable standards and location. The immediate vicinity is dull, but life and colour are not far away. *Sgl 110Lt, dbl 130Lt.*

⌂ **Domus Maria** Aušros Vartų 12; ☎ (5) 264 4880; f (5) 264 4878; e domusmaria@vilnensis.lt; www.domusmaria.vilnensis.lt. This is officially a guesthouse but feels like a hotel. Most of its 39 rooms were formerly monastery cells but those days are long past, although its position on a courtyard immediately behind the St Theresa Church gives it a serenity which will appeal to those wanting a quiet central location. The lounge on the 5th floor has extensive views over the Old Town. The restaurant offers perhaps the closest link to the past with the only decoration on the walls being a crucifix, but it looks down on a well-stocked bar. *Sgl 160Lt, dbl 220Lt.*

⌂ **Ecotel** Slucko 8; ☎ (5) 210 2700; f (5) 210 2707; e hotel@ecotel.lt; www.ecotel.lt. Another example of a hotel aiming at a combination of modernity and economy. It occupies a former shoe factory between the new business district and the Žalgiris Stadium so a 10-min walk is needed to reach anything of interest. Among its unusual features are special rooms for allergy sufferers and extra-long beds for tall people. Expect to see lots of sports groups here. *Sgl 170Lt, dbl 190Lt, trpls 210Lt.*

⌂ **Europa City** Jasinskio 14; ☎ (5) 251 4477; f (5) 251 4476; e city@hoteleuropa.lt; www.hoteleuropa.lt. Although a sister hotel to Europa Royale, this newcomer is much larger and less exclusive and is bound to suffer in comparison. Nothing is wrong with it, but nothing entices either, and whatever the interior, the surroundings are so drab that it really can only suit business travellers rather than tourists. *Sgl 238Lt, dbl 273Lt, suites 342–376Lt, apartments 480Lt.*

⌂ **Mikotel** Pylimo 63; ☎ (5) 260 9626; f (5) 260 9627; e mikotel@takas.lt; www.mikotel.lt. When gentrification finally comes to Pylimo Street and its market, this hotel will be a lovely place to stay. For the time being, it is still an outpost of cleanliness and taste in surroundings that are the complete opposite. The self-catering facilities are a great asset for those wishing to cook some of their own meals and its location halfway between the Old Town and the stations means that some tourists never use a bus or taxi during their entire stay here. *Sgl 110Lt, dbl 140Lt, apartments 230–270Lt.*

⌂ **Panorama** Sodų 14; ☎ (5) 273 8011; f (5) 216 3789; e reservation@hotelpanorama.lt; www.hotelpanorama.lt. For years this was the notorious Gintaras, which seemed oblivious to all the surrounding changes, so sensible travellers who had just come into the bus station rushed by on the way to something more salubrious in town. Now all has changed and one has to wonder why it could not have done so ten years ago. Anyway, its 200 rooms can now be recommended, particularly those on the top floor which have the best views over the Old Town. Photographers should ask to get onto the roof to record them. Others can simply stay in the bar to enjoy the scenery. There is a bank in the foyer so no need to go out to look for better exchange rates. *Sgl 90–139Lt, dbl 120–169Lt, trpls 139–249Lt, suites 159–249Lt.*

⌂ **Senatoriai** Tilto 2; ☎ (5) 212 6491 or 212 7056; f (5) 212 6372; e senator@takas.lt; www.senatoriai.com. This small low-rise hotel profits from an excellent location, being discreetly tucked away down a side street immediately to the rear of Gedimino, just a stone's throw from the cathedral. *Sgl 150–250Lt, dbl 300–350Lt.*

Budget hotels and guesthouses

⌂ **Bernadinų** (11 rooms) Bernardinų 5; ☎ (5) 261 5134; f (5) 260 84 21; e guesthouse@avevita.lt/guesthouse; www.avevita.lt/guesthouse. Offering peace and quiet in the Old Town at a very reasonable price, this is a new guesthouse close to St Anne's Church. Pay a little extra for breakfast and parking in the courtyard. Some rooms are bigger and come with small kitchens. *Sgl 120Lt, dbl 150Lt, trpls 215Lt, suites 230Lt, apartments 400Lt; these prices are reduced by 50% out of season. Breakfast is 7Lt extra.*

⌂ **Jeruzalė** (10 rooms) Kalvarijų 209; ☎ (5) 271 4040; f (5) 276 2627; e jeruzale@takas.lt; www.jeruzale.com. Comfortable budget option 10 mins' drive from the centre, not far from the Calvary Church and trails in the forest. The low price of these 10 rooms means you can

splash out on taxis every day – or catch buses 26, 35, 36 or 50. *Sgl 100Lt, dbl 100–142Lt, suites 214–256Lt.*

⌂ **Pušis** Blindžių 17; ☎ (5) 268 3939; f (5) 272 1305; e pusis@pusishotel.lt; www.pusishotel.lt. A basic, 1-star hotel in Žvėrynas popular in season with Polish tour groups, but quiet out of season and close to lovely Vingis Park. *Sgl 70Lt, dbl 100Lt, suites 170Lt.*

⌂ **Victoria** Saltoniškių 56; ☎ (5) 272 4013; f (5) 272 4320; e hotel@victoria.lt; www.victoria.lt. When this first opened in the mid-1990s it was a welcome and necessary addition to the Vilnius hotel scene with bright décor and friendly service. It now has price and car-parking space going for it, but not much else given that what was novel ten years ago is now standard throughout Vilnius. *Sgl 124–190Lt, dbl 159–207Lt, suites 204–238Lt.*

Bed and breakfast

⌂ **Litinterp** Bernadinų 7/2; ☎ (5) 212 3850; f (5) 212 3559; e vilnius@litinterp.com; www.litinterp.com. Open Mon–Fri 08.30–17.30, Sat 09.00–15.30. This hostel became famous when it opened and has kept ahead of most attempts to compete with it. The location, price and self-catering facilities make it ideal for those wanting a basic but impeccably clean base in the Old

Town, although some rooms are very possibly the tiniest in town. The company also offers rooms in private houses in central Vilnius and Trakai, and has some apartments for rent. Advance bookings for Kaunas, Klaipėda, Palanga and Nida can be made, and car hire, interpretation and translation services are available. *Sgl 80–100Lt, dbl 120–160Lt, trpls 180–210Lt.*

✗ EATING AND DRINKING

The pleasure of dining in Vilnius today is that there is such an unexpected wealth of different kinds of restaurants, all of them striving to be original. It's partly because of the amazing culinary revolution that has taken place since the dull Soviet years that it is so easy to be impressed when you go out for a meal. The art of providing a romantic or a lively evening meal, even the ideal business lunch, is being perfected right across the capital. European and broadly international cuisine dominates, so as not to upset local palates too much, and traditional Lithuanian dishes like the uniquely weighty *cepelinai* are available in an increasing number of rustic-style theme restaurants that are as popular with the locals as they are with visitors. There are some strange absences, however. Asian cuisine is almost exclusively taken up by an inexplicable number of Chinese restaurants, some of them better than others. There is nothing Malaysian or Thai apart from the odd dish on an international menu or rare bursts of 'fusion'. One brave retired Indian air force commander, Rajinder Chaudhary, has struggled with his excellent Indian restaurant, Sue's Indian Raja, in four different locations in the last ten years, and still attracts only expats and tourists. But Vilnius is not just meat and potatoes. Greater awareness about healthy eating ensures that tasty, attractively presented salads are especially easy to find. With one or two exceptions, such as the pricey La Provence, there is not a great deal of variation in what you can expect to pay at the restaurants listed. The price of a three-course meal for two, excluding wine, should come to around 120–180Lt. For bars and clubs, see pages 148–9.

RESTAURANTS

✗ **Belmonto Kriokliai** Belmonto 17; www.belmontas.lt. Incredible amalgamation of both

indoor and open-air folk-style theme eateries, the excellent Vila Gloria restaurant, refreshing waterfall,

4

beautiful countryside and space for everything from conferences to weddings – all just a 15-min taxi ride from the centre of Vilnius.

✗ **Čagino** Basanavičiaus 11; ☎ (5) 261 5555. For authentic Russian dishes and, on Fri and Sat, 'Russian romance' played by a solitary musician with a guitar and a portfolio of popular, sing-along songs, venture a few mins' walk away from the Old Town to this atmospheric subterranean hideaway.

✗ **Čili** Didžioji 5 and Gedimino 23; www.cili.lt. Wander into one of these branches of the phenomenally successful local Čili chain and you'll quickly discover how pizza has become the Lithuanian fast food of choice. But not why. The service is quick and the salads adequate, but the pizzas are nothing really special.

✗ **Čili Kaimas** Vokiečių 8 and Gedimino 14; ☎ (5) 231 2536. Two among a plethora of new theme restaurants offering traditional Lithuanian food, these boast live chickens, pitchforks and even a country-style granny employed full-time at the Gedimino outlet to knit in front of diners. Some people will love Čili Kaimas, run by the popular Lithuanian pizza chain, for its culinary authenticity and its prices. Others will call it village kitsch.

✗ **Da Antonio** Vilniaus 23 and Pilies 20; www.antonio.lt. Excellent Italian dishes served at tables in a pleasantly decorated yet secluded seating arrangement. Come to this quite authentic *trattoria* rather than the homegrown Čili outlets if you fancy a real pizza and bottle of good Italian wine.

✗ **El Gaucho Sano** Pilies 10; ☎ (5) 210 7773. With an unbeatable combination of relaxing atmosphere, spacious seating, meaty food and reliable service, this restaurant set inside the atrium of the Atrium Hotel claims to be Argentinian. That's debatable. But it's certainly perfect for an evening meal with good wine.

✗ **Ephesus** Trakų 15; ☎ (5) 260 8866. Although open until 06.00 every night except Sun, when it closes early at 01.00, this is in fact a conventional Turkish restaurant which has imported not only its menu but also its prices and its generous portions. Even water pipes are available to stress its difference from contemporary Lithuania.

✗ **Fortas** Gedimino 37; ☎ (5) 249 6030. If you happen to be around the central part of Gedimino Avenue and you need an easy bite that's not too challenging, the chain-pub-style Fortas offers an eclectic range of dishes.

✗ **Forto Dvaras** Pilies 16; ☎ (5) 261 1070. A warren of rooms under bustling Pilies Street that offer traditional Lithuanian cuisine such as the famously stodgy *cepelinai* and also *vederai* – pig intestines stuffed with mashed potato. You might even learn what the difference is between Samogitian and Lithuanian food.

✗ **Freskos** Didžioji 31; ☎ (5) 261 8133. One of the great survivors of the Vilnius dining scene, Freskos has seen better days. Housed at the rear end of the Town Hall, it is still popular with expats and diplomats who have litas to spare, and still has a regularly changing menu with dishes to please. But the theatrical décor has worn a little at the edges.

✗ **Ibish** Aušros Vartų 11; ☎ (8) 651 98879. The name is Turkish, but there's little that is genuinely Turkish about this new restaurant close to the Gates of Dawn. Instead, this 'lounge restaurant' boasts more than 100 cocktails to accompany your meal. Try the grilled salmon, which is accentuated by smoky bacon on a bed of lentils and carrots, adorned with lime.

✗ **IdaBasar** Subačiaus 3; www.idabazar.lt. Another of Vilnius's long-time survivors, IdaBasar relies on hearty German cuisine mainstays – and good German beer – to compete with the fresher newcomers. Not a bad option at the southern edge of the Old Town.

✗ **Kineret** Raugyklos 4; ☎ (5) 233 5648. Despite the fact that 40% of the population of Vilnius was Jewish before 1941, Kineret gave the city its first real taste of kosher food when it opened in 2005. There are no meat dishes, just high-quality fish and vegetable courses served with wine from Israel and cosy surroundings. In the inner atrium of the building that houses Kineret, you can still see what remains of Hebrew lettering on what was once the shopfront of a bakery.

✗ **Kinija** Konstitucijos 12; ☎ (5) 263 6363. Possibly the best of Vilnius's countless Chinese restaurants, Kinija is located across the river from the Old Town, close to the landmark Reval Hotel Lietuva. The broccoli, aubergine and seafood dishes really stand out. Wash them down with a large bottle of gassy Tsingtao beer.

✗ **Kristupo Kavinė** Pilies 24; ☎ (5) 261 7722. Though it is called 'Christopher's Café', this is really a classy restaurant next door to the Narutis Hotel on the Old Town's main drag. Rarely crowded, however, it offers beautifully presented dishes on rustic-style linen tablecloths, overlooked by framed sketches of sophisticated couples from the Roaring Twenties.

✗ **La Provence** Vokiečių 24; www.laprovence.lt. Advertising itself as '100% pure gourmet', this relatively pricey restaurant sandwiched between the two constituent parts of the far more informal Žemaičiai serves Provençal and other Mediterranean cuisines. The number of French-speakers regularly to be found here is proof of the high standards and extensive wine list.

✗ **Les Amis** Savičiaus 9; ☎ (5) 212 3738. The best of provincial France has finally reached Vilnius. The family do the cooking and waiting and the menu reflects what could be bought fresh during the day. It's a popular spot, so reserve ahead.

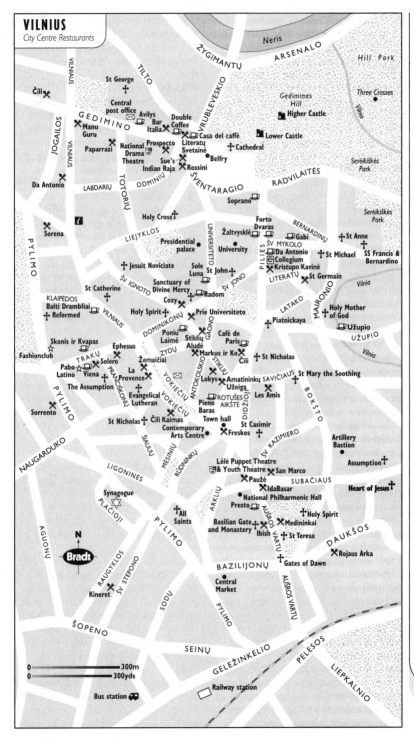

VILNIUS
City Centre Restaurants

Neris

ŽYGIMANTŲ

ŽYGIMANTŲ

ARSENALO

Hill Park

VILNIAUS

TILTO

GRUBLEVESKIO

Gediminas Hill

Three Crosses

St George ✝

Čili ✕

Central post office ✉

Avilys

Bar Italia

Double Coffee

Casa del caffè

Higher Castle ⛰

Vilnia

GEDIMINO

Manu Guru ✕

Paparrazi ✕

National Drama Theatre

Prospecto ✕

Literatų Svetainė

Lower Castle ⛰

JOGAILOS

VILNIAUS

Sue's Indian Raja ✕

Rossini ✕

Belfry ✝

Cathedral ✝

Sereikiškės Park

Da Antonio ✕

LABDARIŲ

ODMINIŲ

ŠVENTARAGIO

RADVILAITĖS

PYLIMO

TOTORIŲ

Sorena ✕

LIEJYKLOS

Soprano ✕

Sereikiškės Park

Holy Cross ✝

Žaltvykslė

Forto Dvaras

Gabi

BERNARDINŲ

St Anne ✝

ŠV MYKOLO

Presidential palace ●

UNIVERSITETO

University ●

Da Antonio

St Michael ✝

SS Francis & Bernardino

PILIES

Jesuit Noviciate ✝

ŠV IGNOTO

Sole Luna ✕

St John ✝

Collegium ⒺCollegium

Kristupo Kavinė ✕

LITERATŲ

St Germain ✕

Vilnia

St Catherine ✝

KLAIPĖDOS

Sanctuary of Divine Mercy ✝

SV JONO

Radom

GRAONO

Cozy ✕

MAIRONIO

LATAKO

Holy Mother of God ✝

Balti Drambliai ✕

Reformed ✝

VILNIAUS

Holy Spirit ✝

DOMINIKONŲ

Prie Universiteto ✕

Piatnickaya ✝

UŽUPIO

Užupio ⚐

Skonis ir Kvapas ☆

Fashionclub ☆

TRAKŲ

Ephesus ✕

Poniu Laimė ✕

Stiklių Aludė ✕

ŽYDŲ

Café de Paris ✕

Vilnia

Markus ir Ko ✕

Čili

St Nicholas ✝

Pabo Latino ☆

Solero ✕

Žemaičiai ✕

FRANCIŠKONŲ

Viena ☆

La Provence ✕

STIKLIŲ

ANTOKOLSKIO

VOKIEČIŲ

Lokys ✕

SAVIČIAUS

Amatininkų Užeiga ✕

St Mary the Soothing ✝

The Assumption ✝

Evangelical Lutheran ✝

VOKIEČIŲ

✉

Pieno Baras

ROTUŠĖS AIKŠTĖ

Les Amis ✕

BOKŠTO

DIDŽIOJI

Sorrento ✕

PYLIMO

St Nicholas ✝

Čili Kaimas ✕

Contemporary Arts Centre ●

Town hall ●

Freskos ✕

St Casimir ✝

ŠV KAZIMIERO

Artillery Bastion

Assumption ✝

NAUGARDUKO

LIGONINĖS

ŠIAULIŲ

MĖSINIŲ

RUDNINKŲ

Lėlė Puppet Theatre & Youth Theatre 🎭

San Marco ✕

Paužė ✕

SUBAČIAUS

IdaBasar ✕

National Philharmonic Hall ●

Heart of Jesus ✝

Synagogue ✡

PLAČIOJI

ARKLIŲ

Presto ⒺPresto

AGUONŲ

N
Bradt

All Saints ✝

PYLIMO

AUŠROS VARTŲ

Basilian Gate and Monastery ✝

Ibish ✕

Medininkai ✕

St Teresa ✝

Holy Spirit ✝

DAUKŠOS

Rojaus Arka ✕

RAUGYKLOS

SV STEPONO

Kineret ✕

SODŲ

BAZILIJONŲ

Central Market ●

Gates of Dawn ✝

AUŠROS VARTŲ

ŠOPENO

PYLIMO

SEINŲ

GELEŽINKELIO

PELESOS

LIEPKALNIO

0 ——— 300m
0 ——— 300yds

Railway station 🚉

Bus station 🚌

✗ **Literatų Svetainė** Gedimino 1; www.literatai.lt. With a view from your candlelit table to the cathedral and a meal prepared by some of the best chefs in Vilnius, the 'Literary Salon' specialises in modern (ie: healthy and not stodgy) Scandinavian cuisine with a good choice of wines. This has been a café for many years. It was from one of these windows that Czeslaw Milosz, the Nobel-Prize-winning poet, witnessed Soviet tanks occupy the city in June 1940.

✗ **Lokys** Stiklių 8; www.lokys.lt. One of the few survivors from Soviet times, 'The Bear' has updated its service standards but not its menu. It is a must for the enthusiastic carnivore. Boar, elk, even bear itself are on the menu. Eat in one of the tiny rooms carved out of the cellar, or on the ground floor in the shadow of a stuffed grizzly. The reasonably priced lunch menu is good quality, although a 20-min wait is necessary.

✗ **Mano Guru** Vilniaus 22; ☎ (5) 212 0126. This restaurant achieved instant success when it was revealed that all the staff were reformed drug addicts and that Mayor Zuokas had promoted this project having seen the success of the idea in Prague. The variety of food is such that one is willing to sacrifice alcohol and to leave by 20.30 which is the state of play here. Fresh fruit and vegetables which seem unavailable elsewhere all turn up with every dish and although meat and fish are served, they almost seem redundant. Puréed soup and the vegetarian main courses are more than enough. Smoking is understandably banned here, a pleasant rarity in Vilnius even in 2006.

✗ **Marceliukės Klėtis** Tuskulėnų 35; ☎ (5) 272 508. Probably the most tongue-in-cheek of the traditional Lithuanian restaurants, and the longest running, this is off the beaten track in a bizarre setting of high-rises a short taxi ride from the centre. The hearty portions, merry atmosphere, live folk music and smiling service are worth the journey.

✗ **Markus ir Ko** Antokolskio 11; ☎ (5) 262 3185. A relaxing, jazzy atmosphere, live piano music and succulent steaks on one of the Old Town's tiniest streets.

✗ **Medininkai** Aušros Vartų 8; ☎ (5) 266 0771. The chefs here like to call the cuisine 'Lithuanian fusion', using imaginative ways to prepare and present traditional local food. With vaulted ceilings littered with frescoes, 18th-century Italian artwork and a peaceful red-brick courtyard open in summer, the Medininkai makes the most of its location in a former monastery near the Gates of Dawn. Another plus is that it is now under the reliable management of the adjoining Hotel Europa Royale.

✗ **Rojaus Arka** Daukšos 3; ☎ (5) 212 0625. Often forgotten since it lies just beyond the tourist trail the other side of the Gates of Dawn, the 'Arch of Paradise' is easy to spot because of its ornately carved doorway. Inside, settle into the quiet, comfortable atmosphere and choose from a short menu of Lithuanian-style dishes.

✗ **Rossini** L Stuokos-Gucevičiaus 1; ☎ (5) 210 7466. Adjoining the Hotel CityPark opposite the cathedral, but with its own separate entrance, Rossini benefits enormously from having one of Vilnius's best-known chefs, Enzo Recupero, who regularly appears in the dining area to add an entertaining panache to the excellent Italian dishes being served.

✗ **Rytai** Naugarduko 22 and Gedimino 49a; ☎ (5) 249 6655. Two of Vilnius's better Chinese restaurants, one near the Parliament, the other on the New Town's eastern edge. Inexpensive delights include a thick, rich chilli seafood soup and a squid dish that comes with oyster sauce and hot paprika. Ask for extra spice.

✗ **Saint Germain** Literatu 9; ☎ (5) 262 1210. This charming little rustic French-style restaurant opened in spring 2005, promoting wine above all else, but also serving fabulous food. It has shelves haphazardly crammed with books and somehow managed immediately to appear old and settled. In the unlikely event that guests prefer to take away the wine rather than drink it on the premises, many varieties are sold by the bottle.

✗ **San Marco** Subačiaus 2; ☎ (5) 264 6418. The new, elegant, centrally situated San Marco restaurant brings creative Italian cuisine to Vilnius in a Mediterranean setting. Opposite the National Philharmonic, it's an excellent choice for a first-class business lunch or evening dining.

✗ **Solero** Trakų 7; ☎ (5) 260 8696. Suddenly, two restaurants appeared in 2005 introducing Spanish cuisine to Vilnius. This is the better, more central of the two, offering delightful tapas like Tabla de Embutidos y Quesos, a delicious plate of Spanish cheeses and Serrano ham, as well as paella, salads and sangria.

✗ **Sorena** Islandijos 4; ☎ (5) 262 7560. Vilnius's only restaurant featuring genuinely authentic cuisine from Azerbaijan, Sorena has slowly earned a reputation for its mouthwatering Caucasian food and friendly service. Named after a heroic army leader in the early history of Persia, there is also an Iranian element to the decoration and the food. Try the Tebriz, a tender roll of beef served on a skewer with a crisp green chilli pepper.

✗ **Sorrento** Pylimo 21; ☎ (5) 264 4737. A calm haven of expensive Italian dining that is in strange contrast to the rest of busy, low-key Pylimo Street. The wood-fired oven by the bar is responsible for some delicious pizzas.

✘ **Stiklių Aludė** Gaono 7; ☎ (5) 262 4501. Run by the plush Stikliai Hotel, the price difference between this beautifully decorated cellar-level tavern and the ultra-posh French restaurant next door seems to be getting wider all the time. The Aludė combines reasonably priced Lithuanian food with good service.

✘ **Sue's Indian Raja** Odminių 3; ☎ (8) 600 27788. Ideally situated opposite Vilnius Cathedral, Sue's offers authentic Indian cuisine that is ahead of its time in the Baltics. If you want hot spices, the Madras and Jhalfarezi dishes will not disappoint, but even for seasoned tastes there will be something special. Try the Fish Amritsari, dipped in a masala of spices and herbs and deep fried.

✘ **Tores** Užupio 40; www.tores.lt. The website, although only in Lithuanian, is so visually dramatic that it is worth watching in its own right. This restaurant manages to reinvent itself several times a day. At lunch during the week, it is probably best to be over 40 and to have plenty of time. These visitors come for the view. Early in the evening the clientele are there to be seen, so can drop in age to around 30. Later an even younger set take over and probably have to be asked to leave at 02.00 which is closing time. Generations do however mix over lunch at weekends, particularly in the summer, when children can play outside.

✘ **Vandens Malūnas** Verkių 100; ☎ (5) 271 1666. Occupying a converted 19th-century watermill in Verkiai Park, this is a popular excursion destination, particularly in summer, when 3 outdoor terraces are open. Traditional Lithuanian fare is served, and there is a good line in freshwater fish dishes.

✘ **Žaldokynė** Molėtai Rd; ☎ (8) 655 09601. One of growing number of out-of-town country inns serving traditional food served in a fun, barn-house atmosphere. This one is 17km north of Vilnius on the road to Molėtai, easily reached by taxi. Go for the Žaldoko Appetiser, a clay dish of sausage, bacon, gherkins, salad and a shot of the house's very own homemade vodka.

✘ **Žemaičiai** Vokiečių 24; ☎ (5) 261 6573. Descend a hazardous flight of steps into a world of traditional food and furnishings from western Lithuania. The choice of seating ranges from throne-like chairs to country-home beds. Expect starchy food and good beer.

Cafés

☕ **Balti Drambliai** Vilniaus 41; ☎ (5) 242 0875. Hard to define, 'White Elephants' is a cellar-level vegetarian café-restaurant with a no-smoking policy but plenty to imbibe. There's also an Indian touch to the décor, which includes a magnificent bar with an elephant's head fashioned out of it.

☕ **Bar Italia** Gedimino 3a; ☎ (5) 268 5824. Squeeze into this tiny but polished caffeine pit-stop close to the cathedral for your espresso, a snack and fresh fruit juice.

☕ **Café de Paris** Didžioji 1; ☎ (5) 261 1021. Café-restaurant attached to the French Cultural Centre; it has a predictably good choice of crêpes and great coffee, but a totally un-French selection of loud background music which may drown out conversation. It's also getting a little worn at the seams.

☕ **Casa del Caffè** Gedimino 1; ☎ (5) 261 1461. Bright, cheerful café tucked just around the corner from Gedimino, on Tilto Street. The buns and coffee are delicious. But it attracts the odd hobo.

☕ **Collegium** Pilies 22; ☎ (5) 261 8334. There is no more convenient place for public internet access in central Vilnius than this cybercafé, which charges 8Lt per hour and is open 08.00–midnight.

☕ **Double Coffee** Pilies 34, Gedimino 5 and 26; ☎ (5) 261 4175. By the time this book is published there will doubtless be several other addresses in Vilnius as this chain expands rapidly throughout the Baltics. Prices are very non-Baltic, in fact rather too British, but clients probably accept this in return for the consistently high quality of the drinks and the service.

☕ **Gabi** Šv Mykolo 6; ☎ (5) 212 3643. A homely retreat on one the Old Town's quietest streets offering unadventurous Lithuanian meals in a fireside atmosphere. Next door is the Amber Museum and St Anne's Church is a few steps away.

☕ **Pauzė** Aušros Vartų 5; ☎ (5) 212 2113. Point to whatever fresh cakes or buns you fancy and take them with coffee or tea. Savory dishes are quickly microwaved. 'Pause' overlooks the busy square in front of the Filharmonija, so the window seats – and especially the balcony in summer – are pleasant for people-watching.

☕ **Pieno Baras** Didžioji 21; ☎ (5) 269 0991. It is amazing how this old café dating from the Soviet days keeps on running. Probably because of its cheap prices and popularity with students. Line up for buns, coffee or cocoa and try to find a seat. Don't expect to find wireless internet here.

☕ **Ponių Laimė** Stiklių 14; ☎ (5) 264 9581. One of the best Old Town cafés for delicious cakes and biscuits with original recipes, 'Ladies' Happiness' is popular with men too. It's also good for lunch, with basic meals on display, weighed and microwaved.

☕ **Presto** Pilies 24; ☎ (5) 210 7779. With its prominent position on Pilies Street, this is one of the more obvious, less atmospheric choices for freshly ground imported coffees and teas – and cakes, breakfast and beer too.

Prie Angelo Užupio 9; ℡ (5) 215 3790. Once part of the arty Užupis district's enigmatic ruins, this is now a richly decorated café serving inexpensive lunches. Found next to the angel statue, it makes for a convenient break while exploring Užupis's oddities.

Radom Domininkonų 16; ℡ (5) 212 0918. Tiny café near the university. Often convenient for a quick bite, but the buns are sometimes not so fresh.

Skonis ir Kvapas Traku 8; ℡ (5) 212 2803. It feels like an upmarket tearoom, tastefully decorated, with teas and coffees from around the world on display. Hidden in a courtyard, it's hugely popular, friendly and serves great meals too.

Sole Luna Universiteto 4; ℡ (5) 212 0925. Situated alongside the university, this Italian café is a particularly recommendable choice for a summertime alfresco drink with a salami and mozzarella ciabatta, which can be enjoyed in the irregularly shaped triple-tier baroque courtyard to the rear. Beer is cheaper before 21.00 every evening, but this is the place to enjoy 4 varieties of grappa or the 30 different wines which sell for less than £10/US$19 a bottle.

Soprano Pilies 2; ℡ (5) 212 6042. For delightful ice cream on a hot day, Soprano is the best parlour in town. But if it's chilly, just take their excellent coffee.

Užupio Užupio 2; ℡ (5) 212 2138. Predictably, the 'local' of Vilnius's bohemian quarter is a favourite with artists and students. Idyllically set by the River Vilnia, it has a spacious beer garden (the only one in Vilnius) and a contrastingly cosy interior, which makes the walk there in winter quite acceptable. Do not be surprised to see the Mayor of Vilnius, Artūras Zuokas, drop in from time to time, even though he could surely afford more lavish surroundings nowadays. Perhaps he likes the deliberately old-fashioned décor, which is such a contrast to the working environment he has established for the council and for the business community on the other side of the Neris River.

Užupio Klasika Užupio 28; ℡ (5) 215 3677. With its top-quality Segafredo coffee and an assortment of homemade pancakes, salads and pasta dishes, this tiny, 5-table café is the perfect pause for breath on a daytime amble through the city. When more than eight people are waiting for food, you may be there for a while. But the relaxed atmosphere and music are somehow conducive to conversation, or to reading the newspaper – or perusing your guidebook for that matter.

Viena Traku 5; ℡ (5) 261 1257. Native American cake expert Franklin Orosco opened this wonderful, casual-minded café in 2005. All the coffee is freshly ground and not kept beyond 14 days after removing from the vacuum packaging. The almond cookies are divine, the Linzer Torte delectable. Great milk shakes, sandwiches and chilli con carne too.

Žaltvykslė Pilies 11; ℡ (5) 268 7173. This establishment, named after a grass-snake, sells itself as a Hungarian restaurant, but is really just an old-fashioned café with cheap meals, popular with university students. These days, there are better places to eat or drink on Pilies Street.

ENTERTAINMENT AND NIGHTLIFE

Vilnius at night is unrecognisable from the quiet backwater is was ten years ago. Dozens of sweaty, pumping new nightspots and atmospheric watering holes seem to open every year, pushing the boundaries of the city centre westwards along Gedimino and eastwards into Užupis. For pre- or post-club relaxation, there is a greater choice of chillout zones, often off the beaten track. At weekends, opening hours extend beyond daylight. Clubbing is in; folk dancing is most definitely out.

There is still plenty of demand for chamber orchestras, contemporary dance, theatre, opera and ballet, however, and there is no more evocative city to combine a concert and an excellent evening meal than Vilnius.

Hardly a week passes in Vilnius without a cultural festival of one sort or another taking place. Unlike in many other capitals of Eastern Europe, these continue through the summer and on into autumn. Whilst the occasional artist from abroad may be engaged to participate, such is the diversity of talent available in Lithuania itself, that even someone from Kaunas or Klaipėda might be seen as an outsider. *VilniusNOW!*, *Vilnius In Your Pocket* and the *Baltic Times* are the best local sources in print for information on events.

OPERA, BALLET AND CONCERTS Inside the colossal **Lithuanian Opera and Ballet Theatre** (*Vienuolio 1;* ℡ *(5) 262 0727; www.opera.lt*), three or four performances a week are held in a programme that is fixed about six months ahead. This extraordinary example of overblown Brezhnev-era architecture hasn't changed structurally, its huge chandeliers still glaring through monumental windows, but fortunately its productions have, with frequent new productions mingling with old favourites. Vilnius attracts some world-class performers, often Russian, though not quite as many as Riga.

Ticket prices are very reasonable, ranging from 10Lt to 120Lt. Operas and ballets are highly popular, but such is the size of the venue it is usually possible to buy tickets once you arrive in Vilnius. The ticket office can be found inside a door at the bottom of the building facing the river. Performances are normally in the original language, with some being contemporary Lithuanian works. The opera is closed in July and August.

The Opera and Ballet Theatre benefits from regular charitable donations from various countries and international corporations, enough to guarantee replacement of some outdated equipment every year. Plush new seats embossed with the opera logo were installed in summer 2005.

The best classical music concerts are held at the **Congress Palace** (*Vilniaus 6;* ↘ *(5) 261 8828*), where the Lithuanian State Symphony Orchestra teams up with local and international musical personages for concerts held throughout the year, except in summer, and the **National Philharmonic Hall** (*Aušros Vartų 5;* ↘ *266 5216*), the city's most impressive concert hall, which hosts everything from pianists and quartets by renowned foreign musicians to full-blown orchestral extravaganzas. On a smaller scale, the **Music Academy** (*Gedimino 42;* ↘ *261 2691*) students and professors give free-of-charge recitals on weekdays during term time.

Always look out for the **St Christopher Chamber Orchestra**, founded in 1994, which brings together several young chamber ensembles, string quartets and solo performers. Its brilliant concerts are performed at different venues in Vilnius as well as abroad.

In addition, concerts and organ recitals are held in several Old Town churches, especially the cathedral, St John's and St Casimir's. At the latter, live music is normally performed every Sunday immediately after the last morning mass ends at around 13.00. Open-air concerts – which take place in the courtyards of Vilnius University and the Chodkevičius Palace, among other venues – are a regular feature of the city's musical life in summertime.

The main venue for large-scale pop concerts is now the **Siemens Arena** (*Ozo 14; www.siemens-arena.com*), a new multipurpose event and conference centre that opened in 2004 opposite the Akropolis shopping complex. In the Old Town, **Tamsta** (*Subačiaus 11a;* ↘ *212 4498*) has built up a reputation for great live blues, rock, hip hop and even gospel, its hip, bohemian and very friendly atmosphere open to any influences. **Brodvėjus** (*Mėsinių 4;* ↘ *210 7208*) is more of a beery pub venue, its younger fanbase bopping around to regular live concerts of local rock music, jazz and blues. The best venue for international and local DJs is **Gravity** (*Jasinskio 16; www.clubgravity.lt*), open only at weekends and famed for its location in a Soviet-era bomb shelter.

FILMS AND THEATRE State-of-the-art multiplexes now dominate the city's film-going scene. The last of the fondly remembered old Soviet-era cinemas are being sold and repackaged. The Lietuva on Pylimo is being turned into shops, the Pergalė on Pamėkalnio has become a new casino and restaurant and the Helios on Didžioji is now an entertainment complex of restaurants, nightclub and strip joint. The last non-multiplex survivor, the Skalvijos opposite the Green Bridge, goes under the hammer in 2006.

There are two multiplexes to choose from in Vilnius, both offering films in the original language with Lithuanian subtitles. An evening out at the cinema is therefore a good evening entertainment option for tourists, though the diet of big-budget

Hollywood movies will not appeal to everyone. Check www.forumcinemas.lt or ☎ 1567 to find out what's on, where and when. **Coca-Cola Plaza**, also known by its old name the Vingis Cinema, has 12 screens and almost 2,000 seats (including a few dozen for the disabled) a short taxi ride from the Old Town at Savanorių 8. A little further away, Forum Cinemas has a second multiplex at the gigantic Akropolis shopping centre.

The **Cinema Spring** festival is an increasingly interesting, week-long annual movie festival with films from around the world, usually taking place in March.

The language barrier should not be seen as a hindrance in the theatre. Many productions are, of course, of foreign classics which will be known to visitors and in other cases the ticket prices are so low that it is worth staying for at least the first act simply to see Lithuanian drama literally in action. The **National Drama Theatre** (*Gedimino 4;* ☎ *262 977*) is the city's biggest theatrical stage, used for plays, modern dance, avant-garde productions and festivals. A statue of three ghostly muses graces the entrance. New management at the **Russian Drama Theatre** (*Basanavičiaus 13;* ☎ *262 7133*) has brought in a more varied programme than just Russian-language performances, while the **Small State Theatre of Vilnius** (*Gedimino 22;* ☎ *(5) 261 3125; www.vmt.lt/en*) is a new stage with repertoire ranging from Chekhov to contemporary Lithuanian plays. The **Youth Theatre** (*Arklių 5;* ☎ *261 6126*) shows cutting-edge plays and innovative productions staged by some of Lithuania's best writers and directors.

Finally, the **Lėlė Puppet Theatre** (*Arklių 5;* ☎ *262 8678*) is a unique and entertaining festival of puppetry for children of all ages – and adults too. Located inside the baroque Oginskis Palace, like the Youth Theatre, it has managed to stay open through good times and bad since it was founded in the 1950s.

BARS AND CLUBS A revolution has taken place in the last five years. Vilnius now offers a wide range of options for the evening and early morning hours. It's no longer just boom-boom techno. DJs play as much cool jazz and lounge music as they do throbbing performances of light and noise. Bars, meanwhile, range from old-fashioned, fireside pubs like Aukštaičiai and Prie Universiteto to more colourfully designed watering holes like Savas Kampas. Cozy, Paparazzi and Pabo Latino are more modern, club-style venues with tasteful, unintrusive chillout sounds, where you can mingle a little conversation with a little dancing and, in the case of the first two, extremely good food.

⊟ **Amatininkų Užeiga** Didžioji 19. A prominent location ensures that this tavern gets a tidy turnover, but the emphasis is on bar food and the beverage of choice is beer. If that's what you want, and you're quick enough to grab one of the tightly squeezed tables on the pavement out front in summer, then this may not quite fall under the label 'tourist trap'.

⊟ **Artistai** Šv Kazimiero 3; www.artistai.lt. The large, buzzing courtyard is the reason to come to this bar and relax during summer sunsets. But a comfortable interior, friendly service and Elvis recurring in the rock 'n' roll music selection should be enough to push you to venture down atmospheric Šv Kazimiero St in winter too.

⊟ **Aukštaičiai** Antokolskio 13; www.aukstaiciai.lt. Popular with expats and the occasional stag group, this cavern of rooms is also a haven of tasty homemade food, ale made on the premises, entertaining open-mic nights and live music – usually one man squeezed into a tight corner surrounded by tables full of jolly folk, young and old.

⊟ **Avilys** Gedimino 5; www.avilys.lt. A popular microbrewery in a cellar close to the cathedral, what you come for at the 'Beehive' is the honey-flavoured or ginseng-spiced beer. It certainly takes precedence over the food, which is tasty but hardly inspiring. The varied bar snacks, which include everything from garlic bread to prawns, may be a better bet to go with the drinks, while the hedonistic 1920s alcohol ads decorating the walls only encourage you to drink more.

⊟ **Bix** Etmonų 6; www.bix.lt. More for those with alternative tastes, this Tarantino-style bar with rock music was founded over ten years ago by the early-'90s Lithuanian group of the same name. Still an exciting venue for a beer, and perhaps even a lurch to the noisy drones on the cellar dancefloor, Bix is a true, unpredictable original.

Brodvėjus Mėsinių 4; www.brodvejus.lt. Attracting a youthful crowd of mostly raucous students, this informal, barn-style venue with regular shows of live music is a good option if you fancy a wild, spontaneous evening.

Cozy Dominikonų 10; www.cozy.lt. As comfortable and relaxing by evening and into the early hours as it is during the day for its morning coffee and well-proportioned meals, Cozy is a warm, glowing chillout zone.

☆ **Entertainment Bank** Pamėnkalnio 7; www.pramogubankas.lt. The rather absurd name belies the fact that this flashy new one-stop entertainment centre in a previously undeveloped corner of the Old Town is popular with young locals with deep pockets. The developers have spared no expense (over €7.25 million) in making this an extravagant venue, where fun-seekers can dine, drink, dance or gamble the day and night away in 2 restaurants, 2 clubs, 7 bars, and a casino without leaving the building.

☆ **Fashionclub** Trakų 2; www.ftv.lt. This exclusive chain of European entertainment venues arrived in Vilnius in 2005 to offer romantic, health-conscious dining, a stylish cocktail bar and a club that hosts fashion shows downstairs. Suitably, this building used to be an 18th-century mansion where glamorous balls highlighted the latest European fashions. The only problem today is the grating Fashion TV music and images beamed from flat-panel screens virtually everywhere you look.

☆ **Galaxy** Konstitucijos 26; www.forumpalace.lt. The largest nightclub in Vilnius, which can absorb 1,000 people or more, opens only on Fri and Sat when it can be sure of this turnout. A privilege card offers discounts once 5,000Lt (£1,000 or US$1,900) has been spent which perhaps indicates the clientele it attracts. The opening until 05.00 makes this financial barrier quite easy to reach. Seating is pretty sparse, so book a table or keep dancing.

☆ **Grand Casino** Vienuolio 4; www.grandcasino.lt. The sophisticated side of Vilnius's new 21st-century casino scene, the Canadian-run Grand Casino entertainment complex promised big things for connoisseurs of gambling and non-gamblers alike when it opened in 2004. Unfortunately, while the casino itself continues to house an attractive collection of card and dice games, the other constituent parts of the complex were temporarily closed at the time of writing due to a financial disagreement. Should the New Orleans nightclub, with its great lighting and entertaining DJs, and the excellent Tokyo restaurant reopen, we recommend both for a quality night out.

☆ **Gravity** Jasinskio 16; www.clubgravity.lt. As famed for its location in a Soviet-era bomb shelter as it is for its international DJs, Gravity attracts young local celebs and a faithful crew of regular party-goers. Found down a 60m tunnel that raises the adrenalin with a thudding bass noise, Gravity is minimalistic and industrial in its décor and unrelenting in its clubbing energy.

☆ **Pabo Latino** Trakų 3; www.pabolatino.lt. Highly popular with stylish 20-somethings, this Old Town nightclub is sumptuously decorated, often more along the lines of an Eastern harem than a Latino dance party, with billowing tents outside in summer and plush cushions and rugs inside. For interesting conversations with beautiful locals, head for the courtyard's wooden steps.

Paparazzi Totoriu 3; www.paparrazzi.lt. Following a brilliantly publicised opening in early 2005, this bar certainly set itself up as the place for the pretentious under-30s to be seen. The bar area has conventional celebrity photos, though nobody seems to have thought about the irony of including Princess Diana in a bar of this name. Those, however, in the toilets will only 'appeal' to those with the most broad-minded of tastes.

Prie Universiteto (also known as The Pub or the Pub'as) Dominikonų 9; www.pub.lt. A busy expat hangout with English-style bar-food during the 1990s, the Pub then changed hands and the food and the music went rapidly downhill. Things are improving, however, and it's still the best venue to watch a live football game on the big screen. It even had a recent evening of alternative music dedicated to the late John Peel.

Prospekto Gedimino 2. Sometimes amazing, sometimes disappointing, Prospekto nevertheless has bags of atmosphere, especially on the new 3rd-floor lounge, where free palm readings and massages occasionally take place on the comfy sofas.

Savas Kampas Vokiečių 4; www.savaskampas.lt. This popular bar serves a wide range of food, including tasty lunchtime hotpots on weekdays. Its cellar closed in early 2005, when the kitchen moved down there as Lithuanians are no longer so keen on eating in cellars. The décor in the expanded ground-floor dining area is as varied as the food.

♀ **SkyBar** Konstitucijos 20 (inside the Reval Hotel Lietuva); www.revalhotels.com. Everybody's favourite cocktail-bar-with-a-view, SkyBar is located at the top of the towering, 22-floor Reval Hotel Lietuva. It opens only at 16.00, but it's where all tours of the city should start or end. Just make your way through the lobby to the speedy lifts on the right. As you enter the bar, seat yourself on the left-hand side for the best view of the neon-lit Vilnius panorama, gazed at through floor-to-ceiling windows.

GAY VILNIUS

In most countries in central and eastern Europe gay scenes have been slow to emerge since the legal restraints of the Soviet era were abolished. In culturally conservative Vilnius, there is barely a scene at all. The hostility the gay community faced in earlier times has still not been eradicated. Gay marches in nearby Warsaw and Riga in 2005 attracted at least twice as many people hurling homophobic abuse at those brave enough to turn up and demand gay rights. Vilnius has never even had a gay march.

The press is hardly leading the way. Occasionally, the daily newspaper *Respublika*, the local equivalent of *The Sun*, runs hysterical anti-gay and anti-Semitic articles written by its editors. The fact that the publication is barely prosecuted and that statements from politicians criticising the articles are painfully slow in coming reveals the lack of understanding in society.

Fortunately, several websites, including www.gay.lt and www.gayline.lt, keep the community together. There is one gay club in Vilnius. Until very recently, its regularly alternating locations had to be kept a tightly guarded secret. Now, however, there is a permanent address.

☆ **Men's Factory** Ševčenkos 16; ☏ (8) 699-85009; www.gayclub.lt. Despite its rather seedy location down an inconspicuous back street a 10-min hike from the Old Town, Men's Factory finally has a fixed abode. The club is modestly sized, but that means it gets tightly packed, especially on the regularly scheduled events nights. Also on the menu are lasers, DJs, stage shows, snow machines and 'sweet surprises'. *Closed Sun–Tue.*

SHOPPING

Vilnius is in general the cheapest of the three Baltic capitals in which to shop, probably because, in both senses of the word, it cannot be spoilt by cruise passengers whose presence always increases prices. Kaliningrad is of course far cheaper still, particularly for amber, since fewer tourists go there and most of what is sold is to local people. Bookshops are usually closed on Sundays, even in mid-summer, but other shops open around 10.00 and close around 19.00, although they will close an hour or two earlier at weekends in the winter. All take credit cards, but are unlikely to accept any currency apart from the local one.

Amber is the best buy from Vilnius. Market stalls with it line Pilies, the main street through the Old Town, but to ensure quality it is best for those without real knowledge of it to use the specialist shops. The **Amber Museum Gallery** at Mykolo 8 is mainly a museum about the mining of amber but it also has a shop with an extensive collection of individual stones or amber set in jewellery. They have an informative website about the origins of amber and their displays at www.ambergallery.lt Almost next door is **Sauluva** at Mykolo 4 with a wide range of **souvenirs**. Look out in particular for beeswax candles and dried flowers. To be tempted before travelling to Vilnius, look at their website (*www.sauluva.lt*).

The **Librairie Française** (*Didžioji 1, opposite the Picture Gallery*) is a somewhat misleading name, since it in fact stokes a wide range of **books** in English, but it is in a very French environment, in fact in the house where Stendhal stayed in 1812; on one side is a French café and on the other, the French Institute. It is part of a group of bookshops originally founded in 1905, when it became legal to sell books in the Lithuanian language using the Roman alphabet. They would face many different censors during the 20th century and only from 1991 have they been free to sell what they want. **Humanitas** (*Vokiečių 2, behind the Old Town Hall*) is the best source for art books, of which there are now a large number in English. The university has its own bookshop **Littera** in the main courtyard, famous more for its elaborate frescoed interior than for what is sells, but it does have a wide range of postcards and books in English on Lithuanian history.

Shopping centres came somewhat later to Vilnius than they did to Tallinn and Riga but will doubtless be just as popular. In fact **Akropolis**, about 3km west from the town centre and which opened in 2002, prides itself on the number of Latvians it now attracts. Those who knew Vilnius in Soviet times will find it hard to believe that such a beautiful complex with space, air-conditioning, and an ice-rink could arise so quickly in its aftermath. **Alcohol**, **clothes** and **fabrics** are the best buys here and full details of all the shops and entertainment are on the website (*www.acropolis.lt*). Opposite the Reval Lietuva and the Best Western hotels, on Konstitucijos, is a somewhat smaller centre, **Europa**, but certainly large enough to stock anything a tourist may want to buy. Akropolis stays open until midnight, Europa until 22.00 during the week and 20.00 at weekends.

WALKING TOURS

Since the Old Town is one of the biggest and most beautiful in Europe, tourists tend to concentrate on the sights and attractions inside it. But the surrounding streets, hills and views offer a great deal too. While the main sights in the Old Town can be covered in one day, more time is needed for venturing beyond it. A route for a day-long walking tour is suggested below, followed by a few shorter ones.

OLD TOWN WALK Start at **Vilnius Cathedral** (*Arkikatedra Bazilika*), a classical structure at the northern edge of the Old Town that was once the site of a revered pagan temple (page 163). The first Christian church was probably built here following the Grand Duchy's initial conversion to Christianity in the 13th century, but most of what you see today dates from around 200 years ago. After Lithuania was occupied by Soviet forces, the three statues of saints that tower over the façade were removed and destroyed, only to be replaced by reproductions of the originals in 1996.

Inside, the impression is of an ornate gallery with oil paintings hung on two tiers, so it should come as no surprise to learn that the building was given the function of art gallery and concert hall under the Soviets. In the first decade after the war it was a garage for truck repairs.

One of the most resplendent of the 11 small chapels is also the oldest, the early 17th-century baroque Chapel of St Casimir, patron saint of Vilnius. A visit to the vaults below reveals an altar once used for pagan rituals and the coffins of royal and noble family members whose lives have become romanticised among Lithuanians. Outside the cathedral, the **Clock Tower** (*Arkikatedros varpinė*), a favourite local rendezvous point, recently got a set of new bells that were blessed by Lithuania's Cardinal Bačkis before they were hung. The tower has a curious history. Its round lower storey, which is pierced by numerous gunports, dates back to the 14th century and belonged to the fortification system of the Lower Castle; it is the only part of it which survives to this day. It was converted into the cathedral's bell tower in the 1520s by the addition of two octagonal tiers. Later a fourth tier was added to house a clock, which still preserves its original mechanism. In 1893, it finally assumed its current appearance when it was crowned with a small steeple.

With your back to the cathedral doors, turn left and head across **Cathedral Square** (*Katedros aikštė*), a vast paved space to the side of the cathedral that makes an ideal starting or finishing point for parades and processions, towards the trees of Kalnų Park. But before you do so, search for the 'miracle stone'. It is said that here in Cathedral Square you can make your dreams come true by finding the slab marked *stebuklas* (miracle), then quickly making a wish while turning 360 degrees clockwise. This paving stone marks the end of the human chain that linked Tallinn, Riga, and Vilnius in 1989, formed by two million Lithuanians, Latvians and Estonians to protest against the Soviet occupation. However, you have to look for the mythical slab yourself, for superstition decrees that no one is allowed to reveal its precise location.

Since 1996, Cathedral Square has been the setting for a monument to Grand Duke Gediminas – a particularly fitting location, as it must be close to the spot where he had his legendary dream about the iron wolf. The commission for the statue was entrusted to veteran sculptor Vytautas Kašuba, who had spent most of his career in America and died soon after the monument was erected. Gediminas is shown with his sword in his left hand, an allusion to his supposed preference for diplomacy over war – though in reality he most probably used both to achieve substantial territorial gains for the Grand Duchy.

With Vilnius being joint Capital of Culture in 2009 the amount of restoration work undertaken before that year is bound to increase. Immediately behind the cathedral is the most ambitious of these projects, the reconstruction of the Renaissance-style **Royal Palace**. A splendid medieval complex that fell into ruin and was finally destroyed by the Tsarist authorities in 1802, the aim is to complete the rebuilding by 2009 – also the date of Vilnius's momentous 1,000th anniversary.

Once inside tree-shaded Kalnų Park, keep left to find the path that winds upwards around the hill to the Higher Castle (*Aukštutinės pilies bokštas*), also known as **Gedimino Castle**, from which the best of the many views of Vilnius can be had (page 160). The viewing platform at the top is worth the struggle to climb steps that are unnervingly narrow at times. The castle also houses a small museum of armoury and a model of medieval Vilnius.

Opened in 2005, a funicular railway leads back down to city level and the spacious courtyard of the **Applied Arts Museum** (*Taikomosios dailės muziejus*, page 159). Enter either this or the **National Museum** (*Lietuvos nacionalinis muziejus*) from the front by first going through one of the gateways (pages 161–2). A stylised statue of Mindaugas guarding the museum entrance was unveiled together with the King Mindaugas Bridge across the road to great fanfare and fireworks in July 2003, marking the 750th anniversary of the coronation that brought Christianity to Vilnius for the first time.

Head back past the front of the Cathedral, diagonally across Cathedral Square, and find the northern end of Pilies, the Old Town's mainly pedestrian-only thoroughfare. A handful of cafés here make a convenient pause for breath and sell good coffee, cakes, lunches and ice cream. Take Bernardinų, the first narrow lane to the left, which snakes past the **Adam Mickiewicz Museum** (*Mickevičiaus butas-muziejus*, page 161) towards **St Anne's Church** (*Šv Onos bažnyčia*), the charming Gothic church that Napoleon famously said he would like to take back to Paris on the palm of his hand (page 165). The more imposing **Bernardine Church** (*Bernardinų bažnyčia*) stands immediately behind it (page 165).

Double back across busy Maironio Street to find **St Michael's Church** (*Šv Mykolo bažnyčia*), which since the Soviet period has housed the Museum of Architecture, interesting as a curiosity since it displays plans of buildings in Vilnius that were never approved. Built by the head of one of Vilnius's great noble families, Leonas Sapiega, as a personal mausoleum in the early 1600s, one or two of the church's lovely details, like the rosette ceiling, are also worth popping in for. Further along Šv Mykolo is the **Amber Museum-Gallery** (*Gintaro muziejus-galerija*), Vilnius's most illuminating museum (and shop) dedicated exclusively to Baltic Gold (page 159).

The street brings you back onto bustling Pilies. Turn left and walk up, pausing at Pilies 26. Known today as the **Signatories' House** (*Signatarų namai*), this was where the 20 members of the Council of Lithuania met in 1918 to sign a declaration on the nation's independence. There is not a great deal in this small museum to see – only to imagine. Even the declaration itself is not on show. It has disappeared, since in Polish and Soviet times it needed to be hidden, and there are various theories as to where it might be. One theory doing the rounds in 2005 was that it might be hidden in the walls of the Lithuanian Language Institute on Antakalnio, near SS Peter and Paul Church. In 1918 the house belonged to a rich architect, Petras Vileisis, whose brother Jonas was one of the signatories. Jonas may have taken the document to him and for safekeeping hidden it within a wall. The first and ground floors of the museum both have exhibition rooms where temporary artistic and photographic displays are held.

Stroll through the arcade over the road to browse through thousands of souvenirs, classier and pricier versions of which are on display in several amber and linen shops along this part of the street. At the top of the arcade, Pilies opens out onto more stalls selling everything from gimmicky ceramics to woolly socks. A lovely row of shops on the left includes a charity shop selling stuffed toys and knick-knacks handmade by the disabled, a tea shop, a gallery showcasing local artists and an irresistible attraction for choc-lovers – a shop with a bounteous display of chocolates of every size, shape and filling. Venture a little further into Bokšto to find the city's eclectic Russian and, round the corner, Polish art galleries.

The downstairs section of the **Šlapelis Museum** at Pilies 40 is a re-creation of the pioneering Lithuanian bookshop established in 1906 by Jurgis Šlapelis and his wife Marija. Displayed in the couple's flat above, which is entered from the courtyard, are books and other objects associated with the national cultural revival they did so much to promote, as well as exhibits from the little-documented inter-war Polish period.

Over the square, standing on a platform above an open-air art market, is **St Paraskeva Russian Orthodox Church** (*Piatnickaya cerkvė*), originally built in 1345, where Peter the Great of Russia supposedly stood as godfather to the christening of Hannibal, the great-grandfather of the Russian poet Alexander Pushkin in 1705. Hannibal was abducted from his home in Africa at the age of seven, rescued from his life as a slave in Istanbul by the Russian envoy and presented as a gift to Tsar Peter.

As the road upwards closes in to become Didžioji, **Vilnius Picture Gallery** (*Vilniaus paveikslų galerija*) lies beyond an unassuming gateway on the left that leads into a grand and elegant courtyard (page 163). Another of the city's Russian Orthodox churches, the Byzantine-style **St Nicolas** (*Šv Mikalojaus cerkvė*), an oasis of candlelit peace away from the bustle of the street, can be explored a short distance further up Didžioji on the left. As with all of Vilnius's Russian Orthodox churches, no concessions are made to Lithuania; everything is written, spoken and sung in Russian.

As Didžioji broadens enough to deserve its name ('great'), boutiques on both sides reveal how many of the Western world's fashion brands are on offer in today's transformed Vilnius. But to discover how most of the city's churches looked 20 years ago, forlorn, dilapidated and empty, take the first street left, Savičiaus. About 100m down on the right is **St Mary the Soothing** (*Marijos Ramintojos bažnyčia*), its courtyard locked and unkempt. The single tower of this late baroque church dates from the mid-18th century and is still tall enough to feature as part of the Vilnius skyline.

Double back to Didžioji, passing the **M K Čiurlionis House** (*M K Čiurlionio namai*) dedicated to Lithuania's most beloved artist and composer (page 160). Another essential museum for art-lovers can be found at number 26. The astonishing legacy of an artist who returned to his home country from America in 1998, the **Kazys Varnelis House Museum** contains an astonishing personal collection of art (page 162). Cross the street to the grand, 18th-century **Town Hall** (*Rotušė*), which today has multiple uses, ranging from classical music venue to contemporary art gallery. The foyer makes an austere setting for often absorbing exhibitions of art and architecture.

Keep heading upwards, bearing left of the town hall, and after a few steps **St Casimir's** (*Šv Kazimiero bažnyčia*) comes into view. This was Vilnius's very first baroque building, modelled on Rome's church of Il Gesu with the characteristically Lithuanian addition of twin spires (page 165). Occupying powers have done some odd things with St Casimir's. During the six months Napoleon was in control of Vilnius the church stored wine for the French army. It was during the Nazi occupation in 1942 that St Casimir's royal lineage was recognised by placing a gold-coloured crown above the central dome. Then, in the Soviet period, St Casimir's became the city's museum of atheism.

An intersection of streets appears further up the hill, with a small parking area in front of the **National Philharmonic** (*Filharmonija*). Take a peek down charmingly narrow Šv Kazimiero Street, which dips back to the left, before approaching Aušros Vartų with its myriad of churches, spires and souvenir shops (seek out the bizarre and cluttered workshop of local craftsman Jonas Bugailiškis at number 17). What immediately catches your eye is the stunning 18m-high baroque **Basilian Gate** (*Bazilijonų vartai*). It leads to a monastery that is used by a small group of Uniate Basilian monks and its rundown **Church of the Holy Trinity** (*Šv Trejybės cerkvė*). Wander beyond the gateway to discover the church and the monastery's calm courtyard. The monastery served as a conveniently isolated prison in Tsarist times and the poet Adam Mickiewicz was held here for a while, a fact recorded on a plaque. Restoration of the church and its 16th-century frescoes is expected to take many years. Another peaceful, leafy courtyard next to the curious **Arka Art Gallery** (*Arka galerija*), immediately before the Basilian Gate, is a relaxing coffee stop served by the Arka café.

Aušros Vartų now takes in the Orthodox **Church of the Holy Spirit** (*Šv Dvasios cerkvė*), the most revered religious building of Lithuania's Russian-speaking community, found through another gateway (page 166). The forms of what is said to be the miraculously preserved bodies of saints Anthony, Ivan and Eustace, who died for their faith in 1347, can still be seen underneath their shrouds. They were murdered by militant pagans on the spot where the Church of the Holy Trinity now stands. At the far end of Aušros Vartų, beyond **St Teresa's Church** (*Šv Teresės bažnyčia*), lies the climax to this pilgrimage between the spires of Vilnius, the **Gates of Dawn** (*Aušros Vartų koplytėlė*), to which the most pious of worshippers crawl in veneration up steps from street level. The gates hold a gold-and-silver image of the Virgin Mary in a chapel that is a shrine for devout Catholics.

Backtrack down past the Philharmonic and take a left on Etmonų, at the end of which stand the Youth Theatre and Puppet Theatre. Both opened many years before independence but have found new audiences as Lithuanians keep up their passionate love of the stage (pages 147–8). Take the passage right, which brings you alongside the Radisson SAS to the rear of the town hall. Head left and left again onto Rūdininkų for two sites that bring back the tragedy of the Holocaust in Vilnius. This was then part of the terror-stricken 'ghetto' where the city's large Jewish population were kept before being herded out for extermination. A map on the wall of Rūdininkų 18, where one of the ghetto gates stood, shows how the streets looked at that time. A courtyard at Rūdininkų 8 was where the cruel process of selection was made. Jewish families were permitted only two children in the ghetto. If there were more, the parents had to choose who was to be taken away and killed. The old and weak – those of no practical use to the Nazis – were also 'selected' here. A plaque on the wall marks this terrible place.

Back on Vokiečių, a broad avenue that is home to more fashionable independent shops and boutiques, the **Contemporary Art Centre** (*Šiolaikinio meno centras*) holds some of the city's most daring modern artwork (page 160). About 50m up Šv Mikalojaus, the second lane on the left, find the oldest Gothic building still standing in Vilnius, **St Nicholas's Church** (*Šv Mikalojaus bažnyčia*), built in 1320 to serve German merchants in the years before Lithuania itself widely adopted Christianity. When Lithuanians' cultural and religious activities were severely restricted during Poland's occupation of Vilnius between the wars, this was the only church where they were allowed to attend mass in their language.

In 2004, a new **Jewish Museum** was opened to the public at Naugarduko 10. Now called the Tolerance Centre (page 161), gradually the collections at the other Jewish museums, at Pylimo 4 and Pamėnkalnio 12, are being transferred here. Some exhibits are moved over each year. If you visit one of these museums, it should be the 'green house' at Pamėnkalnio 12, set back up a hill from the main street. Here you'll find a chilling photographic record of sites where massacres under the Nazis took place. But all three museums stand as a ghostly reminder of what was once a thriving Jewish community. About 200 Jewish communities existed in Lithuania before World War II. Vilnius, where 40% of the population was Jewish, had 105 synagogues and prayer houses and six daily Jewish newspapers, making Vilna, as it was known in Yiddish, the 'Jerusalem of the North'. About 300,000 Jews lived in Lithuania at the turn of the last century. More than 90% of this community was wiped out during the Nazi occupation.

An appropriate few hundred metres away from these memorials to tragedy is Vilnius's strangest statue. It is of the late Californian rock musician **Frank Zappa**, but was in fact unveiled in 1995, two years after his death. He had hoped to visit Lithuania to see it but his final illness prevented this. Find it by turning off Pylimo up Kalinausko; it is in a rather mediocre courtyard behind the first office block on the right. It is probably a suitable compromise for its location. Those who see statutes as a way of the establishment perpetuating itself for ever will probably not be aware of it, and those with a sense of humour will be relieved that the ultimate figure of anti-establishment behaviour will not be forgotten.

Return to Vokiečių via Vilniaus, passing the **Theatre, Music & Film Museum** on your right. The first courtyard on the right after Trakų reveals the location of one of Vilnius's newest and most colourful art shops, **Rūta's Gallery** (*Rūtos galerija*), whose imaginatively styled paintings, sculptures, dishes, handmade jewellery and other items are reasonably priced and not too bulky to take home. Another easily missed courtyard at Vokiečių 20 leads to a church that has served Vilnius's Lutheran community since 1555, known today as the **Evangelical Lutheran Church** (*Evangelikų Liuteronų bažnyčia*). The main point of interest here is the elaborate Rococo altar, built in 1741 by the same architect who designed the magnificent Basilian Gate and the Orthodox Church of the Holy Spirit, Jan Krzysztof Glaubitz. The stunning ornateness of the altar stands out boldly against the whitewashed interior.

Cross to the other side of Vokiečių, doubling back slightly, and dive through one of the archways beneath the residential buildings into a broad courtyard to find the tail-end of Žydų (Jews') Street. This is where the Great Synagogue, the centrepiece of Vilnius's thriving Jewish community, stood before it was badly bombed during the war and finally destroyed completely in the early years of the Soviet occupation to make way for a school. A small monument to the Talmudic scholar Rabbi Elijah, the Vilna Gaon, stands at the back of the school, solitarily lamenting a lost world of 300,000 Jews who lived and worked in confined, cobbled streets that stretched like a maze through this part the Old Town.

Žydų emerges onto the similarly narrow Stiklių, which has an array of poky gift and clothes shops both left and right. Pause for a well-deserved coffee, cake or lunch break at Ponių Laimė on the corner. The tour heads left from Žydų down Stiklių to reach Domininkonų. The focal point for the city's Polish faithful is the cavernous **Church of the Holy Spirit** (*Šventosios Dvasios bažnyčia*), a few steps to the left (page 166), while down the hill on the right, on Universiteto, lies the charming complex of courtyards that makes up **Vilnius University** (*Vilniaus Universitetas*). Before exploring this, however, pop into one of the city's most beautiful baroque courtyards, at Universiteto 2. In summer this is the gorgeous backdrop to the Sole Luna café and makes a wonderful location for a daytime coffee and crêpe or an evening beer.

Vilnius University (page 169) dates back more than 400 years, although the city's history as victim of persecution and occupation ensured that it did not stay open all that time. The Russians closed it in 1832 and it wasn't until 1919, the year after Lithuania won its long-awaited independence, that it reopened. There are 12 courtyards to discover, some more tricky to find than others. Try to visualise the map at Universiteto 7 before entering. In the grand courtyard at the top of the steps is the monumental façade of **St John's Church** (*Šv Jono bažnyčia*), beyond which lies a magnificent interior and intimidating assemblage of ten altars (page 166).

Exit the university where you came in and, opposite, find the **President's Palace** (*L R Prezidentūra*), a building with a history dating back to the 14th century and where Napoleon slept in 1812 on his doomed march to Moscow. Today, after many renovations, it houses the busy offices of the Lithuanian president. It is open on Fridays and Saturdays for pre-booked groups. A tour showing the main reception rooms, the President's Office and the gardens takes about 45 minutes. The furnishings are entirely modern, much of them in oak and birch, but the designs are from the early 19th century. One room has four large portraits of the previous Lithuanian presidents, three from the 1920–40 period and one of Algirdas Brazauskas, in office 1993–98. An even larger painting shows Vytautas the Great riding into the Black Sea, recalling the time when the Polish-Lithuanian Commonwealth stretched that far in the mid-15th century.

FURTHER WALKS

Changing Vilnius walk Of course, there's more to Vilnius than the Old Town. Gedimino Avenue is the city's main drag, extending westwards from the cathedral. It is lined with ever-increasing numbers of classy shops, apartments and mini-malls. Real estate developers are sure that Gedimino will quickly become one long, highly attractive, open-air shopping centre to rival anything Copenhagen or London have to offer. That's ambitious. But with the avenue now physically transformed all the way to the Žvėrynas suburb in the west, the paving evened, underground parking installed and the groaning trolleybuses banished to just one intersection, they are not so far off the mark.

Changes are visible right the way along the street. The Vilnius municipality offices have moved from Gedimino 9 to a new skyscraper the other side of the river, leaving this neo-baroque block to re-emerge as a swanky superstore; one of the city's grimy old cinemas has become a Benetton store; the towering Novotel is a brand new building with fashion shops on the ground floor; and the 19th-century building at Gedimino 20, once the shabby Hotel Vilnius, shines like never before as the multi-million pound commercial and residential Grand Duke Palace.

The most essential thing to see on Gedimino Avenue, however, has stayed structurally unchanged since it was built as a courthouse and prison in 1899. Now housing the vivid and shocking basement-level **KGB Museum** (*Genocido aukų muziejus*), the much-feared building facing **Lukiškių Square** was the Soviet secret service's Vilnius headquarters (page 161). Hundreds of people were imprisoned, tortured and executed in its cells and thousands more were sent to Siberia between the 1940s and the 1980s.

In the middle of the square a giant statue of Lenin gestured with arm outstretched at the KGB building. It was pulled apart by a crane in front of cheering crowds in 1991 and now stands at the Grutas Park of Soviet Statues near Druskininkai.

Gedimino extends beyond the Lithuanian Music Academy, where free public concerts are frequently held in term time, to its westernmost section, which boasts even more boutiques and independent shops. Concealed from view, one of the country's biggest prisons lurks down Ankštoji, a narrow side street to the right.

Before reaching the River Neris, the avenue opens out into **Independence Square** (*Nepriklausomybės aikštė*), bordered on one side by the 'Stalinist baroque'

National Library (*Martynas Mažvydas biblioteka*), built in the 1950s, and on the other by the late Soviet-era **Parliament** building (*Seimas*), which originally housed the Supreme Council of Lithuania. This is where the republic's leaders declared independence from Moscow on 11 March 1990. Barricades were erected to protect the Parliament from Soviet tanks. These giant cubes and slabs of crude concrete remained in place into the early 1990s. Today, a few can still be seen on the side of the building facing the river.

Stroll across the recently renovated old river-bridge into the leafy residential district of Žvėrynas to find the eye-catching onion domes of the Russian Orthodox **Church of the Apparition of the Holy Mother of God** (*Znamenskaya cerkvė*), one of the city's warmest and most appealing churches. As Žvėrynas quickly became the city's first garden suburb, divided into separate plots in the 1890s, this was the first church to be built here, in 1903. To the left, where Vytauto meets Liubarto, and a little to the right stands the tiny, Moorish-style **Kenessa**, built for the Karaite community in 1922, but used as a warehouse during the Soviet occupation.

Žvėrynas, a dense knit of streets, some of them almost rustic with quaint wooden houses, is arranged in a bend in the river. It is an increasingly chic place to live, no more than a square mile wide and very pleasant to stroll around. Find the suspension bridge dramatically spanning the river from grassy banks into the tall pines of Vingis Park on the far side.

Bohemian Vilnius walk
The **Hill of Three Crosses** (*Trijų kryžių kalnas*) is another of Vilnius's dramatic viewpoints, higher than the castle, from which the entire panorama of the Old Town is visible. Reach it via an open-air stadium from the southern end of T.Kosciuškos, or cross a wooden bridge over the Vilnia from tennis courts in Sereikiškių Park and follow the river to the right before finding steep and rickety steps to the top.

The gleaming white crosses are a replacement for wooden crosses first raised here 350 years ago commemorating 14 monks who were dragged from a Vilnius monastery in the 14th century and murdered by pagans. Seven of them were butchered in cold blood, the rest tied to crosses and floated down the River Neris. The crosses were removed by the Soviets in 1950.

Sereikiškių Park borders **Užupis**, another quietly charming part of the city to stroll about. But it has a wacky side too. Užupis is the equivalent of Greenwich Village in New York or Montmartre in Paris, a place with unconventional ideals and creativity. It declared itself the 'breakaway republic of Užupis' in 1998, with its own independence day on 1 April, its own **constitution**, which is nailed to the wall on Paupio Street, and its own flag, president and customs officers – who always seem to be off duty. Its 'national symbol', an **angel** blowing her horn in celebration of freedom and independence, stands atop a column in the central square. The names of everyone who contributed the cash to make it are carved into the base.

Užupis literally means 'the other side of the river'. Up until a decade ago this was one of the most neglected and squalid areas in Vilnius, populated by drunks and criminal types. Today it is prime real estate. Parts are still ruinously rundown, but it is a fascinating place to wander. It might remind you of small towns in Italy, with its smattering of outdoor cafés and boys and girls roaring about on mopeds.

To enter Užupis, pass the white-box **Church of the Holy Mother of God** – a Russian Orthodox church that has over the years been a barracks, a library, a university department and a smithy – and cross the bubbling Vilnia into Užupio Street. The building with the welcoming terrace just across the water is the Užupio Café, frequented by artists, poets and all manner of bohemians. As you cross the bridge, look down at the wall of the near bank to see the Užupis Mermaid, a beautiful little siren who bids adieu to visitors leaving the Old Town.

After the café, at the end of a little alley to the left, is the **Alternative Art Centre**, worth a look for its bizarre 'art' collection. Retrace your steps and just a little up the street at number 5 is the **Užupio Gallery**, a working gallery that features unique enamel items and jewellery.

Užupis is full of lovely courtyards. Don't be afraid to poke your head in and look around. As you face the angel from its front, enter the archway on the right and you will feel as if you've stepped back in time. Notice the water pump, which supplies water for washing dishes and clothes, and for drinking.

Climb the hill and bear right at the fork (bear left to find Tores, the bar and restaurant with the best terrace view in town). Pass the unmarked morgue on the left. When you reach a bus stop and an old payphone, turn right onto Žvirgždyno Street, marked by a small, rusty sign. Fifty metres ahead is the entrance to the **Bernardine Cemetery** (*Bernardinų kapinės*), one of the most serene and beautiful places in Vilnius. It was founded in 1810 by Bernardine monks and stands on the tall banks of the Vilnia, virtually undisturbed by visitors. University professors, artists and scientists are among the people laid to rest here.

21st-century Vilnius walk

Having had foreign monuments stamped all over its streets and squares in the past, Vilnius seems wary of erecting new ones to the grand dukes of its illustrious history or to the national heroes of its fight for survival. But monuments to capitalism, each more impressive than the last, are rising all the time. The riverbank between the southern end of A.Goštauto and the precarious, two-lane Geležinio Vilko is known today as the Business Triangle, crammed with flashy new high-rise office buildings. Close by, the Vilnius Gates (*Vilniaus vartai*), opened in 2006, tower above the Geležinio Vilko underpass.

However, the most visually striking of all these post-millennium skyscraper projects is **Europa Square** (*Europos aikštė*) and the sleek, glass-fronted structures around it. The wall of windows facing recently renamed Konstitucijos (Constitution) Avenue is the new **City Hall**, inside which is an accessible ground-floor room displaying a fascinating model of all the future construction developments in Vilnius. Behind it, at 134 metres, the circular **Europa Tower** (*Europos bokštas*) is the Baltic countries' tallest building. Thirty-three floors up, the panorama of Vilnius from the viewing platform is unrivalled – and it's free to get to the top. Just enter the ground floor and ask the security guard. But attempt this only at weekends; the companies that rent these prestigious offices do not want nosy sightseers getting lost or clogging up the elevators.

Arguably the most comfortable view in Vilnius, however, is from one of the curvaceous, ocean-blue chairs of the 22nd-floor **SkyBar** in the Reval Hotel Lietuva, just across Konstitucijos Avenue from Europa Square. Sitting with cocktail in hand, this is a perfect spot to watch the sunset.

Before 2002, these streets north of the river were a no-go area for most tourists, a scruffy mess of Soviet-era concrete, home to a few straggly shops and a shopping centre that more resembled an indoor market selling clothes, watches and electrical gadgets that had fallen off the backs of trucks.

Much of the ugly concrete is still there. But squeaky clean, colourfully landscaped shopping centres filled with refreshing air conditioning and the sound of running water – in particular the **Central Universal Store** (VCUP) and the **Europa Shopping Centre** – are taking the attention away from the eyesores. The latter include the pedestrian precinct between the refurbished Reval and the Green Bridge, once a futuristic showpiece of the late communist years. Now it is crumbling and cracked and permeated by strip bars. Halfway down the precinct, the **Planetarium** is still operational, despite having a furniture showroom in the lobby.

The **Green Bridge** (*Žaliasis tiltas*) itself is firmly part of the old era, its comical Socialist Realist figures of grim workers and determined peasants a bizarre contrast to the skyscrapers behind it. Why they were not pulled down immediately after the collapse of the Soviet Union, along with Lenin, and deported to the Grutas Soviet theme park is a matter of intense speculation. The authorities say that they stand as a warning to future generations of the horrors (artistic and otherwise) of communist rule. But it is also true that many locals actually see them as genuine works of art, created by Lithuanian sculptors, not imported from Moscow. In a similar way, many residents are proud, not ashamed, of architectural monsters such as the gargantuan **Opera and Ballet Theatre** (*Operos ir baletos teatras*), which virtually overshadows the Green Bridge, or the Parliament building, or even the city's hideous high-rise suburbs, all of which were designed by Lithuanian architects.

The green swathe of riverbank west of the Green Bridge is gradually being put to use. Next to the pedestrian-only **White Bridge** (*Baltasis tiltas*), which daredevil stunt pilot Jurgis Kairys flew under in 1999, are skateboarding, basketball and volleyball courts for restless youths – and '**The Beach**'. In summer, sip on a cold local draught beer under imported palm trees as the sand, brought here in trucks all the way from Lithuania's coastal dunes, tickles your toes.

WHAT TO SEE AND DO

MUSEUMS AND GALLERIES In an irritating overhang from earlier times, most museums are closed on at least one day a week – usually Sunday or Monday – and many for two days; they also close on public holidays. Most do not open until 10.00 and rare is the museum that closes as late as 18.00. Churches are open every day from around 09.00.

Admission prices here are given for adults. Most museums give reductions for children, senior citizens and, providing you have an international card, students and teachers. The websites www.muziejai.lt and www.lnm.lt provide further information.

Amber Museum-Gallery (*Šv Mykolo 8;* ℡ *262 3092; open 10.00–19.00; free admission*) Privately run (it's a shop too), this gallery reveals the history of 'Baltic gold' in several cavernous cellar rooms. You can also find amber here at the gallery in blue, black, white, red and green. It has plenty of unusual, handmade items to choose from including exquisitely designed necklaces, miniature amber musical instruments; even an amber-coloured liqueur in a flask with amber-topped stopper. Each piece comes with a certificate of authenticity.

Applied Arts Museum (*Arsenalo 3a;* ℡ *262 8080; open Tue–Sat 11.00–17.30, Sun 11.00–15.30; admission 6Lt*) Constructed as an arsenal in the 16th century by Sigismund the Old, the more decorative third floor being added by his son a few decades later, this was at the time the biggest building in the Polish-Lithuanian Commonwealth. It was virtually destroyed when the Russians invaded and pillaged the city in 1655, only to be rebuilt 150 years later.

These days it houses a rather austere collection of portraits, but also one or two paintings that are worth the price of admission alone, including canvases by Francisco Ximenez, Luis Morales and the master of Austrian baroque, Johann Michael Rottmayr. Don't miss also one of the best displays of folk art and Lithuanian wooden crosses. Many of these are by Vincas Svirkis (1835–1916), who spent his life roaming the countryside carving saints and religious scenes into the crosses he left behind as he moved from village to village.

Artillery Bastion (*Bokšto 20;* ℡ *261 2149; open 10.00–18.00 except Sun–Mon; admission 2Lt*) In centuries past, this part of Vilnius was infamous for its prostitution and wild taverns. Witches were said to gather here for demonic orgies. The bastion, part of the city's 17th-century defence against invading armies of Russians and Swedes, quickly fell into ruin and was used in the 19th century as a windowless orphanage, then became a rat-infested rubbish dump and public lavatory. The Soviets used it to store vegetables until it was finally restored in 1967. Today, there is not a great deal to see beyond a handful of old cannons, but there is plenty of history to imagine in the darkness. The fat, round walls of the Subačiaus Gate, home to the Vilnius Executioner, used to stand adjacent to the Bastion. With his mask on, he would walk down Subačiaus to Town Hall Square where condemned prisoners awaited their fate. The Slavs who tended to live on Subačiaus said that they knew the executioner's identity, because their dogs would bark at him, mask on or off.

Higher Castle (*Arsenalo 5;* ℡ *261 7453; open 10.00–17.00 except Mon; admission 4Lt*)
A climb via a cobbled path to the top of 50m-high Gediminas Hill rewards with a perfectly situated viewpoint across the rooftops and spires of the Old Town. A recently installed, super-smooth funicular railway, found in the courtyard of the Applied Arts Museum, makes the going easy up to this point. Take the natural next step and scramble to the summit – the viewing platform atop the Higher Castle – and the reward will be even greater.

In this 180° panorama, it is possible to make out virtually every major landmark in Vilnius, from the Gothic spires of St Anne's Church in the east, to the new financial centre rising up from the grassy banks on the opposite side of the river. Vilnius's Soviet-era high-rise housing and Television Tower stand out among the trees on the horizon; if it were not for these, one would have the impression of a city surrounded on all sides by thick forest. As such, the Higher Castle makes an ideal place to begin or end a tour of the city. Normally, in summer, the best light for photography is in the later part of the day.

The museum housed in the castle shows models of the castles of Vilnius as they looked in the 14th and 17th centuries, as well as a display of weapons, armour and a few maps. Other than the tower, little remains of the castle save for the fragments of outer walls.

It can now be taken for granted that the Lithuanian flag will be raised on the castle tower every day. This first happened on 1 January 1919, but following the Polish seizure of Vilnius in 1920, it was not seen again here until 1939. The flag was banned again in 1944 when the Soviets established what seemed to be a permanent occupation, but was courageously raised once more on 7 October 1988, three years before their regime finally collapsed.

M K Čiurlionis Museum (*Savičiaus 11;* ℡ *262 2451; open 10.00–16.00 except Sat–Sun; free admission*) The grand piano on which the gifted Lithuanian composer and painter wrote some of his best pieces is the main object of interest here. Prolific and yet at the same time a sufferer of depression and insomnia, M K Čiurlionis (1875–1911) lived in this small apartment in 1907–08. Fans of his paintings, like the cycle on the signs of the zodiac, will have to travel to the far more interesting Čiurlionis Museum in Kaunas.

Contemporary Art Centre (*Vokiečių 2;* ℡ *262 3476; open 12.00–21.00 except Mon; admission 6Lt*) Right alongside the town hall stands the concrete-and-glass Contemporary Art Centre, which, although an ugly blot on the face of the Old Town, provides much-needed display space for exhibitions that are predominantly, but not exclusively, of the works of living artists. The shows here are usually highly original and often shocking. The gallery's single permanent display is on Fluxus, a bizarre experimental art movement led by the Lithuanian-born George Maciunas, friend of Yoko Ono and John Lennon, which thrived in the US in the 1960s.

Jewish Museum (*Paménkalnio 12;* ☎ *262 0730; open Mon–Thu 09.00–17.00, Fri 09.00–16.00, Sun 10.00–16.00; free admission*) The wooden 'green house' houses a documentary display focusing on Jewish culture and life in Vilnius and Lithuania immediately before World War II and its destruction during the Holocaust. Outside stands a monument entitled Moonlight, which commemorates Chiune Sugihara, the Kaunas-based Japanese diplomat who is credited with rescuing up to 6,000 Jews, by granting them transit visas through Japan and therefore the opportunity to leave Lithuania.

Housed in a tenement building at Pylimo 4 is the Lithuanian State Jewish Museum, on the first floor of which are displays of liturgical objects, dolls used for theatrical performances during the Feast of Purim, prints and drawings of Vilnius's Great Synagogue, and photographs, supplemented by a few tantalising fragments, of the wonderfully elaborate wooden synagogues, all now destroyed, which once graced several Lithuanian towns. Two rooms on the floor above are dedicated to a photographic record of memorial sites throughout Lithuania to victims of Nazism, and to a gallery honouring those who sheltered or otherwise saved Jews.

The **Tolerance Centre** at Naugarduko 10 opened in 2004 and since then the collections found at Pylimo 4 and Paménkalnio 12 have been gradually transferred here.

KGB Museum (*Aukų 2a;* ☎ *249 6264; www.genocide.lt/muziejus; open 10.00–17.00 except Mon; admission 2Lt*) The entrance to one of Vilnius's most essential sites is at the western side of the building, as the front on the square is now a memorial to the many people who died there. In Soviet guidebooks, the building is described simply as 'a municipal institution'. In due course, it is intended to present a full documentary record on Soviet repression against Lithuania (particularly the Siberian deportations), and on the resistance to it. The first part of this exhibition opened in spring 2005.

In the meantime, the cells in the basement, which were used for the imprisonment and torture of political opponents until 1991, can be visited. These include an isolation cell which has neither heating nor windows, a special padded and soundproofed cell for suicide risks, and two cells where water torture was administered in order to keep prisoners constantly awake.

There is documentary material on some of the most prominent victims, while sacks of incriminating documents shredded by the KGB in the final three years of Soviet rule are also on view. A former execution chamber opened to the public in 2003. Great efforts were made to conceal this activity from the other prisoners, including naming the area 'the kitchen' and delaying executions until the spring, when removal and burial of the bodies became easier.

There are short labels in good English throughout the museum, but it is certainly worth hiring the audio guide for a fuller explanation of the terrifying role this building played through the Soviet period in Lithuania. The ticket desk sells several books in English about repression at that time.

Adam Mickiewicz Museum (*Bernadinų 11;* ☎ *279 1879; open Tue–Fri 10.00–17.00, Sat–Sun 10.00–14.00, closed Sun; admission 2Lt*) The famous Polish poet lived here for only two months, in 1822, but this apartment-museum provides the best insight into his life and creative mind to be found in Vilnius. It also shows paintings and engravings that reveal something of everyday life in the city at that time. Poland's greatest national poet is also one of Lithuania's national heroes, as the first words of his best-known epic *Pan Tadeusz* make perfectly clear: 'Lithuania, my homeland, you are like health. Only he who has lost you can know how much you are cherished.'

National Museum (*Arsenalo 1;* ☎ *262 9426; open 10.00–18.00, except Mon–Tue; admission 4Lt*) Curios as diverse as a wonderfully ornate baroque-style sledge from the

18th century, a handprint in iron of Peter the Great made at the opening of a smelting house in Belmontas, built to make guns for Russia's war against Sweden, and a Vilnius executioner's sword are just a few of the exhibits that brighten up the first hall. The sword, made in Germany in the early 17th century, is broken into two pieces, perhaps from a particularly tough neck. Exotic gifts from far and wide that have found their way here include a fan from the Emperor of Japan, presented to the officers of a Russian frigate in 1857, and an Egyptian sarcophagus that was a gift from the Museum of Prague in 1899.

Upstairs, a new exhibition celebrating Vilnius's millennial birthday in 2009 guides visitors through the history of Lithuania starting from 1,000 years ago. Fascinating maps, weapons, portraits, coins and other more unusual objects illustrate the battles against the Teutonic Order, the empire of the Grand Duchy, and everyday life in Vilnius in the centuries since then. The exhibition really emphasises the life of the citizens of Vilnius, the display showing satchels, plates, spoons, scarves and perfume bottles dating back to the 1600s. Another hall shows how rooms in typical Lithuanian farmsteads looked in centuries past. While large families often lived in cluttered surroundings, one room was always kept spotlessly clean in case visitors came to call unexpectedly. For an illuminating tour of the museum, ask for an English-speaking guide.

Pushkin Memorial Museum (*Subačiaus 124;* ☎ *260 0080; open 10.00–17.00 except Mon–Tue; admission 4Lt*) A hike along Subačiaus out to Vilnius's farthest reaches, or a ride on bus number 10 southwards from the cathedral, will take you through the shadowy residential district of Markučiai to a park and a hilltop house. The great Russian poet never lived here, of course, but his son Grigorij (1835–1905) did, together with his wife Varvara (1855–1935). Today, this large, rather rickety wooden house is home to many volumes of Pushkin's works and other curios, the ground floor furnished in the style of the late 19th century. Stroll to the back of the house, past a statue of Pushkin, and the quiet grounds extend to steps leading down to a lake. Paths reach out from here into the surrounding countryside and are a delight to explore.

Radvila Palace (*Vilniaus 22;* ☎ *262 0981; open 12.00–17.00 except Mon; admission 5Lt*) A generally austere collection of art from the 16th century onwards. Built for Jonušas Radvila, Voivod of Vilnius and Grand Hetman of Lithuania, this 17th-century Renaissance-style palace is now used mainly for showcasing 165 portrait engravings of Radvila family members, and also for the odd music concert.

Theatre, Music and Film Museum (*Vilniaus 41;* ☎ *262 2406; open Tue–Fri 12.00–18.00, Sat 11.00–16.00; admission 4Lt*) Despite its name, the 'display' on film is disappointingly cursory, with the briefest of looks at Lithuanian successes during the later Soviet years and virtually nothing on Lithuanian directors and actors since then. This history of the performing arts instead concentrates on the glory days before World War II, with keyboard instruments, still-working musical boxes and musty theatre costumes. One local theatre-turned-cinema director explains his request for subsidies from the Lithuanian government with his idea that 'In future cultural life, films will take the place of the theatre'.

Kazys Varnelis House Museum (*Didžioji 26;* ☎ *279 1644; open 10.00–17.00 except Sun–Mon (by appointment only); free admission*) It would almost be easier to describe what this eclectic art museum does not contain, rather than what it does. From his arrival in the USA in 1949, Kazys combined his work in op art with a passion for collecting just at the time when prices were low and quantities high. He had as much an eye for Chinese painting as he did for British first editions, Italian Renaissance furniture or Lithuanian cartography. Throughout the museum the best of old Europe combines with the best of modern America and the map collection has no equal anywhere. There are 170 maps in total, nearly all of them of Lithuania and the surrounding region. Ample space and light are provided for the fascinating collection of modern art. Although born in 1917, Kazys was still painting in the studio at the top of this house in 2005. The studio can usually be visited, as can the Gothic brick cellars, which date from the 15th century. The museum is open only by appointment so it is essential to email (*kvmuziejus@lnm.lt*) or phone ahead, or make arrangements through a travel agent who works with Lithuania.

Vilnius Picture Gallery (*Didžioji 4;* ✆ *212 4258; open 12.00–18.00, Sun 12.00–17.00, closed Mon; admission 5Lt*) This state-run gallery shows in chronological order the development of painting in Lithuania and there are some real gems to discover, in particular where the main art movements of 19th-century Europe are reflected in Lithuanian art. The gallery's first rooms begin with portraits, some dating as far back as the 16th century. The portraits of former rulers give an insight into the colourful history of the Polish-Lithuanian state.

Artists to look out for include Jan Rustemas, who became head of the city's first department of painting at Vilnius University in 1819. Born in Turkey to Greek parents, he lived in Warsaw and Berlin before bringing influences from these cities to Lithuania. He is credited with steering students away from classicism and towards Romanticism. Vincentas Dmachauskas's intense *Forest Fire* is a dramatic record of the destruction of the country's forests in the 19th century, monstrous fires that were also described by local writers and poets. There are also some evocative impressionist landscapes, such as Juozas Balzukevičius's *Across a Ryefield*.

CHURCHES
Vilnius Cathedral (*Katedros 1;* ✆ *261 1127; open 09.00–20.00*) There is more to this grandiose display of neo-classicism than meets the eye. The Chapel of St Casimir inside is a flamboyant baroque masterpiece with some breathtaking stucco work, while the cathedral's creepy crypt reaches into the bowels of the earth to reveal a fascinating cross-section of history, from the pagan to the present.

The cathedral occupies the site of what was once an ancient, open pagan temple revered by Lithuanians and dedicated to the worship of Perkūnas, god of thunder and fire. According to some accounts, toads, grass-snakes and other sacred creatures were kept nearby, ready for sacrifice on an altar that stood about 5m high. A fire blazed in a hollow in the temple, kept alight day and night. Virgins chosen for their beauty had the task of keeping the temple flames burning. If they failed, they were drowned with a cat and a snake, or were buried alive.

Over the 800 years since these pagan times, five consecutive cathedral buildings have been built on the site, each in turn ravaged by fire, flood or war. Twelve different floors can be identified in the crypt, right down to the pagan altar itself. The earliest floor, dating from the 13th century, is now 3m deep. One or two glazed terracotta tiles that have survived from this time are on show by the entrance. You can also make out the top of the doorway of the very first cathedral, built by Mindaugas, the man who unified the Baltic tribes for the first time. He was baptised with his family around 1251, and erected a cathedral, a square building with a massive tower, shortly afterwards. The pagan lords and tribes were not happy with this sudden conversion, and when they killed Mindaugas ten years later, the building was converted for use as a temple.

Grand Duke Jogaila converted to Christianity in 1387, uniting Lithuania and Poland. He took the name Wladislaw (Ladislaus) and built a church here dedicated to St Ladislaus and Poland's patron saint Stanislaus. This stood until a fire in 1419. Grand Duke Vytautas rebuilt it as a huge, Gothic, red-brick cathedral full of expressive architectural detail. It stood almost 8m taller than the present cathedral, and was completed only in 1430, the year Vytautas died. It was damaged by fire on several occasions in the next 300 years, and was repeatedly rebuilt and restored. But this was marshy ground, and in the mid-1700s the foundations started sinking. Cracks appeared and in 1769 a severe storm blew down the south tower, killing six people.

Extensive reconstruction giving the cathedral its final shape started in 1783, according to a design by Laurynas Stuoka-Gucevičius. His idea, fashionable at the time, was to give the appearance, inside and out, of a real Greek temple. In fact, the neo-classical style is very rare for a cathedral. Stuoka-Gucevičius also designed Vilnius Town Hall, the palace at Verkiai, and also the wonderful circular church in the village of Sudervė, 25km northwest of Vilnius. The cathedral was his last great work.

The great crypt was the final resting place for grand dukes, archbishops, noblemen and their families. There are about 20 vaults under the floor of the naves and chapels. Some have yet to be discovered, undisturbed behind thick walls. The remains of Alexander, Grand Duke of Lithuania and King of Poland at the turn of the 16th century, and the wives of Sigismund Augustus – Elzbieta and Barbora Radvilaitė – were discovered in 1931. They were moved through the crypt to a hauntingly lit mausoleum. Barbora has a special place in the nation's heart. She and Sigismund were married out of love and kept their union a secret from the scheming nobles of the Polish-Lithuanian Commonwealth until she died mysteriously in 1551.

Under the Soviets, Vilnius Cathedral was used as a car repair garage. The three huge statues of saints Helena, Casimir and Stanislaus on the pediment were hauled down and demolished. After Stalin's death in 1953, the building became an art gallery. Finally, during the first congress of national revival in 1988, it was declared that the cathedral would be returned to the Church. Eight years later, after independence, replicas of the saints' statues were returned to their place on the grand façade.

The curious cupola that conflicts with the cathedral's overall design stands out as the stunning baroque Chapel of St Casimir, a survivor of the earlier cathedral building. With red marble from Galicia, black and brown marble from the Carpathian Mountains, lavish stucco and 17th-century frescoes, the chapel is a feast for the eyes. Exquisitely decorated by Italian masters over a period of 14 years from 1622, for the sum of 500,000 gold coins, it was built as a final resting place for the remains of St Casimir, the patron saint of Lithuania, who died in 1484.

Casimir was the youngest son of a wealthy family whose brothers and sisters became kings and queens of European states through lineage and marriage. The pious Casimir, however, was more interested in charity and would go to the cathedral to pray even at night. When he died from tuberculosis at the age of 25, it was rumoured that his coffin could cure illness and disease. A fresco on one side of the chapel shows the legend of Uršulė, a sick orphan who prayed beneath the coffin and found herself miraculously cured. The fresco on the wall opposite shows the moment when the coffin was opened by clergy to see if the body was still well preserved – the sign of a saint. It was, of course, and Casimir was canonised in 1602.

The chapel has some odd features. A 17th-century retable (a decorative panel at the back of an altar) shows a Madonna and Child. The Madonna has a surprisingly broad smile, very unusual for this kind of reverent artwork. In front of it, a silver-coated portrait shows St Casimir with three hands. Some say this was to emphasise his generosity – he gave as if from three hands. Look up into the cupola and you'll see beasts and objects finely moulded from stucco – an elephant for moderation (an elephant never eats more than his/her share), an elk to prevent rash decisions, and a mirror to see both sides of an argument.

The chapel nearest the entrance on the southern side is now known as the 'Deportees Chapel' because of the recent memorials that have been erected there to the many senior figures in the church who were persecuted in Soviet times. One of the statues is of Mečislovas Reinys, who was Archbishop of Vilnius before his arrest in 1947. He died in 1953 in Vladimir Prison near Moscow. Another is of Vincentas Borisevičius, Bishop of Telšiai until he was executed in 1947 for the 'crime' of being a 'bourgeois leader'. His final words were: 'Your hour of victory is brief; the future is mine; Christ will be victorious, just as Lithuania will be victorious.' It would be 40 years before he was proved right.

Church of St Anne (*Maironio 8;* ℡ *261 4805; open 08.30–18.00*) A masterpiece of late Gothic, the enchanting façade features 33 shapes and sizes of red bricks arranged in flamboyant patterns. Its intricate towers, spires and narrow windows were enough to enchant Napoleon, who in an oft-quoted remark said that he wished he could carry it back to Paris on the palm of his hand. He is, in fact, unlikely to have said such a thing, since like the rest of Europe in 1812 he disliked Gothic intensely as an outmoded style. Lithuanians saw Napoleon as a liberator from the grip of Tsarist Russia and probably concocted this story themselves. The French leader stationed some of his cavalry in St Anne's and most of its stained glass was broken and the wax ceilings destroyed by the soldiers' campfires.

The mystery of who designed the church endures to this day. One tale tells of a talented young Lithuanian apprentice named Jonas who helped his master from Belarus in the initial stages of construction before going to study architecture abroad. On his return he mocked his old master's work and completed the church in a flourish while the offended master vanished for several years. During this time Jonas married the master's daughter and settled into the family home. Late one stormy night, the master returned and insisted on Jonas showing him the brickwork. On the scaffolding, the more Jonas enthusiastically explained his work, the more envy the master felt. Eventually he pushed Jonas over the edge. Jonas caught hold of a piece of overhanging wood, but the master took a brick and brought it crashing down on Jonas's head. This tale of the outré may be mere legend, but it is strange how the lower part of the façade appears so much more austere than the rest. It is also true that in written records there were two architects, one known simply as 'Johannes', the other not mentioned at all.

Bernardine Church/Church of SS Francis & Bernardino (*Maironio 10;* ℡ *260 9292; open 08.30–18.00*) More than just the Gothic backdrop to St Anne's, the Bernardine Church is impressive in its sheer size. The vaulting is wondrous, but tragically the rest of the interior did not escape the ravages of the centuries. Fire, war and neglect left it to rot until 1994 when it was returned to the brethren of St Francis. Students from Vilnius Art Academy have slowly been renovating it ever since. Mass in English is held here every Sunday at 17.00.

Church of St Casimir (*Didžioji 34;* ℡ *212 1715; open 10.00–18.00*) The oldest baroque church in Vilnius, St Casimir's was founded by Jesuits in 1604. Named after Lithuania's patron saint, who had just been canonised, it's modelled on Il Gesu in Rome, the Jesuits' much-imitated mother church, but with characteristically Lithuanian twin spires set on top. St Casimir's has suffered many abuses through the centuries, including 20 years of humiliation as the Soviets' museum of atheism. Locals especially recall the prime exhibit – a re-creation of Inquisition torture implements, displayed to show the cruelty of the medieval Catholic Church. Now it is back in the safe hands of the original owners. The glittering crown on the central dome symbolises the royal family that Casimir came from (see *Vilnius Cathedral*, page 163). It was placed there in 1942.

Church of St Catherine (*Vilniaus 30; closed to the public*) This rather intimidating structure originally belonged to a Benedictine convent founded in 1618. Following a series of fires, it was rebuilt between 1741 and 1753 by the Vilnius-born Polish architect

Jan Krzyzstof Glaubitz, who also designed the extraordinary Basilian Gates. In order to overcome the restricted nature of the site, he adopted an audacious design based on a nave which is as high as it is long. The exterior features an elaborate rear-facing gable as a counterbalance to the majestic twin-towered façade. The interior is richly furnished, but has not been accessible for many years because of ongoing restoration work.

Church of the Holy Spirit (Catholic) (Dominikonų 8; ℩ 262 9595; open 07.00–18.00) A Dominican friary established in Vilnius in 1501 gave Dominikonų Street its name. Its extravagant Church of the Holy Spirit, a lavish display of baroque furnishings and decoration that are almost rococo in appearance, is a suitable setting for several hauntings and unexplained events. The interior was ravaged by fire in the 18th century and almost completely remade. Its huge crypt, which extends underground even beyond the walls of the church, was used to bury corpses from the Napoleonic wars and, before that, plague victims. The bodies remain incredibly well preserved, stacked up on top of each other. It is not possible to go down there.

Strangely, the church was not closed by the Soviets and remained a place of worship throughout the last century. Today it is the religious heart of Vilnius's Polish community. The eye of the visitor is drawn immediately to the altarpiece, which depicts a vision of Christ as he appeared in a miracle to a local nun in 1931. The painting, *Divine Mercy*, was completed by the Vilnius artist Eugenijus Kazimierovskis (1873–1939) in 1934 but only after ten attempts to portray the vision as accurately as possible. The inscription '*Jezu ufam tobie*' means 'Jesus, I trust in thee'. To the Polish community, the wide rays of red and white light represent their flag. The painting was hidden in the countryside through most of the Soviet period, only being brought back to this church in 1986 at the beginning of the perestroika period. Its long-term location is a matter of considerable dispute, as a chapel over the road has been built to house it but the Polish community is eager to keep it where it now stands and where Pope Paul II saw it on his 1993 visit to Vilnius.

Statues of King David and angel musicians adorn the beautifully carved case that protects an organ made in 1776 by Adam Casparini. This is the oldest organ in Vilnius and a model of it is being built for Christ Church at the University of Rochester, New York. It should be finished in 2008.

Church of the Holy Spirit (Orthodox) (Aušros Vartų 10; ℩ 212 7765; open 08.00–18.00) The most revered of the city's Russian Orthodox churches stands in a peaceful courtyard away from the bustle of Aušros Vartų Street. There is not actually a great deal to distinguish it from the surrounding Catholic churches, it having been rebuilt by the genius of the late baroque period Jan Krzysztof Glaubitz after a fire in 1749. But the most important feature makes it a popular place of pilgrimage for Orthodox Christians – the well-preserved bodies of saints Anthony, Ivan and Eustace, killed by pagans in 1347 for not renouncing their faith. The three lie in a glass-topped case shrouded in red most of the year, in white during Christmas and black during Lent. Should you be in Vilnius on 26 June, however, visit this church to feel the healing spirit that is said to envelop it when the bodies are unveiled.

Church of St John (Šv Jono 12; ℩ 261 1795; open for services Sun 11.00–13.00) Immediately after Grand Duke Jogaila shed his pagan beliefs to convert to Christianity in 1387, he commissioned this church, completed 40 years later. Originally Gothic, the awe-inspiring baroque façade you see today was designed once again by Jan Krzysztof Glaubitz, in the 1740s. The interior, accessible from a university courtyard, boasts a high altar consisting of no fewer than ten interconnected altars. One of the many memorials inside is dedicated to the memory of Adam Mickiewicz.

Church of SS Peter and Paul (*Antakalnio 1;* ↘ *234 0229; open 07.00–19.00*) One of Vilnius's most stunning baroque churches, with twin-tower façade and a central dome, the magnificent Church of SS Peter and Paul was completed in 1685. It was built on the site of a wooden church that had been burned by pillaging Russians during their destructive invasion 30 years earlier. This was a time of almost constant war, but churches like this continued to rise up. The man who commissioned the Church of SS Peter and Paul was Mykolaj Casimir Pac, Field Hetman of the Grand Duchy of Lithuania. His appeal to the Mother of God above the church entrance is not for strength in war, but for an end to war: 'Regina pacis fundanos in pace' ('Queen of peace, protect us in peace'), although this could simply have been a playful pun on the patron's name.

Mythological scenes and strange creatures, flowers, trees, and over 2,000 human figures in stucco decorate the rich interior. Baroque also placed a lot of emphasis on death, which accounts for the array of skulls, skeletons, dragons and demons immediately on the left and right as you walk in. Criminals were not allowed to enter any further into the nave than this point and the ugly images were meant to remind them of the consequences of sin.

In the amazing figures and images in stucco, stories can be made out. Many relate to the sea, since Peter and Paul were both fishermen, and possibly the main curiosity in the entire church is an enormous, boat-shaped chandelier, hanging from the cupola like a grand cluster of jewels, magnificently catching the light.

If the bottom of the kettledrum close to the altar to Mary on the left appears blackened, this is because it also doubled in times of war as a cooking pot and a bath for the soldiers.

Gates of Dawn (*Aušros Vartų 12;* ↘ *212 3513; open 09.00–17.00*) One of the essential sights on any trip to Vilnius, the 16th-century Gates of Dawn – originally part of the city's fortifications – now hold a small chapel housing a gold-and-silver holy image of the Virgin Mary, the Madonna of Mercy, which overlooks the street through open windows. Locals cross themselves every time they walk underneath it, while the most devout of worshippers crawl piously on their knees up steps from a doorway on the left. Unless you want to crawl too, climb past them to inspect the miracle-working icon up close. Afterwards, pass out of the gates to find part of the original city wall stretching down a dark back alley towards the Artillery Bastion.

LANDMARKS
Europa Tower (*Konstitucijos 7a;* ↘ *248 7171; open at weekends; free admission*) Thirty-three floors up in the Europa Tower, the tallest skyscraper in the Baltic states, completed in 2004, the view of central Vilnius is unrivalled. It's perfect for a bird's-eye perspective on where the best vacant lots of real estate are hiding. And getting to the top is free. There is only one restriction: the Europa Tower is a caffeine-fuelled office building, which means that the resident companies do not want unruly groups of sightseers milling around, clogging up the lifts. So access to the public is only at the weekend. Otherwise, groups can call ahead to book visits on weekdays.

After an ear-popping elevator ride to the top, the open air is invigorating. The 33rd floor is an open terrace facing southwards, while the vista to the north is from office space that can be rented out for seminars or private parties, for which food and drink can be ordered from one of the eateries in the Europa shopping centre below. Both views stretch the full 180 degrees.

It's the panorama to the south that grabs the attention, taking in the Old Town, the river and the brand new smattering of nearby skyscrapers. From this height, however, some of the buildings become virtually indistinguishable and the tall glass barrier also slightly obscures the visibility. But it's the thrill of standing on one of the highest viewpoints for hundreds of kilometres around that you should come for.

Looking north, you can see Vilnius's ragbag of old and new suburbs – the tumbledown wooden shacks of Šnipiškės, which will soon disappear to make way for new buildings, and in the distance masses of identical Soviet-era residential blocks.

Gariūnai Market For years one of the biggest open-air markets in eastern Europe, these days Gariūnai is dominated by poor-quality products from China and Turkey. The sprawling market stands in the shadow of the city's water-heating plant, about 10km west of the city centre on the road to Kaunas. The stalls sell pushchairs, lightbulbs, pirate DVDs, hi-fis, bad coffee, you name it. Some of the clothes sellers have recently gone upmarket with permanent stalls that actually resemble small shops. The rest, though, is set up from scratch early in the morning, which explains why so many of the salespeople yawn at you. In the early 1990s it was rumoured you could buy weapons here by finding the man with the toy gun on his bonnet. The best times to go are weekend mornings; by noon the market is closing up. Watch your wallet/handbag.

Paneriai (*Agrastų 17;* ↘ *260 2001*) Out in the forests to the southwest of Vilnius lies the village of Paneriai, consisting mostly of close-knit wooden houses, unpaved streets, a railway track and stray dogs. Close by, about 100,000 people were murdered in a clearing, their bodies burned in pits. Most of them were Jews from Vilnius – a fact ignored in the wording on the memorials here until 1990. In fact, a dance hall was raised on the site in the early Soviet period. Today, the pits are displayed, the whole place eerily quiet except for the occasional passing train. It is notoriously hard to find due to the shameful lack of signposting. Take a train going to Trakai and get off at the Paneriai stop. Walk along the lane that runs more-or-less parallel to the tracks in the same direction the train is heading. The memorial lies at the end of the road, after about a kilometre. A small branch of the Lithuanian State Jewish Museum displays some photographs, but it has no set opening times and is closed in winter.

Television Tower (*Sausio 13-osios 10;* ↘ *252 5333; open 12.00–21.00; admission 15Lt, children 6Lt*) Venture out into the 'sleeping districts' of Vilnius's high-rise suburbs at least once during your stay and experience this Soviet vision of the 1970s space age, with an unequalled panorama from its 55th-floor restaurant. Christened Paukščių Takas, Lithuanian for 'Milky Way', when it opened in 1980, the restaurant is 165m up and rotates slowly so that a full circle is completed in 50 minutes. On a clear day you can see up to 70km in every direction (don't come if the sky is thick with cloud), when you will discover just how amazingly green Lithuania really is. Coniferous forests stretch out to the horizon. The Old Town and Vilnius's landmark buildings are clearly visible just to the east. Beyond, you can spy on Belarus, the last dictatorship in Europe, only 40km away.

Before you shoot up in the high-speed elevator, you have a choice at the reception of either paying the entry fee and then having the freedom of the menu, or taking one of four set meals for about double the price, which includes the entry fee. We recommend the former, since the set meals are more a convenient tool for the restaurant when coping with groups.

The wording on the menu is worth the price of admission alone. 'Meat collection' consists of 'fried pork, fried neck with dried plumps'. The wonderfully titled 'Mischief of frost' is 'fruit and berry ice cream, berries and fruit'.

Before you leave, pay your respects to the 14 Lithuanian civilians who died here defending the Television Tower from Soviet tanks on the night of 13 January 1991. A small exhibition remembering this tragic event can be found on the ground floor. Outside, granite markers show the precise places where the victims were crushed beneath tanks or shot. Sadly, the surroundings look a little unkempt, weeds protruding through the concrete blocks.

However, the tower comes to life in December when it becomes what is claimed to be the tallest artificial Christmas tree in the world, with fairy lights stretching up its entire height.

Verkiai Palace (*Žaliųjų ežerų 47;* ☏ *271 1618; open 09.00–17.00 except Sat–Sun; admission 3Lt*) The remains of a superb classical mansion stand on a hill just to the north of Vilnius. The land here belonged to grand dukes until 1387, when Jogaila, on his conversion to Christianity, granted it to the new diocese of Vilnius to be used by the bishops as a summer residence. In 1780, a huge palace was constructed here, but Napoleon's soldiers ravaged it in 1812. Soon after that the central part of the palace was pulled down.

Today, the rooms in the remaining wings of the palace contain a great deal of handsome, intricate woodwork and some attractive painted ceilings. There's also a lovely view of the forested River Neris valley below, and at the very end of the ridge is a fireplace surrounded by stones. A legend tells how a sacred fire was once tended on this spot by a pagan priest and beautiful virgins.

Walk down the long flight of steps to an old mill, recently renovated into a restaurant, named Verkių Vandens Malūnas. It serves delicious homemade meals and has peaceful outdoor seating overlooking the river in summer.

Vilnius University (*Universiteto 3;* ☏ *261 1795; open 09.00–17.00 except Sun*) The oldest university in eastern Europe is a maze of 12 courtyards, corridors, halls and towers. It is a delight to explore and usually no-one will mind if you do. An absurd practice of selling tickets at the gate was recently established, but we recommend you walk directly through with a sense of purpose, pretending you're a visiting professor or a mature student. A basic map of the complicated layout is at Universiteto 7.

Founded by the Jesuits in 1570 and given university status in 1579, Vilnius University has not always been allowed to flourish and contribute to the cultural, social and political life of the city. Many of its students and professors have aided the resistance against virtually every occupation, often to find themselves persecuted, even executed. The entire university was closed by the Russian Tsarist authorities in 1832 for backing the failed rebellion the year before. It stayed closed until 1919, the year after Lithuanian independence was regained.

At the far end of the initial Sarbievijus Courtyard is the lovely Littera bookshop, whose walls and ceiling were painstakingly decorated by local painter Antanas Kmieliauskas in preparation for the university's 400th birthday in 1979. In fact, the university as a whole is in good condition because of the extensive renovations made in time for that event. Another artist, Petras Repšys, created the stunning fresco cycle in the Centre for Lithuanian Studies next door, working at it for nine years, finishing in 1985.

Up a flight of steps from the Sarbievijus Courtyard is the Great Courtyard, dominated on one side by the monumental baroque façade of St John's Church. There is an almost Mediterranean flavour to the open arcades around the courtyard, while faded frescoes from the 18th century show figures who influenced the early part of the life of the university. An arch in the western side of the courtyard leads to a small but charmingly leafy courtyard beside the Observatory, the walls of which are decorated with the signs of the Zodiac.

CEMETERIES Vilnius has a number of cemeteries set amid the hills around the city centre that are really worth visiting, if time permits, for they reflect aspects of the city's tumultuous history. Reach Antakalnis Cemetery by walking beyond the Church of SS Peter and Paul up busy Antakalnio Street, bearing right onto L Sapiegos then turning right onto progressively quieter Kuosų and Kariu. The Bernadine Cemetery is found, eerie and cut off from the rest of the city, in Užupis, at the end of a little lane off Polocko Street. Rasa Cemetery is best reached by strolling up Rasų Street away from Subačiaus in the Old Town.

Antakalnis Cemetery (*Antakalnio kapinės*) A calm and peaceful place that brings together much of Vilnius's modern history, the biggest public cemetery in Vilnius has elegantly carved old memorial stones covering the rolling, tree-shaded landscape, the crosses and tombs adorned and inscribed in Lithuanian, Russian and Polish. Following the paved path into the cemetery, you find a series of identical stone crosses over to the left dedicated to Polish soldiers killed during World War I – as bloody and tragic a conflict in Eastern Europe as it was in the West. By taking paths to the right, you'll find broadly chiselled Soviet-era statues in the Socialist Realist style, commemorating those poets and political leaders who toed the party line. Cut into a hill at the cemetery's heart is a sweeping, semi-circular memorial to the 14 people who died defending the Television Tower and the Parliament building in January 1991.

Bernardine Cemetery (*Bernadinų kapinės*) Beautifully perched on a high bank above the little River Vilnia, at the far end of the quaint suburb of Užupis, is this tranquil spot, tightly packed with lopsided metal crosses and tiny, uneven plots. Founded in 1810, this quiet retreat holds the last resting places of university academics and painters. Over the long years, trees have gently elbowed their way between the tombs, making them even more irregular, gradually spilling through railings that fence off the graves. Desolate and wonderfully gloomy, you will find no calmer place in Vilnius.

Rasa Cemetery (*Rasų kapinės*) Deceptively isolated, this hill of crosses contains the graves of famous Lithuanians like Jonas Basanavičius, the founder at the end of the 19th century of the first Lithuanian-language newspaper *Aušra* (Dawn). He lies close to the chapel, while uphill from the main entrance lies the tombstone of revered painter and composer M K Čiurlionis. Right next to the entrance, however, is a more controversial site – the family plot of the Polish leader Josef Pilsudski, the man responsible for Poland's annexation of Vilnius in 1920. He was buried in Krakow, but his heart was cut out and buried here, in this tomb. Rasa Cemetery has been a place of spiritual reverence also during troubled times. More daring Lithuanians gathered here in October 1956 to protest against the suppression of the Hungarian uprising.

EXCURSIONS FROM VILNIUS

Vilnius offers a wide choice of places to visit for a half- or full-day excursion and it is well worth extending a short break to allow time for these. Kaunas definitely requires a full day and staying the night is also worthwhile to give more time to cover what it offers. A half-day in Trakai is enough for seeing the spectacular Island Castle, but not for walking around the lake and the charming village. Europa Park can be covered in half a day; about two hours is probably sufficient to cover the array of sculptures, but in good weather a leisurely day could happily be spent there.

EUROPA PARK (*Off the road that passes Verkai and the Green Lakes (follow the signs), 10km north of Vilnius;* ℡ *237 7077; www.europosparkas.lt; open 09.00–sunset; admission 20Lt*) There's a lot of talk about the concept of Europe in Lithuania, just as there is in the other EU countries. Here, however, it is brought to life just a few kilometres from the 'centre of Europe' as defined in 1989 by the French National Geographic Institute. Although only about 10km north of Vilnius, access by public transport is very difficult, so it is worth joining a group tour or sharing a taxi with others. Europa Park is an open-air museum of mostly bizarre modern sculptures in a woodland and meadow setting (take insect repellent in July), with exhibits specially created for the site by around 100 different artists from 30 countries around the world.

Founded in 1991, it is the brainchild of the Lithuanian sculptor Gintaras Karosas who had conceived the idea a few years earlier while still a teenager and who did much of the preparatory work of clearing the site with his own hands. He created the pivotal *Monument of the Centre of Europe* which features a pyramid and indications of the direction and distances to a range of worldwide capitals, of which the furthest away is Wellington in New Zealand. Karosas was also responsible for the heavily symbolic *Infotree* by the park entrance, which has gained an entry in the *Guinness Book of Records* for being the world's largest artwork of television sets. There are 3,000 in all, arranged (when viewed from above) in the shape of a tree, with a decaying statue of Lenin in the middle.

Chair Pool by the American Dennis Oppenheim is the most popular work, and also the most humorous, as its subject is exactly what the title suggests, a giant chair with a small pool instead of a seat. The success of this led to the commissioning of a second composition from Oppenheim, *Drinking Structure with Exposed Kidney Pool*, consisting of a hut dipping down towards the water. Other sculptures guaranteed to catch the eye are Magdalena Abakanowicz's *Space of Unknown Growth*, a group of 22 concrete boulders; Jon Barlow Hudson's *Cloud Hands*, which consists of four granite blocks seemingly suspended in the air; and the 6m-high *Woman Looking at the Moon* by the Mexican Javier Cruz.

KAUNAS With Kaunas, Lithuania's second city, only 90 minutes by train or bus from Vilnius, it is a pity not to spend a day there, or at least to linger awhile after arriving at Kaunas Airport, where more and more flights from Western Europe are now landing. In the immediate aftermath of independence in 1991, it has to be admitted that Kaunas was very slow to change and the distance between it and Vilnius seemed, in a metaphorical sense, to grow each year. From around 2000, this pattern has begun to change and the sudden influx of no-frills airlines into the local airport since 2005 will doubtless accelerate this process. The trebling of property prices within the three years 2003–06 is a further sign of rapid change.

Getting there and away Local buses link the airport with the town centre, and long-distance ones leave every half hour for Vilnius. There are also about eight trains a day between Kaunas and Vilnius. The railway and bus stations are close together in both towns, so it is possible to travel by train in one direction and by bus in the other. Several local trolleybuses go from the bus and railway station to the Castle, where it is possible to start a walk which finishes back at the station. This is described below. Most museums close on Monday, and some on Tuesday too, so these days should be avoided for visiting Kaunas. The website (*www.kaunas.lt*) gives exact opening times for all museums. The Bradt guides to *Vilnius* and *Lithuania* both have full chapters on Kaunas for those able to stay longer.

What to see Kaunas is divided into the Old Town, **Senamiestis**, where every century from the 15th to the 19th is represented, and the New Town, **Naujamiestis**, which is mostly 20th century, although its layout of long straight roads was established in 1871. Kaunas was the 'provisional' capital of Lithuania from 1920 to 1940, when Vilnius was occupied by the Poles and the grand buildings in the new part of town basically reflected a view that it was likely to become a permanent capital.

The **Castle** looks as though it has withstood endless sieges; in fact its run-down state simply results from neglect since the mid 19th century when the Russians stopped using it for defence purposes against the Germans. It is now being restored so the original layout from the 14th century has become clearer. **Town Hall Square** is about 200m away; it looks unchanged since 1800 when much of it was built. As private houses were limited to two stories, the 53m tower on the **Town Hall** itself makes it look taller than it really is. For those of average height or less, a trip down the tortuous staircase to the cellars is worthwhile, where the **Ceramics Museum** has both a permanent display and regular exhibitions of contemporary artists. On the south side, behind the statue of Jonas Maironis, Lithuania's most famous poet, is the **Literature Museum** which also covers books written by Lithuanians in exile. On the north side is the **Postal Museum**, which goes back to horse-drawn carriages but also covers more recent means of communication such as the fax and telex. Finally on the east side is the **Pharmacy Museum**, where a 19th-century dispensary has been redesigned.

The **cathedral** is on the corner of the square and Vilniaus. It is unusual for having a totally Gothic exterior and a largely baroque interior. A short detour is worth making along the fourth street to the right, Zamenhofo, named after the founder of Esperanto, who lived in Kaunas. This leads to the **Folk Instruments Museum**, where the staff are often willing to demonstrate the various exhibits. As Vilniaus comes towards the New Town, the former **Presidential Palace** is on the left, with statues outside of its three occupants. This is now a museum commemorating the 1920–40 period when it was in use.

The mile-long **Laisvès Alèja**, like Vilniaus, a pedestrian precinct, goes from one end of the New Town to the other, although cars can cross it at several intersections. The buildings here are clearly those of a former capital city. The first large one on the left is the **Zoological Museum**. The collection is extensive, but so gloomily displayed that it really will only interest taxidermy fanatics. Next is the **post office** with its display of all the stamps issued by Lithuania since independence was restored. Many of these can still be bought there, together with first-day covers. The park opposite the post office commemorates Romas Kalanta, a 19-year-old student who burnt himself to death here in 1972 as a protest against the Soviet occupation. The 19 stones which make up the memorial represent each year of his short life.

At the fountain that marks the crossroads with Daukanto, a detour to the left is necessary to see the **Military Museum**. This is pictured on the back of the 20-lit note. Westerners will be most interested in the section on Napoleon who conquered this area *en route* to Moscow in 1812 and then lost it a few months later in his ignominious retreat. A larger area, however, is devoted to the two local heroes pictured on the 10-lit note, the pilots Darius and Girenas who lost their lives in a crash over East Prussia, when they had nearly completed, after 37 hours, a non-stop flight across the Atlantic. The wreck itself, together with the mangled remains of what they took with them on the flight, are all on show here.

At the back of this building is another which houses the **Čiurlionis Art Museum**, named after the person who is both Lithuania's most famous composer and artist, even though he died when he was only 36 years old. Both can be appreciated here, as can a collection of wooden religious artefacts from much earlier times. Over the road is the **Devils Museum** where the 2,000 figures collected by one person obsessed with this theme take three floors to show. Do not miss Stalin and Hitler dancing on a map of Lithuania.

The square that marks the end of Laisvès Alèja is dominated by the church **St Michael the Archangel** which can in fact be seen along its entire length. Clearly built as a Russian Orthodox Church at the end of the 19th century, it was in fact given to the local Catholic community in 1990. The crypt now houses the **Museum of the Blind**, totally based on sound, smell and touch. The very Soviet building on the right hand side of the square is the **Žilinskas Museum**, named after a Lithuanian exile who bequeathed his collection of 16th–20th-century art to Kaunas. The statue of a naked man in front of the museum still causes controversy, which was presumably its initial purpose.

TRAKAI Set on a slim peninsula between sparkling lakes and forests, the picturesque village of Trakai (*www.trakai.lt*) is reason alone to visit Lithuania. Its biggest attraction is the awe-inspiring Island Castle, a truly magical sight filled with enchanting medieval atmosphere. Wooden bridges connect the castle with the rest of the village and leaping from them into the clear water in summer is almost irresistible. Yachts for hire and paddle boats circle Lake Galvė's 21 islands.

The castle keeps its fairy-tale quality in the depths of winter under a thick blanket of snow, the villagers out ice-fishing and the landscape deserted, making the whole adventure of coming here infinitely more personal.

There is a distinctly exotic flavour to Trakai, thanks to the presence of the Karaites, a community of Turkic settlers whose ancestors were taken as bodyguards by Vytautas the Great on his march south to the Crimea in 1398. They had converted to a branch of reformed Judaism in the 8th century and their oriental-looking prayer house, or Kenessa, built in the 18th century, and a Karaite museum are located on Karaimų Street. Their characteristic, colourful wooden houses, each with gable ends and three windows facing the street, line Karaimų. Perhaps the Karaites' most lasting legacy in Lithuania is culinary – the ubiquitous '*kibinai*', Cornish-pasty-shaped pastries filled with juicy meat.

Getting there and away The 25km journey from Vilnius by bus or by train takes around 30 minutes. You might even take the bus in one direction and the train in the other, since the stations stand close together in both Vilnius and Trakai. A local bus covers the 2km between the bus station and the footbridge to the castle, but the walk through the village is much more pleasurable. Renting a car for the day is more advisable than hiring a taxi, since this will give the freedom to explore the beautiful surrounding landscape. Parking near the castle costs 5Lt.

Eating and drinking Lunch or dinner in Trakai is now an appetising prospect. The range of restaurants has improved considerably since 2004, most serving traditional Lithuanian and Karaim food.

✕ **Akmeninė Užeiga** On the Vievis road, 2km from Trakai; ☏ (8-614) 86654. Oddly, this enviably situated restaurant, hotel, sauna and wine cellar on the shores of Lake Akmena, arguably the most beautiful body of water in Trakai, is not signposted at all. But that makes it one of the best-kept dining secrets in the country. Find it after turning right on the roundabout on the far side of Trakai. Pass the lake, climb a slope and it's on the left. It's a fabulous spot to dine, with two tables out on a pier on the water and more on the grassy bank with a fine view of the lake. Try the 'Baked pike-perch with Indonesian sauce', 'Fresh salmon Tatar' or the mouthwatering 'Braised mussels in mustard sauce'.

✕ **Apvalaus Stalo Klubas** Karaimų 53a; ☏ (8-528) 55595. The strangely named Round Table Club is a classy restaurant on the quayside directly facing the Island Castle. It has both a formal dining room that is frequently empty and a pizza restaurant popular with the masses. The formal section serves particularly good fish dishes.

✕ **Csarda** Aukštadvario 28a; ☏ (8-616) 55366. A Hungarian restaurant in Trakai is curious enough, but its location beside a busy Leader Price superstore when there are so many appealing locations for miles around is positively bizarre. Since the terrace overlooks the parking area, winter is a far more appealing season to dine here, the cosy tavern-like interior based around a central fireplace. The food? Not bad, and reasonably priced.

✕ **Kibininė** Karaimų 65; ☏ (8-528) 55865. This long-standing Karaite restaurant with dark, barn-style interior has achieved cult status due to the fact that only two dishes have ever been on the menu – '*kibinai*', of course, and a meat-and-veg stew served in a clay pot. Order both, since they are equally delicious, and why not wash them down with Lithuanian vodka?

✕ **Kiubėtė** Vytauto 3a; ☏ (8-528) 59160. Situated on Lake Totoriškių, just off the beaten tourist path, the big attraction here is the unique pie that this charming, authentic Karaite restaurant is named after. The tasty traditional dish comes from recipes handed down from owner Ingrida Špakovskaja's great-grandparents. Ingrida is one of the few remaining Karaim still living in Trakai.

✕ **Žvejų Namai** On the Trakai road, 2km from Vievis; ☏ (8-528) 26008. At the 'home of the fishermen' don't

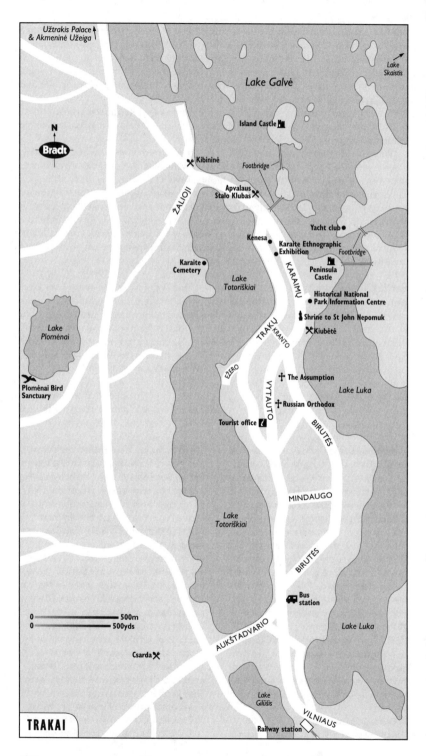

Užtrakis Palace ✦
& Akmeninė Užeiga

Lake Galvė

Lake
Skaistis

N
Bradt

✕ Kibininė

Island Castle 🏰

Footbridge

ŽALIOJI

Apvalaus
Stalo Klubas ✕

Yacht club ●

Kenesa ●

Karaite Ethnographic
Exhibition ●

Footbridge

Karaite ●
Cemetery

Lake
Totoriškiai

KARAIMŲ

Peninsula
Castle 🏰

Historical National
● Park Information Centre

Lake
Plomėnai

TRAKŲ KRANTO

🛐 Shrine to St John Nepomuk

✕ Kiubėtė

EŽERO

✈ Plomėnai Bird
Sanctuary

VYTAUTO

✝ The Assumption

Lake Luka

✝ Russian Orthodox

Tourist office ℹ

BIRUTĖS

MINDAUGO

Lake
Totoriškiai

BIRUTĖS

0 ————— 500m
0 ————— 500yds

🚌 Bus
station

Lake Luka

Csarda ✕

AUKŠTADVARIO

Lake
Gilūšis

VILNIAUS

TRAKAI

Railway station ▱

174

go looking for veal. It's fish on the menu. And only fish. And only one kind of fish: trout. Catch your fish and order it cooked in the style of your choice – trout Mexican, trout Scottish, salted trout, rapidly salted trout, trout soup, it's up to you. A kilo of fish costs 29Lt, whichever way it's prepared.

What to see and do The spectacular **Island Castle** dates from the 14th century, but was partially destroyed with Russia's invasion in 1655. From a distance, the extensive renovation work done between 1951 and 1962 – with Kremlin money, astonishingly enough, repairing a symbol of serfdom and national identity at the height of Soviet repression – appears to have been an amazing success. Up close, however, the lack of harmony between the original lumps of stone and modern factory-made bricks is obvious. But it is the awesome view of the castle from afar that all visitors remember, a sight that must have shaken the knees of any potential attacker.

When it was constructed on a cluster of three small islands, the 4m-thick walls literally rose up from the water. Every man coming to Trakai was ordered to bring a stone the size of a sheep's head or larger. The 30m-high keep was the residence of the Grand Duke, connected to the rest of the castle by a drawbridge. Steps leading down to the water where a boat was waiting was a possible secret escape in time of battle.

Vytautas the Great's escape from the Island Castle was far more remarkable, however. His ambitious cousins Jogaila and Skirgaila had taken it as theirs and then tricked Vytautas and his father Kęstutis into coming to negotiate for it, imprisoning them in the castle dungeon. Vytautas was a rare man in those days, wearing his hair long but without a beard. One night, his brave wife Anna, in the company of a serf girl, demanded to see her husband. Vytautas and the girl switched clothes, and the future grand duke slipped away undetected. When the cousins learned of this illustrious escape, they had both Kęstutis and the poor serf girl killed.

There were, in fact, three castles in Trakai. The ruins of the older **Peninsula Castle** can be strolled round or clambered over, a short walk upshore from the first bridge to the Island Castle. Covering 4ha, with 11 towers rising above the treeline, this was one of the biggest castles in the region. One story goes that it was built because Kęstutis's wife Birutė, the headstrong girl whom the impetuous grand duke had abducted as a pagan flame-tending maiden, wanted a bigger house. But thanks to the Christian Crusaders, it was badly damaged in 1390, just eight years after it was completed. Vytautas repaired it, but it was finally destroyed by the Russians in 1655.

All that remains of **Senieji Trakai** (literally Old Trakai), the first castle known to be built in Trakai, is a circular mound, at the centre of which now stands an 18th-century neo-Gothic church. This wooden castle was Kęstutis's residence and Vytautas's birthplace, built by Grand Duke Gediminas early in the 14th century. It can be found 3km from the town by taking a signposted lane to the left after exiting Trakai on the road back to Vilnius.

Walking away from the Island Castle down Karaimų, a track leading left after a short bridge leads to the haunting **Karaite Graveyard**. In contrast to the pristine cemeteries of the Lithuanians, this one is captivatingly overgrown, the headstones disappearing into the grass on the edge of the lake. It is a Karaite tradition to pray while touching the grave with a tissue, but it is also important to let nature take its course around the stone rather than keep it prim and tidy. After this, wander a few steps further up Karaimų and indulge in the Karaite dining experience at Kibininė.

Back in the other direction, past the castle, the **Karaite Museum** can be found at Karaimų 22. It is a fascinating mishmash of evocative old photographs, jewellery and a few weapons too. The community's 18th-century Kenessa stands nearby, on the same side of the street.

Further on, the little-visited, slightly shabby **Church of the Visitation** stands away from the road on a quiet hill. Originally dating from the time of Vytautas the Great though extensively altered in 1718, it is the unassuming home for an extraordinary painting of the Madonna and Child, also known as the **Madonna of Trakai**. Said to be a gift from a Byzantine emperor to Vytautas the Great, this is unlikely, it probably dating from the 16th century, its silver covering added in the 18th, as was the fashion.

Information and maps

Historical National Park Information Centre
Karaimų 5; ☎ (8-238) 55776. Maps of the town and its attractions are available. *Open Mon–Thu 08.00–12.00 and 12.45–17.00, Fri 08.00–12.00 and 12.45–15.00.*

Tourist Information Centre Vytauto 69; ☎/f (8-238) 51934; e trakaiTIC@is.lt; www.trakai.lt. Some English is spoken. *Open in summer Mon–Fri 09.00–18.00, Sat 10.00–15.00; in winter Mon–Fri 08.00–17.00.*

KERNAVĖ The first capital of the united Lithuanian tribes is about 50km northwest of Vilnius. It can be driven to on a leisurely minor road that stretches through rolling countryside beyond the capital's outer suburb of Pilaitė. There are several places to stop along the way. Sudervė is a lovely village beside a lake that is dominated by a unique round church designed by Laurynas Stuoka-Gucevičius (1753–98), the young classical architect who also redesigned Vilnius Cathedral.

Further down the road, an old oak wood and runic stone can be explored near Dūkštos (find the roadside sign saying *ąžuolynas*). A trail leads between these majestic oaks, while the mysterious stone with its so-far-untranslated runic script probably dates from the 3rd or 4th century AD, the time when Goths established their dominions across whole swathes of Eastern Europe.

Kernavė (*www.kernave.org*) is a tiny village set on a terrace above the green and grassy valley of the River Neris. The reason for visiting is a series of five mounds at the ridge of the valley that hint at a lost city. An observation platform and information point reveal the whole panorama, from which you are free to descend into the landscape and explore. Each mound has a name, not all of them accurate. The wooden castle that once stood here rested on Mindaugas's Throne Mound, whereas Castle Mound was more likely to have been home to quite a sizeable medieval population. A Lithuanian pagan mystic named Lizdeika was said to have lived on Hearth Mound, always tending a sacred flame. But Lizdeika Mound probably had a defensive purpose. Confusing? An excellent archaeological museum adjacent to the site provides plenty of explanatory information, but unfortunately it is closed for extensive renovation until 2008. However, the excellent website compensates for this temporary loss.

Archaeological finds have determined that the site was inhabited in the Neolithic period, as far back as 9000BC. The peaceful pagan town and trading centre that prospered here in the Middle Ages was raided, ransacked and badly damaged by Crusaders in 1365, then again in 1390. It never recovered after the second blow and gradually vanished. The mighty army of Crusaders from western Europe who dealt it consisted of mercenaries from Germany, France, Italy and England – including the future Henry IV. This was the army that marched on to Vilnius to inflict such devastation on the Crooked Castle and the Upper Castle.

Tourist Information Centre Kerniaus 4; ☎ (8-382) 4731; e kernave@taigaeurobaltika.com. Some English is spoken. *Open May–Sep, 10.00–18.00 except Sun.*

5

Kaliningrad

For 46 years between 1945 and 1991 the Soviet Union occupied the Baltic states of Estonia, Latvia and Lithuania and also incorporated part of the former German province of East Prussia, renaming the town of Königsberg as Kaliningrad. Confusingly they used this name, too, for the surrounding region or *oblast*. A cultural and political uniformity was quickly imposed on all these territories and most former links with the outside world curtailed. Kaliningrad suffered most in this respect, with travel there even for Soviet citizens being difficult. Its history as a major German city was ignored; in the town centre British bombing in August 1944 and the final battle for the city in April 1945 left many buildings totally or largely destroyed. Much of what could have been restored was subsequently removed to make the break with the long German past even stronger. Tallinn, Riga and Vilnius were still granted a history, albeit a distorted one as the Soviet Union was unhappy to publicise the period between 1920 and 1940 when these towns were not part of it. Many of their pre-war inhabitants, however, were unable to enjoy it, having been murdered in the Holocaust, or deported to Siberia in 1941, or having fled west ahead of the Soviet army in 1944.

From around 1960, the Soviet authorities allowed travel to Tallinn, Riga and Vilnius but with a maximum stay of three nights. Travel between the cities was by air or on overnight trains. Longer stays were rarely granted to prevent serious contacts being established with the local populations. Tours always started and finished in Leningrad (now St Petersburg) or Moscow to stress the Soviet nature of the programme and to minimise the Baltic element. Travel outside the capitals only became possible in the 1980s towards the end of the Soviet period. Tourists first came to Kaliningrad from 1991 as the Soviet Union fell apart and the military were no longer able to prevent this. As Kaliningrad was a major naval base on the front line with NATO, admitting tourists was out of the question before then. The occasional visitor from Scandinavia came in the 1950s and 1960s but, in comparison, Tibet, North Korea or Albania seemed wide open in those days. Many former East Prussians were desperate to return and 64,000 Germans came to visit in 1992. Their largely hostile reports, and continued bitterness at what many regarded as an illegitimate occupation of their homeland, initially discouraged more general tourists. Now with many business, academic and voluntary organisations working towards reconciliation and with the successful rebuilding of several pre-war monuments, the image of Kaliningrad has greatly improved and visitor numbers are likely to increase again.

THE STATUS OF KALININGRAD

Independence in Estonia, Latvia and Lithuania brought an immediate influx of tourists to their capitals from all over the world, many taking tours that visited all three. Arrivals came to be counted in millions rather than in thousands. This added to the determination of the local town councils to eradicate the recent Soviet past. Cyrillic road signs were torn down, hard currencies introduced and visas abolished for most visitors. Active tourist boards were established, eager to work with the travel industry and with travel writers. In these capitals, the new private sector quickly adapted to tourism so that by 1994 visitors had no problem in finding a luxury hotel or a small two-star one, eating Chinese or Italian food, and reading a Western newspaper on the day of publication. Tourist visits are now similar to those in Stockholm, Lübeck or Kraków, with ample scope for specialist and general groups or individuals preferring to stay on their own.

World War II left savage human scars across the region but fortunately there was little fighting in the three other Baltic state capitals so an architectural heritage stretching back for eight centuries welcomes all visitors. Many of the sites are within walking distance of each other and of the hotels which visitors are likely to use. Others are cheaply and easily reached by public transport.

The transformation in Kaliningrad would be, and remains, more ambivalent. British bombing and bitter fighting in April 1945 left the town centre a shell. By the end of the Soviet period most of the inhabitants were from Russia, a few from the other Soviet Republics. In 1991 they were suddenly cut off from home by three foreign countries – Lithuania, Poland and Belarus. Renewed contact from Germany with this former part of East Prussia was as much a threat as an opportunity. The year 1992 brought visions of Kaliningrad becoming the 'Hong Kong of the Baltics' but realism on the spot and indifference in Moscow soon put paid to this. A new role was not found during the 1990s but there is now greater optimism as it becomes a pilot region in testing links with the surrounding EU.

The problems the rest of Russia faces are equally acute in the Kaliningrad region: nearly half the working population earns less than £65/US$100 a month, a sum which is regarded as a realistic minimum wage. The old age pension, if it is provided on time, is £33/US$50 a month. Tourists will appreciate the massive grants the Germans have provided in the last ten years as they admire the restored cathedral and the enlarged History Museum. They will enjoy the restaurants and the many 24-hour shops. Königsberg is methodically and aesthetically returning to many parts of Kaliningrad. Yet the abandoned fields in much of the countryside and the dismal blocks of flats in many of the suburbs show that little has changed for much of the local population. In some ways, Russia has left Kaliningrad behind. Those who never knew the Soviet Union can still take the chance to see Lenin looking down on most town hall squares, even though he was removed in 2005 from the Kaliningrad town centre where he otherwise would have obstructed the view of the new orthodox cathedral. They can still do serious shopping in local markets as peasants prefer to bypass the official distribution structures. They can wonder why the name of the town has not been changed, since Kalinin, as a close associate of Stalin, hardly inspires reverence any more. Kant would be the obvious person to choose in renaming the town as the philosopher is respected by both the Germans and the Russians, but some local residents claim that the town is not yet worthy of his name (see page 179). Tourists need not worry whether it is or whether it is not, but for the sake of the local residents let us hope for not too long a delay. A move in this direction was taken in 2005 when his name was given to the university.

HISTORY

The history of the former German town of Königsberg began with bloodshed in 1255 and ended with bloodshed in 1945. The establishment of the first settlement by the Teutonic Knights was to lead by 1283 to the complete annihilation of the Prussian tribes. In 1945 the Germans would in turn be annihilated by Soviet troops at the end of World War II. In the intervening 700 years, war would generally pass the town by, its few temporary occupiers having established their authority in battles elsewhere.

Membership of the Hanseatic League from 1340 ensured close relationships with all the other large ports along the Baltic coast and a common adherence to Lutheranism after the Reformation. It also ensured extensive trading links with Britain. During this long period of time, Germany and Russia would usually be friends, uniting just as easily against the French as against the Poles. Loyal former residents always refer to 700 years of German history, yet such rule can hardly be seen as continuous. For much of the 15th century, local rulers had to swear allegiance to the Polish crown. The Swedes followed in the 16th century and were only finally driven away in 1679. The first Russian occupation lasted four years, between 1758 and 1762. In 1807 Napoleon occupied the town for 39 days. Far worse than any occupation was the plague that killed a quarter of the population in 1709.

LEARNING AND CULTURE Albertina University, founded in 1544, was a constant feature of the town's history. Foreign occupiers always respected it and eagerly encouraged its work. It was equally well known throughout Germany. It pioneered in many fields, being one of the first to lecture in German instead of Latin, to introduce science degrees and to admit women students. Throughout its 400-year history, any prominent writer, historian or scientist living in Königsberg had a post at Albertina. Its academic standards were only to slip twice during this time. An honorary degree was awarded to Napoleon's General Pierre Daru who led the forces that occupied Königsberg. In the university's final 12 years between 1933 and 1945, the teaching was as dominated by Nazi ideology as it was in all other German universities.

The original 16th-century buildings of the university were beside those of the cathedral in the heart of the old town. These were all destroyed during the fighting at the end of World War II, including a library of over half a million books. As part of the 300th anniversary celebrations in 1844, further faculties were built on the northern side of the Pregel River and some of the buildings survived the war and are still in use. These followed other institutions that had been founded earlier in the century, such as the botanical garden and the observatory built by Germany's most famous astronomer, Friedrich Wilhelm Bessel (1784–1846).

The philosopher Immanuel Kant (1724–1804) was undoubtedly Königsberg's most famous resident and probably the only one ever to achieve fame outside Germany. He stayed loyal to the town throughout his life and never accepted posts elsewhere. In fact he went further than this and hardly left the town, indicating in many of his writings that travel would not have broadened his mind. Marxist philosophers see him as a precursor to Hegel and then to Marx himself. Because of the Russian occupation he was, like all other residents for that four-year period, a Russian citizen. One hundred and fifty years later these two factors would be crucial. During the Soviet period between 1945 and 1990, he was the one famous former resident who could officially be commemorated. His tomb outside the cathedral, erected in 1924 on the 200th anniversary of his birth, was not destroyed and his work continued to be published.

Kant was renowned for his rigid schedule and his regular companions. His butler always woke him at 04.45 each morning and he was always in bed by 22.00. He never married, to his regret, but he consoled himself with the thought that staying single kept his mind more alert. He held the Chair of Logic from 1770 until his death in 1804, the year of which he had actually predicted. He had a regular circle of friends whom he entertained each Sunday. Amongst these were two Englishmen, Joseph Green and Robert Motherby, whose shipping business, originally based in Hull, brought grain and herring to Britain. They had lunch with him every Sunday for about 20 years. In the 19th century their successors started a regular steamer service between Hull and Königsberg, profiting in particular during the Crimean War when Königsberg was the only source of Russian goods.

The second most famous resident of Königsberg was Heinrich Schliemann, who will always be associated with the discovery of Troy. He spent two crucial years there from 1853 to 1855, helping the Russian government break the British and French blockade of Russian ports during the Crimean War. Königsberg, being German, could not be cut off from trade in this way and he used it to import crucial war materials into Russia.

The most famous visitor to Königsberg was Peter the Great, who came in 1697 *en route* to western Europe. A Russian trading community had already been settled in the town for over a hundred years and was sufficiently large to hold regular church services. Officially he came incognito, but being some 2m tall (well over 6ft) and bringing an entourage of 400, this pretence was impossible to maintain. He did enjoy disguising himself in a range of unlikely occupations but wildly drunken behaviour was on several occasions to let him down. On his visit to Königsberg the German court presented him with amber jewellery and horses from the famous breeding centre in East Prussia, Trakehnen. Later they would present him with the Amber Chamber, which would adorn the summer palace at Tsarkoye Selo for two centuries, before being brought back to Königsberg by German troops in 1942. After his 1697 visit, Peter the Great continued his journey to Holland and England, settling in Deptford for several months to study shipbuilding. He would send students from St Petersburg to study at Albertina University but this link was broken in 1720 as too few Russian students had sufficient knowledge of German to follow the courses. It was restored during the Tsarist occupation (1758–62) when Russian students attended Kant's lectures.

EXPANSION AND PROSPERITY The 19th century was one of fame in every commercial and intellectual field for Königsberg and the city enjoyed peace and prosperity throughout these hundred years. 'First' and 'largest' are adjectives that need to be used again and again. At the beginning of the century, in 1809, the famous Königsberg marzipan was first produced. At the end of the century, in 1895, Germany's first electric trams operated here and then, two years later, the first 11 women graduated from Albertina. Well before the end of the century, the port handled more grain and wood than any other in Germany whilst at the same time 'Gräfe und Unzer' had become the country's largest bookshop. Shipbuilding, printing, railway engineering and textiles were the industries that enjoyed particular success. The opening of the railway link with Russia in 1861 greatly expanded the scope of the port, as did the construction of the canal to Pillau (Baltiysk) on the coast. Uniquely it could guarantee ice-free access throughout the winter. The first British steamer had in fact arrived seven years earlier in 1854 and trade with Russia through the port would greatly increase following the completion of the railway link.

Culturally, Wagner, Schumann and Liszt paid several visits for performances of their works; Bizet's *Carmen* was successfully performed in 1879 after its initial failure in Paris. In architecture, the Luisenkirche and the Stock Exchange are the most famous of a wide range of impressive 19th-century buildings that are still in use.

Königsberg remained untouched by World War I, although it was sufficiently close to several battles for it to be used as a military relief station and for its hospitals to be greatly expanded. Under the Versailles Treaty of 1919, independence was restored to Poland after over a century of German and Russian occupation. This led to the division of East Prussia and its capital Königsberg from the rest of Germany. Although links with the 'mainland' were assured, Königsberg was forced to look for closer trading links with the new Baltic states of Lithuania, Latvia and Estonia and also with the Soviet Union. There are few realistic portrayals of the 26 years Königsberg was still to exist as a German city. The many memoirs that the exiles would produce after World War II present an idealised picture of a prosperous town with no crime, no tension and where the sun always shone. One writer does in fact admit that she cannot recall a rainy summer's day, so happy are her recollections of her childhood in Königsberg. There is no doubt that much was achieved there and evidence of this can still be seen in many parts of the town, despite the later bombing. One mayor, Hans Lohmeyer, was in office from 1919 to 1933 and he relentlessly drove the town forward. In Carl Gördeler, his deputy from 1922 to 1930, he had an equally active supporter. (Gördeler then became Mayor of Leipzig and, had the July 1944 plot to kill Hitler succeeded, he would have been nominated as German Chancellor. He and several other East Prussians were among the many executed for their role in the plot.)

Lohmeyer built a new main railway station, probably the first in Germany with non-smoking waiting rooms, and with a bowling alley. He foresaw the role air travel would play so gave his city a large airport. He realised the need for close links with the new Soviet government so helped to establish Deruluft, a joint venture with them which operated regular flights to Moscow. The two-storey road and rail bridge across the River Pregel, which is still in use, was built at his instigation. His most famous achievement was the annual Ostmesse, the export trade fair that dominated trade to and from the city throughout the inter-war period. First opened in 1920, by 1923 it was attracting 2,500 exhibitors and continued operating until the autumn of 1941.

Yet an honest portrayal of the city between 1919 and 1939 has to reflect the developments that hit the whole of Germany. The rampant inflation of 1923 destroyed many long-established businesses and then unemployment in the early 1930s provided the breeding ground for Nazism. The Nazis' main opponents both on the streets and in the ballot box were the Communists. None of the centre parties appeared to offer solutions to the ever-worsening crisis. At the Ostmesse in 1932, many stands were empty and an art exhibition had to fill up the empty space.

THE NAZI ERA In the last free election to be held in Königsberg the Nazis were elected on 5 March 1933, with 54% of the vote. Democracy and racial tolerance died that night throughout Germany. Opposition to the Nazis was dealt with as ruthlessly in Königsberg as elsewhere. Mayor Lohmeyer was sacked on 9 March. On 10 May a book burning was organised on the Trommelplatz, the main parade ground. Any books which could be stigmatized as 'Un-German, Jewish or Bolshevik' went up in flames. Sixteen staff at the university were immediately sacked on account of their political views or racial background.

The most famous Jew who left Königsberg in 1933 was the songwriter Max Colpet who wrote 'Where Have All the Flowers Gone' for Marlene Dietrich. In his American exile he went on to write for Charles Aznavour and to translate *West Side Story* into German. A five-year-old Jewish girl who also left in 1933 later achieved prominence as Lea Rabin, wife of the Israeli prime minister. By the end of the year, the Hansaring had been renamed Adolf Hitler Strasse, to mark the supposed permanence of the Nazi regime.

On 7 November 1938 a junior diplomat, Ernst von Rath, was shot in the Paris Embassy and died two days later. He had joined the Nazi Party in 1932 whilst a student in Königsberg. His assassin, Herschel Grynzpan, was a young impoverished Polish-Jewish refugee who had just been expelled from Germany with all his family. This murder gave the Nazis a pretext for launching a new wave of attacks on all Jewish businesses and synagogues in Germany, on what later became known as Kristallnacht. The date of 9 November was already symbolic in German history since on that day the Kaiser had abdicated in 1918 and in 1923 Hitler had launched his unsuccessful 'Beer Hall Putsch'. Because of von Rath's links with East Prussia, these attacks were particularly brutal in Königsberg and the main synagogue was totally destroyed. Destroyed, too, were any hopes some maintained that Nazism could be tamed. For those happy to support the Nazi regime, Königsberg would survive for another six years. For anyone else, Königsberg as a cosmopolitan, racially diverse city, rightly proud of its past and present, died in November 1938.

Kaliningrad HISTORY

5

Until 1944 one can almost say that Königsberg 'enjoyed' the fruits of World War II. The destruction of Poland reunited East Prussia with the Reich and the advance into Russia again brought the Baltic states under German influence. 'Bombing' was what relatives in Hamburg or Berlin suffered, but it did not initially touch Königsberg. Food supplies were ample and prisoners provided cheap labour on the farms and in the factories. With most opponents of Nazism having been exiled by 1939, there could be no focus for any opposition and little need for it given the high standard of living enjoyed by most of the population. The year 1944, however, was a turning point. The defeat at Stalingrad in early 1943 and continuing German losses on all fronts after that could no longer be concealed from the population at large.

August 1944 presented the local authorities with an acute dilemma – how should the 400th anniversary of the founding of Albertina University be celebrated? In the past such celebrations had been particularly flamboyant and had been well documented for posterity. To continue in a similar vein might be seen as tasteless in the middle of an increasingly desperate war, yet to ignore the occasion could be termed defeatism. Gauleiter Erich Koch took the second option, even sanctioning new buildings for the university. He probably bore in mind Hitler's interest in Frederick the Great and the commitment the emperor had shown to the 200th anniversary in 1744. At one of the formal ceremonies, Koch presented three statues, of Kant, Copernicus and Hitler. In the British air raids that followed two weeks later, most of the university was destroyed, but two of these statues survived intact. Hitler did not.

The Royal Air Force launched two major bombing attacks, on the night of 26–27 August 1944 and again on 29–30 August. The desolation these caused can still be seen all too clearly in the former Old Town by the river. All the streets were destroyed and only the shells of the cathedral and the castle remained. The cathedral was rebuilt from 1991, but the castle was torn down in the late 1960s; none of the university buildings survived. Refugees from Lithuania started to come into East Prussia. Wild cattle, abandoned by their owners, drifted across the countryside. The Russians slowly encircled the town, the last train to Berlin leaving Königsberg on 22 January 1945. The next one would not leave until August 1991.

Even during the following two months, reality was evaded. Food and fuel supplies were adequate, the zoo sold annual season tickets valid until December 1945 and hairdressers required clients to make appointments two weeks in advance. Children, as normal for January, built snowmen at the side of the streets and passing soldiers handed out chocolate bars to them. Officially nobody could plan to escape, but 100,000 East Prussians did so via the port of Pillau which stayed in German hands until the end of the war.

The occupation of Königsberg came quickly and brutally; after a three-day siege the German commander, General Otto Lasch, formally surrendered to the Russians on 10 April 1945. He spent the next ten years in prison and then wrote his memoirs, which still remain contentious amongst the *Vertriebene*, the exile community who fled to West Germany. With 35,000 troops and no air cover against the 250,000 Russian force, the result of the battle could not be in doubt. Some argue that, with an earlier surrender, there would have been less suffering in the town as the Russians would not have felt so vengeful. Others argue that Lasch could have disobeyed Berlin earlier and arranged for a more orderly civil evacuation, as happened in other East Prussian towns. Cynics claim that he fought until his own life was in danger and then surrendered. Hitler had ordered him to fight to the last man, but he was one of many German commanders not to carry these orders out, even though he pursued such a policy further than was necessary.

The defence of Königsberg did not prevent war crimes being carried out to the last minute. In early April 1945 resources were still found to force-march 5,000 Hungarian prisoners from Königsberg to Pillau. Some 2,000 perished *en route* and most of the remaining 3,000 drowned in the sea or were murdered on the beach. Only 13 were rescued by extremely brave local villagers.

SOVIET RULE Although leaflets dropped by Russian aircraft before the final attack promised a quick and pleasant return to civilian life, the population of Königsberg was exposed to every possible form of human depravity as the Russian troops arrived. Women were 'lucky' if they were only raped by one soldier. Men forced into work brigades were similarly fortunate in that this ensured just enough rations to survive. Stalin is alleged to have encouraged his troops with the slogan, 'Take these blonde German women. They are all yours.' Soldiers could loot at will and understandably took the chance to do so. If there was one German word that they all learnt it was Uhr ('watch') but their interests could not be expected to stop there. Most had spent the last years seeing town after town destroyed by the German Army and few would not have had many relatives killed. Despite the siege and the earlier bombing, Königsberg still had a modern vibrant feel to it. Russian troops expecting an impoverished German proletariat found thousands of townhouses full of clothes, china, furniture and jewellery. One soldier wrote home, 'It is hard to know where to look first when you enter a German house. Do you realise that they all have pianos the size of tables?' Some items were unknown to them, particularly to soldiers from central Asia. They had never seen bicycles or flushing toilets and were equally inept with both.

For about a week, Russian troops were allowed to rampage as the German army had done on their territory for the previous four years. Under the circumstances their behaviour was perfectly comprehensible, even though it can in no way be condoned. Königsberg was the first major German town to surrender. The soldiers knew that it was going to be incorporated into the USSR. Like Berlin and Dresden, in 1945 the town was to pay a particularly high price for its Nazi past. It would soon pay an even higher one.

If law and order were quickly restored, food supplies were certainly not and mere survival became a total preoccupation for the German population of around 100,000 who remained in May 1945. Survival was only possible through ingenuity and barter. Elderly relatives were abandoned so that their clothes could be sold and then their corpses would be cannibalised. (Only those who died of typhus could expect a burial.) Pets had to be eaten, as did any non-poisonous plants. Everyone turned their hands to thieving as honesty could only lead to starvation. The three letters LSR daubed across makeshift air-raid shelters were a familiar sight in the town since this was the German abbreviation for such cellars (*Luftschutzräume*). Under the occupation it soon came to mean *Lernt Schnell Russisch* ('quickly learn Russian').

In the early days of the occupation, it was assumed that the remaining German population would be allowed to stay. In fact, some German refugees who had reached what was now western Poland were returned. By 1946, though, the German population in the city had dropped to around 25,000. Relations between the Russians and the Germans became remarkably cordial and reminiscences from both sides dating from that time testify to this. The Russians needed the Germans for their skills and for their local knowledge. They admired their resilience and cleanliness. No Russian would regularly clean the doorstep and pavement outside his house, let alone outside a bombsite. Only the Germans could find the sewers, operate the drainage systems and restore production in the amber mines. When the Königsberg trams started to operate again in the summer of 1946, there were 400 German staff and only 70 Russians. The Germans needed the Russians for regular supplies of food and money, so became the workers, tradesmen and nannies that could ensure this.

The early Russian settlers had mixed backgrounds. Some soldiers simply stayed on, attracted by a potential lifestyle unlikely to greet them elsewhere in the Soviet Union.

Those who had been imprisoned by the Germans, and could therefore be judged as traitors by the Red Army, felt less threatened here as their past could be more easily falsified or ignored. New settlers were positively encouraged from summer 1946. Those from a country background admired the asphalt and cobbles which were as novel to them as bicycles and flush toilets had been to the troops a year earlier.

The Germans still went to church, although the Russians by and large did not. There were of course no orthodox churches and many Russians feared that expressions of religious belief might prejudice their future careers. A German club was founded in February 1946 and some Russians also attended. Genuine relationships between both communities started to be formed. There were again grounds for optimism. Such hopes were shattered in July 1946. Königsberg was renamed Kaliningrad (**Калининград**) in honour of Mikhail Kalinin who had just died (of natural causes). He had been a senior member of the Soviet Politburo, a man of little vision, but of great staying power. Confusingly, the same name was given to the new surrounding region (*oblast* in Russian). Although every other town and village in East Prussia, and all the streets, would now receive Russian names, many were better honoured. Insterburg, the second-largest town in the former East Prussia, was renamed Chernyakhovsk after a noted commander, Ivan Chernyakhovsky, who fought heroically in many battles on the Eastern Front and died of his wounds in February 1945. Only the rivers and the town gates kept their German names after 1947 so the Pregel still ran through the town centre, overlooked by the Brandenburg Gate.

In the same month, the whole oblast of Kaliningrad was declared a military zone. A barbed-wire fence along the entire length of the new border with Poland went up in September 1946, dividing families and cutting the link with Germany. The following winter was, as elsewhere in Europe, a bitter one, and many were to suffer almost as badly as they had done in the summer of 1945. Many older people felt there was no alternative to suicide, particularly as rations were often restricted to 'specialists'. ('Parasites' were expected to fend for themselves.) In the countryside, conditions were worse as the months of hard frost and deep snow prevented any cultivation. Yet some Russians started to learn German and in June 1947 a German newspaper, *Neue Zeit* ('New Times'), was founded with six Russian staff and four Germans. Its contents were largely translations from Russian papers, but its publication did suggest a long-term future for the German community.

The complete opposite was made clear on 10 October when Stalin suddenly ordered what would now be called ethnic cleansing. On 22 October, the first special train left for Germany and many others were to follow. By March 1948, the policy had by and large been carried out, with only a few specialists allowed to stay a little longer because their expertise was still needed. Kaliningrad became a unique region of Europe in many ways. It had been ethnically cleansed with total success and with the full agreement of the wartime Allies. It became a community with no past and with minimal links to the outside world. Guidebooks and school textbooks would talk of Kant being born in Kaliningrad in 1724, but no other reference was made to the German era or even to the Seven Years War when the Russians previously occupied Königsberg. Lhasa, Pyongyang and Tirana suddenly appeared cosmopolitan in comparison as they did at least see regular delegations from abroad and occasional groups of tourists. Public displays of religion ceased as the German churches closed in 1948 and were restored only 40 years later when the Russian Orthodox Church took over some of the churches whose fabric could still be saved.

We must hope that those settlers who came in their twenties and are now retired will write up their experiences. For the time being, our knowledge of the next 40 years is restricted to the few official documents that have entered the public domain since the downfall of the USSR. Because of the military sensitivity of the area, minimal information was published during the Soviet era and there was no way in which it could be checked. We now know the background to the dynamiting of the castle ruins in 1969, which aimed to remove a clear visual link to the German past, but with the reopening of the university in 1967 skilful students would in due course track this history down. The Bunker Museum was also opened in 1969, at the site of the German surrender. It displayed large-scale models of the fighting in Königsberg. In 1974 came a museum dedicated to Immanuel Kant which could not conceal his German surroundings, although he was portrayed as a 'citizen of all Europe' because of his fame. In 1975 a second German was commemorated, the astronomer Friedrich Wilhelm Bessel (1784–1846), when a memorial plaque was erected on the site of his former observatory written in both Russian and German. (In 1989 Kaliningrad again had a Bessel Street, as it had before the war. A crater on the moon also bears Bessel's name.)

The destruction of churches continued until 1976. The last one to be blown up was the Lutherkirche, a beautiful neo-Renaissance building dating from 1907 which had not been seriously damaged during the war. The stagnation and inertia that took over during the later Brezhnev years in the USSR did not particularly affect Kaliningrad, any more than the earlier Khruschev thaw had done in the 1960s. The military maintained such a tight grip that political changes in Moscow were largely irrelevant. For the same reason, Kaliningrad was hardly to enjoy the perestroika ('reform') and glasnost ('openness') that characterised the final years of the Soviet Union in the late 1980s. Had visitors been allowed then, they would have found some lighter reading in the bookshops and a few Russian Orthodox services taking place in the former Lutheran churches. That tourists were still not allowed, under any circumstances, speaks volumes.

After the failed military coup in Moscow in 1991, Kaliningraders were polled by a local newspaper and asked for their views: 25% were saddened at its failure, 25% were glad and 50% did not care. An older generation had known political terror under Stalin and then years of political inertia following his death in 1953. Younger people had known only the inertia, being totally cut off from foreigners and the more radical outbursts that flowered from time to time elsewhere in the Soviet Union.

MODERN PROBLEMS The year 1991 should have forced a break with this tradition. With the formal demise of the USSR at the end of December and the establishment of the various independent republics, Kaliningrad was now cut off from the rest of the Russian Federation by three foreign countries: Lithuania, Belarus and Poland. It had to adapt to new circumstances in the same way that Königsberg/East Prussia had done in 1919. Yet no new Hans Lohmeyer was forthcoming who could successfully maintain links with Moscow whilst at the same time achieving the local economic autonomy needed to trade successfully with western Europe. There was talk of the town becoming the 'Hong Kong' of the Baltics but Moscow did not grant the full range of tax-free privileges that such a project needed.

Initially the sudden influx of high-spending nostalgic German tourists saved the town from making serious economic decisions. Some 64,000 came in 1992 and similar figures lasted for several more years. Many German charities became active and some businesses from Germany started to invest as low labour costs compensated for all the bureaucratic hurdles that still needed to be overcome. There are other resources, too. Amber is a unique and valuable local product and the legal sales abroad guarantee a regular income. Other export products such as timber have to compete against those from Poland and the Baltic states where an efficient business ethos has quickly taken root. Income is clearly also derived from smuggling as local cigarettes are known to have worldwide distribution networks.

Ten years after the fall of communism, around 2000, there was still no alternative to take its place in Kaliningrad. The private sector, being so corrupt, did not contribute

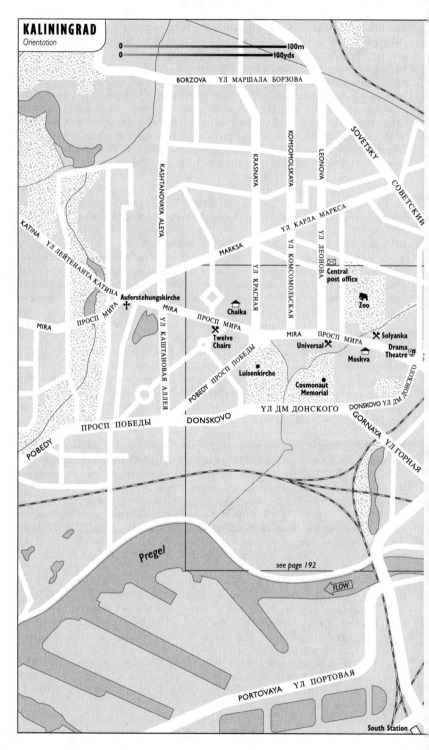

Patriot

УЛ ОЗЕРНАЯ
OZERNAYA

УЛ НАРВСКАЯ

NARVSKAYA

УЛ ГОРЬКОГО
GORKOVO

УЛ ТЕЛЬМАНА
TELMANA

ПРОСПЕКТ

Upper Lake

УЛ А НЕВСКОГО

NEVSKOVO

✗ Francis Drake

North
Station

Fighting
Bulls

✝ Orthodox
Cathedral

Central Market

Amber
Museum

Vasilevsky Square

Ploshad Pobedy
ПЛ
ПОБЕДЫ

CHERNYAKHOVSKOVO

УЛ ЧЕРНЯХОВСКОГО

Distillery

УЛ ПРОЛЕТАРСКАЯ

LITOVSKY VAL

Schiller
Statue

🏛 Town Hall

Post Office

Titanic

Valencia

PROLETARSKAYA

УЛ КЛИНИЧЕСКАЯ

Lower Lake

LENINSKY

footbridge

War Memorial

University

Supermarket

Bunker
Museum

Kaliningrad ⌂✗

Monopol

History &
Art Museum

KLINICHESKAYA

УЛ ГАГАРИНА
GAGARINA

ЛИТОВСКИЙ ВАЛ

УЛ ФРУНЗЕ

FRUNZE

'The Monster'

MOSKOVSKY

МОСКВСКИЙ ПРОСПЕКТ

MOSKOVSKY

Art Gallery

ЛЕНИНСКИЙ ПРОСПЕКТ

Oceanography
Museum

Cathedral ✝

Pregel

Pregel

Former Stock
Exchange

OKTYABRASKAYA

LENINSKY

N

Bradt

Brandenburg
Gate

BAGRATIONA
УЛ БАГРАТИОНА

DZERZHINSKOVO

УЛ ДЗЕРЖИНСКОГО

Pregel

Philharmonia

sufficiently to a tax base that could in turn drive the public sector out of its torpor. There was a general expectation that either Moscow or the EU would in due course bail out Kaliningrad; there was certainly no attempt to turn to self-reliance, nor were closer links established with other potential markets beyond Germany. The EU was seen as a threat, not as a possible stimulus.

However, as EU membership for its neighbours became more likely and then a fact in 2004, Kaliningrad began to reinvent itself. The awkward clash of two anniversaries in 2005 – the 750th anniversary of the founding of Königsberg and the 60th of its 'liberation' by Soviet forces – was a further stimulus for presenting a more attractive face to the outside world. Projects such as the building of the new Russian Orthodox Cathedral beside Victory Square, which had hardly seen any activity for years, were suddenly completed. The opening of a truly five-star hotel on the coast at Svetlogorsk enabled foreign rulers to be entertained at the same level as their predecessors in the 19th century had been, and so Presidents Chirac and Schröder attended a summit there in July 2005.

The year 2002 had brought Kaliningrad to the attention of the West in the context of imminent EU membership for its two neighbours Poland and Lithuania. Kaliningrad residents, unlike other Russian citizens, did not need visas to travel to either country and this enabled them to travel to other parts of Russia. EU policy, however, dictated that visas would be required in accordance with practice on other borders. By the autumn of 2003, a compromise was finally reached and transit arrangements through Lithuania were agreed. As long as they do not leave the train in Lithuania, residents of Kaliningrad are automatically issued transit visas free of charge. Germany remained the major trading partner in the West and the major supporter of any charity work. Whether for ringing bells in the cathedral or for ringing birds at the Rybachy Sanctuary, it is German money that is being provided.

Yet 'Königsberg' will never take over Kaliningrad as so few people on any side would wish for this. 'Königsberg' has returned and is making its presence felt where it is most welcome: in the churches, on the farms, in the factories and in museums. History begins again in 1255 and not in 1945. 'Königsberg' remains sensibly absent from the civil administration, from education and above all from the military. Agnes Miegel (1879–1964), Königsberg's most famous poet, wrote during her final years in exile: 'Königsberg, you are NOT mortal', and she has turned out to be right.

Königsberg and Kaliningrad began to co-operate in 1990. The commemorations in 2005 brought them closer than they had ever been during the previous 15 years. Exhibitions from Germany are now welcome in the main museums and galleries. Some Russian street names are being dropped in favour of German ones. A Gorki Street is a Hoffman Street, named after the 19th-century poet Ernst Hoffman. On 28 December 2005 an air service, first started 85 years before, was restored to Berlin. Königsberg and Kaliningrad now happily coexist, as Russians and Germans have so often done in the past, but it is safe to predict that they will never embark on cohabitation.

PRACTICALITIES

MONEY AND BANKING Roubles can easily be obtained in the Baltic states, in Poland and also through some banks in western Europe. At the Lithuanian and Polish borders, the local currencies can be exchanged into roubles, otherwise it is difficult to change anything apart from American dollars and euro. A few exchange bureaux will accept other currencies such as British pounds but give very poor rates. Travellers' cheques can only be exchanged at a few banks so are best avoided. Reliable ATM machines suddenly sprouted up across the city in 2005. Credit cards are accepted by the main hotels and restaurants. The rouble has been very stable since 1999, maintaining a rate of around US\$1 = RUB28. In spring 2006, €1 was worth RUB35 and £1 sterling around RUB50.

COMMUNICATIONS

Telephones Calls from Kaliningrad to foreign countries require an international access code of 810 and then the relevant country code and foreign number. Russian dialling codes all changed in late 2005. Calls made to Kaliningrad from abroad require the country code for Russia which is still 7 then the Kaliningrad area code which is now 4112 followed by the local number.

Direct dial is available to countries abroad from some hotels but charges vary widely and should be checked before using the phone. There is often a three-minute minimum charge, even if the line is engaged or not answered. At telephone centres around the town, charges are lower and English or German are usually spoken. There are telephone centres in the main railway station, the Central Post Office (*Leonova 22*), and in the Kaliningrad Hotel. All have extensive opening hours. In 2005 they charged around 30p/US\$0.50 per minute for calls to western Europe.

Useful telephone numbers

Fire	01	Ambulance	03
Police	02		

Post The postal service out of Kaliningrad has greatly improved since 2000 even though everything goes via Moscow. Allow two weeks for cards to reach western Europe, slightly longer for elsewhere. Charges are very low, even for air mail. Stamps are not sold at kiosks or hotel reception desks so have to be bought at post offices. The two main post offices in Kaliningrad are not in the town centre; the main one is near the zoo at Leonova 22 and another is in the main railway station to the south of the town centre. A third one has recently opened opposite the Central Market on Chernyakhovskovo.

Internet Internet cafés have not yet caught on in Kaliningrad but most telephone centres, such as those at the Kaliningrad and Moskva hotels, provide internet facilities. Expect to pay around 75p/US\$1.20 an hour.

CONSULATES There is no British or American consulate in Kaliningrad so any emergency assistance has to be provided by the relevant embassy in Moscow. In 2006, there were Danish, German, Lithuanian, Swedish and Polish consulates in Kaliningrad.

HOSPITAL AND PHARMACY

✚ **Klinicheskaya Hospital** Lower Lake, near Amber   ✚ **Apteka Pharmacy** Mira 98; ☏ 21 7883
Museum; ☏ 43 4556

RELIGIOUS SERVICES There was no public worship in Kaliningrad until the end of the Soviet era in the late 1980s when some of the former German churches were taken over by the Russian orthodox community. Some services are now held in German in the cathedral.

TOURIST INFORMATION There are no tourist information offices anywhere in Kaliningrad. It is therefore advisable to pre-book a transfer on arrival and a guide for a day or two to get used to the town layout, public transport and to be up to date on concerts. Kiosks sell town plans in Russian, and sometimes in German or English as well, but these can be several years out of date so may not show new hotels. A local publication *Welcome to Kaliningrad* is distributed through the larger hotels. It consists mainly of advertisements in Russian but there are short descriptions in English of the major attractions and a helpful map with roads given in both Cyrillic and transliteration. *Kaliningrad In Your Pocket* is no longer available in print but can be consulted on the website (*www.inyourpocket.com*).

TRANSPORT

AIRPORT There is no public transport to the international terminal, which is about 2km from the domestic terminal. Whilst some taxis wait for the flights from Berlin and Warsaw, it would be unwise to rely on them and a transfer should be pre-booked through a travel agent abroad. Major rebuilding of the airport is planned for 2007, to give it a 'spoke and hub' role between western Europe and Russia.

PUBLIC TRANSPORT An efficient and extensive network of buses, trams and trolleybuses covers the town with very low fares. A ticket in 2005 cost ten roubles, the equivalent of £0.20/US$0.35, however long the journey. Tickets are bought on board, not beforehand in kiosks. The main bus station, beside the railway station, serves other towns and villages in the region. Timetables are clearly listed there, but only in the Cyrillic alphabet, as they are in the railway station; there is no written guide to these services. Do not expect English or German to be spoken either in the bus station or in the railway station.

TAXIS These are now metered and are reasonably priced by Western standards. A short journey within the town centre should not cost more than £3.50/US$5.00 or around £4.50/US$7 to the more distant hotels. Unlike in the Baltic states, most people get a taxi from a rank or on the street. It is not common to phone for them, except from the suburbs where they would otherwise be difficult to find.

ACCOMMODATION

HOTELS (see also pages 209–10) Visas are issued only with confirmed accommodation and approval from the Ministry of the Interior. Local agents arrange this through tour operators abroad who then in turn arrange for visas to be issued by the local Russian Embassy. To avoid extra visa charges, bookings should be made at least six weeks before the planned date of arrival. It is therefore not practical to book hotels directly since they cannot offer this visa service. Prices given are those likely to be charged abroad by specialist travel agents who work with Kaliningrad. They usually include breakfast. There is little seasonal variation although hotels get very heavily booked from mid-June to mid-August, the German holiday season. The distinction between prices for foreigners and those charged to Russians was abolished in 2005.

Chaika (25 rooms) Pugacheva 13; ☎ 35 2211; f 35 2292; e rezerv@hotel.kaliningrad.ru; www.hotel.kaliningrad.ru. This was a hotel in German times and was renovated in 1995 to what must have been its former standards. The surrounding area was and is a quiet, affluent suburb, largely untouched by bombing or fighting during the war. The décor remains German in all the rooms and German is the only foreign language spoken by the staff. Breakfast is adequate, but not generous, and an extensive menu is available for other meals. The main road into town is a walk of 500m or so away, but then there are plenty of bus routes and passing taxis. It also has several 24-hour shops. Nearer at hand are several bars and restaurants, all with a calm, elderly clientele. Visitors who want to turn the clock back to the Königsberg era will be very happy in this hotel. Although it is under the same management as the Kaliningrad Hotel, and therefore shares its email and website addresses, these two hotels could not be more different. *Sgl US$55, twin US$70.*

Comandor (24 rooms) Schastlivaya 1, ☎ 34 1815; f 34 1808; e comandor@gazinter.net; www.comandor.gazinter.net. This is without doubt Kaliningrad's best hotel, situated 20 mins' drive north from the town centre in a new smart suburb. It will suit those determined to have no contact with contemporary Russia: a portrait of Peter the Great dominates the reception area and all prices are quoted in US dollars. Anyone paid in roubles is unlikely to be able to afford to enter. The hotel has an underground car park, several private dining rooms, satellite TV in all rooms and a large swimming pool. *Sgl US$90, twin US$110.*

🏠 **Deima** (64 rooms) Tolstikova 15; ☎ 71 0814; f 71 0700; e deima.tour@mail.ru. The location of this hotel could not be more dire – in the middle of a dreary housing estate about 3km from the town centre – but standards inside are more than adequate compensation. Furnishings are modern and the staff welcoming, although only in German as none seem to speak English. The hotel is on several bus routes, but as taxis rarely cost more than US$1 into town, this is hardly a major bonus. *Sgl US$55, twin US$65.*

🏠 **Kaliningrad** (200 rooms) Leninsky 81; ☎ 35 0500; f 35 6021; e rezerv@hotel.kaliningrad.ru; www.hotel.kaliningrad.ru. For the time being, this is by far the largest hotel in the whole region. All rooms are adequately furnished and many have good views towards the cathedral. Phones in the rooms each have separate numbers not linked to the main switchboard, so if calls are expected from abroad, these numbers should be passed to relevant contacts on arrival. The

exchange bureau handles currencies other than US dollars and German marks but not at competitive rates. Hotel staff and those in the shops speak adequate English or German. *Sgl US$75, twin US$90.*

🏠 **Moskva** (127 rooms) Mira 19; ☎ 35 2300; f 35 2400. Tourists and business visitors were all greatly relieved when renovation here was finally completed in spring 2002. Twelve years after opening to the outside world, Kaliningrad finally had a normal hotel, with all the facilities that tourists and business travellers require, and perhaps even more important, staff who appear committed to their job. It is therefore surprising to find it under the same management as the Kaliningrad Hotel. Care too has been taken with the design of both the rooms and the public areas. The location, opposite the zoo, is very convenient for many sites, for public transport and for shops. *Sgl US$50, twin US$70.*

🏠 **Patriot** (154 rooms) Ozernaya 25; ☎ 32 8707; f 27 5023. For visitors on a budget this hotel is ideal. It is clean, well maintained and adequately furnished. Most rooms have a fridge for families wishing to prepare picnics. It is a high-rise surrounded by others, about 2km to the north of the town centre. For many years, locals who could afford it came here for dental treatment as the surgery was regarded as one of the best in town but it moved out in 2003. The café has an unexpectedly wide menu with most main dishes costing around £0.75/US$1.20. *Sgl US$30, twin US$40.*

EATING AND DRINKING

For ten years from 1991, when Kaliningrad first opened to the West, the food available was universally dull. In the last few years, however, it has undoubtedly improved, as local people demand the standards they find elsewhere and a higher standard of living enables them to afford variety. The return of German food is not surprising as part of the increasing interest in the city prior to 1945. What is sad is the lack of restaurants representing other parts of the former Soviet Union. Georgian or Central Asian dishes would be a great bonus. Southern Europe is beginning to make its presence felt, and this trend is to be welcomed. Most of the irritants of eating in Soviet times have gone. Service is fairly quick, the menu does represent what is available and there will never be a problem finding a table. In most places, the menu will only be in Russian, but there will at least be the consolation that costs are so low that if a mistake is made, it will not be costly to order another dish.

Restaurants

✕ **Francis Drake** Sovietsky 19; ☎ 21 8353. Only the names of the dishes here and the pictures on the walls have any link with Britain. A Sir Drake salad for US$3.50 is a mixture of meats, tomatoes and mayonnaise. A Manchester for a similar price is a fillet of pork, mushrooms, sour cream and garlic. The ice cream has fortunately no hint of Britain in it. Transportation problems have prevented the flow of British beer so far

but hopefully this will be resolved before long.

✕ **Kulinaria** in the Kaliningrad Hotel. On the ground floor with a street entrance to the right-hand side of the hotel, the colours of the ingredients and of the décor at this self-service establishment used to make a refreshing contrast to the drab exterior surroundings. Now the whole neighbourhood has brightened up so it fits in well. Although a wide choice of cold meats is

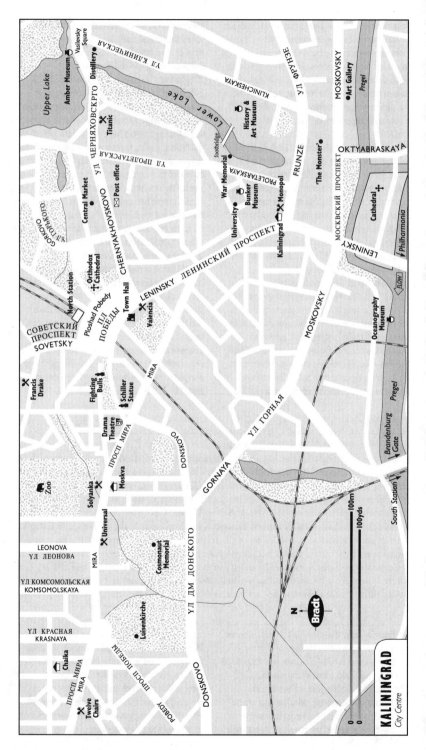

KALININGRAD
City Centre

Bradt

N

100m
100yds

offered, vegetarians will not be made to feel a nuisance here. Lingering here in the winter is not possible as no tables are provided, only stools and a counter. However, tables are provided outside during the summer.

✗ **Solyanka** Prospekt Mira 26; ☎ 27 9203. Self-service restaurants in Russia tend to be basic, but the Solyanka has definitely broken with this pattern. Cleanliness is taken to an obsession, in the toilets as much as in the restaurant itself. Menus are only in Russian, but with the clear displays, this hardly matters. A wide range of hot main courses is available for about US$3.50 each and there are also even cheaper snacks, while beer is around US$1.40 depending on the brand. Smokers are segregated into a glass-covered alcove. A board at the entrance invites job applications from potential waitresses and cooks. The salary offered of 8,000 roubles a month, about US$280, clearly gives the management a good choice as service always seems to be friendly and efficient.

✗ **Titanic** Chernyakhovskovo 74; ☎ 53 6768. The décor was meticulously planned before this restaurant opened in the summer of 2000. The designer clearly did more than see the film to have constructed the 'life boat alcoves', to have reprinted the old menus, and to have varnished the wood on the stairs. If the food is not quite first class, it is well above steerage. The veneer is almost April 1912 and when the restaurant opened it was a complete contrast to the rugged surroundings of the nearby market where the elderly attempted to supplement their minimal pensions by selling knitwear and vegetables. Like so much else in Kaliningrad, by 2005 the market had much less of a steerage feel to it.

On the opposite side of the road are exchange bureaux with long opening hours and usually the best rates for dollars and euro.

✗ **12 Stuliev** (12 Chairs) Prospekt Mira 67; ☎ 21 09031. Named after one of the few satirical novels published in Soviet times, this small cellar-bar mixes the old and the young, locals and tourists. The menu is a mixture of German and Russian, the décor and music likewise, so perhaps this is a portent of continuing future collaboration. Whilst vodka is the usual US$1.75 for a large measure, it is worth spending a little more on one of the 50 cocktails in which the restaurant specialises. Salmon salad accompanies them well. A bucolic evening here can happily be concluded with ice cream drenched in a liqueur.

✗ **Universal** Prospekt Mira 43; ☎ 21 6921. As this restaurant is part of a casino, smart dress is required and expect a search for weapons on entry. However it seems that the gamblers subsidise the food, which is extensive and freshly cooked. The restaurant is in fact a balcony overlooking the gamblers so the extravagance of new Russia can be safely viewed from a distance.

✗ **Valencia** Ploshad Pobedy 1; ☎ 43 3820. Most tourists visiting the Baltics want to forget previous holidays in Spain, but for those who cannot, southern warmth and a predictable menu of pancakes, paella and strong red wine is always on offer here. Their hours, too, are Spanish, as they close at 02.00 and happily serve both late lunches and late dinners. Local people always recommend it to Western visitors, on the assumption that they are looking for the familiar rather than the unusual.

ENTERTAINMENT AND NIGHTLIFE

MUSIC Most concerts take place at the Philharmonia, converted from the former Church of the Holy Family. Over the next few years, more will take place in the cathedral, now that the roof is complete and the interior largely restored.

THEATRE The Drama Theatre at Mira 4 performs only in Russian but its repertoire is international and with cheap tickets. An enjoyable evening can be spent there even without following all the dialogue.

CLUBS AND CASINOS As clubs and casinos are the centres for criminal activity, they are usually best avoided by visitors, except for those in hotels, which restrict entry to guests and carefully vetted local people. The Universal, mentioned above for its restaurant, checks all guests for weapons and is therefore secure.

WALKING TOURS

A one-day walking tour is suggested and a day excursion to the coast is also outlined. About four or five days are needed to do justice to the town and the surrounding area. Other places in the Kaliningrad region (*oblast* in Russian) are beyond the scope of this book but offer a worthwhile extension to visitors with the extra time.

ONE-DAY WALKING TOUR A sightseeing tour of Kaliningrad has to start at the lobby of the Kaliningrad Hotel.

Those who came in the early 1990s, when the town was first open to tourists, might really have wondered whether such a visit was worthwhile. The hotel lobby could perhaps be passed off as mediocre. When they went outside, what stood before them and beside them was the Soviet Union at its very worst. Concrete was the sole building material and it was abused in many forms. To the left, the view was of an abandoned 16-storey tower block, an unfinished bridge and an enormous parking lot for trucks. Ahead was a wide straight road across a small island leading towards anonymous suburbs. To the Germans who had lived here before the war, sacrilege had been committed. This was their beloved Kneiphof, the island that had been the heart of Königsberg with the cathedral, castle, university and a cluster of surrounding lanes. Only the shell of the cathedral then remained, surrounded by an unkempt garden; its sole use was as a playground for local children, who could enjoy many variants of hide and seek. To the right a slightly less nondescript road offered a few shops with the relief of stone and granite. Few would imagine that it had once been the location of Germany's largest bookshop, Gräfe und Unzer.

The mood of the exiled Germans on their return – 64,000 came in 1992 – is perhaps best summarised by their most famous representative Marion Gräfin Dönhoff who became well known as the publisher of the weekly *Die Zeit*. After her visit in 1991, she wrote, 'If I had been parachuted into this town and asked where I was, I would have perhaps replied Irkutsk. Nothing, absolutely nothing, reminded me of old Königsberg.'

The contemporary visitor will be much happier, mainly thanks to the fund-raising and reconciliation initiated by Marion Dönhoff since that visit. Through her paper, and by lobbying the German government and private foundations, funds have been raised to rebuild the cathedral and many other former churches. The local administration started to make serious efforts at renovating this area in 2004 and doubtless this will continue for several more years. No longer does it shame Kaliningrad. The **cathedral** (Кафедральный, *open daily 09.00–17.00*) must be the first port of call on any tour as by 2005, in time for the 750th anniversary of the founding of Königsberg, it had been largely rebuilt to its pre-war format.

Construction of the cathedral started in 1333 and was completed in the comparatively short period of 50 years. The first organ was installed in 1535. The early site bore an uncanny resemblance to the vista that greeted tourists in the early 1990s – an austere stone building with little decoration surrounded by greenery. It had as much military as religious significance, proving the power of the Teutonic Knights over the Prussian heathens. The oak piles, topped with copper, which form the foundations, are a credit to the advance in civil engineering at that time. They continued to support the increasing weight of subsequent builds, although it has been calculated that the cathedral has sunk 1.7m over 700 years. Finance was soon a problem and had to be resolved by the sale of papal indulgences. In 1410 there was the first service of remembrance, to those who had died at the Battle of Grünewald, which saw the end of the Teutonic Knights as a major force in the area. The Reformation was eagerly taken up in the 1520s with Christmas 1523 being celebrated in German, a very popular move according to surviving reports. A second 58m tower was added in 1540.

Much of the interior was destroyed by fire in 1544 but it was again quickly rebuilt within six years and then expanded over the next century, when a larger organ was added and the clock built on the South Tower. It became the aim of every famous resident to be buried behind the gold altar.

However, Kant, as a non-believer, never entered the building and his funeral procession stayed outside. The last restoration of Kant's tomb was carried out in 1924 and it was little damaged during the war. It can be seen beside the cathedral wall. (The Nazis left it intact after exhuming his skull to check on Kant's Aryan origins.)

There was minor damage to the cathedral during the French occupation at the beginning of the 19th century, when it was variously used as a stable, a prison and a hospital. Whilst Königsberg expanded in every other field over the next 100 years, it was only between 1903 and 1907 that the cathedral received much needed maintenance and rebuilding. It was the first time it had been cleaned since 1695 and many frescoes were discovered as a result. The devotion of the population to the cathedral is best summarised in the writings of the poet Agnes Miegel, born in Königsberg in 1879, who stayed until she was forced to flee in February 1945. 'You are always part of my life, like my father and my mother. Your bells wake me in the morning and send me to sleep in the evening.'

The RAF raids in August 1944 seriously damaged the cathedral but in no way destroyed it. The library, for instance, remained intact. There was no direct hit but fire spread from neighbouring buildings, which destroyed all the woodwork and led to the collapse of the roof. The site was abandoned after the war and some of the bricks were casually looted; others were specifically taken for use in various Soviet cities. The cobbles from the surrounding streets were relaid in Moscow's Red Square. The surrounding area was cleared in 1972, probably in preparation for the destruction of the site.

During the Soviet era, there was considerable dispute about the future of this ruin. Some felt it symbolised both the powerlessness and irrelevance of both Germany and religion. Others felt it was an inappropriate reminder of these former phenomena. In Kaliningrad *en route* to Britain in 1973, President Brezhnev certainly expressed his eagerness to destroy it, having just four years previously ordered the destruction of the castle ruins. Perhaps it was Kant's tomb that saved it, a complete and restored monument to the precursor to Marxist philosophy, beside a ruin of what he opposed.

Much of the vaulting collapsed in 1975 and some minimal restoration was done in 1976. Arguments went on as late as 1994, well after the demise of the Soviet Union, when views were still expressed that the whole area should become a sculpture park. However, that year saw the first service being held since the war and the burial of joint Russian and German capsules which included a memorial to the suffering of the German population. Four bells were restored during the following year and since then the roof has been completed and a museum has opened in the South Tower. An Orthodox chapel has been built in the North Tower, a compromise from the original Russian demands that the whole cathedral should be Orthodox. In mid-2002, work was concentrating on the interior windows and walls. The baptistery was completed early in 2000 with four stained-glass windows. The original designs were followed by local Russian glaziers and they depict John the Baptist, Konrad von Tierberg, the founder of Königsberg, and Martin Luther. Services and concerts now take place regularly. Both Lutheran and Orthodox services are now held in the cathedral.

The cathedral museum already occupies several rooms in the South Tower and is regularly being extended. It shows the 1903–07 rebuilding plans, as well as others proposed earlier which were not in fact carried out. It also outlines plans for the next few years, including archaeological excavations under the former castle and university. One room is devoted to Königsberg city life around the cathedral and shows an extensive china and postcard collection. Several rooms are devoted to Kant. It is fortunate how much material on these subjects survived during the Soviet period or was taken west by refugees in 1945. The whole collection is well lit and generously displayed. Labelling is, however, only in German and Russian.

German visitors always look east from Kneiphof island, to the former Lindenstrasse, now **Oktyabraskaya**. The remaining brick building facing the bridge dates from 1905 and was a Jewish orphanage for around 45 children. The synagogue,

KÖNIGSBERG RAID OF 29–30 AUGUST 1944 1,900 miles, 176 aircraft, 485 tonnes of bombs, 16 minutes and 400 acres of devastation. This calls, and without apology, for yet another misquotation of the Prime Minister's famous epigram. Never has so much destruction been wrought by so few aircraft at so great a distance, in so short a time. Königsberg, the capital of East Prussia, the greatest port in Eastern Germany, and the base for nearly 50 enemy divisions, is practically no more. Königsberg, the administrative centre of that province of Germany which has been the malignant breeding ground of the arrogant military caste, a town which has stood unchanged for 600 years, has to the benefit of mankind, been wiped out overnight.

The effects of this blow cannot be measured merely in acres, it is a pincer movement on the grand scale. Königsberg may have been just another strategical target to Bomber Command, though a large and important one at that, but it was also a tactical target for the Russians of absolutely first-class importance. The Russian victories of June and July brought them to within 100 miles of the town and within sight of the German frontiers; so did this great port with its ample dock facilities, miles of marshalling yards and modern factories, become of paramount importance to the armies desperately trying to stem the Russian advance.

With the few railways between Berlin and the front choked with supplies in one direction and the evacuation of such of the frightened populace as were allowed to go in the other, the port became the only means of relieving this bottleneck. Through its docks came the armour, the supplies and the reserves so urgently needed to re-equip the tattered divisions after their long retreat. Through its docks must go such of the much needed agricultural produce as could be salved from this fertile but threatened area. Meanwhile the armament and engineering works were ideally situated for the maintenance and repair of unserviceable armour brought back from the front.

The Königsbergers, busily engaged in digging trenches, with their eyes turned fearfully towards the east, and the British heavily committed nearly a thousand miles away in the opposite direction, can have had little thought of danger from the west. The shock of discovering that Bomber Command could meet the needs of the western armies, engage in the battle with the flying bombs and at the same time join in on the Russian front, will not have been confined to those who actually felt the blows.

Indeed to judge from the lack of comments in the press and on the wireless, it has left the enemy speechless.

Perhaps the best way of all of considering the effect of this raid is to ponder on what would have been the reactions of the Germans, and indeed of this country, had the Russians flown to Bremen before us and utterly destroyed it.

which had been built a decade earlier, was destroyed by the Nazis on Kristallnacht, 9 November 1938.

The street was also famous for the house of Käthe Kollwitz, an artist born there in 1867. Although she moved to Berlin in 1891, she kept close links with Königsberg until the rise of the Nazis. She never made a secret of her left-wing views, and her paintings – similar in many ways to those of the English artist L S Lowry – show the suffering of working-class people under various regimes. She was invited to Moscow in 1927 as part of a delegation to the celebrations of the tenth anniversary of the Russian Revolution. She courageously stayed in Germany during the Nazi era, feeling she would be more of an embarrassment by staying than by going into exile. Her work was banned from public exhibition during this time. Despite this political background, her house was not restored during the Soviet period and she was never mentioned in local publications of that era.

Looking south from the island, the former **Stock Exchange**, painted in a light-blue pastel, stands out on the riverbank. As a contrast to German Gothic and Soviet concrete, it is a welcome Florentine renaissance façade and was built in the 1870s, when the town's prosperity was at its height. Like the cathedral, it is built on a foundation of deep piles; the exact number used was 2,202 and they are mostly 4.5m (15ft) deep. Statues were erected beside the four corners of the building, which depicted four continents, and hence the extent of Königsberg trade at the time, but these did not survive the war. The ground floor of the building is now a pretentious restaurant, Monetny Devor, one of the few places where the local rich like to flaunt themselves. Unlike their counterparts in other Russian cities, successful business people in Kaliningrad tend to enjoy their wealth discreetly.

Walking north, back across the river, an incomplete Soviet-era office block, the '**Monster**', as it is usually now called, dominates the skyline. It is built over the foundations of the famous **castle** (*Schloss* in German) that has haunted contemporary Kaliningrad. The castle dated from 1257 and dominated the German town throughout its history. All major ceremonies of state took place in its main reception room. Peter the Great stayed there and Frederick the Great accepted the surrender of the Russian army there at the end of the Seven Years War. In 1904 Russian and German Social Democrats were tried there, accused of smuggling Lenin's fledgling journal *Iskra* ('The Spark') into Tsarist Russia. The castle housed the Prussian Museum and then, during World War II, the Amber Chamber, which had been brought back from Tsarskoye Selo, outside Leningrad, by German troops. The museum curator, Dr Alfred Rohde, vowed he would not leave Königsberg in 1945 without his treasure but neither he nor the chamber was ever seen again. One mosaic panel was finally rediscovered in Bremen in 1997 and was sent back to Russia in April 2000 in return for paintings taken by the former Soviet government which had belonged to the Bremen Art Gallery before the war. A small panel has been rebuilt for the Amber Museum in Königsberg but a full restoration was carried out for Tsarskoye Selo in 2003.

The former Amber Museum, which was also housed in the castle, boasted about 100,000 items, of which 11,000 were fortunately taken to Göttingen University in late 1944 for safe keeping and therefore survived. The rest of the collection was either destroyed or disappeared.

Much of the correspondence between Moscow and courageous local architects about the proposed destruction of the castle and a suitable replacement has recently come to light. To the politicians, the building represented 'centuries of German militarism and plunder' which should be replaced by a large modern civic building to display Soviet power in what had been the heart of the German city. The political activities of the exiled East Prussians in West Germany clearly influenced the final decision to remove all traces of the castle in 1969. They used the castle tower as the logo on all their campaign literature that lobbied vocally and frequently for the then West German government to continue its policy of regarding East Prussia as being 'temporarily under Soviet administration' rather than as being lost for good. It therefore made political if not aesthetic sense for this symbol of former German power to be eliminated. Architects pointed out the many historical links the building had with Russia, as outlined above, and how a Soviet war memorial could be incorporated into a restored building. Their pleas were ignored and a budget agreed for a **new town hall**.

The 25-year saga that followed showed Soviet planning and political bigotry at its very worst. An initial budget of 1.6 million roubles (about £500,000 or US$1 million at the official rate of exchange in 1969) was agreed for a 16-storey building. Over the first two years, around 1,100 concrete pillars, each 8m in length, were dug into the marshy ground beside the castle. Cynics were soon to point out that they did not have the firmness of those laid by the Germans 700 years before. Twenty workers were employed on the site between 1972 and 1976 and they completed six storeys. The next ten storeys took a further five years so the basic structure was finished in 1981. By then costs had increased to nine million roubles, a surprisingly capitalist problem in a country that had been cut off from a market economy for 30 years. There was no money for moving the local government and none for installing electricity and heating. In 1988 money was found to furnish half the building but this work was not completed by the time the Soviet Union collapsed in 1991. Nothing was done to the building until 2005 when refurbishment slowly began. Many residents would have preferred to see it destroyed.

Turning right along Moskovsky for about 100m, leaving behind the Monster and the Kaliningrad Hotel, the first major building on the right-hand side is the **Art Gallery**. Soviet money fortunately did not run out here and the gallery opened in 1989, just in time to give a final overview of art throughout the USSR at that point. Every former Soviet republic is represented, both by paintings and by applied arts. Ceramics and glass are both well covered, but more surprising are the copies of imperial china and lacquer. This style of china with its gold leaf represents a style of life to which few in Kaliningrad can or could ever relate. The gallery holds many exhibitions of children's art. They are now encouraged to paint Königsberg as well as Kaliningrad. The exploits of the Teutonic Knights provide ample material for them to portray happily. One of the most famous local artists is Boris Bulkagov, born in 1944, whose pictures are marked by his almost total use of dark colours. One of the rooms is a gallery where contemporary artists can sell their pictures.

Cross Moskovsky and head towards the **Lower Lake**, called Schlossteich or 'Castle Lake' in German times. The surroundings of the lake had been made communal in 1900 and the path around it built in 1937. The History and Art Museum, on the eastern side of the lake, can easily be identified as a former German concert hall.

The nondescript five-storey building on the western side used to be the town's most famous hotel, the Park, where on different occasions both Hitler and Molotov regularly stayed. Because of the notoriety of its former guests, this is now an office building.

The **History and Art Museum** (Историкоху дожественный музей) has been totally transformed since the Soviet period. Most labels are in English and German. It originally consisted of the remains of the Prussian Museum collection, which had previously been housed in the castle. This was largely an archaeological collection, so did not cause political problems. It in fact enabled Soviet historians to claim a Slavic rather than a German origin for many of the artefacts. The museum has recently undergone considerable expansion, showing not only extensive material from pre-war Königsberg, but also from the early Soviet period in the 1950s. One can only hope that what is portrayed as a typical apartment from the 1950s is no longer typical of homes in the town outside. Fabrics, furniture, paintings and crockery from both eras have been salvaged. Some 'bourgeois' exhibits such as refined table linen and advertisements are displayed, as well as examples of the inflation banknotes from 1923 when they had to be constantly recycled and overprinted. Programmes and layouts are displayed for the major annual trade fair, the Ostmesse, which took place every autumn between 1920 and 1941.

The Königsberg room in other respects still shows considerable political bias. Far more is shown of the rise of the Communist Party than that of the Nazi Party, but no attempt is made to assess the Communists' failure to overcome the Nazis in the years prior to 1933. The banners, the photographs and the pamphlets all date from earlier. Some items would seem more appropriate for a car-boot sale than for a serious town museum. Beer mugs and ashtrays seem an odd choice of exhibit but anything gathered from former Königsberg has a magical significance for those who still remember it.

The Soviet room is now frank about issues that were formerly taboo. There are photographs of the destruction of the castle, and portraits of both Stalin and Khrushchev, leaders whose pictures were not shown elsewhere in the later Soviet times. Other exhibits have not been changed since the 1980s and are reminiscent of the Moscow 'Exhibition of Economic Achievements'. Several cosmonauts came from Kaliningrad so photographs of them with the Politburo abound and a display case is devoted to the presents given to them by visiting foreign statesmen, such as a cigar from Fidel Castro and a ring from Le Duan, the Vietnamese Prime Minister. The shop and stalls within the museum offer a variety and value impossible to find elsewhere in the town. They offer good selections of amber, lacquer, woodwork and paintings and some books likely to be of interest to foreigners.

Cross the lake on the footbridge and note the modest **war memorial** to the left. It commemorates Colonel Tulan and his French regiment that fought as part of the Soviet air force in 1942–44. In February 1944 the regiment was named Normandy Neman, the Neman (or Niemen) being the river that traditionally divided Russia from Germany (and which now divides Lithuania from Kaliningrad). The memorial notes that the regiment made 5,000 sorties, fought in 869 battles and destroyed 273 German aircraft.

Next cross Proletarskaya which leads into the **university**. The buildings here date from the 19th century and were designed by August Stüler, one of the pupils of Karl Friedrich Schinkel, Germany's most famous architect of the early 19th century. They were all completed within a year between 1858 and 1859. Although seriously damaged at the end of the war, they could have been restored to show the original Italian façade but this was not done. It is necessary to wander inside for any memories of the 19th century. In the square which the university buildings surround, old sculptures are being restored and new ones being created. The original statue of Kant disappeared at the end of the war, but Marion Dönhoff paid for a replacement to be provided in 1992. Kant's name was given to the University in 2005. This replaced a statue of Ernst Thälmann which had been there for most of the Soviet era. He was the leader of the German Communist Party during the 1930s and he died in a concentration camp in 1944.

In the centre of the square is the entrance to the **Bunker Museum** (Ълиндаж Ляша, *open daily 10.00–17.00*), sometimes called the Lasch Bunker after General Lasch, who had it built as his headquarters for the final defence of Königsberg in 1945. Several of the rooms are much as he would have left them on 10 April 1945 after signing the capitulation and surrendering himself to what would turn out to be ten years' imprisonment. The heating pipes, the telephone wires and the electric cables have all remained intact. When the museum opened in 1967, it provided the only picture of former Königsberg that local residents were allowed to have, with detailed models of the town layout and of the military formations. Even a German slogan (*Wir kapitulieren nie* – 'We will never surrender'), daubed on a wall, is included. The smallest exhibit is a ticket for the last train to Berlin that left on 22 January 1945. The leaflets dropped by the Russians stressed the futility of continued fighting and promised food supplies and family reunions to all who surrendered. Recently the museum has been extended to show the burial sites of troops from both sides.

Leave the museum in a westerly direction towards Lenin Prospekt. On the far side of the road is the town's major supermarket (BECTEP), open daily until 23.00. Turning left takes one back to the Hotel Kaliningrad after 100m. Readers of Russian will find the kiosks along here a good source of books, maps and magazines.

A SHORT WALK Another sight within walking distance of the hotel is the **Oceanography Museum** (Музей истории мирового океана, *open daily except Monday, 11.00–17.00*) based in and around the ship *Vityaz*. This is now permanently moored on the Pregel about 700m from the hotel. During 2000 and 2001 the exhibitions were considerably extended and now include new buildings on the shore. *Vityaz* was built as a cargo boat in Bremerhaven in 1939 and launched with the name *Mars*, after a river in western Germany rather than the planet. It was never used as a cargo carrier, being taken over as a troop ship on the outbreak of war. In March and April 1945 it made several trips between Pillau, the port on the coast nearest to Königsberg, and Denmark, rescuing about 20,000 civilians from the oncoming Russians. When the British liberated Denmark from the Germans, they took over the boat and renamed it *Empire Forth* but it only stayed in British hands until February 1946 when it was 'returned' to the Russians, being seen as based in territory now belonging to them. This British name would have been most appropriate for the Russians in view of the territory they seized at the end of World War II, but they renamed it firstly *Equator* and then *Vityaz* ('Noble Warrior').

It was moved to Vladivostok and between 1949 and 1979 made constant oceanographic expeditions to the Pacific Ocean. It also made pioneering visits to Osaka and to San Francisco in 1958, the first in each case since the start of the Cold War. Jacques Cousteau was invited on board in Mombasa in 1967, again a symbol of an easier political climate. Its last expedition finished in Kaliningrad harbour where it would rot for ten years, becoming known as the 'rusty tin' until a restoration programme began in 1990. This was completed in 1994, partially with the help of surviving members of the *Mars* crew. (Meanwhile another *Vityaz* was built in 1981 and is now part of the Russian Black Sea fleet based at Novorossisk.)

The exhibitions are not limited to the life of the ship. One room covers the history of oceanography, the laboratories ships included, and two earlier boats that carried the name *Vityaz*. Pictures show the startled reaction of the inhabitants of New Guinea in 1870 to a white man when the captain of an earlier *Vityaz* landed. They assumed he had come from the moon, as his skin was a similar colour. The researches beneath the Pacific, including the measurement of the Marianas Trench, are covered extensively. The new political climate means that life on board in any era can be shown honestly, and where appropriate, ridiculed. The whims and needs of all former commanders, Tsarist, Nazi or Soviet are not hidden, be they for an absurdly large piano, a shredding machine or a portrait of Lenin. Mess rooms, too, with appropriate memorabilia, have been rebuilt. The museum authorities hope to set up a British room, if enough material from the 1945–46 period can be provided.

The 60th anniversary in 1999 of the building of the ship was a suitable pretext for further enlargement of the collections. One theme is 'Maritime Königsberg', showing the expansion of the harbour, firstly in 1901 when the canal to the sea at Pillau was widened, and secondly in the 1920s when Königsberg became eastern Germany's major port, following the loss of Danzig and Memel (now Gdansk in Poland and Klaipėda in Lithuania respectively) at the end of World War I. Many of the buildings dating from those times, such as the grain silos, can still be seen along the riverside. In 2000 a miniatures gallery was added with replicas of ships from Egypt, Greece, Japan and Fiji. More familiar to British visitors will be the models of the *Revenge* and of Elizabeth I knighting Francis Drake. Columbus and Queen Isabella have not been forgotten, nor has the *Santa Maria*. April 2000 also saw the conversion of several cabins into displays of coral reefs, sharks' jaws and underwater geological discoveries.

In July 2000 the opening to the public of a B-413 submarine greatly increased the scope of the museum. Originally built in 1969, it then travelled almost as much as *Vityaz*, being a frequent visitor to Cuba. The B-413 was the Soviet answer to the

NATO Foxtrot submarines, being able to carry 22 torpedoes and to launch them from a depth of 100m. Only the small and the agile will be able to enjoy the displays on board as the interior has been maintained as closely as possible to the original. It is hard to believe that it housed 80 men for nine-month journeys; only the captain and the KGB agent had single rooms. An exhibition honestly portrays the history of the Russian/Soviet navy from 1834 until the present day. Tragedy and triumph are covered in equal measure.

The museum complex around *Vityaz* is probably the most dynamic institution in the whole Kaliningrad oblast. Each year there is expansion, the exhibits are regularly updated and the publications show a professionalism totally lacking elsewhere. In 2001 the Whale Pavilion was opened; it displays a whale 17m long which was captured in 1975 but which was then buried in the sand along the Baltic coast for the next 25 years in the hope that eventually a home would be found for it. The central museum building opened in 2003, covering in greater detail the whole field of oceanography and also introducing the theme of global warming. By 2006 another building will be open, in which the exhibition will cover the maritime history of Königsberg and Kaliningrad. Other plans are to restore a fishing trawler and to cover the field of space exploration as several of the leading USSR cosmonauts were born in Kaliningrad. The museum website (*www.vitiaz.ru*) provides current information on the whole site. By 2006 a whole day was needed to do justice to the different collections.

WALKS FURTHER AFIELD Many other sights within the city are just too far to walk from the Kaliningrad Hotel but can be easily reached by bus or taxi. Tour operators abroad can pre-book English-speaking guides with their own cars and this is the most convenient way to visit other sites in the town and also for visits along the coast. The following itinerary can be done in a long day, or be divided into two days.

The first port of call must be at the **Amber Museum** or **Музей янтаря** *(open daily except Mon 10.00–17.30)* housed in the Dohna Tower, one of six similar 19th-century fortifications that still dominate the city skyline. (General Dohna fought against Napoleon.) It replaced an earlier museum, which had been beside the mines at Yantarny on the coast. A few items come from the pre-war museum, which had been housed in the former castle.

Amber has formed the one thread that binds together the history of the region. Since 90% of the world's amber production comes from this area, its value was an incentive for many generations of conquerors and would-be conquerors. The Prussian tribes traded it with the Romans, who saw magical and practical value in it. Tacitus and Pliny the Elder both refer to it and gladiators wore it. Amber would become an important ingredient in medicine, in agricultural fertilisers and in varnish. It would strengthen fishing nets and be used in fumigation. The museum therefore presents a 2,000-year artistic and political history of the region through the 6,000 amber products displayed. The natural history goes back millions of years to the formation of fossilised resin, which is the basis of amber.

The most interesting exhibits are those from the Soviet period; models from Aesop's fables such as 'The Fox and the Grapes' are a surprising legacy but more obvious ones are the model Kremlins, dams, pylons, nuclear icebreakers and power stations with smoking chimneys. Examples of gifts to foreign dignitaries include jewellery boxes with the hammer and sickle emblem and statues of Soviet leaders. None have been deposed from the museum so Lenin, Stalin and Khrushchev sit peacefully side by side. There are some replicas of famous pieces in the Hermitage and Kremlin collections. The largest of these weigh over a kilo. Clearly the lost Amber Room cannot be forgotten in these surroundings, so some of the original panelling has been copied and paintings show how the complete original looked when it was displayed at Tsarskoye Selo, outside St Petersburg.

Do not miss the museum shop before leaving. Its lack of taste rivals that of much of the collection and the use of amber dust as a painting material enables 'pictures' to be sold very cheaply.

The museum is on Vasilevsky Square, named after the commander responsible for the final victory over the Germans. The memorial at the centre of the square commemorates this victory, in particular 216 Heroes of the Soviet Union and 20 who received this award twice. On the opposite side of the road from the museum is a distillery; its shop sells vodka liqueurs at prices low even by Kaliningrad standards. Perhaps it is just as well nobody can really tell how dependent the local economy is on drink and cigarettes smuggled out to Poland and then on to the rest of Europe.

Proceeding west from the museum, along Chernyakhovskovo, the **Central Market** (Центральный рынок) is on the right-hand side of the road after about 800m. Between the first and second world wars, the halls housed the famous Ostmesse, an annual trade fair which brought together major traders from East Prussia with their opposite numbers in the Baltic states and the Soviet Union. Being the largest building in Königsberg, it was also the centre for all political rallies during both the Weimar Republic (1920–33) and the subsequent Nazi era. President Ebert opened the building and the first fair in 1920 and Hitler and Himmler spoke here on several occasions.

Now it has a largely local function and for tourists gives a clear indication of what is available and what is fashionable. The 2,000 stands within the halls are clearly regulated with prices listed and satisfactory hygiene. A guide is useful since, when prompted, an otherwise banal stand can suddenly produce caviar or silk at prices much lower than elsewhere. Good picnic ingredients available here include German sausage, Polish ham, Lithuanian fruit, local cheeses and the famous Russian black bread. Few tourists can take advantage of all the fresh fish that arrives here at least once a day.

Chernyakhovskovo continues to Ploshchad Pobedy (Площадь Победы; 'Victory Square') the former Hansaplatz, which Gauleiter Erich Koch renamed after himself in 1933. It had by then become the business and administration centre of the town. In 2005 there were discussions about renaming the square so that the link with Soviet times could be broken. 'Redeemer' or 'Cathedral' Square seemed to be the most likely names, if there is to be a change. On the north side of the square, a dominating statue of Lenin used to make clear who were now the masters here but he was removed in 2005 to allow a proper view of the Orthodox Cathedral completed during that summer. Boris Yeltsin laid the foundation stone for this cathedral but lack of funds delayed progress on the building during the later 1990s. There are no chairs as believers stand through the service. In the garden to the southeast of the square stands a statue of Mother Russia; she replaced Stalin on this plinth in 1974.

The former **North Station**/Nordbahnhof, built in 1930, still functions as such but it now also includes offices of several government departments and private businesses. Foreign businesses such as the Hamburg Chamber of Commerce are in a new building behind the station on Sovietsky Prospekt (Советский проспект). The **town hall** building on the south side of the square dates from 1923 and is one of very few to have served the same function both in German and in Soviet/Russian times.

Leaving Victory Square to the west, along Prospekt Mira (Проспект Мира; 'Peace Avenue') note first the bronze **statue of the fighting bulls** on the right-hand side of the road. They are the work of sculptor August Gaul whose bronze animals became famous all over Germany before World War I. In early Soviet days the statue was moved to the zoo, but it was returned here to its original location in the late 1970s. Local people now read a contemporary theme into the statue, seeing it as a representation of Kaliningrad locked into battle with Moscow. Behind the statue note the baroque entrance of the former courthouse which dates from 1913. Beside the courthouse are the former postal headquarters constructed in 1924. This building now houses the senior staff of the Baltic Fleet so is one of the best maintained in the whole town centre.

The next major building on the right-hand side is the **Drama Theatre**, built in 1927 but given its current bolshoi façade by the Soviet regime. In the six years prior to the Nazi regime every German actor of note played here and the Soviets continued the high standards, once it was finally reopened in 1980. On the other side of the road is a **statue of the German writer Friedrich Schiller** (1759–1805) which was allowed to stay during the Soviet period, probably because his work was regarded as very 'progressive'. A rather implausible story is told to explain its survival at the end of the war: the words 'don't shoot' were allegedly daubed across it in both German and Russian.

Prospekt Mira now widens and soon the entrance to the **zoo** (**Зоопарк**) comes up on the right-hand side. (*Open daily at 09.00, closing at 21.00 May–Sep, at 17.00 during other months.*) It was founded in 1896 and is the only institution in Königsberg/Kaliningrad to have had a continuous history through German, Soviet and now Russian times. It might well be the world's first theme park; its early posters were decades ahead of their time, the funfair was always as crucial as the collection of animals and no secret was ever made of its commercial intent. Slot machines competed with donkey rides, cycle races and tennis tournaments. There were free family days when cooking facilities would be provided, thereby encouraging long stays and extensive patronage of the fairground attractions. Within two years of its opening, it sold 25,000 annual season tickets, a present for which every young Königsberger yearned at Christmas. Its flamboyant first director Hermann Claass stayed in charge until his death in 1914, never letting his commercial flair interfere with the expansion and maintenance of the collection. Within a year of the opening there were 983 animals and by 1910 this number had increased to 2,126, including two Siberian tigers donated by Moscow Zoo.

It closed on the outbreak of war in August 1914 but popular demand and the elimination of any threat from Russia enabled it to reopen in July 1918, before the end of that conflict. It was completely rebuilt during the 1930s and these buildings largely remain despite the zoo being a battleground in April 1945. The zoo stayed open throughout the war this time and the Soviet government even presented two elephants in 1940, while the cynical Nazi–Soviet pact was still in effect. Annual season tickets were printed for 1945 and were sold from Christmas 1944 until the following March. The director throughout the war was Dr Hans-Georg Thienemann whose father Johannes was founder of the bird sanctuary at Rossitten (see page 208).

Many stories circulate about the number of animals who survived through May 1945 – most of course were killed by the starving residents. Four is the most quoted figure, representing a hippopotamus, a deer, a fox and a badger. Several Russian soldiers tried to feed the hippopotamus, which had apparently lost its appetite. Conventional nourishment failed, but a fortnight of vodka, allegedly four litres a day, succeeded in reviving it. The hippopotamus is now therefore the zoo's logo. In the midst of the tragedy that engulfed Königsberg in the summer of 1945, it is good to find one amusing story.

The zoo reopened in 1947, it is claimed with a collection of 2,000 animals, though this figure is now doubted. For the local population, it is again a major attraction although they must feel frustrated at the rather run-down air it now presents. Around 300,000 come each year and a pet shop has been added to the traditional attractions. With a brochure printed in colloquial English, it is, however, well in advance of other Kaliningrad tourist sites in attracting foreign visitors. They are promised 'baboons with colourful bottoms' and 'apes who so closely resemble humans that they look like someone you have probably met before'. Hermann Claass would be proud of the marketing flair shown by his Russian successors.

Almost opposite the zoo south of Prospekt Mira is the **Cosmonaut Memorial**, its circular format with the space in between portraying the journeys around the globe that Kaliningrad's most famous sons accomplished in the 1970s. One, Alexei Leonov, was the first to leave a spaceship while it was in orbit. Another, Victor Patzayei, was killed in a failed landing when his rocket returned to earth.

Leaving the zoo and continuing along Prospekt Mira out of town, Germany begins to take over the architecture from the Soviet Union. After 200m on the left, the **Luisenkirche** makes this point emphatically. It was built around 1900, paid for largely by one benefactor, Louis Grosskopf. He founded a cigar factory in 1857 but expanded the business so successfully that by 1900 he was employing 400 people there and had opened 18 shops around the town. The consecration of the church in 1901 commemorated the 200th anniversary of the crowning of King Frederick I in 1701. The German community worshipped here until 1948 when it was turned into a storeroom for gardening tools used in the surrounding park. Its conversion into a puppet theatre in 1976 possibly saved it from destruction as that was the last year in which German churches were still being pulled down.

A further kilometre along the same road brings up on the left the first new church to be built since the war. It uses the German name Auferstehungskirche ('**Church of the Resurrection**') and was completed in 1999 on land that had earlier been a German cemetery. The large Lutheran exile community in Germany had wanted to re-establish a church in Kaliningrad, theirs having been the predominant religion in the former East Prussia since the 16th century – both Martin Luther's son and daughter had been active in the area and were buried in Königsberg. Every former church considered for this gave rise to considerable difficulties. The current Russian organisation was in some cases not willing to move; in others the bureaucratic and financial hurdles in rebuilding turned out to be too great.

The church now serves a local Russian community, the Volga Germans, who have settled in Kaliningrad with the hope of eventually being resettled in Germany, and the increasingly large number of Germans who now work in Kaliningrad. Attending a service or a concert, or seeing all the voluntary activities that take place during the week, shows how strongly German/Russian reconciliation can work. The altar is of great significance, being assembled from bricks taken out of eight different ruined churches.

The oldest church in East Prussia, the **Juditterkirche**, is another kilometre or so along Prospekt Pobedya, but on the right hand side. The Juditter suburb, (renamed Mendeleevo (**Менделеева**) was as sought after by successful Germans as it now is by successful Russians. The area offers space, greenery, cleanliness and above all privacy. The public parks near to the church rivalled the zoo as an attraction for children. Reminiscences from former East Prussians tell of collecting anemones in spring and acorns in autumn, of climbing trees, of open-air concerts, and the climax of the afternoon, buying peppermint drops and lemonade at the sweet shop. The church dates originally from the 13th century with the tower being added at the turn of the 15th century. It was extensively restored in 1906 and this revealed wall paintings which had been hidden for centuries. Although the church was totally untouched by the war and fighting, much of the intricate woodwork was plundered in the immediate aftermath and then 35 years of complete neglect left little of the former interior. Germans were allowed to continue worshipping here until their expulsion in 1948.

The ruins were given over to the Orthodox Church in 1984 and a basic restoration was completed in 1988. Services started in 1986, the first to be held in the Kaliningrad region since 1948. Official atheism had therefore lasted 38 years. It would take another two or three years before any other churches reopened. Given the vigorous support that the local Orthodox community gives to the church, the building is unlikely ever to return into Lutheran hands. However, the German cemetery beside the church is being slowly restored and a memorial plaque is planned to all Germans killed in Königsberg at the end of the war.

Another visit should be made within the town and that is to the **Brandenburg Gate** (it has kept the same name in Russian) situated south of the river on Ulitsa Bagrationa (**Улица Багратиона**) near to the main railway station. Architecturally, it has nothing in common with its Berlin namesake although being as large, trams and cars also go through it. Like six other similar gates that date from the early 19th century, it is a red-brick structure built so well that it survived both the RAF bombs and the subsequent Soviet onslaught. It even retains two statues, of General von Boyen and General von Aster, two prominent 19th-century commanders.

Even though Lenin no longer dominates the square in front of the North Station, Kalinin still has to have his glory here in front of the **South Station** (**Южный Вокзал**). As most visitors, whether local or international, will arrive here or at the neighbouring bus station, he could always claim to be more prominent. The interior of the station was completely rebuilt in time for the 2005 celebrations, but surprisingly it has a very Soviet feel. Marble and chandeliers predominate. A small railway museum was opened in summer 2000 with two restored steam engines and the promise of more. Given the number of engines abandoned in marshalling yards around the country, it is a pity that this museum has not been enlarged. A large post office is at the western end of the station complex and beside it is an antique shop, full of Königsberg and Soviet memorabilia. There is another antique shop on the opposite side of the square, beside which is one of the larger bookshops in Kaliningrad.

The current home of the Kaliningrad Philharmonic Orchestra is in the former Kirche zur Heiligen Familie ('**Church of the Holy Family**'), known as Philharmonia in Russian. It is on the same road as the Brandenburg Gate, Ulitsa Bagrationa, and it is a walk of about 700m from there or from the station. Originally one of four Catholic churches in Königsberg built around 1900, it was saved from serious damage at the end of the war because it was surrounded by narrow streets. It therefore avoided the worst of the fighting and the bombardments. In the early 1970s, whilst other churches in Kaliningrad were still being pulled down, restoration started here and in 1980 it opened as a concert hall. An organ was added in 1982 and good standards of maintenance have been upheld ever since, together with equally good standards of catering in the crypt-café underneath.

EXCURSIONS FROM KALININGRAD

If time allows for only a one-day trip outside the town of Kaliningrad, this must be to **the coast and along the Curonian Spit** (**Крушская коса**) towards the Lithuanian border. It should be done by car and with a guide since it involves a number of stops and signing in many places is not good. Such a trip can start in **Yantarny** (**Янтарный**), which will very likely be the backbone of the Kaliningrad area's economy for the next 100 years, when the amber mine there is expected to run out. Known as Palmnicken in German times, the village is on the coast about 35km kilometres from Kaliningrad. Its wealth is well disguised since the village houses have a forlorn look and its roads are poorly maintained. Bomb damage was minimal so older German tourists can recognise the layout and again enjoy Sunday afternoons along the beach.

There is now just one large opencast mine in use, producing about 450 tonnes of amber a year, about 90% of world production. Water has now seeped into the others, although Russian children follow their German predecessors in collecting amber pieces from the beach when they have been washed up after storms.

There is a somewhat precarious viewing point from which the whole mine can be seen; strong footwear is necessary to reach it and an equally strong constitution to tolerate the dire environmental pollution that it causes. The site was privatised in 1990 and then renationalised three years later with the hope of returning most of the profits into government hands. The Baltic Germans in the 13th century had similarly tried to control this trade and although they publicly hanged private traders, they were as unsuccessful at controlling it as their contemporary Russian successors. A small shop near the site is sometimes open for the purchase of amber; otherwise the Amber Museum in Kaliningrad is the best source.

If ever a reward could be made for the town in the Kaliningrad region least affected by the Soviet occupation it must go to **Rauschen** or as it is still officially called, **Svetlogorsk (Светлогорск)**. Its role as a seaside resort did not alter, and having official Soviet status as a spa town, money could always be found for maintenance. The Russian name translates as 'bright city', the German one as 'to rustle'. Both are equally appropriate for a well-designed, spacious town full of trees and shrubs. A good regular train service operates from Kaliningrad and the town is small enough to be explored *in toto* on foot. It was the introduction of this train service in 1900 that brought day-trippers from Königsberg to Rauschen and so made it less exclusive than it had been in the 19th century. The Soviet Union, rather than Russia, intrudes with the street names. Marx, Lenin, Kalinin, Gagarin and the October Revolution are all remembered but, unlike in most other towns of the region, the statue of Lenin has been removed. Perhaps he may in due course be replaced by Prussia's King Friedrich Wilhelm I who first made the town famous in the early 18th century. Otherwise one could be in any small German town on the Baltic coast. At weekends, the town is as lively in the winter as it is in the summer. Its year-round population is some 4,000 compared with 2,500 before the war, but this trebles in the summer season when Russians come from all over the federation for their holidays and for medical treatment. Svetlogorsk likes to think of itself as the Sotchi of the north, rivalling this Black Sea resort in its facilities and in its prestige.

The red-brick Gothic church was designed by August Stüler, famous for many grander buildings in Berlin. It was consecrated in 1907, converted into a sports centre after the war but was then given to the Orthodox Church in 1990. Chamber music concerts are held there throughout the year. A second church was built in 1994 as a memorial chapel to 25 children killed when a military aircraft crashed into their kindergarten in May 1972. Following normal Soviet practice, no official mention of the crash was made at the time. The photographs inside are of the children and their teachers, but there are none of the air crew who also all died.

The promenade by the sea, with its funfair, sundial and stairway decorated with mosaics has survived largely intact. Some villas and sanatoria are newly built but most of the grand wooden villas with their intricate window designs and elaborate roofs date from around 1900. They are all at a discreet distance from each other, allowing for extensive shrubbery and flower gardens between them. Some are now in private hands, some still belong to state organisations, but all can be proud of their paintwork and varnish.

Sculpture from Rauschen's most famous artist, Hermann Brachert (1890–1972) has survived throughout the town. He fell out of favour with the Nazi regime on account of the pessimistic tone of many of his pieces. They did not allow him to teach or exhibit but fortunately they did not destroy his work and some of his most moving sculptures date from that era. He worked with equal effect in marble, limestone and bronze. His house in the neighbouring village of Otradnoye (**Отрадное**), formerly Georgenswalde, is now a museum.

Oktyabrskaya Ulitsa (**Октябрьская Улица**) is the main shopping street and it is very clear which shops are for the German tourists and which for the local population. Number 13 has the best bookshop in the whole region with excellent and cheap English–Russian dictionaries. The street also has a very Soviet cafeteria with tin trays and poor lighting. As a full meal from an extensive menu can, however, be had for about £0.50/US$0.90, it seems churlish to complain. Those who do can turn instead to a pretentious café with the surprising name of the Lame Horse (Хромая лошадь) where a mediocre German meal can be obtained for around £6/US$9. Cynics might claim that 'lame' refers to the level of service and cuisine.

A 20km drive from Rauschen/Svetlogorsk is needed to reach the start of the Curonian Spit at **Zelenogradsk (Зеленоградск)**, formerly Cranz. Not being granted any special status during the Soviet period and having been the scene of serious fighting in April 1945, what was once a glamorous, vibrant resort soon became a neglected village. It is changing much more slowly than other places in the region. The young people drifting around the streets clearly do not represent the success stories of the new regime. The Russian name translates as 'Green City', which perhaps aptly sums up the weeds growing in the streets and the moss that has gripped many former villas. A grotesque concrete walkway along the coast offers no consolation after seeing the main street through the town.

The **Curonian Spit**, however, will without doubt be worth the drive from Kaliningrad. Visitors with more time may well consider continuing their tour to Nida, just over the Lithuanian border. The spit is an 80km tongue of land which divides the Baltic Sea from the Curonian Lagoon. Half the territory belongs to Kaliningrad and half to Lithuania. The history of the spit shows nature at its most brutal. Humans fought the elements rather than each other in this area. Most visitors travelling on a calm summer's day will see an alternation of dunes and forests, interspersed with the occasional village. It is hard to believe that a graveyard of whole villages lies beneath the sea and sand just a few hundred metres away.

That nature was finally controlled here is due to one man, Franz Epha (1828–1904), whose plans for forestation took 40 years to implement between 1860 and 1900, but which finally made the area secure. The Prussian regime encouraged the work initially to safeguard the road to the end of their empire and also to provide good communications with St Petersburg. If the rail network had developed sooner, this work might never have been carried out. Epha's work has been respected by all the governments that have ruled here since, by Nazis as much as by Communists, and now by the new independent regimes. A sand dune that was named after Epha shortly before he died has retained its name throughout the subsequent century, not being changed in the Soviet era. The isolation of the area at that time also spared it from development so animals roamed at will. Wild boar, beavers and elk now predominate in the pine forests, which take up 71% of the land on the Russian side. The spit is designated by both Russia and Lithuania as a national park and a small tax is charged for entry by car. Cars were banned from the spit between 1920 and 1940 so access was then by boat, bicycle or on horseback.

There are two main villages on the Russian side of the spit between Zelonogradsk and the Lithuanian border, Lesnoy (**Лесной**) and Rybachy (**Рыбачий**), Sarkau and Rossitten in German. In Lesnoy new money flaunts itself behind formidable metal grilles. One of the villas belongs to the Moscow Central Bank. It shows reasonable taste in architecture though one must regret the passing of many of the former more modest houses in the village.

Halfway between Lesnoy and Rybachy is the **Spit Museum**, founded in 1987 in what had formerly been a Communist Party guesthouse. The first German guidebook to the area, produced in 1996, tells visitors not to be put off by the austere concrete exterior and that it really is worth entering. This is true. The year 1987 was sufficiently into the glasnost era for a detailed and honest history of the area to be given. An extensive collection of photographs, models and stuffed animals covers contemporary and past natural history.

More unexpected is the history of the gliding centre which was founded in Rossitten in 1920. This resulted from the ban on motorised aviation in Germany

Thomas Eichelbaum

My family left East Prussia in 1938 when I was aged 7: refugees from Hitler's Germany. We were to settle in New Zealand, on the opposite side of the world. My father had a globe of the world, and I was worried about where we were going, because looking at New Zealand on the globe, it seemed people had to walk upside down. My father said that wouldn't be a problem, and it wasn't; not being able to speak the same language was a greater worry, for a while. But New Zealand turned out to be a great choice for our new home.

Exactly 60 years later I returned to the place of my birth for the first time. My wife and I flew to Vilnius, then were driven to Kaliningrad, the city where I had been to kindergarten and (for two years) to school. As we crossed the border and moved deeper into the former East Prussia a number of memories came back. The light blue of the sky, the shape of the clouds, captured by pictures my grandfather used to paint, some of which we still have. Farmers haymaking, stacking the hay in round haystacks and transporting it by horse-drawn carts. Storks nesting on telegraph poles, some with large chicks. Swallows. Cobbled streets. As it grew dark, the road sweeping through avenues of trees in the countryside, the headlights catching reflector paint; vague childhood recollections of trips with my grandparents from Königsberg to Insterburg (Chernyakhovsk) to visit my grandparents there. We reach our hotel in Kaliningrad late at night and, despite the excitement, sleep well.

The next day, with our guide, we set out to look at Kaliningrad. The guide assures us that the trams have been replaced, but they seem to have been modelled on the ones I knew. I have a book with me, *Königsberg in 144 Pictures*, and recognise many of the buildings, although others have been destroyed. Some of the streets are familiar to me; Steindamm where my father had his office. Here the buildings have all gone, but the former shape of the streets is clear and unchanged. We come to the Hufenallee with its distinctive winding stretch and instantly I know where we are. I say to our guide, we are close to the zoo – around the next corner we come to the zoo entrance through which I was often taken as a child; it seems unchanged. A few minutes later, an unforgettable indescribable moment, we are outside the apartment building where my family was living in 1938.

stipulated by the Versailles Treaty at the end of World War I. Although neither German nor Russian historians like to dwell on the matter, there was close co-operation between the USSR and Germany throughout the early inter-war period here. Soviet pilots came for training and Germans were in return invited to the Soviet gliding school in the Crimea. There had been similar co-operation between Imperial Germany and Tsarist Russia for a time after 1895 when gliding first began in this area. A recently erected plaque commemorates a world-record eight-hour flight undertaken in 1925 by a local pilot, Ferdinand Schulz. The inscription, carved in both German and Russian, proclaims that 'gliding should overcome frontiers and bring nations together'.

Seven kilometres further along the road towards Rybachy, the **bird sanctuary** founded by the German Ornithological Society in 1901 continues its work and welcomes visitors and helpers. It broke an earlier culture amongst the fishing community of killing local birds, mainly crows, for food. Now they are ringed and then released. The first and most famous director, Johannes Thienemann, ringed 103 himself in 1903. By 1936 this annual total had reached 140,000. The larger birds included seagulls, sparrowhawks, kestrels and buzzards. Regular smaller ones were robins, thrushes and wagtails. Thienemann was soon able to work out the migratory routes of the white stork through Hungary, Egypt and Kenya to South Africa. He remained as director until 1929. The German staff all fled in 1945 and it was not until 1956 that the sanctuary was reopened by the Russians. They gave it the name Fringilla, from the Latin for chaffinch which is one of the most common birds to be found there. In 1991 the very precise statistic was provided that 1,672,071 birds had been ringed since the reopening. Its traps are thought to be the largest in the world, one being 100m deep, 30m wide and 15m high. The birds fly in totally unaware that they are in a trap so around 60,000 can be ringed each year. The traps are relocated each season, facing north in the spring and south in the autumn to catch the birds on both their outward and return migrations. The large nets are renewed each year; songbirds in cages entice the migrants. By 2002, a lot of the exhibition material had been translated into English as well as into German. British and German researchers are now regularly at work there. Electronic chips are beginning to replace rings but the enormous cost of tracking them is limiting this research.

Just outside the sanctuary, the **Museum of Russian Superstition** opened in May 2002 with a collection of 70 wooden carvings of spirits linked to water, forests and fields. It is planned to broaden the field of carving, so soon it should also have domestic utensils. The building is of course totally wooden.

In **Rybachy/Rossitten** itself, several wooden houses have preserved their original 19th-century carvings. The main building of interest is the red-brick village church, consecrated in 1873, and like the one in Svetlogorsk/Rauschen it was designed by August Stüler. The building was never damaged and the vicarage beside it is still intact. Even the bell and the windows remain. It was not used between 1945 and 1963 when it was taken over by the 'Dawn of Communism' fishing collective as a storage depot for their nets. In 1990 it was given to the Orthodox Church.

The **Lithuanian border** is a further 16km from Rybachy so this village is an appropriate point to finish the tour. By the summer of 2006 it may well be possible to return from Rybachy to Zelenogradsk by boat along the sea coast or along the lagoon. Another likely route is across the lagoon to Polessk. This second route would offer a semicircular journey starting to the west of Kaliningrad and then finishing in the east. In the summer of 2005 it was still necessary to retrace one's steps by road but the variety of tracks through the forest or along the dunes offer so many tempting stops that this is hardly an imposition.

ACCOMMODATION IN SVETLOGORSK/RAUSCHEN
It is quite possible to visit Kaliningrad on a daily basis from Svetlogorsk by local train or vice versa. Svetlogorsk is developing as a health centre and as a summer holiday resort, both for Russian and for German tourists. It is attractive in winter, too, particularly after a snowfall, as temperatures rarely drop much below freezing point and day trippers from Kaliningrad keep it lively year-round. The dialling code for Svetlogorsk is 01153 and the '0' is still used when phoning from abroad.

Azur Coast (6 rooms) Dynamo 1a; ☎ 21523; f 21522. This large villa was opened as an exclusive hotel in 1999. Whilst only small, it offers the full range of hotel services. Its private grounds are sufficiently extensive to ensure privacy and tranquillity. With prices not being much higher than those in conventional hotels, the luxury is well worth the modest extra cost. *Sgl US$45, dbl US$60, luxury US$80.*

Baltic Pearl (20 rooms) Baltiskaya 15a; ☎ 21351. Without doubt, this is the most pleasant hotel in the whole Kaliningrad region. It is surrounded by woodland but is only 10 mins' walk from the town centre. The family feel is unexpected and most welcome. The hotel offers ample grounds, a large indoor swimming pool, a sauna and a billiard room. Prices for meals and refreshments are very low, tea in spring 2002 costing 16c a cup and coffee 20c. *Sgl US$45, twin US$75.*

⌂ **Rauschen One and Rauschen Two** (54 rooms) Kaliningradsky 70; ☎ 21580/21564; and Lenina 48; ☎ 33452. These two hotels are within a few hundred yards of each other and were formerly Soviet trade union hotels. They are now largely used by German tour groups spending a night *en route* to the Baltics. This is why they have only a German and not a Russian name. They have both been sufficiently modernised to make a longer stay possible but neither has any really appealing features. *Sgl US$45, twin US$75.*

⌂ **Rus** (37 rooms) Verestschagin 10; ☎ 21445; f 21418; e hotel_rusy@baltnet.ru; www.rus-hotel.narod.ru. This new hotel is the place to be seen for young successful Russians. Everything is built on a lavish scale and its private grounds stretch to the sea. A winter garden is the most novel feature. It of course has a casino, tennis courts and a restaurant with an extensive wine list. The hotel achieved notoriety in February 2000 when Anatoly Sobchak, the former mayor of St Petersburg, died there from a heart attack after an evening of over-indulgence. He had been helping with Vladimir Putin's presidential campaign. *Sgl US$80, twin US$130.*

Appendix I

LANGUAGE

Of necessity these are only basic words and phrases. Consult a dictionary if you would like to learn more.

USEFUL EXPRESSIONS

English	Estonian	Latvian	Lithuanian
hello	*tere*	*sveiki*	*laba diena*
goodbye	*nagemiseni*	*atā*	*viso gero*
good morning	*tere hommikust*	*labdien*	*labas rytas*
good evening	*head õhtust*	*labvakar*	*labas vakaras*
goodnight	*head ööd*	*ar labu nakti*	*labanakt*
yes	*jah*	*jā*	*taip*
no	*ei*	*nē*	*ne*
please	*palun*	*lūdzu*	*prašau*
thank you	*tänan*	*paldies*	*ačiu*
How much?	*Kui palju*	*Cik?*	*Kiek tai kainuoja?*
When?	*Millal?*	*Kad?*	*Kada?*
Where?	*Kus?*	*Kur?*	*Kur?*
Excuse me please	*Vabandage palun*	*Atvainojiet, lūdzu*	*Atsiprasau*
I do not understand	*Ma ei saa aru*	*Nesaprotu*	*As nesuprantu*

USEFUL WORDS

English	Estonian	Latvian	Lithuanian
airport	*lennujaam*	*lidosta*	*aerouostas*
bus station	*bussijaam*	*autoosta*	*autobusu stotis*
railway station	*raudteejaam*	*dzelzceļa stacija*	*geležinkelio stotis*
toilet	*WC*	*tualete*	*tualet*
beer	*õlu*	*alus*	*alus*
coffee (with milk)	*kohv (piimaga)*	*kafija (ar pienu)*	*kava (su pienas)*
drinking water	*joogivesi*	*ūdens*	*vanduo*
juice	*mahl*	*sula*	*sultys*
mineral water	*mineraalvesi*	*minerālūdens*	*mineralinis vanduo*
wine (red, white)	*wein (pumane, valge)*	*vīns (sarkans, balts)*	*vynas*
sugar	*suhkur*	*cukurs*	*cukrus*

AI

English	Estonian	Latvian	Lithuanian	Russian
1	üks	viens	vienas	один [adeen]
2	kaks	divi	du	два [dva]
3	kolm	trīs	trys	три [tree]
4	neli	četri	keturi	четыре [chyetiyryeh]
5	viis	pieci	penki	пять [pyat]
6	kuus	seši	šeši	шесть [shest]
7	seitse	septiņi	septyni	семь [syem]
8	kaheksa	astoņi	aštuoni	восемь [vosyem]
9	üheksa	deviņi	devyni	девять [dyevyat]
10	kümme	desmit	dešimt	десять [dyesyat]

English	Russian
hello	Здравствуите [zdrahstvooytyeh]
goodbye	До свидания [dasvidanya]
good morning	Доброе утро [dobriy dyen]
good evening	Добрый вечер [dobriy vyechyer]
goodnight	Спокойной ночи [spahkoynigh nochee]
yes	да [da]
no	нет [nyet]
please	Пожалуйста [pazhalsta]
thank you	Спасибо [spahseebah]
How much?	Сколько? [Skol ka?]
When?	Когда? [Kagda?]
Where?	Где? [Gdyeh?]
Excuse me please	Извините, пожалуйста... [Izveeneetye, pazhalsta]
I do not understand	Я не понимато [Ya nye panimayu]
airport	аэропорт [aeroport]
bus station	автовокзал [avtovokzal]
railway station	вокзал [vokzal]
toilet	туалет [tualyet]
beer	пиво [peeva]
coffee (with milk)	кофе (молоком) [coffee (molokom)]
drinking water	питьевая вода [peetyeva-ya vada]
juice	сок [sok]
mineral water	минеральная вода [meenyeralna-ya vada]
wine (red, white)	(красное, белое) вино [(krasna-yeh, byela-yeh) veeno]
sugar	сахар [sahar]

Appendix 2

GENERAL BOOKS

Baddiel, David *The Secret Purposes* 2005. The story begins in Königsberg shortly before the War.

Dönhoff, Marion *Before The Storm: Memories of my Youth in Old Prussia*. Much of the literature on their former Heimat (homeland) produced by East Prussians is tendentious and superficial but voluminous. Dönhoff is an exception, and fortunately one that has been translated into English. She has written many other books about both Königsberg and Kaliningrad but these are only in German.

Eksteins, Modris *Walking Since Daybreak*. For the human dimension of the occupations during the 20th century, this is unlikely ever to be surpassed.

Kirby, David *The Baltic World 1772–1993*. Covers earlier history.

Königsberg Merian Live series. The best German guidebook. The many still in circulation that date from the early 1990s should be treated with great caution. The writers are still embittered about the loss of the area and the whole Soviet period is described in totally hostile terms.

Koster, Baldur *Königsberg; Architectur aus Deutscher Zeit* 2000. The definitive book on German architecture, it was the result of four years work there and shows how much has remained.

Landsbergis, Vytautas *Lithuania, Independent Again* 2000. Vytautas was the first Baltic independence leader to have written his memoirs. Walking the calm streets of Vilnius now, it is all too easy to forget the struggles needed to remove the Soviet occupiers. Music and politics have always been linked in his life so it is not surprising that two chapters in this book are called 'Debussy and Despair' and 'The Power of Music'. A third has the title 'Čiurlionis' in recognition of Lithuania's most famous composer.

Manthey, Jürgen *Königsberg, Geschichte einer Weltbürgerrepublik* 2005. The year 2005, being the 750th anniversary of the founding of Königsberg, produced a number of commemorative books. Manthey's account is likely to be the definitive history of the German period for many years to come.

Mason, Pamela *Puppet Maker* 2005. A novel set in London and Latvia in the 1990s with flashbacks to pre-war Latvia.

Miegel, Agnes *Spaziergange einer Ostpreussin* Those with knowledge of German are recommended this. Miegal was a famous poet who lived in Königsberg before the war and these are her recollections of the 1920s there.

Palmer, Alan *Northern Shores* 2005. Effectively summarises a thousand years of very complicated history around the Baltic Sea.

von Rauch, George *The Baltic States, Years of Independence*. Recommended for more detail on the 20 years of independence the Baltic States enjoyed between 1920 and 1940.

The Baltic States, Estonia, Latvia, and Lithuania Routledge, 2002. Three books brought together in one volume. Each provides short general histories on each country and then greater detail on the Soviet occupation and the transition to independence.

Unwin, Peter *Baltic Approaches* 1995. Unwin's many visits to the area and much research allows him to put the sudden transition of 1990–1 into a longer-term perspective; the book has in no way dated. His chapter on Kaliningrad is one of the very few sources in English on this area.

Wieck, Michael *Zeugnis vom Untergang Königsberg*. The best account of life and death in Königsberg at the end of the war written by a Jew who was under equal threat from both the Nazis and then from the Russians.

TRAVEL GUIDES Individual guides to Estonia, Latvia and Lithuania have been published by Bradt, offering in-depth coverage of each country. New editions of these books are published regularly.

Baister, Stephen and Patrick, Chris *Latvia: The Bradt Travel Guide* Bradt Travel Guides, 2005. All corners of Latvia, from the capital, Riga, to the 13th-century town of Cēsis, Sigulda National Park, the lakes of Latgāle and the coast at Jūrmala.

McLachlan, Gordon *Lithuania: The Bradt Travel Guide* Bradt Travel Guides, 2005. Highlights of this rapidly changing country include medieval cities, national parks, pristine beaches and colourful local festivals.

Taylor, Neil *Estonia: The Bradt Travel Guide* Bradt Travel Guides, 2004. A practical guide to Estonia's complex history and many attractions: Tallinn; the unspoilt countryside and islands; German manor houses and elegant resorts.

MAPS Jāņa Sēta in Riga publish atlases of the Baltic states and individual town plans for each capital and for many smaller towns as well. Their maps are available at Stanfords in London, Bristol and Manchester and all over the Baltic states. Their shop in Riga is at 83–85 Elizabetes iela. The Estonian map specialists are Regio, whose main outlet is the Apollo Bookshop at Viru 23, close to the Viru Gate. They publish historical as well as contemporary maps of Tallinn. They also sell through Stanfords shops in the UK (*www.stanfords.co.uk*). There are no similar publishers to these two in Vilnius or in Kaliningrad, although a wide selection of locally produced maps is available. In Kaliningrad it is possible to buy bilingual maps produced in Germany giving both the former and the current names of all the streets in the town centre.

LOCAL PUBLICATIONS *Tallinn In Your Pocket* and the parallel publications for Riga and Vilnius are essential purchases on arrival. They cost only about £1.50/US$2.50 and this cover charge enables them to comment freely on local restaurants, museums and shops without being beholden to advertisers. They appear bimonthly and are all on the website (*www.inyourpocket.com*) so this should be consulted for up-to-date information before departure. The *City Paper* covers all three Baltic capitals in one publication and, combined with practical information, has a wide range of articles on contemporary political topics. Its price is around £1.75/US$3.00 which again ensures editorial integrity. Its website (*www.balticsworldwide.com*) provides a far wider range of restaurant and hotel reviews than the written publication.

Kaliningrad has still to realise the potential of providing tourists with nice books as souvenirs of their visit. A locally produced guidebook in Russian has still to appear, let alone one in German or English. In Kaliningrad itself, visitors should look out for *Königsberg/Kaliningrad Now*, an excellent introduction to contemporary and former art and architecture produced by the local branch of the Centre for Contemporary Arts. This book was produced with a one-off subsidy for the 2005 celebrations but hopefully tourists in later years will still be able to obtain copies. Sets of postcards are easily available, both of pre-war Königsberg and of contemporary Kaliningrad. The cathedral has produced, in German only, a few booklets on its history.

From around 2000, the other three capitals began producing a plethora of large photographic albums and manageable booklets, a trend that showed no signs of abating in 2005. In Tallinn the little book *The Living Past of Tallinn* by Elena Rannu skilfully portrays the high life and the low life of the Upper Town throughout its history. Gustav German's *Estonia* published in 1996 in fact concentrates on photographs of Tallinn just before new building, rather than just restoration, took over in parts of the town. Sulev Maevali's *Architecture and Art Monuments in Tallinn* was first published in 1986 but it is regularly updated and has no equal in its detailed descriptions of church interiors. For exteriors turn to *History Reflected in Architecture*, which is in fact a catalogue of a photographic exhibition held in Tallinn in 2005. Tallinn deserves a lively book on its history but for the moment has to do with the rather ponderous *History of Old Tallinn* by Raimo Pullat published in 1998.

Most visitors to Riga return with the two books written by Andris Kolbergs called *The Story of Riga*. One covers the history of the Old Town, the other Riga's expansion in the 19th century. Both are well illustrated with prints and contemporary photographs. A worthy extravagance for the coffee table is *Art Nouveau in Riga* by Janis Krastins which covers every building in this genre. *Riga: A City to Discover* by A Bruders manages to include 300 original photographs in a book almost pocket-size. *The Jews in Riga*, published by the Jewish Museum in 1991, covers all buildings linked with their history, both those still in use and those destroyed during the war. It also has a very useful history of their community.

It would be impossible to leave Vilnius without buying a baroque book. The best is *Baroque in Lithuania*, which concentrates on architecture. *Baroque Art in Lithuania* covers porcelain, tapestry and painting. *Lithuania: Past, Culture, Present* does manage to do justice to all three ambitious themes within the space of 270 pages, both in the text and in the illustrations. The title *Lithuania: Facts and Figures* hardly sounds inviting but, although it is an official publication, it is written in a lively manner and has far more photographs than statistics. *Vilnius*, an annual publication in English of the Lithuanian Writers' Union, translates the best writing of the previous year and also has commentaries on art and film. *Vilnius 13.01.91* is a grim photographic reminder of the violence the capital had to endure in defending its independence from Soviet forces. (No individual authors are listed for these books as they all have several contributors.) The website www.booksfromlithuania.lt lists all Lithuanian fiction recently translated into foreign languages.

Many guidebooks produced in the Baltics suffer from the problem of being written for a local audience and then simply translated. Tomas Venclova's *Vilnius* is a clear exception to this pattern; having lived in exile in the USA from 1977 to 1990, he is able both to draw on his local knowledge and to present it warmly to an outside audience. He has a wide canvas, with an excellent historical introduction and a large number of drawings and photographs.

The various chapters earlier in this book include details of local bookshops with the best selection of recent English-language publications. The www.amazon.com and www.amazon.co.uk websites are always up to date on material in English on each of the Baltic countries and the parallel www.amazon.de site similarly covers books published in German. The website www.amazon.fr covers the more limited, but now increasing number of books published in French on the Baltics.

WEBSITES

Baltic Times	www.baltictimes.com
City Paper	www.balticsworldwide.com
Estonian Tourist Board	www.visitestonia.com
Eurolines buses	www.online.ee/eurolines.com
In Your Pocket	www.inyourpocket.com
Latvian Tourist Board	www.latviatourism.lv
Lithuanian Tourist Board	www.tourism.lt

Index

Page numbers in bold indicate major entries; those in italic indicate maps